RHETORIC AND THE RULE OF LAW

Rhetoric and the Rule of Law

A Theory of Legal Reasoning

NEIL MacCORMICK

OXFORD
UNIVERSITY PRESS

OXFORD
UNIVERSITY PRESS

Great Clarendon Street, Oxford OX2 6DP

Oxford University Press is a department of the University of Oxford.
It furthers the University's objective of excellence in research, scholarship,
and education by publishing worldwide in

Oxford New York

Auckland Cape Town Dar es Salaam Hong Kong Karachi
Kuala Lumpur Madrid Melbourne Mexico City Nairobi
New Delhi Shanghai Taipei Toronto

With offices in

Argentina Austria Brazil Chile Czech Republic France Greece
Guatemala Hungary Italy Japan Poland Portugal Singapore
South Korea Switzerland Thailand Turkey Ukraine Vietnam

Oxford is a registered trade mark of Oxford University Press
in the UK and in certain other countries

Published in the United States
by Oxford University Press Inc., New York

© Neil MacCormick 2005

The moral rights of the author have been asserted
Database right Oxford University Press (maker)

Crown copyright material is reproduced under Class Licence
Number C01P0000148 with the permission of OPSI
and the Queen's Printer for Scotland

First published 2005

British Library Cataloguing in Publication Data

Data available

Library of Congress Cataloging-in-Publication Data

MacCormick, Neil.
Rhetoric and the rule of law : a theory of legal reasoning / Neil MacCormick.
p. cm.
Includes index.
ISBN 0–19–826878–5 (alk. paper)
1. Law—Methodology. 2. Law—Philosophy. 3. Rule of law. I. Title.
K213.M284 2005
340'.11—dc22

2005011130

Typeset by Newgen Imaging Systems (P) Ltd., Chennai, India
Printed in Great Britain
on acid-free paper by
Biddles Ltd, King's Lynn

ISBN 0–19–826878–5   978–0–19–826878–9

1 3 5 7 9 10 8 6 4 2

Preface

It has been my huge good fortune to have held a Leverhulme Personal Research Professorship, first from 1997 to 1999, but then secondly with an extraordinarily generous renewal of it by the Leverhulme Trustees for a further period from September 2004. This followed an interval of five years during which I served as a Member of the European Parliament for Scotland. I record my very warm thanks to the Trustees, and also to Professors Barry Supple and Sir Richard Brook, successively Directors of the Trust, for their kindness and encouragement.

This is the second book in a quartet on the theme 'Law, State, and Practical Reason', and I hope the third, *Institutions of Law*, will appear within eighteen months of this one. *Rhetoric and the Rule of Law* is a book that has been taking shape for a long time—around twenty-five years. My *Legal Reasoning and Legal Theory* first appeared in 1978, and since then I have received the benefit of many critical reviews and comments, both supportive and corrective. Instead of producing a new edition of that work, I have, with a certain change of perspective, sought to respond in a new form to elements of the debate provoked by *Legal Reasoning*. Through invitations to make academic visits in many parts of the world, I have had the opportunity to discuss basic questions about legal reasoning with a wide diversity of colleagues, too many to contemplate naming individually. Many other authors have at the same time been publishing wise and learned books and journal articles on many aspects of legal reasoning. Judges in courts everywhere have become more explicit in their reflections about their reasoning and argumentation, and have joined issue with the scholars on many occasions. They continue, of course, to write and issue opinions on cases they decide, furnishing an astonishingly rich repository of examples of practical argumentation at work.

I have learned at every turn from the work and contributions of scholarly and judicial colleagues, and have tried to be as explicit as possible in the text and the footnotes of this book in acknowledging and responding to what I have read or heard. The Index of Names functions in part as a kind of roll of honour to colleagues. Many, however, must be the ideas and influences that have affected my thinking and writing in ways I have not been able to recall while writing and revising this text—I apologize unreservedly to all to whom I have been thus unintentionally discourteous.

I have also accumulated so many intellectual debts and debts of friendship and hospitality over the ages that it is impossible adequately to thank everyone involved. With a fresh apology to anyone whom I have inadvertently omitted, I must at least acknowledge the following long list: Aulis Aarnio, Ruth Adler, Robert Alexy, Manuel Atienza, Fernando Atria, Hans Baade, Jack Balkin, Zenon Bankowski, Garrett Barden, John Bell, Joxerramon Bengoetxea, Jes Bjarup,

Mogens Blegvad, James Boyle, Beverley Brown, Stephen Burton, Tom Campbell, Emilios Christodoulidis, David Dyzenhaus, Ronald Dworkin, Carla Faralli, John Finnis, Michael Freeman, Åke Frändberg, David Galbraith, Peter Goodrich, Ron Griffin, Les Green, Knud Haakonssen, Andrew Halpin, Herbert Hart, Graham Hughes, Bernard Jackson, Nils Jareborg, Heike Jung, Urpo Kangas, Martin Krygier, Niki Lacey, Eerik Lagerspetz, Douglas Leggatt, Brian Leiter, Sanford Levinson, David Lyons, Michael Machan, Alastair MacLeod, Geoffrey Marshall, Stuart Midgley, Bob Moles, Michael Moore, George Mousourakis, David Nelken, Patrick Nerhot, Byung-Sun Oh, Russell Osgood, Alan Paterson, Enrico Pattaro, George Pavlakos, Aleksander Peczenik, Bill Powers, Joseph Raz, Michael Roumeliotis, Wojciech Sadurski, Burkhard Schäfer, Mike Sharlot, Raimo Siltala, Sundram Soosay, Bob Summers and all members of the 'Bielefelder Kreis' not otherwise mentioned here, Victor Tadros, Alice Tay, John Touchie, Michel Troper, Takeshi Tsunoda, Kaarlo Tuori, William Twining, Sebastian Urbina, Scott Veitch, Vittorio Villa, Neil Walker, Alan Watson, Ota Weinberger, Jim Weinstein, Jerzy Wròblewski, and Mark Yudof. Some of these are, alas, no longer alive to be thanked in person, but my gratitude to them endures. A particular word of thanks is due to Sundram Soosay for exhorting me not to be content with a simple 'collected essays' format, but to revise the whole body of work with a view to restating a theory of legal reasoning grounded in the institutional theory of law.

That is advice which I have tried to follow, and I present this book as a compendious contemporary statement of a theory of legal reasoning as a branch of practical reasoning. It is not just a collection of loosely connected essays, but a substantial reworking of ideas I have developed over the years and aired in lectures, papers, and chapters in other books. Legal reasoning matters, among other reasons, because it is a key to the possibility of a genuinely objective Rule of Law mediated through the reasoned judgments of the courts. In trying to delineate the character of genuinely persuasive (but not demonstrative) arguments in a legal context, I have drawn many examples from judgments in decided cases. These are indeed principally from the jurisdictions of the United Kingdom, but I have kept at least half an eye directed across the Atlantic, and given some attention also to the European Union and some of its other Member States. It is sometimes said that the account of legal reasoning to be found in books such as the present is skewed by the fact that it takes its evidence of the character of reasoning exclusively from judicial opinions in the higher appellate courts. Thus it is not representative of the real day-to-day business of the law. But the point of the present work is not to be in that way representative. It is to establish a view of what are the elements of strength and weakness in argumentation that enable us (if we can at all) to discriminate between better and worse arguments, more and less rationally persuasive ones. For this qualitative appreciation there is no better source material than the type of carefully considered arguments to be found in the opinions of judges in higher tribunals.

The book bears the title it does partly because of the theme developed in Chapter 2, but also partly as a salutation to the memory of Chaim Perelman. Perelman befriended me as a junior colleague at a Scots Philosophical Club conference in Stirling in 1976, and encouraged me to develop thoughts on legal reasoning of a kind generally inspired by his 'new rhetoric'. Chapter 9 began as a paper on 'the reasonable' at a seminar in his national Centre for Studies in Logic in Brussels in 1982. Chapter 2, under the name 'Rhetoric and the Rule of Law' that has now been appropriated for the whole book, was initially a paper presented to the special Perelman Symposium at the 'Paideia' World Congress in Philosophy in Boston in 1998, after a prior airing in MacQuarie University, NSW. Traces of other papers written at Perelman's prompting are more diffusely spread through the book. I hope the use of the term 'rhetoric' in a rather broad sense, and without much allusion to rhetorical classics other than Perelman's work, will not be found too inappropriate by purists.

Finally, my thanks to Gwen Booth, John Louth, and other colleagues at Oxford University Press for editorial patience in the face of authorial delays.

Edinburgh   Neil MacCormick
January 2005

Acknowledgements

Various of the chapters in this book are more or less substantially rewritten versions of work published earlier, and are published in this form with the consent of previous publishers, which consent I gratefully acknowledge, as follows.

Chapter 2: 'Rhetoric and the Rule of Law' in David Dyzenhaus (ed.), *Recrafting the Rule of Law* (Oxford: Hart Publishing, 1999) pp. 163–77, having been presented to the Perelman symposium at the 'Paideia' World Congress in Philosophy at Boston University in August 1998, and made available for publication in the Conference Proceedings.

Chapter 3 has not been previously published, but was prepared in an earlier form as the John Dewey Lecture for the year 2000 in the University of Minnesota, an invitation by which I was much honoured.

Chapter 4 contains elements drawn from the following Articles that appeared in the *International Journal for Semiotics and Law* as follows. 'Notes on Narrativity and the Normative Syllogism' *IJSL* 4 (1991) 163–74; 'Legal Deduction, Legal Predicates and Expert Systems' *IJLS* 5 (1992) 181–202; and 'A Deductivist Rejoinder to a Semiotic Critique' *IJLS* 5 (1992) 215–24. Copyright was held by the original publishers, Deborah Charles, of Roby, Merseyside, UK, but subsequently transferred to Kluwer Academic, hence published here by kind permission of Springer Science and Business media, to the extent of overlapping material. A similar paper 'Legal Reasoning and the Institutional Theory of Law' appeared in P. Koller, W. Krawietz and P. Strasser (eds) *Institution und Recht, Rechtstheorie, Beiheft 14*, pp.117–39, Published by Duncker & Humblot GmbH, Carl Heinrich Becker Weg 9, 12165 Berlin (1994).

Chapter 5 is substantially new but had its origin in, and partly overlaps with, 'Universalisation and Induction in Law' in C. Faralli and E. Pattaro (eds), *Reason in Law-Proceedings of the Conference Held in Bologna, 12–15 December 1984* (Milan: Dott. A. Giuffrè Editore, 1987) pp. 91–106; published by Giuffrè Editore, Via Busto Arsizio 40, 20151 Milan, Italy.

Chapter 6: 'Legal Decisions and their Consequences: from Dewey to Dworkin' *New York University Law Review* 58 (1983) 239–58 (Originally a John Dewey Lecture, delivered in the Law School of New York University in 1983).

Chapter 7: 'Argumentation and Interpretation in Law' Kluwer Academic Publishers, *Argumentation* 9 (1995) 467–80, by kind permission of Springer Science and Business media. Also 'Argumentation and Interpretation in Law' in *Ratio Juris* 6 (1993) 16–29 by kind permission of Blackwell and Co., 108 Cowley Road, Oxford OX4 1JF.

Chapter 8: 'Why Cases have *Rationes* and What These Are' by Neil MacCormick, from *Precedent and Law* edited by Goldstein, Laurence (Oxford: Oxford University Press, 1987).

Chapter 9: This is a partly rewritten version of 'On Reasonableness' in Ch. Perelman and R. Vander Elst (eds), *Les Notions à Contenu Variable en Droit*, with kind permission by the publisher, Etablissements E. Bruylant, Brussels; a later, adjusted, version entitled 'Reasonableness and Objectivity' was published in a special issue of *Notre Dame Law Review* in honour of Kent Greenawalt— Volume 74, Number 5, *Notre Dame Law Review* (June 1999) 1575–603.

Chapter 10 is substantially new but had its origin in, and partly overlaps with, 'On Coherence in Legal Reasoning' in W. Krawietz *et al.* (eds), *Theorie der Normen* (Berlin: Duncker und Humblot, 1984) pp. 37–53.

Chapter 11: 'Time, Narratives, and Law' in J. Bjarup and M. Blegvad (eds), *Time, Law and Society* (*ARSP-Beiheft 64*) pp. 111–25, by kind permission of Franz Steiner Verlag (Postfach 10 10 61, D-70009 Stuttgart).

Chapter 12: Kluwer Academic Publishers: 'Defeasibility in Law and Logic' in Z. Bankowski, I. White and U. Hahn, *Informatics and the Foundations of Legal Reasoning* (Dordrecht: Kluwer, 1995) by kind permission of Springer Science and Business Media.

Chapter 13 is substantially new but had its origin in, and partly overlaps with 'Can Judges Make Mistakes?' in H. Jung and U. Neumann (eds), *Rechtsbegründung—Rechtsbegründungen* (Baden-Baden: Nomos Verlaggesellschaft, 1999) pp. 76–89; in its first existence, it was the annual lecture for 1986 of the Centre for Law and Society of the University of Edinburgh.

Chapter 13, together with Chapter 6, supersedes my 'The Limits of Reason: A Reply to Dr Knud Haakonssen', in *Archiv fuer Rechts- und Sozialphilosophie 67* (1981) 504–9, which responded to Haakonssen's 'The Limits of Reason and the Infinity of Argument', in the same volume at 491–503; in attending to persuasiveness rather than demonstrativeness of arguments throughout the present work, I am greatly indebted to this piece by Haakonssen.

Contents

Table of Cases

1

Prologue: Institutional Theory and the Lawmaker's Perspective

Introduction

Indefinite imprisonment without charge or trial is anathema in any country which observes the rule of law. It deprives the detained person of the protection a criminal trial is intended to afford. Wholly exceptional circumstances must exist before this extreme step can be justified.[1]

These words (by Lord Nicholls of Birkenhead) address one of the profound challenges faced by contemporary law. Can the Rule of Law be upheld in the face of contemporary dangers arising from terrorism and of concerns about public safety? By what arguments can lawyers and judges engage with this problem? Are they objective and interpersonally testable, or purely subjective and political, having no special legal quality? To answer such questions calls for a broad understanding of the character of legal arguments.

This book offers a theory of legal argumentation. It revises the positions presented in my *Legal Reasoning and Legal Theory* of 1978, taking account of significant critiques of that work and responding to work by other scholars. The trajectory of my thought has been away from some elements of the legal positivism expounded by H. L. A. Hart and the value-scepticism derived from David Hume that formed the backcloth to the argument in *Legal Reasoning and Legal Theory*. The basic forms of legal argument still appear to me to have been well described in the 1978 book. Now, however, it seems to me that the whole enterprise of explicating and expounding criteria and forms of good legal reasoning has to be in the context of fundamental values that we impute to legal order. Reasoning about the application of law in the light of such values is persuasive,

---

[1] *A (FC) and others v Secretary of State for the Home Department* [2004] UKHL 56 at para. 74. Lord Nicholls was one of eight (out of nine) Law Lords who concluded that the circumstances were not sufficiently exceptional to justify detention without trial or charge of foreign nationals reasonably suspected of terrorist connections when British citizens under the same suspicion were not subjected to the same regime. The arguments they deployed take a prominent part among those discussed throughout the present book. Preferring a more memorable name than '*A(FC) v Home Secretary*,' I call it the '*Terrorist Suspects* case'.

not demonstrative, and in that sense the present book is a contribution to the 'new rhetoric' pioneered by my late friend and respected senior colleague Chaim Perelman, along with Lucie Olbrechts-Tyteca. Some arguments are genuinely better than others, although it is often possible for reasonable and highly experienced judges to differ about the right conclusion to reach. In such cases, decisions must still be made, with finality but without infallibility, because it is in turn reasonable to use such methods as majority voting to settle a matter that has to be settled in the interests of justice and good order.[2]

This all has a bearing on the Rule of Law. Respecting the Rule of Law is of profound political value in states or confederations of states, such as the European Union. To have properly published and prospective laws, equality of citizens before them, and limitation of official power with respect to them, are foundations for democratic liberty and essentials for a stable economy. This would not be possible if laws and arguments about them gave only a sham of intelligibility. In that case, once it came to applying them, anything would go, on account of the radical indeterminacy of legal texts and absence of any reasonable grounds for preferring one construction of them to another.

The post-positivistic view of law presupposed for the purpose of this inquiry about legal arguments goes by the name of 'the institutional theory of law'. A brief account is necessary here to disclose the assumptions about the character of law that animate the rest of the book and underpin the study of legal reasoning that it offers.

1. Institutional Theory

Law is institutional normative order. The most salient and commonly discussed example of law, the municipal law of the modern state, has special features, and it is appropriate to this book's purpose to focus mainly on these, and on similar features of such durable supranational organizations as the European Union. But at this preliminary point, a more general view is appropriate.

Two closely related ideas, those of 'legal order' and 'legal system', are essential to this view. Legal order is an instance of normative order. It obtains when life in a given society proceeds in an orderly way with reasonable security of mutual expectations among people, on the ground of reasonable conformity by most people to applicable norms of conduct. This presupposes a conception of law as in some degree systematic and orderly, a body of norms orderly and systematic in character. If people believe in, and orient their conduct toward, a body of norms regarded as a system of law, this is one way of achieving a measure of order and

---

[2] Scott Veitch challenges the need for reaching a final decision in closely disputed cases, and does so on account of a particular liberal perspective on the Rule of Law. This is an important challenge, to be dealt with in later chapters of the present work. See S. Veitch, *Moral Conflict and Legal Reasoning* (Oxford: Hart Publishing, 1999) 169–71.

security among them. This is possible even in large-scale societies most of whose members do not have any face-to-face acquaintance with each other. A legal system is not, of course, a tangible physical entity. It is an ideal construct, or thought-object. A legal system belongs to the real social world, as distinct from a pure world of ideas, to the extent that a corresponding legal order exists, however imperfectly. To assert that a 'legal system' exists somewhere is one way of accounting for such social order as is found there. One significant element in the orderliness around us can be 'legal order'. Two conditions have to be satisfied for this to be so.

The first is this: there are many norms of conduct relevant to people's activities, and their activities largely conform to what the norms require. Moreover, whether actually conforming or not, and whether aware of a specific relevant norm or not, people are aware that there are norms relevant to what they do. What they do is accordingly either lawful or unlawful, or in some other way legally effective or ineffective. A general awareness of this informs much of what they do, and in particular the way in which they respond to and pass judgement on what other people do (and even what they do themselves).

The second is as follows: all of the numerous norms of which we speak are considered as being in some way interconnected. They belong together as forming in some way a single body of 'law'. It is in the articulation of the one body that we utilize the idea of 'system'. The 'we' who utilize the idea of system are those involved in some way in the scholarly or professional study of law, that is, in 'legal science'. The systematization of law and legal understanding has been an ongoing task of legal science in many forms over three millennia.

We need not pretend that there is one single true vision or version of legal system; there have been many illuminating accounts of one or another aspects of this idea or family of ideas. What is offered here is a model based on the idea of institutional normative order. The first element in this deals with the attempt to secure impartial and respected judgment in cases of dispute or controversy about the meaning of a norm in a practical context, or about its fair application to a particular case. It also deals with situations where someone refuses voluntary compliance with back-up sanctioning or remedial norms, even though there is no serious doubt or dispute that a breach of a norm has occurred that warrants a sanction or remedy. Here too we need some form of third party intervention of an impartial kind. Mere uninvolved bystanders or chosen arbiters might sometimes be enough for these needs, but where there is refusal of voluntary compliance, or no reason to suppose that voluntary compliance will be forthcoming, more is needed. There has to be some way of calling on a person or group with acknowledged authority to take decisions in such cases, without blatant prejudice on one side or another. They have to be endowed with sufficient personal or traditional or other standing, or sufficient power, or the backing of those who do exercise sufficient power, to make any decision that is issued effective even against the recalcitrant, at least in most cases.

This can, in many settings, not only that of the sovereign state that is master over a defined territory, reach a certain threshold of organization. This is the point at which criteria exist settling such points as

- which individuals, with what qualifications, are competent to act in an adjudicative role;
- in what circumstances they are able to exercise this competence; and
- what, if any, formalities of a procedural kind have to be observed to invoke the adjudication process, to carry it on in an unblemished way, and to bring it to a conclusion. Such a conclusion takes the form of the issuance of some decision or order that is binding on those to whom it is addressed.

At this point, we may say that institutionalized adjudication exists in and for the relevant setting. Those who can do the job of judging in the regulated way constitute collectively an adjudicative institution; the appropriate exercise of their power under proper procedures and other required conditions yields valid adjudicative decisions (or 'judgments'). Thus may we characterize 'adjudicative institutions', that produce 'institutional judgments'.

In the present model, these are fundamental to institutional normative order. Across the threshold mentioned, we move from informal, non-institutional, normative order into the institutional version. Once this transition is made, two problems almost automatically arise, the problem of identity and that of change. The problem of identity concerns the possibility of settling at any moment in time whether any particular norm or normative proposition is relevant and binding for institutional adjudicators. Assuming that adjudicators are not deemed competent to pass judgement on just anything, and that their office has emerged in the context of some broad understanding of a sphere of activity and a correlative sphere of competence, this will require definition both positively and negatively. Positively, what counts as a satisfactory ground or reason for decision? Do such grounds include norms or normative propositions of some kind? And what does not so count as a relevant or adequate reason? What if any norms that might be appealed to are ruled out as irrelevant to this decision-making process?

We may indeed stipulate as a condition of effective institutionalization that there be acknowledged, but not necessarily very exact or detailed, criteria of inclusion and exclusion. H. L. A. Hart suggested for this the useful terminology of 'criteria of recognition',[3] discriminating between recognized norms and those that are not recognized as binding for adjudicators to apply. They may also allow that some norms are permissible, but not obligatory to apply. To the extent that we are able, in relation to some adjudicative institution, to specify such criteria, we are able to impute a certain identity to the body of reasons of decision, including norms and normative propositions, that are in use.

---

[3] See H. L. A. Hart, *The Concept of Law* (Oxford: Clarendon Press, 2nd edn 1994) 95–6.

The problem of change arises from the felt need of humans to adjust their expectations to a changing natural, technological, and social environment. To some extent, adjudicative institutions can deal with this, for example, to the extent that they include need for change and adaptation among the reasons that are accepted as relevant. But anything that amounts to a reform, deliberately setting adjudication on a new path from that which has prevailed previously, is likely to call for some different process of deciding upon and announcing change. It is almost inevitable that an announcement of such a change will have to take the form of some kind of generally stated norm that is to be applied so as to override prior recognized reasons to the extent of any conflict. Again, this can come to be institutionalized, again through a clarification of criteria that settle

- which individuals, with what qualifications, are competent to act in a norm-changing role;
- in what circumstances they are able to exercise this competence, and what, if any, formalities of a procedural kind have to be observed to invoke the norm-creating process, to carry it on in an unblemished way, and to bring it to a conclusion.

The conclusion, in this case, involves promulgation of a norm or set of norms explicitly aimed at guiding the adjudicative institutions, and also, more than likely, the population whose lives are affected by the adjudicators.

In the model so far, nothing is said about separation of the personnel operating these institutions. That the creation of new norms is an in-principle distinguishable activity from that of applying existing ones (or working with other recognized grounds of decision) does not mean that there have to be different people doing the different things, and in many contexts they will not in fact be so. But the differentiation of the functions does make possible some form of constitutional provision for separation of the powers involved among agencies with entirely or largely different personnel. The liberal-democratic state as it has developed since the seventeenth century has been marked by efforts to achieve a workable, if nowhere absolute, separation of functions among different institutional agencies. This involves exclusion of (most) persons holding office in one agency from also holding office in or performing functions of another. The 'separation of powers' in this sense has, in details at least, been differently conceptualized and differently put into practice in different constitutional traditions, representing different strands in a broader tradition of free government under a constitutional state or *Rechtsstaat* or 'law state'. In one form or another, a separation of powers is an essential element in the Rule of Law. Those who apply the law, interpreting and developing it as they go along, should be different people from those who enact it.[4]

---

[4] The idea of the 'Rule of Law' in use here and in the rest of the present book is more fully stated in chapter 3 of N. MacCormick, *Questioning Sovereignty: Law, State, and Nation in the European Commonwealth* (Oxford: Oxford University Press, 1999) (pp. 27–48). There is also an excellent account

Across many durable forms of institutional social activity and collective or corporate groups or enterprises, but to a particularly high degree in states, we find institutional normative orders that approximate to this model. To repeat a point already made, this is not just an abstract matter of the normative system as a pure thought-object. The idea of such a system gives a framework for understanding life within the state or relevant collectivity as being orderly, albeit imperfectly so. The conduct of individuals and of groups does conform to some extent to the patterns set in what we deem norms of the system, people can be understood as acting upon reasons that the system characterizes as good or appropriate reasons for action, and so on. Moreover, this again is not simply a matter of detached understanding from an observer's viewpoint. It is also a practical understanding from a participant's viewpoint. Members of groups can direct their own conduct with regard (not necessarily absolute and slavish regard) to what they understand as norms of the system. In framing expectations about others' conduct, they can, in a more or less conscious way, assume the similar self-direction of those others to what are understood as relevant norms. Thus an understanding of a normative system and an understanding that others understand it similarly and similarly give it practical regard contribute to, or are even constitutive of, a certain orderliness in conduct. The participants sustain among themselves a shared or common order. They do so by exhibiting regard for a conception of system as something normative for them. This is significant, but not all encompassing or absolutely overriding, among the reasons for action they have and the ways of acting they regard as reasonable.

Sometimes, a contrast is drawn between an 'institutional' and an 'interpretative' approach.[5] No such contrast is appropriate to the ideas advanced here. The idea of institutional order (like the related idea of institutional facts) depends on how humans act and interpret their own actions and those of others. An institutional order amounts to a shared framework of understanding and interpretation among persons in some social setting. As a normative order, it is in continuous need of interpretation, and as a practical one, in continuous need of adaptation to current practical problems. Such interpretation engages interests and values of great importance to individuals and groups. Hence, especially in the context of

---

of the 'liberal Rule of Law' in Scott Veitch, *Moral Conflict and Legal Reasoning* pp. 137–40. This captures the concept well in the context of showing some of the difficulties it can pose for a satisfactory approach to legal reasoning. Another recent and powerful argument drawing out the relevance of Rule of Law to autonomy of the person is in Sebastian Urbina, *Legal Method and the Rule of Law* (Dordrecht: Kluwer Academic, 2002) 225–43.

[5] See Ronald Dworkin, 'On Gaps in the Law', in P. Amselek and N. MacCormick (eds), *Controversies about Law's Ontology* (Edinburgh: Edinburgh University Press, 1991) 84–90, at p. 85 contrasting 'institutional fact' and 'interpretive fact'. In fact, it now seems to me that the 'institutional' approach is in a broad way compatible with the methodology of Dworkin's interpretative approach to political philosophy as most recently expounded in R. Dworkin, 'Hart's Postscript and the Character of Political Philosophy' *Oxford Journal of Legal Studies* 24 (2004) 1–37. The argument in the present book will, I hope, largely exhibit that compatibility.

adjudication, it is accompanied by a practice of argumentation, and of decision-making among rival arguments on issues of interpretation and of practical decision-making.

It is then a question what are good arguments, and how we can distinguish good from bad arguments in these issues of interpretation and practical decision-making. The study of good and bad arguments has over the years been carried on under the name of 'rhetoric'. Hence this book offers itself under that title. But it does so also with reference to the 'Rule of Law'. According to the 'ethics of legalism',[6] there are specific social and moral values that depend on upholding and sustaining institutional normative order, for the sake of peace and predictability among human beings, and as a condition for, but not a guarantee of, securing fairness among them.

2. The Lawmaker's Perspective

Much of what is written both about the Rule of Law and about legal reasoning takes for granted the forum of adjudication. But that of legislation matters scarcely less. As I mention in the Preface, my academic study of these matters was interrupted between 1999 and 2004, but in a way that turned out to be incidentally beneficial to it. In June 1999, I was elected one of the eight Members of the European Parliament for the constituency of Scotland. That Parliament was originally little more than a consultative assembly. But it is now (particularly since the entry into force of the Treaties of Maastricht of 1991, Amsterdam of 1997, Nice of 2000, and the Treaty of Accession admitting ten new Member States in 2004) a full-blown legislative assembly. It exercises the power of legislative co-decision with the Council of Ministers over most aspects of European Community law, save for the law governing the Common Agricultural Policy and the constitutional treaties themselves. It is a remarkable legislative chamber, making laws for about four hundred and fifty million people in twenty-five Member States speaking twenty-one official languages, and acknowledging many more minority languages and lesser-used languages. It will soon expand by admitting two new members (Bulgaria and Rumania), and Turkey's application is still pending, but looks likely to proceed successfully. It was, to say the least, a fascinating and daunting experience to expose theories about law that I had developed over many years to the rough-and-tumble world of legislative politics. At least in some degree, the present work reflects the changes of perspective that opened up to me.

There is one lesson that parliamentary experience speedily imparts. A parliamentarian's fellow citizens are convinced that legislative decisions make a real difference to their lives and fortunes. It would otherwise be difficult to explain the great effort that is put into lobbying parliamentarians and drawing to their

---

[6] See N. MacCormick, 'The Ethics of Legalism' *Ratio Juris* 2 (1989) 184–93.

attention the impact that a decision one way or another will have on a certain interest. For example, let us look at a possible reform of product liability law in the European Union. At present, the law of the European Union includes a Directive on Product Liability, establishing strict liability for consumer injuries caused by product defects (the Product Liability Directive of 1985, amended in 1999 to include primary agricultural products). The Directive also, however, allows, in respect of technological innovation, a 'development risk' defence to a claim for damages by an injured consumer against the producer of a product that caused injury. The general rule is that liability under the Directive is strict, and conditional only on proof of causation and damage. But if the producer shows that the matter concerns a design defect rather than a manufacturing flaw, a defence is possible. The defence consists in showing that the defect in the product could not possibly have been foreseen or guarded against in the contemporary state of scientific knowledge at the time the design was developed.

A possibility for reform in this was raised in Parliament in Spring of 1999, and in July of that year the European Commission put forward a Green Paper describing experience with the Directive since its enactment and inviting interested parties to respond to a series of questions about particular issues. In response to such a 'green paper', Parliament's practice is to make an initial response of its own. It refers the matter to one of its standing committees, which appoints one of its members as *rapporteur* (reporter) to draft a response. The draft is first debated in the committee then debated in the whole house as amended in committee, and either adopted with or without further amendment, or rejected. As it happens, I was appointed *rapporteur* on the Product Liability Green Paper. In that capacity, I had it borne in on me quite forcefully that not a few fellow-Europeans are greatly exercised about the question whether to retain or to abolish the 'development risk' defence. Representatives of manufacturing firms, and confederations of manufacturers in various sectors, beat a path to my door and loaded my mailbag heavy with representations. They suggested that failure to retain this defence would chill initiative and industrial development, in particular in fields like pharmaceuticals and biotechnology.

Consider, they said, even the most cautious developer of some new medicine that promises treatment for hitherto untreatable diseases or conditions. Suppose that, in course of the process of development and testing, this paragon takes every possible test and precaution, allowing for every possible risk known to contemporary science. If even this exactingly cautious developer can be held liable for damage that no precaution could have guarded against in the prevailing state of scientific knowledge, then, according to manufacturers' representatives, the burden of strict liability will prove too great. It will bear down especially heavily on smaller and more innovative firms. The pace of scientific, technological, and finally industrial innovation will slow down, or development will move away to other jurisdictions and less regulated environments. Europe will be the loser, the European consumer included. The evidence from the USA, with its fierce product liability regime and the costs this imposes on American business, is cited to back up the argument. 'No tort tax in Europe', demand the lobbyists.

The consumers' organizations and their champions lined up on the opposite side of the argument. They drew it to my attention that the development risk defence is an unfair infringement of the underlying principle of a strict liability regime in product liability. For strict product liability is essentially a way of spreading risks, as well as a way of encouraging maximal care in manufacturing and product-development processes. And yet the risk-redistributive function is switched off in the very case where it is most appropriately used, where a new-developed drug does devastating harm to some of its users. 'Remember thalidomide', they said. Where insurance or pricing-policy by the manufacturer might have established a fund to compensate the injured through a small unit cost spread over many other purchases of the same or similar medicines, the injured are left to cope with their own loss, backed only by public health and welfare systems, or private first-party insurance schemes.

While further evidence was being accumulated, and analyses made of the vast body of evidence elicited by the Commission in the form of the responses to its Green Paper, it was too soon for a final judgement on this question. For its part, the Parliament urged the Commission to carry on a further dialogue about the whole issue, and to return in due course with proposals grounded in hard evidence, well-considered reasons of principle. Above all, these have to establish a clearer vision of the place the product liability regime occupies in the context of the law of obligations in the various countries of the EU.

This shows how useful a role lobbyists and lobbying organizations can play in sharpening awareness of the multiple considerations that bear on a legislative decision of this kind. After all, one seeks a yes/no answer to a question concerning something like abolishing or keeping a certain defence in the context of a regime of civil liability. Legislators and lobbyists have positions that are open to abuse, no doubt, and the legislator who surrenders independence of judgment is the worst of scoundrels. But a legislative process in which real value is set upon ensuring that decision makers act with knowledge of the potential impact of their legislation on the interests of those they represent cannot do without lobbying.

However that may be, and whatever be in the long run the better view about the development risk defence, it is jurisprudentially illuminating that such watchful attention is paid by so many and such diverse organizations to the European law-making process. There could be no clearer sign that people believe legislative change makes a real difference. They think it affects what people do, and what claims they can make of each other. They think it has real impact on the economy and on the economic and other interests and behaviour of people and firms and governments. They think they can predict the kinds of changes it can make. That is why they care whether or not new legislation is introduced.

One example may stand in place of many possible ones. How to define counterfeiting and piracy; how to deal with exhaustion of trade marks; how to set up regulations for e-commerce that adequately protect consumers without terrifying small and medium-sized enterprises away from the internet; how to establish a fair regime of copyright for the digital age; how far, if at all, computer software should become patentable. On all these and many other matters, the European Parliament's Committee on Legal Affairs and the Single Market deliberated long and carefully during the legislative term 1999–2004. Its members exchanged genuine arguments rather than heated mutual denunciations. In the end, reports were brought to the full plenary session of Parliament for the perhaps more formal and conclusory exchange that can take place in the debate there before votes are cast and decisions finally taken. Always it was understood that decisions make a difference, and always there are lobbyists and others to tell about the difference it will make.

It cannot be taken simply at face value that everybody is correct about this. There may be all sorts of symbolic and other reasons that better explain what is really going on than the simple belief I have ascribed to people. There may be interests simply in the process itself. Lobbyists persuade clients that they give value by alerting parliamentarians to the meaning of issues before Parliament. Parliamentarians are flattered to think they do make a difference, and so on. Moreover, everybody knows that the job of legislation is never completed when the text of a statute leaves the legislature. In due course problems, foreseen or unforeseen by the legislature, will arise concerning the exact scope of a legislative text, or its exact application to some situation that arises and that has significance enough for a party affected to litigate the question. The final process of concretization or determination (*determinatio* in the Thomistic usage drawn to our attention by John Finnis[7]) will still have to take place through judicial decision. In future, reliable commentaries on the legislation will give an account of the judicial glosses and explanations or interpretations that now contribute to the body of law that the legislation has called into being.[8]

Actually, the process of determination is even more extended in European law, in the case of those enacted laws that are termed 'Directives' in the European Treaties. For these are themselves framework laws[9] enacted by Council and Parliament that require to be transposed into the several national laws by appropriate legislative processes in each Member State. The transposition process is a part of the *Stufenbau*, that is, the step-by-step process from abstract general enactment to particular decisions in concrete cases.[10] Hence, from the very start, the belief that legislation changes something about the way we live must be a qualified

---

[7] Compare J. Finnis 'On "the Critical Legal Studies Movement"' *American Journal of Jurisprudence* 30 (1985) 21–42.

[8] On the process of 'completion' of law-making by the judiciary who interpret the text issued by the lawmaker, see D. N. MacCormick and R. S. Summers (eds) *Interpreting Statutes: A Comparative Study* (Aldershot: Dartmouth Publishing Co. 1991) at 487–90.

[9] Under the new Constitution of the European Union, if it is ratified and comes into force, the term 'Framework Law' will replace the old term 'Directive'. (Treaty Establishing a Constitution for Europe, 2004, Article I–34).

[10] The idea of building law step-by-step, that is '*Stufenbau*', was developed by Hans Kelsen from an idea put forward by Adolf Merkl. For a helpful discussion, see Peter C. Caldwell, *Popular Sovereignty and the Crisis of German Constitutional Law* (Durham N. C. and London, Duke University Press, 1997) p. 92.

one. It changes things in a certain direction, perhaps, but we cannot be sure exactly what change it will in the end have made, how broad its impact, with what exact effect in concrete situations as these will arise in the domains affected. But being not sure exactly what change a decision makes is not the same as not being sure if it makes a change. No crops will grow if I sow no seed, but something will happen if I plough the field and sow some seeds. Whatever seed I sow, I cannot be sure in advance just how my crop will turn out. To be sure that something of a certain general kind will happen is quite compatible with being unsure, and indeed with its being uncertain, what exactly will happen.

One of the most commonly heard pleas by citizens, and one of the most commonly announced promises by legislators, concerns 'legal certainty'. Lobbyists, especially those representing industry, are concerned that new legislation not introduce uncertainty into the law. Uncertainty is costly from a business point of view. If law is to be changed, let it be done in a way that is straightforward to understand and to act upon, with reasonable security that action oriented toward the new law will not be disappointed when adjudicators come to interpret and apply the new law. Lawmakers for their part promise that they are keeping the need for legal certainty and legal security at the forefront of their attention. All this is, indeed, much as legal thinkers like Lon Fuller[11] would lead one to expect. As a philosopher of law among the ranks of lawmakers, I always had a certain inclination to remind colleagues that certainty is unattainable, and that the most one can do is aim to diminish uncertainty to an acceptable degree. What degree is acceptable depends on the fact that other values, including justice in the light of developing but currently unforeseen situations, are at stake. Even this modest role of avoiding needless uncertainty would, however, be viewed most suspiciously by many legal thinkers of the present epoch, especially those aligned with 'Critical Legal Studies', as will appear in what follows. Is limited uncertainty achievable and acceptable?

---

[11] L. L. Fuller, *The Morality of Law* (London and New Haven, Conn.: Yale University Press, revised edn, 1969).

2

The Rule of Law and the Arguable Character of Law

Introduction

The Rule of Law is a signal virtue of civilized societies. Where the Rule of Law obtains, the government of a state, or of a non-state polity such as the European Union, or of political entities within states, such as England, Scotland, Wales, or Northern Ireland within the United Kingdom, is carried on within a framework laid down by law. This gives significant security for the independence and dignity of each citizen. Where the law prevails, you know where you are, and what you are able to do without getting yourself embroiled in civil litigation or in the criminal justice system.

There cannot be a Rule of Law without rules of law. These may take the form of provisions in treaties or on constitutional texts or in acts of legislation or in judicial precedents. Values like legal certainty and legal security can be realized only to the extent that a state is governed according to pre-announced rules that are clear and intelligible in themselves. They must also form part of a legal system characterized by consistency among its many rules, and by a certain overall coherence of principle in the system as a whole. So rules alone are not enough in themselves. From a moral point of view, legal certainty and legal security are of considerable value because of the quality of life they facilitate for citizens, in the ways mentioned a moment ago. By contrast with morality, or moral order, legal systems do comprise, among other things, a large body of authoritatively enunciated rules. These are often backed up with a great body of carefully recorded precedents in the reports of judicial decisions, and with legal-doctrinal discussions of the principles and values explored in the precedents and implicit in legislation. All this establishes a framework for reasonable predictability in one's life and reasonable protection from arbitrary interventions either by public officials or by private citizens.

A case can be made for the view that moral judgement is quite particularistic, with each decision depending on its own particular facts and circumstances, and leading to action on the basis of a sound judgement about the reasons for decision present in each context of decision.[1] This view is contestable (and I for one do not adhere to it), but at least we can agree with those who hold it that morality lacks anything like a statute-book, and does not afford libraries full of recorded decisions to serve as precedents. So, that part of moral particularism which claims that moral judgement proceeds without recourse to an established set of rules and principles may be accepted.[2] In accepting it, we at once acknowledge a great and important difference between legal order and moral order. We also find an aspect of law that has moral value. For it is morally of value to people to have common rules available for such purposes as to regulate the allocation of possessions among people, or to deal with complex coordination problems like those posed by motor vehicle traffic on contemporary roads and streets.[3] Law does not, of course, have conclusive moral value, since legally established rules can sometimes, perhaps even often, fall some way short of any reasonable moral ideal, and can even stand condemned by that test sometimes.

This does not mean that the law is always certain while morality is uncertain. The reverse is sometimes the case. Even though law comprises or includes a large body of rules, it can also be a site for bitter and drawn-out arguments and disputes. The proper interpretation and application of legal rules, and the proof and interpretation of facts relevant to law-application can be hugely problematic. Theories about the indeterminacy of language cast doubt on the possibility of the legal certainty proclaimed by supporters of the Rule of Law. Problems become apparent as arguments are raised to cast doubt even on what have hitherto seemed law's most cherished certainties. No less ancient than recognition of the Rule of Law as a political ideal is recognition of law's domain as a locus of argumentation, a nursery of rhetoric in all its elegant and persuasive but also sometimes dubious arts. Then rhetoric can be turned in on itself.

Argument from commonplace propositions or starting points (*topoi*) is common in rhetoric, but the commonplace truths of everyday thinking may sometimes appear to be in flat mutual contradiction. We have just identified a case in point. The idea of the arguable character of law seems to pour cold water on any idea of legal certainty or security. If there can be no legal certainty, how can the Rule of Law be of such value as is claimed? What prospect can there be of reconciling these two? Rhetoric itself would be the discipline to apply in trying to find a convincing reconciliation or equilibrium between two commonplaces in apparent mutual contradiction.[4] This introductory chapter will therefore apply some

---

[1] See for a recent and very powerful representation of this view, Jonathan Dancy, *Ethics Without Principles* (Oxford: Clarendon Press, 2004).

[2] Compare Dancy, *Ethics Without Principles* pp. 82, 190, further discussed in Chapter 5 section 1, below.

[3] See T. Honoré, 'The Dependency of Morality on Law' *Oxford Journal of Legal Studies* 13 (1993) 1–13.

[4] Compare Ch. Perelman and L. Olbrechts-Tyteca, *The New Rhetoric: A Treatise on Argument* (trans. J. Wilkinson and P. Weaver), (Notre Dame, Ind. and London: University of Notre Dame Press, 1969) 83–5.

reflections on rhetoric and argumentation in law with a view to mapping the road to a possible reconciliation.[5]

1. First Commonplace: The Arguable Character of Law

Law is an argumentative discipline. Whatever question or problem is in our mind, if we pose it as a legal question or problem, we seek a solution or answer in terms of a proposition that seems sound as a matter of law, at least arguably sound, though preferably conclusive. To check whether it is sound or genuinely arguable, or perhaps even conclusive, we think through the arguments that could be made for the proposed answer or solution. We can then test the arguments we have developed by constructing all the counter-arguments we can think of. If this be said on one side of the argument, that will be said on other side. By thinking out what seems to be the strongest argument or strongest arguments on that side, we test the strength of the arguments on this side. By figuring out the counter-case they have to meet and, if possible, defeat, lawyers get their arguments into the best shape possible. One's opinion about the strength of a case depends on an evaluation of the rival strength of competing sets of arguments. It can also depend (when there is an issue concerning proof of facts) on one's opinion as to the strength or weight of the evidence in relation to the facts that are in issue. It can further depend on the probability that, as proved, they will fit well the legal argument one wishes to make.

This is not an exact science, for it is not a science at all but a practical skill, a practical art. Yet it very much depends upon knowledge and learning (law is not inaccurately called a 'learned profession'). Legal arguments are always in some way arguments about the law, or arguments about matters of fact, of evidence, or of opinion, as these have a bearing upon the law, or as the law has a bearing on them. To know, and indeed to be intimately familiar with, a great body of legal learning is essential both to the making, and also to the evaluating, of high quality arguments in law. Legal science, the structured and ordered study of legal doctrine, is therefore one essential underpinning of law as praxis. Many persons of deep learning evince little flair for forensic argumentation; some persons of considerable flair and skill lack the application fully to master the law. It is the combination that is required.

A process of evaluating the relative strength of competing arguments is bound to be a matter of more-or-less, a matter of opinion, calling for judgement. If arguments often seem close-matched, how can we tell for certain which is the

---

[5] The chapter is a considerably modified version of one presented to the Perelman Symposium at the 20th World Congress in Philosophy, held in Boston in August 1998, and published both in the proceedings of the Congress and also, in another variant, in D. Dyzenhaus (ed.), *Recrafting the Rule of Law: The Limits of Legal Order* (Oxford: Hart Publishing 1999) 163–95.

stronger? The answer is that we can scarcely ever say with certainty, not as we can in demonstrative arguments,[6] where acceptance of premises as axiomatic or as empirically true allows us to derive from them a conclusion that cannot be doubted so long as its premises stand. In law, subjective conviction is possible on occasion, where for you or for me a certain body of arguments points firmly to a certain conclusion, and all the counter-arguments that have been put to us or that we can think of seem fatally weak by comparison. This can be a shared or inter-subjective certainty, when a community of experts[7] shares such a view, to the point even of treating it as practically axiomatic. But such a shared conviction, such a shared attitude of being certain about something, is not what is meant by certainty in the other sense: that which is certainly true, whether anyone actually believes it or not.

All this is, I suppose, relatively commonplace among those who have any interest in law, whether as a subject of study or as a practical profession. It is the kind of common opinion which leads on to related positions such as these: (a) that the law is not logical; (b) that logic contributes nothing to legal argument; (c) that law has nothing to do with truth, only with what can be proved according to the law's processes and standards of proof, applied to whatever evidence the law characterizes as relevant and admissible. Whether such derived positions really are necessary corollaries of our commonplace starting point is far from obvious, and issues concerning logic will be disputed in the third and fourth chapters of this book. But the starting point itself will stand as one key element in what must be grasped by one who would understand the nature and character of law as practical activity. This, therefore, is our initial commonplace about law: so far as law is that which underlies legal claims or accusations and legal defences, law is something arguable, sometimes, but not always, conclusively, always at least persuasively.

2. Second Commonplace: The Rule of Law

To the first must then at once be posed the second, antithetical, commonplace we already noted about the Rule of Law. Where there is in some polity a body of established and acknowledged law that is supposed to govern the dealings of persons in all capacities in that polity, a strict observance of all those laws, especially their strict observance by those who hold governmental power, is of inestimable

---

[6] Ronald Dworkin is a particularly forceful proponent of the well-taken point that the non-demonstrative character of legal arguments is not a bar to their being nevertheless sound arguments, in a context in which one sound argument can genuinely defeat another. See *Law's Empire* (1986: London, Fontana Books) pp. 9–15, and compare S. Guest, *Ronald Dworkin* (Edinburgh: Edinburgh University Press, 1991) pp. 141–4.

[7] Compare Aulis Aarnio, *The Rational as Reasonable* (cited hereafter as *Rational as Reasonable*) (Dordrecht: Kluwer Academic, 1987) pp. 221–5.

value. Where the law is faithfully observed, the Rule of Law obtains; and societies that live under the Rule of Law enjoy great benefits by comparison with those that do not. The Rule of Law is a possible condition to be achieved under human governments. Among the values that it can secure, none is more important than legal certainty, except perhaps its stablemates, security of legal expectations and safety of the citizen from arbitrary interference by governments and their agents.[8] For a society that achieves legal certainty and legal security enables its citizens to live autonomous lives in circumstances of mutual trust.

Where the Rule of Law is observed, people can have reasonable certainty in advance concerning the rules and standards by which their conduct will be judged, and the requirements they must satisfy to give legal validity to their transactions. They can then have reasonable security in their expectations of the conduct of others, and in particular of those holding official positions under law. They can challenge governmental actions that affect their interest by demanding a clear legal warrant for official action, or nullification of unwarrantable acts through review by an independent judiciary. This is possible, it is often said, provided there is a legal system composed principally of quite clearly enunciated rules that normally operate only in a prospective manner, that are expressed in terms of general categories, not particular, indexical, commands to individuals or small groups singled out for special attention. The rules should set realistically achievable requirements for conduct, and should form overall some coherent pattern, not a chaos of arbitrarily conflicting demands.[9]

Many people, and certainly I for one, find attractive both the commonplace and the counter-commonplace stated above. I do believe in the argumentative quality of law, and find it admirable in an open society. We should look at every side of every important question, not come down at once on the side of prejudice or apparent certainty. We must listen to every argument, and celebrate, not deplore, the arguable quality that seems built in to law.

But I also believe in the Rule of Law, and think that our life as humans in community with others is greatly enriched by it. Without it, there is no prospect of realizing the dignity of human beings as independent though interdependent participants in public and private activities in a society. Dignity of that sort and independence-in-interdependence are, to my way of thinking, fundamental moral and human values. How is it possible to believe in both? Can this be anything other than wishful believing? These are the questions that lie before us. Can we reconcile the commonplace of the 'Arguable Character of Law' with the ideology of the 'Rule of Law'?

---

[8] Compare J. Raz, 'The Rule of Law and its Virtue', in Raz, *The Authority of Law* (Oxford: Clarendon Press, 1979) pp. 210–29.

[9] The *locus classicus* for this type of account remains L. L. Fuller, *The Morality* (New Haven, Conn.: Yale University Press, revised edn, 1969) ch. 2.

3. Toward Reconciliation

(a) Rhetorical theories

The strategy of trying to reconcile competing commonplaces that I shall adopt here depends on acknowledging a fundamental constraint on the process of legal argumentation. This constraint is to be found in the so-called 'special case thesis' suggested by Robert Alexy.[10] That is to say, legal argumentation must be acknowledged to be one special case of general practical reasoning, and must thus conform to conditions of rationality and reasonableness that apply to all sorts of practical reasoning. This implies at least that there may not be assertions without reasons— whatever is asserted may be challenged, and, upon challenge, a reason must be offered for whatever is asserted, whether the assertion is of some normative claim or a claim about some state of affairs, some 'matter of fact'.

Thus it is a restricted version of the Arguable Character of Law that will be reviewed and defended here. The argument will be confined to considering what is rationally arguable. To say this is to distinguish between the use of words as mere weapons of intellectual coercion or deceit, and their use as instruments of reasonable persuasion, where coercion appears only in the sense of the compelling force of an argument. It is the latter, argument as rational justification, which will be reviewed here. And the issue will be whether there can be a 'Rule of Law', if 'law' is a matter of what is arguable in this sense. It will remain an open empirical question whether or how far actual advocates and judges in any particular state confine their use of argumentation to the domain of the practically reasonable.

Notwithstanding the restriction to what is rationally arguable, the very idea of law as arguable leads us at once to consider the rhetorical character of legal argumentation. Wherever there is a process of public argumentation, there is rhetoric. The modern rediscovery of rhetoric as a legally significant discipline owes much to reflection on legal reasoning. Theodor Viehweg, drawing on Aristotle, has drawn attention to the significance of *topoi*, or 'commonplaces' in rhetorical arguments.[11] An argument for a particular rule or proposition can be supported by reference to some accepted *topos*, and arguments progress by

---

[10] See R. Alexy, *Theory of Legal Argumentation* (trans. R. Adler and N. MacCormick), (Oxford: Clarendon Press 1989), pp. 5–10, 212–20, 294–5 (cited hereafter as *Argumentation*); and compare N. MacCormick, *Legal Reasoning and Legal Theory* (cited hereafter as *Legal Reasoning*) (Oxford: Clarendon Press, 1978; 2nd edn, 1994), making substantially the same point (pp. 272–4); Alexy's *Theorie der juristischen Argumentation* was first published in 1978, almost exactly contemporaneously with *Legal Reasoning and Legal Theory*, so we each came to much the same view by independent processes of discovery.

[11] See T. Viehweg, *Topik und Jurisprudenz* (Munich: C. H. Beck, 5th edn, 1974) pp. 15–26; also 'Some Considerations concerning Legal Reasoning', in G. Hughes (ed.), *Law, Reason and Justice: Essays in Legal Philosophy* (New York: New York University Press, 1969) pp. 257–69 at 266–8; here, '*topoi*' is translated as 'points of view'; see also Alexy, *Argumentation* pp. 21–4.

working towards, or from, such commonplace positions. In law, there are maxims and long-standing principles and presumptions, such as 'a person is to be presumed innocent until proven guilty', 'no one can give a better right than he/she has himself/herself' or 'a later law derogates from an earlier one' or 'no one should profit from another person's loss', and such like. Likewise, there are well-established argument forms such as *argumentum a fortiori*,[12] *argumentum a maiori ad minus*,[13] *argumentum per analogiam*,[14] and the like. An argument in such a recognized form starting from or working toward a recognized *topos* is well calculated to be persuasive in its given context. The present argument itself starts from two ideas that seem to me well-established commonplaces among those who think, even sporadically, about law.

Using a concept not far removed from that of 'commonplace', Duncan Kennedy suggests that common law arguments typically proceed through the adduction of standard 'argument bites'. These tend frequently to be found in matching pairs, so that a persuasive legal argument will be an aggregation of argument bites constructed relatively to the fact-situation in question. No sooner is that done, however, than someone constructs a counter-argument using a similarly contextually appropriate set of counter-arguments in the form of matching but opposite 'bites'.[15] James Palmer has suggested that this insight might be exploited in harnessing information technology and artificial intelligence to assist in processes of legal reasoning. Intelligent knowledge-based systems can be envisaged that would generate a battery of relevant argument bites for adduction in relation to problems in given domains of law. So far, at least, there is no suggestion that the evaluation of competing arguments constructed in this way could or should be delegated to computers. Rather, the aim is to ensure that lawyers and judges would come to the task of constructing their final arguments to lay before a court, or to deploy in justification of a decision, with a thoroughly worked-over checklist of available arguments based on prior practice (precedent) and, where appropriate, statute-law.[16] The present argument as posed so far itself takes two

---

[12] That is, argument from a stronger hypothesis to a weaker one, which is presumed to be tenable if the stronger one is. If a person were acquitted of manslaughter in circumstances of involvement in a suspicious death, then *a fortiori* he or she must be presumed innocent of murder in the factual situation in issue (and would be protected on 'double jeopardy' grounds if fresh charges were raised on the same facts).

[13] That is, argument from the greater to the lesser. If a vehicle is licensed to carry sixty passengers, then it must be lawful to carry thirty in it.

[14] Argument by analogy, argument from like case to like case. If you can grow turnips successfully on a given piece of ground, it is reasonable to suppose that you can also grow carrots there. Legal argument by analogy is discussed in Chapters 8 and 11 below.

[15] See D. Kennedy, *A Critique of Adjudication* (cited hereafter as *Adjudication*) (Cambridge Mass.: Harvard University Press, 1997) pp. 137–56, and note other 'CLS' authors and works cited at p. 393; as Kennedy fully acknowledges, the fundamental insight here goes back at least as far as to the early work of Karl Llewellyn—see, e.g., Llewellyn, *Jurisprudence: Realism in Theory and Practice* (Chicago: Chicago University Press, 1962) pp. 70–1).

[16] See J. Palmer, 'Artificial Intelligence and Legal Merit Arguments' D. Phil. Thesis (Oxford University, 1998) pp. 109–28.

bites or *topoi* and sets them in mutual opposition. The question is where this apparent contradiction can lead us to in the end.

Certainly, one should bear in mind Josef Esser's teachings concerning the importance of *Vorverständnisse*, 'pre-understandings', the taken-for-granted assumptions that enter any judgment of what is acceptable in the setting of legal argumentation—and in the preference of one method of arguing over another in a particular case. Once premises and mode of argument are settled, it is relatively easy to produce an argument that satisfactorily justifies the conclusion reached. But the problem then becomes one about the reasonable choice of premises and method, so there must be inquiry into pre-understandings.[17] Aulis Aarnio has suggested that in the end these may simply have to be assessed as the 'form of life' that they constitute.[18]

In several outstanding contributions to the 'new rhetoric' Chaim Perelman emphasized that arguments are necessarily addressed to an audience, and that persuasiveness is audience-relative. This is specially obvious in legal practice, where trained advocates put cases before courts as persuasively as possible, and judges decide after weighing their rival arguments on points of law. In systems where juries are responsible for the determination of facts, or of legal conclusions reached through their own findings of fact in the light of law as explained by the presiding judge, the rhetorical character of forensic argumentation is yet more salient. But from the point of view of practical rationality, the immediate and concrete persuasiveness of an argument is not necessarily the same as its sound-ness. The issue for a theory of reasoning-as-justification is not what argument actually persuades a particular judge or jury, but what ought to convince any rational decision maker. In this connection, Perelman postulates a 'universal audience' as providing the ultimate test: whatever argument would convince the audience of all intelligent and concerned persons, evaluating issues in a disinter-ested way, is a sound one.[19]

More or less contemporary with the early work of Perelman and Olbrechts-Tyreca on rhetoric was Stephen Toulmin's on the uses of argument. This offered a way of narrowing the apparent gap between the supposedly timeless pure rational-ity of formal logic and the context-bound character of rhetorical argumentation and persuasion. Toulmin proposed a reinterpretation of traditional logic as a sort of normative ordering of thought processes and public presentations of reasons, a process that regulates moves in the play of arguments. Rather as a ticket entitles one to undertake a certain journey by train or plane, appropriate forms of argument supply warrants that entitle one to move from premises to conclusions.

---

[17] J. Esser, *Vorverständnis und Methodenwahl in der Rechtsfindung* (Frankfurt/Main: Suhrkamp, 1970), pp. 3–20.   [18] Aarnio, *Rational as Reasonable* pp. 213–18.

[19] Ch. Perelman and L. Olbrechts-Tyteca, *La Nouvelle Rhétorique* (Paris: Presses Universitaires de France, 1958), *The New Rhetoric: A Treatise on Argument*, (trans. J. Wilkinson and P. Weaver), (Notre Dame, Ind. and London: University of Notre Dame Press, 1969), see pp. 76–86 on the 'universal audience').

The validity of the move depends on the soundness to its context of the warrant produced.[20]

The rhetorical turn in analysis of practical reasoning must not be understood as reducing the rational acceptability of an argument to its actual persuasiveness, if that means whether or not it persuaded (or failed to persuade) a particular concrete person on a particular occasion. 'Rhetoric' has a bad name among many people because of the notorious possibility that a good speaker can win an audience round with a bad case. Studying rhetoric can thus seem like passing on recipes for how to make the worse seem the better reason, or how to use eloquence to browbeat a gullible audience into accepting a conclusion that is not well supported by the grounds available to support it. One way to counter this is to relate persuasiveness to an ideal or a universal audience. If what you said had to be persuasive in the sense of 'persuasive on the same terms to everybody' (not just to your particular audience of the moment) your tricks would find you out. Yet there is a difficulty about using as a test 'the universal audience', or even some supposed consensus of reasonable contemporaries. To do so seems question-begging, since we possibly have to work out what would persuade the universal audience by reference to what is sound, rather than vice versa. Moreover, we have no guarantee that a contemporary consensus, where it exists, is correct. On the other hand, recent 'critical' approaches to legal thought typical of the late twentieth century urge that the claim to an objective soundness of legal reasons is the grandest rhetorical turn of all.

This point of the 'Critics' has in part been noted already. Often a set of persuasive reasons or 'argument bites' can be built up to give strong support for one solution to a legal problem or controversy. But in any actual or imagined situation of controversy, we can find a matching counter-reason or counter-bite for each of them. So the problem is not to uphold a soundly arguable case at the expense of a manifestly weaker case. Rather, it is all too often a matter of choosing between two strongly arguable and strongly argued cases, in a dialectical situation in which each argument made by either party is firmly countered by a good argument proposed by the other. Perhaps, therefore, as Jack Balkin and Peter Goodrich contend, it is only by reference to considerations of ideology extraneous to law that one can come to a justified decision at all. Then the ultimately justifying ground is a particular ideology, not law as an ideologically neutral ultimate ground of appeal.[21] Hans Kelsen's brief discussion of interpretation in *The Pure Theory of Law* points in the same direction as this 'critical' line of thought.[22]

---

[20] S. E. Toulmin, *The Uses of Argument* (Cambridge: Cambridge University Press, 1958) pp. 94–145.

[21] See J. Balkin, 'The Crystalline Structure of Legal Thought' *Rutgers Law Rev.* 39 (1986) 195; 'Nested Oppositions' *Yale Law Journal* 99 (1990) 1669; 'Ideological Drift and the Struggle over Meaning' *Conn. Law Rev.* 25 (1993) 369; Compare Kennedy, *Adjudication* pp. 133–8, and see Peter Goodrich, *Reading the Law: A Critical Introduction to Legal Method and Techniques* (Oxford: Blackwell, 1986) pp. 213–23.

[22] See H. Kelsen, *The Pure Theory of Law* (trans. M. Knight) (Berkeley and Los Angeles: University of California Press, 1967), pp. 251–4 on the 'political' character of interpretative decisions taken within the framework of statute law.

(b) Proceduralist theories

A procedural approach to practical reasoning may, however, provide a partial solution to the problem concerning what is persuasive in an objective sense. There are various 'proceduralist' approaches, but they have in common a concern with understanding the constraints on practical reasoning that have to be acknowledged if it is to yield rationally acceptable conclusions in an interpersonal context. So a starting point is indeed the rhetoricians' emphasis on the interpersonal context of argumentation. In its light, the concept of universality has two uses. First, it demands universalizability of reasons—for the present instance of circumstances C to count as a reason now for reaching decision D, and acting on D, it would have to be acceptable to hold a decision of type D appropriate whenever an instance of C occurs. Second, it suggests a way of testing whether it is warranted to assert that D is appropriate whenever C obtains. This universalized reason, by its terms, will be applicable to all instances of C, not just the single instance now under attention. The interests, feelings, and opinions of all human beings are therefore potentially at stake, and one can ask whether the formula '*Whenever C, then D*' could be rejected by anyone who is willing for everyone to have the same opportunity to challenge practical principles of decision.[23]

As Jürgen Habermas and like-minded thinkers such as Robert Alexy argue, it may be possible to test practical propositions by reference, at least in principle, to the interests, feelings, and views of the totality of persons in any way affected by or concerned with them. Habermas's move is to propose a test by reference to dialogue in an 'ideal speech situation', envisaged as one in which all forms of coercion or interpersonal power or domination are put aside for the purposes of conducting (or imagining the conduct of) interpersonal discourse. Analysis of the necessary constraints on such a discourse yields a procedural approach to testing the kinds of principles that rational discourse-partners could accept, acknowledging the types of desires and interests they actually have.[24] Important in this is the idea that accepted principles or commonplaces (*topoi*) should be subject to challenge, but are considered acceptable until successfully challenged. Such challenges might be on the ground that they cannot pass the test of universalizability or on the ground that they owe their origins to past or present social power-relations that would themselves have been rejected in the ideal speech situation.[25] A similar, but simpler and thus more persuasive, idea is that of T. M. Scanlon.[26] He suggests that an action is wrong if any principle that permitted it would be one that, just by

---

[23] Compare Alexy, *Argumentation* pp. 65–9, 146–7, 267–77, MacCormick *Legal Reasoning* pp. 76–86.

[24] J. Habermas, *The Legitimation Crisis* (trans. A McCarthy) (Cambridge: Polity Press, 1988), pp. 109–12; compare Alexy, *Argumentation* pp. 111–37.

[25] See Alexy, *Argumentation* pp. 151–3, 204–5.

[26] See T. M. Scanlon, 'Contractualism and Utilitarianism', in A. Sen and B. Williams (eds), *Utilitarianism and Beyond* (Cambridge: Cambridge University Press, 1982) pp. 103–28; and *What We Owe to Each Other* (Cambridge, Mass.: Harvard University Press, 1998). Since no actual agreement or contract is involved in such reasoning, and obligations generated by or under it are not in fact

reason of its permitting such an action, could be reasonably rejected by any person whose aim was to find principles for the general regulation of behaviour that others, similarly motivated, could not reasonably reject.[27]

It is doubtful whether any such procedural approach wholly disposes of recourse to personal feelings or subjective intuitions. For one has to interrogate the grounds that would lead one to reject a certain principle oneself, and still the question has to be faced what it is 'reasonable' for anyone to reject given the feelings and pre-understandings that each person brings to the judgement-seat. The procedure of procedurally testing arguments seems to face the risk of leading into an infinite regress. But it is surely a merit of such procedural approaches that they both postpone and narrow down appeals to intuition[28] or to gut-feeling. They enable us to scrutinize claims about what is reasonable in the light of acknowledged constraints of rational discourse. Commonplace principles are still needed as starting points, but they are challengeable within the argumentation.

Rationality of argumentation introduces another significant constraint. Although any particular practical dilemma or topic of concern falls to be considered on its own merits, and subjected to procedures such as we have considered so far, one must recall that the universals (*whenever C, then D*) that we work toward cannot be envisaged as one-off isolated commitments. We who decide them do so as part of an ongoing and interpersonally engaged social life in which decisions and dilemmas are recurrent in character. This has a strong bearing on what one can reasonably accept or reject in terms of Scanlon's meta-principle or Habermas's ideal speech situation. So one's principles and rules of decision and of conduct have to belong in a body of practical thought and commitment that is internally consistent, and characterized also by a certain overall coherence.[29] This implies at least some guidelines about priority rankings and procedures to determine relative weights of practical reasons in order to resolve prima facie conflicts.

Here, it is useful to remind oneself of the starting point of the present train of reasoning. We started from a puzzle about the apparent conflict between law as that which is arguable, and law as that which guarantees security and stability in social life within a state under the Rule of Law, or 'law-state'.[30] The context so far has been that of a somewhat abstract consideration of the idea that the study of

contractual in character, it seems to me regrettable that this style of procedural testing of practical principles has been dubbed 'contractualist'; but its value as a mode of reasoning is unaffected by the name it bears. Compare MacCormick, 'Justice as Impartiality: Assenting with Anti-contractualist Reservations' *Political Studies* 44 (1996) 305–10.

[27] Quoted from T. M. Scanlon, 'Promises and Contracts', chapter 3 of P. Benson (ed.) *The Theory of Contract Law* (Cambridge: Cambridge University Press, 2001).

[28] M. J. Detmold, *The Unity of Law and Morality* (London: Routledge, 1984) at pp. 115–22 rightly stresses the element of intuition in judgement, but leaves too wide open the scope for its exercise.

[29] See A. Peczenik, *On Law and Reason* (Dordrecht/Boston/London: Kluwer Academic Publishing, 1989).

[30] Elsewhere, following Åke Frändberg, I have suggested adopting the term 'law-state' as English translation of the German *Rechtsstaat*. See N. MacCormick, *Questioning Sovereignty* pp. 9–11. See again pp. 27–48 for an extended account of the Rule of Law as a politico-legal value.

rhetoric could cast light on the character of argument in law. We have considered how far a procedural or a discourse-theoretical development of ideas that emerged from the 'new rhetoric' might offer the hope of an acceptable rational framework for our argumentation in law and indeed in other practical domains.

The legal context, however, is one in which the recently mentioned idea of coherence has a particular and obvious significance.[31] In a legal argument, no one starts with a blank sheet and tries to work out a reasonable conclusion *a priori*. A solution offered must ground itself in some proposition that can be presented with at least some credibility as a proposition of law, and such a proposition must be shown to cohere in some way with other propositions that we take to state established laws. Legal argument makers and decision makers do not approach problems of decision and justification in a vacuum, but rather in the context of a plethora of material that serves to guide and to justify decisions, and to restrict the range within which the decisions of public agencies can legitimately be made.

The material in question comprises constitutions, treaties, statutes of state or sub-state parliaments, regulations and directives of supranational entities, and the multitudinous reports of decisions by judicial tribunals, recognized in some systems as 'precedents' in the sense of a 'formal source of law'. These are used in practically all systems of law at least as one kind of relatively (more or less) authoritative guide to interpretation of statutes, constitutional articles, and other formally binding legal provisions.[32] It also includes treatises and other scholarly writings on law by acknowledged legal experts.

(c) Laws

It is trite to say that this mass of material is not and cannot be imagined to be self-interpreting and self-applying. It is law viewed at what Ronald Dworkin suggests we should call the 'pre-interpretive' stage.[33] In the perspective of the 'Rule of Law' ideal, it has to be comprehended as the raw material of a 'legal system'. As a system, we must suppose it to take the form of a body of material relevant to particular human concerns within traditionally understood branches or domains of law, such as property, contract, family law, criminal law, administrative law.[34] These, at any rate, are typical branches of the law of states, not that states alone have law (in the sense of 'institutional normative order'). States are

---

[31] See Kennedy, *Adjudication* pp. 33–4; N. MacCormick 'Coherence in Legal Reasoning', in W. Krawietz et al. (ed.) *Theorie der Normen* (Berlin: Duncker & Humblot, 1984) pp. 37–53 and 'Time, Narratives, and Law', in J. Bjarup and M. Blegvad (eds), *Archiv für Rechts- und Sozialphilosophie Beiheft 64, Time, Law, and Society* pp. 111–25, or Chapter 11 below.

[32] See D. N. MacCormick and R. S. Summers, *Interpreting Precedents: A Comparative Study* (cited hereafter as *Interpreting Precedents*) (Aldershot: Dartmouth Publishing Co., 1997).

[33] R. Dworkin, *Law's Empire* (Cambridge, Mass.: Harvard University Press, 1986) 65–6.

[34] See J. Wróblewski, *The Judicial Application of Law* (cited hereafter as *Judicial Application*) (Z. Bankowski and N. MacCormick (eds)) (Dordrecht/Boston/London: Kluwer Academic, 1992), 75–85.

territorially organized coercive associations of human beings, which makes the Rule of Law especially important in their context. The governments of states (and thus the human beings who perform governmental roles) are empowered to act authoritatively towards others. Moreover, they can back their assertions of authority with decisions to deploy organized coercive power, and with threats to do so. In this context, the demand for rational justifiability of governmental action is an urgent one if government is not to be the mere mask of tyranny. Hence it has come to be generally understood as legitimate to demand that any governmental act be warranted by explicit provisions that use specific terms and that stipulate clearly specified circumstances that must obtain to mandate, to permit, or to authorize decisions that affect other citizens. Where a discretionary element is involved in such empowerment, it must be a discretion that obtains only within quite clearly stated limits. Provisions of this kind, especially when specifically enacted by some legislative process, but also when they can be derived in reasonably definite terms from other materials such as precedents, are typically called 'rules', in contradistinction to other kinds of norm, such as conventions, standards, values, or principles.[35]

A legal rule is a normative provision stated in or constructed from a recognized legal source that has the form of linking a determinate normative consequence to determinate operative facts. It is in the nature of a rule to provide that whenever a certain state of facts obtains, a given normative consequence is to follow therefrom. To put this in a standard form: 'Whenever *OF* then *NC* '. This is somewhat more precise than the model earlier suggested in relation to universalizing one's grounds of action in a situation where a practical decision is called for—then it seemed enough to think of a decision 'D' being justified whenever certain circumstances 'C' obtain. Legal rules do all bear on decision, but by no means all of them do so directly. They may prescribe conditions in which ownership of property is acquired, or circumstances that amount to breach of contract, or frustration of contract, and so forth. These are included in what I call 'normative consequences', and it is in relation to those normative consequences that the law makes acts and events of the specified kind 'operative facts', that is, facts that operate in law to bring about the relevant consequence. In the next chapter, as we shall see, it is often necessary to refine this refinement still further, by unpacking what I am here treating for relative simplicity as a lumped-together bundle of operative facts into all the component elements that the law specifies.

At the heart of the liberal idea of free government, and at the heart of the distinction between free and despotic governments, is the idea that when governments act towards citizens, their action must be warrantable under a rule that exhibits the structural characteristics we have noted. This holds good also when government, usually through the agency of law courts, purports to regulate or pass

---

[35] For a clarification of these distinctions, see N. MacCormick, 'Norms, Institutions, and Institutional Facts' *Law and Philosophy* 17 (1998) 1–45.

judgment on claims and complaints and demands made by citizens against other citizens. In such a case, too, the Rule of Law demands that there be some rule to warrant the claim of one person against another if adjudication of the claim is liable to issue in an enforceable order against that other. (For example, if it takes the form of an award of compensatory or punitive damages or that of an injunction or an interdict.)

Codes and statutes of the modern period, and other similar materials, represent an institutional response to the ideology[36] of the Rule of Law as a condition of liberty. The state that governs through law takes care to provide in advance the texts that contain (or can be read as containing) rules that warrant public interventions in private lives, whether such interventions be prompted by public authorities or by private litigants. The security for individuals that is thus guaranteed consists in the fact that rule-application evidently requires the prior existence of specific facts instantiating the relevant rule's generically stated operative facts '*OF*'. Thus, for example, a statute may provide a remedy for persons who suffer discrimination in their employment 'because of sex'. Under such a statute, no action to implement the normative consequence(s) that the rule provides for can be justified unless in a particular case some act of discrimination has occurred, has occurred in the context of an employment relationship, and is attributable to the sex of the person discriminated against—but what does 'sex' mean for this purpose?[37] Or there may be a rule that provides for nullification of a driver's licence and for some other penalty within a range determined at a judge's discretion when a person drives a motor vehicle while impaired by the consumption of alcohol beyond a specified proportion in her/his bloodstream. In that case, no penalty is legitimately exigible from a particular person except if on appropriate proof it is warranted by her/his having been in the condition specified, and having 'driven' a 'vehicle' while in that condition. Can this be applied by analogy to a horse-rider?[38]

If the Rule of Law is to be actually a protection against arbitrary intervention in people's lives, it seems clear that it is not in practice enough to demand that the operative facts did on some occasion actually happen or obtain. It is necessary that some specific and challengeable accusation or averment of relevant facts be made to the individual threatened with action. This in turn must be supported by evidence in an open proceeding in which the party charged may contest each item

---

[36] 'Ideology' in this context is of course not used in its pejorative sense. Compare Wróblewski, *Judicial Application*.

[37] See *Oncale v Sundowner Offshore Services Inc.*, (1998) 523 US 140, L. Ed 2d 201 118 S. Ct. 998 where the Supreme Court held that same-sex harassment amounted to a breach of the anti-discrimination provisions in Title VII of the Civil Rights Act 1964.

[38] See *State v Blowers* ((Supreme Court of Utah, 1986), 717 P. 2d 1321; 1986 Utah Lexis 781; 31 Utah Adv. Rep. 42; 71 ALR 4th 1121) on the question whether a person riding a horse while drunk can be said to be drunk in charge of a 'vehicle'; J. Palmer, *Merit Arguments* pp. 36–8, cites a fascinating run of precedents from various jurisdictions illustrating the indeterminacy of the predicate 'drive' in the context of judicial determinations about the statutory offence committed by those who 'drive' a motor vehicle while disqualified from doing so.

of evidence both one at a time and in the cumulative effect of the totality of items adduced, and may offer relevant counter-evidence as she/he chooses. Moreover, it must also be possible to challenge the relevancy of the legal accusation or claim. Such a challenge is to the effect that, whatever may be the facts of the matter, the legal materials that supposedly warrant the assertion of a rule governing the case do not warrant it at all in the alleged, or the actually proven, state of the facts.

Here we move on to the familiar terrain of the relative indeterminacy of law.[39] This indeterminacy is in a curious way magnified by the very same considerations that lead to the demand for determinate law. For the dialectical or argumentative character of legal proceedings is a built-in feature of a constitutional setting in which citizens are able to challenge any case laid against them. They can do so if they have an unfettered right to challenge any allegations of fact and the assertions of law that government agencies, either of their own volition or at the instance of private litigants, put forward as entitling them to intervene coercively in their lives or affairs. A vital part of the guarantee of liberty in the governing conception of the Rule of Law is that the opportunity to mount such a challenge on fair terms and with adequate legal assistance be afforded to every person.[40] And yet that same governing conception calls for relatively clear and determinate law in the form of pre-announced rules.

Hence legal indeterminacy is not merely (though it is also) a result of the fact that states communicate their legal materials in natural ('official') languages, and that these are afflicted with ambiguity, vagueness, and open texture.[41] It also results from, and is in some measure magnified by, the due recognition of the 'rights of the defence' in every setting of criminal prosecution or civil litigation. Every doubt that can be raised against prosecutor or plaintiff, whether concerning fact or concerning law, is a doubt that may be raised by the defence. Conversely, it is also the case that, wherever there seems to be a significant point of justice or of public order in issue, the plaintiff or prosecutor has reason to seek in the materials of the law some provision that will, upon some reasonably arguable interpretation,

---

[39] See S. J. Burton, *An Introduction to Law and Legal Reasoning* (cited hereafter as *Introduction*) (Boston/Toronto: Little Brown & Co, 2nd edn, 1995) pp. 27–8, 54–8, 77–85.

[40] For example, in the Charter of Fundamental Rights of the European Union, now Part II of the Treaty Establishing a Constitution for Europe, Article II-107 prescribes that

'Everyone whose rights and freedoms guaranteed by the law of the Union are violated has the right to an effective remedy before a tribunal in compliance with the conditions laid down in this Article.
'Everyone is entitled to a fair and public hearing within a reasonable time by an independent and impartial tribunal previously established by law. Everyone shall have the possibility of being advised, defended and represented.
'Legal aid shall be made available to those who lack sufficient resources insofar as such aid is necessary to ensure effective access to justice'.

[41] Compare H. L. A. Hart, *The Concept of Law* (Oxford: Clarendon Press, 2nd edn, 1994) ch. 7, and compare B. Bix, *Law, Language, and Legal Determinacy* (Oxford: Clarendon Press, 1993) pp. 7–35, MacCormick 'On Open Texture in Law' in P. Amselek and N. MacCormick (eds), *Controversies about Law's Ontology* (Edinburgh: Edinburgh University Press, 1991) pp. 72–84.

provide an adequate ground for the civil action or criminal prosecution that is brought in the given case. And the defence will then again challenge what it characterizes as a strained or illegitimate reading of the law according to how courts, lawyers, and citizens have previously understood and acted upon it.

Thus emerge contests over proper interpretation of legal materials, over the proper drawing of inferences from evidence, over evaluation of conflicting pieces of evidence, over the proper characterization of facts proven or agreed, or over their relevance to the legal materials adduced.[42] These contests are not some kind of a pathological excrescence on a system that would otherwise run smoothly. They are an integral element in a legal order that is working according to the ideal of the Rule of Law. For this insists on the production by governments of an appropriate warrant in law for all that they do, coupled with the right of the individual to challenge the warrant produced by government.

We may now move towards a conclusion. What we see is how legal processes move through a chain of putative certainties that are at every point challengeable. No claim or accusation may be made without proper citation of the legal warrant that backs it and without giving notice of the allegations of fact in virtue of which it is asserted that the law warrants the conclusion proposed (by prosecutor or by plaintiff). This has the full logical certainty that inheres in syllogistic form.[43] There is a rule 'Whenever *OF* then *NC* ', cited by prosecutor or plaintiff in indictment or in pleadings, and it is there also alleged that *OF* has occurred in a concrete case at a specified time in a way that materially involves the accused person or defendant. So the relevant normative consequence *NC* ought to be implemented as demanded. This is the standard legal syllogism[44] variously embodied in criminal or civil pleading and procedure.

But the conclusion is only as good as the premises, and these may be problematized. The idea of the Rule of Law that has been suggested here insists on the right of the defence to challenge and rebut the case made against it. There is no security against arbitrary government unless such challenges are freely permitted, and subjected to adjudication by officers of state separate from and distanced from those officers who conduct prosecutions. In litigation concerning private law, a similar requirement appears in the need for visible impartiality of the judge between the contending private parties.

After hearing evidence and argument, the court must decide. In deciding about problematic matters (to be considered in detail in the next chapter), the court may find it necessary and proper to develop a new understanding of the law, and thus set a new precedent, that may confirm or qualify prior understandings. At the end, the case is either dismissed as inconclusive, the defendant being absolved, or some order is made by the court and justified in the light of law as clarified through

---

[42] Compare MacCormick, *Legal Reasoning* pp. 65–72.

[43] But compare for an opposed view B. S. Jackson, *Law, Fact and Narrative Coherence* (Liverpool: Deborah Charles, 1988) pp. 37–60; discussed in Chapter 4 below.

[44] Compare Kennedy, *Adjudication* pp. 101–4, Burton, *Introduction* pp. 43–58.

resolution of the problems posed. And then there is in effect a concluding syllogism. But it is rarely if ever identical with the starting syllogism. It is a new defeasible certainty that has emerged from posing problems about the old defeasible certainty and resolving them by rational argument.[45] From confronting law's arguable character, we move to restating a new putative certainty after admitting and dealing with doubts about the old.

In the upshot, it has to be recognized that the original representation of the Rule of Law as antithesis to the Arguable Character of Law was a misstatement in the emphasis it gave to certainty in law. That is not the only value of, or present in, the Rule of Law, though it is one benefit which people rightly look to legislators and judges to confer on them so far as possible. All the care in the world may be devoted to preparing the source materials of law by legislators, drafters, or judges writing opinions that attempt to state a holding or *ratio* with exemplary character. Whatever care is taken, the rule-statements these yield as warrants for governmental action aimed at vindicating public or private right are always defeasible, and sometimes defeated under challenge by the defence. Law's certainty is then defeasible certainty. Its being so is not, after all, something that contrasts with the Arguable Character of Law, but something that shares an underlying ground with it. That ground is a conception of the rights of the defence built into the ideology of the Rule of Law in its guise as protector from arbitrary action by governments.

In a recent extremely important essay, Ronald Dworkin has proposed that 'legality', alias the Rule of Law, is the political value that lies at the heart of any interpretative attempt to understand and characterize law. It is out of rival conceptions of legality rather than by way of some kind of empirical description of things as they are or of the semantics of ordinary language that we develop different possible philosophies of law.[46] The greater or lesser strength of a philosophical approach depends on the soundness or attractiveness of the conception it proposes of an important fundamental political value considered alongside of other important values like democracy, liberty, or equality. The methodology that I follow in this book chimes quite closely with this idea of Dworkin's.

My earlier *Legal Reasoning and Legal Theory*[47] suggested that a discussion of the canons of good legal reasoning, even if attached closely to a particular legal system, cannot be simply descriptive, however faithful it tries to be to the material it uses in evidence for its claims. In explicating standards for good arguments that one considers to be acknowledged by judges and lawyers, one inevitably commits oneself to a view of what *is* a good argument. In that case, apparent counter-examples

---

[45] On defeasibility, see Chapter 12 below.

[46] See R. Dworkin, 'Hart's Postscript and the Character of Political Philosophy' (cited hereafter as 'Hart's Postscript') *Oxford Journal of Legal Studies* 24 (2004) 1–37.

[47] Oxford: Oxford University Press, 1978; revised edn, 1994; on methodology see p. 13. See also MacCormick 'Ethical Positivism and the Practical Force of Rules' in T. Campbell and J. Goldsworthy (eds) *Judicial Power, Democracy and Legal Positivism* (Aldershot: Ashgate/Dartmouth, 2000) 37–55 at 53–4.

from decided cases or judicial dicta can be rebutted by explaining why they are actually instances of bad arguments, not good arguments according to the true criteria. The present work is a fresh treatment of the theme of good and bad arguments in legal reasoning, aiming to take into account some of the main criticisms my position has attracted over the years, and to rethink aspects of that position on broader grounds.

I certainly stand by the methodology of 'rational reconstruction' as I would now describe what I was trying to accomplish in *Legal Reasoning and Legal Theory*. This approach aims to address rather than avoid (far less declare misdirected) the challenge launched by Dworkin concerning interpretivism. It acknowledges that reflecting on the Rule of Law is necessarily engaging in a discourse concerning what is of value, and that any opinion concerning this value will shape one's attempts to produce a theory of legal reasoning or of law.

To say a little more about 'rational reconstruction', this is an approach developed by a group of like-minded scholars in relation in the first instance to studying the activity of interpretation itself.[48] As I would now characterize this, it is a method for dealing with the interpretation and elucidation of large bodies of data or material in the context of the humanities. A case in point is the above-mentioned mass of materials available for study as 'law'—materials that might be called 'raw law'.[49] Such materials are typically at first sight confused and disorderly, and gappy in places. The task of elucidation and explanation involves selection from the unanalysed mass and then reconstructing them in a way that makes them comprehensible because parts of a coherent and well-ordered whole.

This is an intellectual process involving a new imagining and describing of the implicit order in potential disorder, based on some principles or values ascribed to the whole and its parts. It is not a literal rebuilding of something originally present that has somehow fallen apart.[50] In the context of the present discussion, I would certainly assent to Dworkin's observation that 'Legality is sensitive in its application, to a far greater degree than liberty, equality or democracy, to the history and standing practices of the community which aims to respect the value, because a political community displays legality, among other requirements, by keeping faith

---

[48] See D. N. MacCormick and R. S. Summers, *Interpreting Statutes: A Comparative Study* (cited hereafter as *Interpreting Statutes*), (Aldershot: Dartmouth Publishing Co., 1991), ch. 2 'On method and Methodology', by Z. Bankowski, D. N. MacCormick, R. S. Summers, and J Wróblewski; compare also MacCormick and Summers, *Interpreting Precedents* ch. 1.

[49] See MacCormick, 'Four Quadrants of Jurisprudence' in W. Krawietz, D. N. MacCormick and G. H. Von Wright (eds), *Prescriptive Formality and Normative Rationality in Modern Legal Systems* (Berlin: Duncker & Humblot, 1994) 53–70.

[50] Compare MacCormick, 'Reconstruction after Deconstruction: A Response to CLS' *Oxford Journal of Legal Studies* 10 (1990) 539–58 at 553–8. William Lucy ascribes to me and others a notion of rational reconstruction as a 'good faith rebuilding of the law from the sometimes imperfectly expressed statements of it contained in judicial decisions and statutes'. It is more than that, though perhaps the word 'reconstruction' invites misunderstanding. W. Lucy, *Understanding and Explaining Adjudication* (cited hereafter as *Understanding and Explaining*) (Oxford: Oxford University Press, 1999) p. 3.

in certain ways with its past.'[51] The issue is, in what ways faith is to be kept, and with what regard to such values in mutual tension as that of trying to create and sustain law that has a good degree of certainty and predictability and that of insisting that legal processes must listen to all reasonable arguments.

William Lucy in a wide-ranging account of theories about adjudication assigns me to the camp of what he calls 'orthodoxy', along with Ronald Dworkin and Joseph Raz, ranged against the 'heresy' of the Critical Legal Studies movement. The four points that, for him, identify the orthodox amount to the views that laws do constrain adjudicators, because they are relatively determinate, and can be applied within a framework of justifying arguments that lead to reasonable pre-dictability of the uses of state coercion.[52] If that is orthodoxy, the argument advanced in this chapter shows that I am justly assigned to that camp. Heretics, by contrast, believe that legal practice and adjudication are a field open to full-scale political contestation. For my part, having taken a vigorous part in electoral polit-ics all my life, and even having succeeded in being elected to serve a term in the European Parliament, I believe that the cause of political reform is better served by activism outside the law classroom. What goes on in classroom or courtroom has also a political aspect, in that it concerns the good of the polity and the develop-ment of what is implicit in the settled law. I repeat my agreement with Dworkin's remark about 'keeping faith in certain ways with its past'. Activist legal politics is about changing or shaping the direction of the future by reforming some of the inheritance from the past. If it is orthodox to respect that difference, then ortho-doxy is of considerable value. Lucy suggests, however, that my position is some-what precarious because of a relatively recent renunciation of Humean non-cognitivism in respect of value judgements. Quite correctly, he says that I need to clarify what I actually think about the character of politico-legal values and the role they play in legal reasoning.[53] Fernando Atria has made a substan-tially similar point.[54] In the present book I implicitly abandon the Humean non-cognitivism that I espoused in *Legal Reasoning and Legal Theory* (see Chapter 6 below). Yet I remain attached to the prospect of marrying in some way (yet to be fully explored) Adam Smith's account of moral sentiments with a Kantian univer-salistic moral philosophy modified to allow of defeasible universalism (see Chapters 5 and 12 below). In these and other ways I attempt to improve on what I have written before, in the process aligning myself closer to Ronald Dworkin's position than I have previously thought right.

These are points to develop in due course. The conclusion of this chapter is a preliminary one. From a starting point of the rhetorical contrast between two

---

[51] Dworkin, 'Hart's Postscript', at 35

[52] Lucy, *Understanding and Explaining* p. 3. Steven J. Burton, on account of his admirable *Judging in Good Faith* (Cambridge: Cambridge University Press, 1992) deserves a place in the front line of the 'orthodox'. See pp. 229–33 on politics as distinct from law.

[53] Lucy, *Understanding and Explaining* pp. 149–50.

[54] See F. Atria, *On Law and Legal Reasoning* (Oxford: Hart Publishing, 2002) 172–83.

apparently opposed commonplaces, the argument has sought to achieve a reconciliation between them. This has involved unravelling their real point in the legal context. There is a risk of misunderstanding the 'Rule of Law' as an ideal taken in isolation. Then, perhaps, we stress its more static aspects, that promise legal certainty and security of legal expectations. But it has a dynamic aspect as well, illustrated by the rights of the defence, and the importance of letting everything that is arguable be argued. In this dynamic aspect, the arguable character of law is no antithesis of the Rule of Law, but one of its components. This, however is only a pretence at reconciliation if the 'orthodox' view about legal reasoning is not itself sustainable.

For it to be sustainable requires a thorough examination of the elements of sound legal arguments. Can these ever be conclusive and demonstrative? Can they be genuinely sound or persuasive in the objective sense even when they are not demonstrative? In one of its many senses, 'rhetoric' is the study of non-demonstrative but persuasive arguments. By discussing the place of the 'legal syllogism' in the next two chapters, I shall establish the genuine but modest part logically demonstrative reasoning plays in legal argumentation. Having identified the points at which the syllogism stops working, I shall establish what other issues have to be dealt with through persuasive modes of argumentation, and how they are to be dealt with. This will in the end lead to conclusions about the true reconcilability of rhetoric and the Rule of Law.

3

On the Legal Syllogism

Introduction

Has reasoning of a syllogistic kind any place in law? In the last chapter I depicted legal rules as taking the form 'Whenever *OF* then *NC*'. Given this depiction, you would think law application must be an intellectually simple procedure. All you have to do in any case is establish that the fact situation *OF* obtains, and then *NC* must follow. This is nothing more than the 'hypothetical syllogism' of traditional logicians.

'If *OF* then *NC*
OF
therefore *NC*.'

This chapter will develop arguments for thinking that reasoning in this form (which will be developed in a somewhat more elaborate way) is indeed central to legal reasoning. This amounts to taking a very old question and giving it a highly unfashionable, perhaps an outrageously archaic, answer. The question: 'is legal reasoning in any interesting sense syllogistic?' The answer: 'Yes'—at least, 'Yes, with reservations and qualifications'.

This answer can gain a certain initial plausibility by reference to a live example. Here is a short excerpt from a recent decision of the Inner House of the Court of Session dealing with an appeal from an industrial tribunal.[1]

In deciding on the compensatory award, the Tribunal had to apply section 123(1) of the Employment Rights Act 1996 which, so far as material to this appeal, provides as follows: 'the amount of the compensatory award shall be such amount as the tribunal considers just and equitable in all the circumstances having regard to the loss sustained by the complainant in consequence of the dismissal in so far as that loss is attributable to action taken by the employer.' The Tribunal therefore had to consider two main questions; namely, whether the respondent's dismissal was one of the causes of his wage loss in the period after January 2001; and, if it was, what compensatory award would be just and equitable in all the circumstances. The former question was one of fact. The latter was one of discretion.

---

[1] *Dignity Funerals Ltd v Bruce* 2004 SC(D)5/10; 2004 SLT 1223; opinion of Lord Gill, Lord Justice Clerk.

The Court takes a fairly plain view of the tribunal's duty in face of the relevant statute. If the 'question of fact' is answered one way, the 'question of discretion' arises and has to be decided by the tribunal, and if not, not. The implicitly syllogistic structure here looks obvious.

John Dewey, however, once proposed that lawyers ought to abandon ancient but misleading formalisms and devote themselves to what he called 'a logic of prediction of probabilities rather than one of deduction of certainties'.[2] Dewey's paper is one of the great foundational texts of American legal realism. I follow him in thinking the certainty we can have in law is, at best, qualified and defeasible certainty. Perhaps this was the very thing he had in mind. Surely it was at least a part of what he had in mind. Anyway, it became a dominant theme in American jurisprudence right through the twentieth century that logic and formalism had no place in law. Dewey was one of those whose words were often quoted to reinforce the point; Oliver Wendell Holmes Jr. was another, and Karl Llewellyn a third. With a trio of such luminaries, it is an uphill struggle perhaps to propose any other view and hope for a hearing.

Nevertheless, there is a strong case for a different view, as falls to be argued here. What needs to be grasped is that the syllogism plays a fundamental structuring part in legal thought, though not all of such thought is exhausted by the structure alone. Formal logic and deduction do matter in law. Certainly, to acknowledge this does not require one to deny the massively important part played in law by informal reasoning, probabilistic reasoning, rhetoric in all its senses and modes. So far from requiring denial of that, an appreciation of the central place of the legal syllogism is a condition of understanding them in their legal setting.[3]

1. The Legal Syllogism

Surely it must be a very general principle of legal procedure in all systems of law that a pleader cannot rely on a statute without saying on what statute she relies, and quoting its relevant parts. To commence proceedings about some legal matter, one must name and cite any statute that one's case relies on. This principle holds in every system of which I know anything,[4] and indeed would have to hold in anything that could be imagined as really a legal system. Let us put this a little more in context. Statutes issued by legislatures everywhere have the feature of

[2] See John Dewey, 'Logical Method and Law' (cited hereafter as 'Logical Method and Law) *Cornell Law Quarterly* 10 (1924–5) 17 at p. 26; there is some further discussion of this in Chapter 6 below.

[3] Compare A. Soeteman, *Logic in Law* (Dordrecht: Kluwer Academic Publishers, 1989) on the mutual interdependence of deductive and non-deductive elements of reasoning in the legal context.

[4] Compare R. S. Summers and M. Taruffo, 'Interpretation and Comparative Analysis', in N. MacCormick and R. S. Summers (eds), *Interpreting Statutes: a Comparative Study* (Aldershot: Dartmouth, 1991) 461–510, esp. at 490–1, on invariant elements present in judicial decisions across nine different legal systems.

being ordered series of sentences usually called something like 'sections' or 'articles' or 'paragraphs', often with sub-sections built in as well, and usually with some system of numbering. Generally put, statutes are sequences of sentences susceptible of being understood as normative in import, and amounting to some kind of a normative schema when read as comprising a cluster of sets of sentences together, and all the more when taken as a whole. Statutes purport to be issued to set new norms of conduct and of liability in what is conceived as an ongoing legal order. The content of the surrounding legal order is modified by enactment of the statute into the system.

This lets me focus a little more tightly the above-asserted principle that one cannot rely on a statute without saying on what statute one relies. In order to say how one relies on a statute, one must specify which sections (which sentence or sentences in the statute-text) are considered relevant and applicable to the case one is pleading. This is true equally of criminal prosecutions, of administrative proceedings, and of civil litigation; prosecutor or public agency or private litigant must tell the court what bit of the statute—which of its numbered sentences—are supposed to be in issue.

Then let me add a further point. There have also to be some relevant issues of fact. What is in issue may be an accusation that a crime has been committed contrary to a statute's provisions. It may be a demand for a declaration that some administrative act is either valid or challengeable under a statute's provisions. Or somebody may be claiming that because of a statute this party is entitled to a certain remedy (e.g. an award of damages) against that other party. Whatever it is, the proceedings will be incoherent or a sham unless the party raising a matter before a court makes some allegations of fact that are capable of being tried and determined. Moreover, those allegations of fact obviously have to be relevant to the statutory sentences cited as being those on which prosecutor or agency or private litigant has cited in the proceeding in question.

Perhaps nobody will doubt this. Perhaps these remarks deserve no more than reproach for labouring the obvious, in relation to which none will dispute the trivial point that is being made. Perhaps so, perhaps not—but what truly deserves attention here is the idea of what is 'relevant'. What is the test of this? How do we know what is relevant? How is one to raise 'relevant' allegations of fact to be tried by a court in relation to some provision or provisions in a statute?

The answer is obvious, and not especially surprising. You read the statute to find out what is relevant.

Let us take as an example an imaginary and slightly schematic version of a statute that might belong to some Member State of the EU, by means of which it transposed into domestic laws the provisions of the Product Liability Directive discussed in the Prologue above. Suppose the statute says in section *n*

(1) If any article is a product, and if it is in the possession of or being used by any consumer, and if the consumer suffers injury that is caused by a defect

in the product, then the producer of the product shall be liable to compensate the consumer for the injury suffered, and this liability is not conditional on any proof of fault on the producer's part. *Let us call this the 'strict liability rule'.*

We can imagine such further sub-sections as:

(2) If a consumer injured by a product is unable to discover the identity of its producer, or if the producer is insolvent, then the consumer shall be entitled to the same remedy against the person who supplied the product as would have been available against its producer. *Let us call this 'the substitute liability rule'.*

(3) If an injury to a consumer caused by a product is attributable to a defect intrinsic to the design of the product, and if the producer is able to show that the possibility of such an injury so caused was incapable of being foreseen in the state of scientific knowledge available to the producer at the time at which it was designed, the producer shall not be liable under subsection (1) of this section of this statute to compensate any consumer so injured. *Let us call this the 'development risk defence'.*

(4) If, at the time at which a consumer has suffered such an injury as is contemplated in subsection (3) of this section, the producer had become aware of the possibility of the product causing damage, and if the producer had not taken all reasonable steps (the burden of proof whereof shall rest with the producer) to warn all consumers of the risk in question, the producer shall be liable under subsection (1) of this section, and subsection (3) shall cease to have application. *Let us call this the 'no reasonable warning exception'.*

It is surely obvious that no competent lawyer could, or would think she could, seek a remedy for an injured person by virtue of this statute unless she were willing to make allegations that link the particular circumstances of the injured person to the very categories deployed in the terms of the statute. These categories are person, injury, consumer, producer, product, defect, and cause. To engage this statute, what must be alleged is that a person P, the plaintiff or pursuer, has suffered an injury, that P was a consumer who had a particular item in his possession or use in the character of consumer, that the cause of the injury was a defect in that item, and that the item was a product produced by the defendant, who was in the statutory sense the producer of the product. It will not be necessary to allege that the producer was at fault. If P were unable to identify the producer, or if the producer were insolvent, then under the 'substitute liability rule', it would be necessary to allege that one or other of these facts obtained, and that the defendant in the action had supplied the product to P.

Amidst all the variations that there are of procedural law, it is difficult to imagine a legal system that does not in some way require a plaintiff at some point to put down such allegations reasonably concisely in writing and intimate them to the defendant. In turn, the defendant must decide whether to admit them, or to deny them and leave it to the plaintiff to try to prove them in some form of trial of factual issues. Or, of course, in the envisaged situation the defendant might invoke my section *n*(3), the 'development risk defence'. To do so would require one to allege that the defect, if any, was a design defect and that in the state of scientific knowledge at the time of the design it would not have been possible to have known or guarded against the risk involved. P can in turn simply deny this and leave it to the defendant to prove the facts required for this defence, or could in turn invoke the 'no reasonable warning exception' in subsection (4). This requires alleging that the defect had been discovered by the material time, but no warning had been given in such a way as to come to P's attention. Finally, D might reply that D had taken all reasonable steps to communicate with all possible users of the product. Unless a settlement were achieved to the satisfaction of both parties, the case would eventually go to trial, and the outcome would depend on the question which party could prove to the appropriate standard of proof the facts contained in the allegations.

It has been said that the initial pleadings in a case amount to an attempt to construct a legal syllogism.[5] It is easy to see why. Statutes typically deal in terms of universals—'whoever is a consumer, whoever being a consumer suffers an injury, whenever the injury results from a defect in a product, the producer of the product that does injury is liable without proof of fault to compensate the injured consumer'. From the infinity of particulars in the world, one who wishes to apply a statute must select a set of particulars that instantiate the universals—consumer, injury, cause, product, producer—deployed in the statute, and must prove events and facts that substantiate the alleged particulars as instances of the universals.

The logical form of this can be represented in various ways: the major premiss is the statute. It is necessarily universal in its terms. Earlier, this was presented in a very simple-minded way as simply linking a set of lumped-together operative facts with the normative consequence that is to follow from them. (If *OF* then *NC*.) But to develop the argument, it will be better to break the parts of the rule down into more refined components that will help highlight the logical character of what is going on. Thus one might schematically represent the statutory provision in the following way: *for all c, for all p and for all t, if c is a consumer of products and if t is a product, and if p is the producer of t, and if c is injured and if the cause of c's injury is a defect in p, then p is liable to compensate c.*

The allegations of fact in pleadings amount to a set of minor premisses that are necessarily particular, for it is a particular plaintiff who seeks compensation from a particular producer. So what has to be alleged is that each of the universals of the statute is instantiated in the particular case. Connie is a consumer, Connie has

---

[5] See D. M. Walker, 'The Theory of Relevancy' *Juridical Review* 63 (1951) 1 at p. 3, discussed in N. MacCormick, *Legal Reasoning and Legal Theory* (Oxford: Clarendon Press, revised edn, 1994) 71–2. Walker's observations are particularly addressed to the Scottish system of pleading in civil cases, but the point is a generalizable one.

been injured, Connie's injury was caused by a defect in this thing, this thing is a product, Paul is the producer of this thing. The claim founded on these allegations is the conclusion of the syllogism: Paul is liable to compensate Connie for the injury she suffered through this cause. If it comes to litigation, the very point is to establish the soundness of that very claim, and thus to persuade the court to make an award of damages commensurate with the pecuniary value set upon the injury and its deleterious consequences for Connie. So far as concerns justifying claims, or justifying judicial decisions about them, the same goes. Assume on some ground that a certain statute ought to be obeyed in a given territory. Then to show that a given case is one that instantiates the operative facts stipulated in universal terms in the statute is to show that the normative consequence attached by statute to these operative facts ought to be suitably instantiated also. An order of the court giving appropriate such effect is therefore justified as a matter of law.

This chapter took shape in an earlier incarnation as the year 2000 Dewey Lecture of the University of Minnesota. As I travelled to Minneapolis to deliver the lecture, it so happened that the news of the day was the decision by Judge Thomas Penfield Jackson in the Federal District Court in Washington DC in the *Microsoft* antitrust case. The Conclusions of Law stated by Judge Jackson include:[6]

The United States, nineteen individual states, and the District of Columbia ('the plaintiffs') bring these consolidated civil enforcement actions against defendant Microsoft Corporation ('Microsoft') under the Sherman Antitrust Act, 15 U.S.C. §§ 1 and 2. The plaintiffs charge, in essence, that Microsoft has waged an unlawful campaign in defense of its monopoly position in the market for operating systems designed to run on Intel-compatible personal computers ('PCs'). Specifically, the plaintiffs contend that Microsoft violated § 2 of the Sherman Act by engaging in a series of exclusionary, anticompetitive, and predatory acts to maintain its monopoly power. They also assert that Microsoft attempted, albeit unsuccessfully to date, to monopolize the Web browser market, likewise in violation of § 2. Finally, they contend that certain steps taken by Microsoft as part of its campaign to protect its monopoly power, namely tying its browser to its operating system and entering into exclusive dealing arrangements, violated § 1 of the Act.

Upon consideration of the Court's Findings of Fact ('Findings'), filed herein on November 5, 1999, as amended on December 21, 1999, the proposed conclusions of law submitted by the parties, the briefs of *amici curiae*, and the argument of counsel thereon, the Court concludes that Microsoft maintained its monopoly power by anticompetitive means and attempted to monopolize the Web browser market, both in violation of § 2. Microsoft also violated § 1 of the Sherman Act by unlawfully tying its Web browser to its operating system.

The terms of sections 1 and 2 of the Act are not explicitly stated here, but are alluded to in unmistakable terms. The argument is legally formalistic in presentation, if somewhat informally presented from a logician's point of view. Its basic structure is unmistakable, and is that which I am describing here.

---

[6] *United States v Microsoft Corp.* 87 F. Supp. 2d 30 (DDC 2000) ('Conclusions of Law').

Some may find the usefulness of this example weakened by the fact that the judgment of Judge Jackson was speedily vacated on appeal to the D.C. Court of Appeals, on the ground *inter alia* of improper conduct by the judge:[7]

[W]e vacate the Final Judgment on remedies, because the trial judge engaged in impermissible ex parte contacts by holding secret interviews with members of the media and made numerous offensive comments about Microsoft officials in public statements outside of the courtroom, giving rise to an appearance of partiality. Although we find no evidence of actual bias, we hold that the actions of the trial judge seriously tainted the proceedings before the District Court and called into question the integrity of the judicial process. We are therefore constrained to vacate the Final Judgment on remedies, remand the case for reconsideration of the remedial order, and require that the case be assigned to a different trial judge on remand.

This, however, merely shows that judges can make mistakes of more than one kind, including failure to sustain the integrity of judicial proceedings by actual or apparent bias or prejudice.[8] It also shows that a formally proper structure of argument can coexist with material impropriety in the conduct of the case, or indeed some error of argumentation in establishing one or more of the premises. However, the process of reversal by the Court of Appeals exhibits substantially the same form, this time without (one hopes) material impropriety: if a judge is found to have given the appearance of partiality, his/her judgment must be quashed. This judge gave the appearance of impartiality, therefore his judgment must be quashed.

In any event, the relevance and applicability of the syllogism strikes me as very clear, barely disputable. But perhaps it is scandalous nonsense after all. Ought one to be worried that it seems like an absolute revolt against Dewey's logic of probabilities not certainties,[9] an absurd throwback to formalism and slot machine jurisprudence? At best, perhaps, it says something about statute law, and might be meaningful for some kind of codified system of a civilian type. But it is wholly out of sympathy with the spirit of the common law. Anyway, what about the fact that law is an interpretative concept and all legal reasoning is interpretative and value-laden through-and-through?

We shall turn to these problems shortly. Whatever is to be said about them, a position has already been established that makes it possible to say a little more about the idea that law can actually make a difference. The lobbyists whose activity was noted in the Prologue, it turns out, really are on to something. It is not just a matter of symbolic triumphs and disasters, not just a matter of wool-pulling over the eyes of gullible clients or vainglorious deputies in Parliaments, even if there is

[7] *United States of America v Microsoft Corporation* US Court of Appeals, DC Circuit, (2001) 253 F. Ed 34 (DC Circuit).

[8] One may compare the error by Lord Hoffmann for not recusing himself from hearing the appeal in *Pinochet's* case, in which an organization of which he was a trustee was involved. (*R v Bow Street Magistrate ex p. Pinochet (No 2)* [2000] 1 AC 119). See also, on the general issue of judicial mistakes, Chapter 13 below.   [9] Dewey, 'Logical Method and Law'.

always some possibility that either or both of these is in the air as well. What we change in changing the law of a state, or of a federal or confederal union, are the possible grounds of legal arguments and the legal claims and decisions that these arguments can support.

Our imagined Product Liability law makes it possible for consumers to raise claims of liability against manufacturers and other producers despite absence of any allegation of fault, and perhaps in the absence of any possibility to make an allegation of fault stick. If the 'development risk' sub-section is added, it enables a manufacturer or producer to set up a defence in the case of new-designed products that will work in the cases it covers as a possible exception to strict no-fault liability. This does not tell us for certain or at all what will be the incidence of claims, or the number of situations in which (if available) the development risk defence will be usable or used, nor with what success. But the bare possibility in law of claims and defences and the like is one that affects things like insurance markets and exposures to risk of manufacturing firms, and so on. We should be far from surprised by the apparently widespread belief that changes in laws can have real impact on relations in economy and society, and that the direction of the change and its impact can also be foreseen, even if not with exactness and certainty.

2. Law as Interpretative?

The issue of exactness and certainty brings me back to the point about law's interpretative character.[10] Of course law is not an exact science, and of course legal decision-making and legal justificatory reasoning lack the demonstrative character that their construction in syllogistic form would seem to attribute to them. What account can be given of this? The answer is clear in principle. Observe this—what has been discussed hitherto is the process of pleading, that of setting out a claim that depends on the statute's being applicable to a particular case. But one must attend not only to the making of a claim, but also to the making of a decision about the claim. What kind of justification is possible for a decision to accept and enforce such a claim, or indeed for a decision to reject it? The assumption so far has been that all the points of a claim prove uncontroversial and all the matters that require proof have in fact been proven. But that is what can never be assumed in advance.

For each concept, each universal like 'consumer', 'producer', 'product', 'injury', 'cause', we have to supply a particular instantiation in the case we put forward.[11]

---

[10] For this idea, the juristic community in general is, and I in particular am, indebted to Ronald Dworkin's *Law's Empire* (Cambridge Mass.: Harvard University Press, 1986), though the word 'interpretative' is preferable on etymological grounds to, 'interpretive'.

[11] See the critique by Patricia White, book review, *Michigan Law Review* 78 (1979–80) pp. 737–42, of my earlier statement of the present point (*Legal Reasoning and Legal Theory*, ch. 2), in which she brings out forcefully the significance of 'universal instantiation'.

But each such term is subject to interpretation, and this is interpretation in the light of an understanding of the point of the law, its fit with the surrounding law, and a sense of justice appropriate to the legal domain in question. There may be current disputes about terms and concepts in their general usage—for example, law-talk abounds with rival theories of causation. Maybe the answer in a given case will turn upon a general theoretical point of this kind, and the deciding court will have to decide what is the theory of causation that is proper to interpretation of the concept 'cause' as it is deployed in this statute. It is always possible that a claim can be problematized on a general issue of interpretation of this kind. When it is, there can't be a good decision of the case till the rival views on interpretation have been given a proper hearing and consideration, and a conclusion reached and justified.

To look again at *Microsoft*, we find, shortly after the 'conclusions of law' quoted earlier, the following elucidation of 'monopoly power':

The threshold element of a section 2 monopolization offense being 'the possession of monopoly power in the relevant market', the court must first ascertain the boundaries of the commercial activity that can be termed the 'relevant market'.

In this case, the plaintiffs postulated the relevant market as being the worldwide licensing of Intel-compatible PC operating systems. Whether this zone of commercial activity actually qualifies as a market 'monopolization of which may be illegal', depends on whether it includes all products 'reasonably interchangeable by consumers for the same purpose'. See *Rothery Storage and Van Co.* v. *Atlas Van Lines Inc.* ('Because the ability of consumers to turn to other suppliers restrains a firm from raising prices above the competitive level, the definition of the "relevant market" rests on a determination of available substitutes.'[12])

In his succeeding analysis of the details of the case before him, Judge Jackson indicates his acceptance of this interpretative gloss upon the statute as providing a sound basis for his own reasoning.

A closely related possibility, similar but not identical, concerns the way in which the particulars of a case unfold. There is an inevitable narrative character about any attempt to grasp, let alone prove, events that happened in the past. Legal cases most usually concern events that happened earlier than the litigation concerning them, and hence the task of pleading and of proving a case involves the construction of narratives[13] and the use of narratives of witnesses in building the case. However the story comes out, with whatever solidity on some points and shakiness on others, it is quite likely that in the end the particulars are seen in a somewhat different light from that in their initial summary. Then the question may arise: 'but does that really count as an instance of the concept in question, given the sense we ascribe to it in the statute?'

Suppose a Member of the European Parliament buys a laptop computer for use in her parliamentary office, but sometimes take it home. One day she is writing

---

[12] Cited above, n. 6.   [13] See Chapter 11 below.

some family letters on it at home when it goes on fire, and burns her, and corrupts a whole lot of data that she urgently needs for parliamentary business. Do any of her injuries, and, if so, which of them, count as injuries suffered by her in her character as a consumer?

In such problems of classification (in French, '*qualification*',[14] 'characterization' in the terminology of the conflict of laws) there is a double interpretation afoot. On the one hand one considers the sense of the statute to see if this is the sort of situation that comes within the intendment of the statute. On the other hand, one is interpreting the situation as a social situation of a kind that may or may not come within what we typically see as consumer protection. Perhaps the grandest example of such a 'problem of classification' was *Brown v Board of Education of Topeka*,[15] where the Warren court gave its celebrated ruling on the question whether segregated education for black children counted as 'equal treatment' for the purposes of the equal protection of the laws guaranteed by the Fourteenth Amendment of the United States' constitution.

Taking the running example of *Microsoft*, one might note the following element in the judgment:

If the defendant with monopoly power consciously antagonized its customers by making its products less attractive to them—or if it incurred other costs, such as large outlays of development capital and forfeited opportunities to derive revenue from it—with no prospect of compensation other than the erection of barriers against competition by equally efficient firms, the court may deem the defendant's conduct 'predatory'.

That section of the judgment, read together with the succeeding paragraphs, is a paradigm case of the type of argument I am drawing attention to here. Scarcely less relevant, indeed, is the finding by the Court of Appeals that Judge Jackson's indiscretions in the case 'seriously tainted the proceedings before the District Court and called into question the integrity of the judicial process'.

Another variant on this type of problem arises from the use of so-called 'standards' in statutory provisions. For example, the hypothetical product liability statute with which we are working contains the provision that was dubbed the '*no reasonable warning exception*' to the development risk defence. To invoke this, a defendant corporation will have to show that it took all reasonable care to warn users of the product of a design defect in it, once that has come to the corporation's attention. In any given case, once evidence has been led to show what steps were taken in the way of warning consumers, and when these were taken, and with what effect in alerting consumers to the risk, a question remains. Does that degree of care count as reasonable? This is not so much a classification as an evaluation, but it is again one that is steeped in interpretative reasoning (see Chapter 9 below). On the one hand, one has to consider the scheme of the statute to see what kind of

[14] See M. Troper, C. Grzégorczyk and J-L. Gardies 'Statutory Interpretation in France' in D. N. MacCormick and R. S. Summers (eds), *Interpreting Statutes: A Comparative Study* (Aldershot: Dartmouth, 1991) 171–212 at 198–9. [15] (1954) 347 US 483.

risks it is dealing with, and in what context it puts in issue the duty to warn. On the other hand, one has to consider the general idea of reasonableness in law and the kind of care commonly looked for in a situation like that of a manufacturer. It might well make a difference what kind of product is concerned, and how easy it is to contact known purchasers. Cars, for example, are different from farm-fresh foods, and these again are different from drugs, and drugs from computers, and so on.

In all the kinds of interpretative reasoning that we are considering, it is not only the case that one has to reach an interpretative conclusion before one can apply the statute to the case in hand, or conclude that it is inapplicable. It is also the case that such conclusions can themselves be justified by argument and by weighing and balancing the case for each of the possibilities in play. Arguments concerning the internal self-consistency of the law are in play. Also in play are arguments concerning the overall coherence of the statute in the light of its underlying principles and in the light of other fundamental principles of legal order, especially those that are most relevant to the statutory domain. Hypothetical cases may be raised that suggest the unacceptability of one interpretation and the preferability of its rivals. The implications for the legal system and for social life of a ruling one way or the other are tested, and in some cases, full-blown consequentialist arguments may be appropriate.[16]

So in the end, it is not the legal syllogism that alone determines the outcome of the case. Some or all of the terms in the statute will have to be interpreted, and the facts of the case must be interpreted and evaluated to see if they really count, if they really fit the statute. Reasons can and should be given for preferred interpretations that are decisive in a case. The rest of this book explores the issue, 'What sorts of reasons are appropriate to this task?' The reasons for reading the syllogism in a certain way are, it may be said, the real reasons of the case. They belong in a logic of probabilities, not certainties, so that is in the end the decisive logic of the matter.

Why then insist on the syllogism at all? The answer should be obvious: it is what provides the framework in which the other arguments make sense as legal arguments. We go back to the point about what could possibly count as applying a statute at all. We go back to the issue of a conceivable procedure for raising a case with a view to implementing a statute. That has an intrinsic logic of its own within which it is clear why the interpretative points and arguments have a real bearing as legal arguments. Moreover, this helps to remind us why it is so important for a lawyer to be meticulous in sifting through every one of the universals or concepts deployed in a statute, and figuring out their relevant ordering and mutual interaction or super- and subordination. Cases are won and lost through meticulous care—or its lack—in following through every concept that counts, and testing rigorously for each one what particulars will count as an instance of that concept.[17] Of course, that does not mean that it is necessary or even best to set out real legal

---

[16] See Chapter 6 below.
[17] Compare Robert Alexy, *Theory of Legal Argumentation* (trans. R. Adler and N. MacCormick) (Oxford: Clarendon Press, 1989) at p. 222–30.

arguments in rigorously syllogistic form. How to present the case belongs more to rhetoric than to logic, but the most effective rhetoric is likely to be that which rests on a clear understanding of the implicit logic of the process.

To summarize, if the legal syllogism is taken as exhibiting the framework of all legal reasoning that involves applying law, there is a limited number of ways in which problems can arise that require in-principle non-deductive, that is, rhetorical or persuasive, reasoning to resolve them. Reverting for schematic purposes to the simplified formula 'Whenever *OF* then *NC* ', the following four ways exhaust the possibilities concerning challenges that can be raised in any contested case:

1. No instance of '*OF* ' as alleged in indictment or pleadings has been proven (up to the required standard of proof) to have existed, taking account of all relevant and admissible evidence, including any evidence in rebuttal adduced by the defence. (We may call this the 'problem of proof'.)

2. What has been alleged, whether or not proved, is not properly characterized as an instance of '*OF* ' in the sense proper to the law. (We may call this the 'problem of classification', or of 'characterization', or of 'qualification'.) Where '*OF* 'is or includes a value-expression, or 'standard', such as 'reasonable', 'fair', 'equitable', or the like, and the issue is whether the conduct (and so on) complained of was actually reasonable, it is better to consider the relevant problem one of 'evaluation'.

3. The case as presented depends on reading the acknowledged rule 'Whenever *OF* then *NC* ' according to a particular interpretation of '*OF* ' or of '*NC* ' or both. But this is a misinterpretation, and there is in fact a more legally acceptable interpretation according to which the defence ought to be absolved from the accusation or claim presented against it. (We may call this the 'problem of interpretation'.)

4. Success in the claim or prosecution depends on reading authoritative legal materials as though they generated a rule 'Whenever OF then NC' such that the allegations of criminal guilt or civil liability are relevant given the facts alleged, or even the facts proven; but no such norm can properly be read out of the adduced materials as a reasonable concretization of them or determination from them. (We may call this the 'problem of relevancy'. As framed, it is a kind of problem that arises mainly in common law systems, or in non-codified parts of other legal systems, such as French administrative law, developed through the jurisprudence of the *Conseil D'Etat*.)

3. Common Law Difference?

Finally, I face the last objection. This concerns the special character of the common law. Syllogisms, it is said, are all very well for statutes and codes. But the common law is different. Common law is about cases and analogies, about pattern-matching across similar but subtly different narratives. The deep idea is to treat like cases alike and different cases differently, the lawyer's skill lies in developing the relevant likeness and skirting the decisive difference. All this is true, though it must not be forgotten that common law systems do also contain statutes. Nowadays, most departments of law are structured by statutes, or prominently contain important reforming statutes, and this is true across all branches of the law, in common law systems as much as in mixed systems[18] or pure civilian ones. The few excerpts from the *Microsoft* case themselves reinforce this point. So it will be a bit anomalous if what counts as a well-reasoned case differs radically depending on whether or not a statute is in play. Still, if that is how things stand, that is how they stand, and one must simply work the anomaly into one's overall view.

As usual, though, I think the differences are overstated. In most common law systems, and mixed systems as well, a fair part of the basic elements of criminal law and the law of obligations, contract, and torts, and related subjects, still rests on cases and commentaries more than on statutes. What would be odd would be if, in these domains, people were somehow less able than in others to rely on the law as comprising some framework of reasonably predictable rules for the conduct of their life. Since the law of obligations is at the heart of business and commercial life, the problem would be acute. But it does not seem to exist. Indeed, it does not exist.

The point about common law systems is that they treat judicial precedents as 'sources of law'. This means that general rules of conduct and of liability are supposed to be implicit in the cases, wrapped up in the judicial opinions pronounced by judges in their deciding of cases. Textbooks and commentaries on the law are written on the footing that a proposition of law can be sufficiently supported by citing a case which is 'authority' for that point, though it may be controversial whether any commentator's proposition exactly catches the true *ratio decidendi* of the case cited. Anyway, propositions of any substance and generality are usually built up by citation of and reference to several cases, perhaps a 'leading case' and several satellite cases further explaining and interpreting the leading case. Whether this is a credible way of reading precedents is a question to be considered later in this book, in Chapter 8.

Suffice it for the present to deny that the common law can be conceived as a legal domain without any rules. That is not the problem. Rather, the rules are themselves expounded by an interpretation of the cases, and hence almost any formulation is challengeable by reference to a rival interpretation of the same material. The device of legislation is one that delivers to the law-using community

---

[18] Mixed systems are those that derive partly from the (originally Roman) civil law and partly from Anglo-American common law, e.g. Scots Law, South African law, the law of Louisiana or of Ceylon. See R. Zimmermann, K. Reid and D. Visser (eds) *Mixed Legal Systems in Comparative Perspective: Property and Obligations in Scotland and South Africa* (Oxford: Oxford University Press, 2005).

an authoritative text to guide and structure deliberation, the text itself comprising explicit norms of conduct and of liability. By contrast, the common law as a body of case law has no such explicit norms laid down in its authoritative texts, the law reports.

In Scots law, indeed, the greater part of the law concerning serious crimes retains the character primarily of case law. This does not exclude a relevantly syllogistic approach to the framing of indictments and conduct of trials. A recent remarkable example concerned the trial and appeals relative to the explosion that occurred on board Pan Am flight PA 103 London–New York on 21 December 1988 over Lockerbie, killing all the crew and passengers, and residents whose homes were struck by falling wreckage. This led to a famous trial at Camp Zeist in the Netherlands before a special statutorily empowered court of four judges sitting without a jury. One of the two accused in this so-called *Lockerbie* case was acquitted, the other convicted. He appealed, but without success. Lord Justice General Cullen framed the issue in these terms:[19]

At the trial, as in all criminal trials in Scotland, the burden of proving the guilt of the accused lay on the Crown, and so remained throughout the trial. In order to secure a conviction against either accused, the Crown had to succeed in proving his guilt beyond reasonable doubt. Corroboration, that is to say, evidence coming from at least two independent sources, was required to prove the essentials of the Crown case. In the present case these were, in relation to each accused, first, that the crime of murder had been committed and, secondly, that the accused in question was criminally responsible for its commission. Applying these tests, the trial court held that the guilt of the appellant had been proved, but acquitted his co-accused.

[30] As the trial court explained in para [2] of the judgment, it was not disputed, and was amply proved, that the cause of the disaster was the explosion of a device within the aircraft. Nor was it disputed that the person or persons who were responsible for the deliberate introduction of the explosive device would be guilty of the crime of murder. The matter at issue in the trial therefore was whether or not the Crown had proved beyond reasonable doubt that one or other or both of the accused was responsible, actor or art and part, for the deliberate introduction of the device.

In this light, it is material to take note of the charge that was laid against the accused:

[3] The charge narrated that the appellant, having formed a criminal purpose to destroy a civil passenger aircraft and murder the occupants in furtherance of the purposes of Libyan Intelligence Services, while acting in concert with others, did certain acts. These included the purchasing on 7 December 1988 of a quantity of clothing and an umbrella in shop premises known as Mary's House at Tower Road, Sliema, Malta; entering Malta on 20 December 1988 at Luqa airport while using a passport with the false name of Ahmed Khalifa Abdusamad; residing overnight at the Holiday Inn, Tigne Street, Sliema, using this

[19] *Megrahi v HMA* Appeal Court, High Court of Justiciary, 2002 JC 99 at 111, the following quotation being from 2002 JC at 103–4.

false identity; and placing or causing to be placed on board an aircraft of Air Malta flight KM180 to Frankfurt am Main Airport on 21 December 1988 a suitcase containing said clothing and umbrella and an improvised explosive device containing high performance plastic explosive concealed within a Toshiba RT SF 16 radio cassette recorder and programmed to be detonated by an electronic timer, having tagged the suitcase or caused it to be tagged so as to be carried by aircraft from Frankfurt am Main Airport via London Heathrow airport to New York. The charge went on to state that the suitcase was thus carried to Frankfurt am Main Airport and there placed on board an aircraft of PanAm flight PA103 and carried to London Heathrow airport and there in turn placed on board an aircraft of PanAm flight PA103 to New York; and that the improvised explosive device detonated and exploded on board the aircraft while in flight near to Lockerbie, whereby the aircraft was destroyed and the wreckage crashed to the ground and the passengers, crew and residents were killed. The [appellant was convicted, but the] appellant's co-accused, Al Amin Khalifa Fhimah, was acquitted of that charge.

Clearly, the only problematic element in this case concerned issues of proof, and these were indeed massively problematic. Totally unproblematic was the definition of murder, and its applicability to a case of deliberately causing an explosion on a plane during a flight. If the acts charged were committed as charged, they certainly constituted a murder, indeed a multiple murder. But the evidence depended on long and finely drawn out chains of circumstantial evidence. It remains a matter of public controversy whether the charge was indeed proved beyond reasonable doubt in the case of the unsuccessful appellant, Abdelbaset Ali Mohmed Al Megrahi. But the logic of the universal premiss that defines and prohibits murder, the minor premiss alleging specific acts by the accused that clearly constitute murder, and the conclusion that adequate proof of the specific acts is therefore proof of guilt is uncontested and uncontestable. That is what brings about the sharp focus on the elements of the proof and the question whether the standard 'beyond reasonable doubt' is satisfied.

In areas defined by case law and legal doctrine rather than by statute, both in matters of criminal law and in matters of civil law, there is a clear need for procedural provisions essentially the same as those we explored with regard primarily to statute law. Whoever initiates litigation at common law also must intimate to defendant and court the basis of the claim in issue. There must be some allegations of fact, and some claim concerning their legal relevancy, as amounting to the commission of some crime, or a breach of some civil law duty causing harm, or a breach of some contract validly agreed between the parties, or whatever. Even if there is not a statute available to be used as the major premiss in such a way of pleading a case, there has to be some explicit or implicit major premiss grounded in case law and doctrine. The idea of an accusation, a claim, or a decision justified in law presupposes, as will be argued in Chapter 5, some conception of 'universalizability'. For this claim to be justified given these facts, any case with materially similar facts has to be likewise acknowledged as a justified claim. This is the flipside of the 'like cases alike' principle noted earlier.

Whether any implicit premiss can in fact be spelled out and justified as a sound proposition of law becomes, then, the key question in a disputed matter of common law. All the panoply of arguments we already took into account will again be deployable. If our asserted proposition is inconsistent with pre-established law, that will be fatal to it, so interpretative argument will seek to explain and distinguish ostensibly adverse precedents, or advocate their overruling where that is competent. The strong coherence of the proposition with pre-existing law will tell in its favour, and argument by analogy has a special value here. The point of analogies is that they can draw out implicit principles, and indeed only where there turns out to be similarity of principle between two or more apparently like cases is there a relevant legal analogy. Hypothetical examples will test the implications of the principles and propositions suggested and will enable us to test their acceptability by reference to the underlying values we ascribe to common law doctrines, and more full-blooded consequentialist arguments of legal policy are also relevant.

In the nature of the case, the premisses of any syllogism we start from in common law adjudication are weaker and more tentative or defeasible than in reasoning with statutes. But it is no less true that we aim towards a concluding syllogism whose premisses have the full solidity that a good legal argument can secure. The elements of such interpretative arguments are not essentially different as between common law cases and statute-based cases within common law systems. It would be quite extraordinary if anything else were the case.

4. Institution and Reason

Chief Justice Coke, in a famous confrontation with King James I and VI, rebuked the monarch for ignoring the fact that the common law is a system of 'artificial reason and judgment'. However intelligent the king, however gifted in 'natural reason', he could not decide cases between his subjects legitimately if not steeped in 'artificial reason'. Coke had quite a good point—but of course, the contrast cannot be absolute. Artificial reason does not contradict natural reason, but supplements it. Legal order is institutional normative order. The institutional agencies that shape legal order, roughly assignable as these are into the traditional trinity of legislature, executive, and judiciary, construct norms for human conduct of a kind that differ critically from the moral norms and customs that would prevail in a wholly autonomous interaction of humans. They differ critically, just because they are interpersonally authoritative, relatively determinate, and equipped with agencies to enforce and interpret them, these agencies being in turn the creatures of institutional norms. That is the sense in which they are 'artificial', and give rise to an 'artificial' system of reasoning.

No legal norm can be interpreted reasonably in abstraction from its place in a larger whole. As will be seen in Chapters 7 to 11, this accounts for the omnipresence in law of arguments from coherence. These look to ensuring that a proposed ruling or interpretation makes good sense, indeed the best sense possible, in the context of the 'local' part of the system—the statute read as a whole, the particular branch of common law, and the closely comparable cases. They also concern, more generally, an effort to ensure that the system as a whole hangs together well. The idea of 'system' or 'order' is itself an internal element in practical legal argumentation, not just in theoretical conceptions of law. Again one can see the point about 'artificial reasoning', not in the sense that we are dealing with some curious sort of artefact, but in the sense that a lot of knowledge of the law and how it has developed is already presupposed in interpreting even a single text. The whole of the law comprises many parts, and without comprehension of the parts the whole makes little sense. Equally, however, one cannot make sense of any part without regard to its place in the whole. This so-called 'hermeneutic circle' explains why law is so frustrating and difficult a subject to commence studying. (But so are all the humanities.)

4

Defending Deductivism

Introduction

It is an old saying that 'hard cases make bad law'. Its original meaning concerned cases in which the law had a hard impact on some person whose situation aroused sympathy. In such cases there was an inevitable, and often strong, temptation to offer a strained interpretation of the law to avoid the hard effect in the individual case. The slogan 'hard cases make bad law' amounted to an exhortation to refrain from bending the law on account of exceptional individual hardship. *R v Dudley and Stephens*,[1] discussed in later chapters, gives an example. The shipwrecked sailors, desperate for water, all facing apparently certain death, kill the weakest of their number and drink his blood. Subsequently they are rescued. Later they are arrested, indicted, and tried for murder. Should the law be interpreted as allowing a defence of necessity in such a case?

The Chief Justice of England in 1884 held that it should not, arguing that such a defence would inevitably set up a situation where, in emergencies, every person would become judge of his/her own right to survive at someone else's expense. The accused were convicted and sentenced to death. A hard case, indeed—but one that was not permitted to make bad law (law that would allow the defence of necessity in such a case. But the hardness of the law was mitigated through exercise of the prerogative of mercy. The sentence was commuted to one of life imprisonment, and the prisoners served only about six months following their trial.)

A similar, if less dramatic, firmness in the face of temptation to trim was shown in *Daniels v White and Tarbard*,[2] discussed extensively in my previous work on legal reasoning.[3] The purchaser of a bottle of lemonade that contained carbolic acid was injured by drinking it. So was his wife. They sued the manufacturers, who were found to be not liable on the ground that they had not been culpably careless in their manufacturing and bottling processes. The publican was, however, liable to the purchaser (but not his wife) under the Sale of Goods Act, as seller of defective goods that caused damage.[4] The judge acknowledged that the law was 'rather hard' on the publican, who was 'a perfectly innocent person in the

---

[1] [1884] 14 QBD 273.   [2] [1938] 4 All ER 258.
[3] N. MacCormick, *Legal Reasoning and Legal Theory* ch. 2.
[4] Strictly 'goods sold by description' that were not 'of merchantable quality'.

matter', but considered that the law was too clear to admit of any conclusion other than that of seller's liability. Again, a hard case that failed to make bad law—on one view of good law, that is to say.[5]

'Hard case' has over the past few decades changed its meaning, under the influence of Ronald Dworkin, who suggests (in effect) that such cases provide occasions to make good law.[6] A hard case is now understood as a case where some difficulty of interpreting the law has arisen, where there are strong arguments for each of the rival understandings or interpretations of the law put forward by or on behalf of the parties. Dworkin's own most recent example concerns the position of Mrs Sorenson, who has been injured by taking a certain generic drug, which is currently being manufactured by several large pharmaceuticals companies. Assuming it to be clear that she has suffered long-term damage to her health caused by the drug in question, she has a problem. She has used different versions of the drug from different manufacturers, does not know for certain which manufacturers made the drugs she used, but does know that several were involved. Can she then sue the whole set of drug companies that make this drug, claiming a proportionate contribution to her award of damages from each, proportionate to the respective manufacturer's market share? One argument turns on the theory that compensation under tort law is about assignment of risks. Drug companies make substantial profits from sales of drugs, but in circumstances in which there are risks of drugs proving harmful to some persons using them as prescribed medicines. It is seriously arguable that a principle of proportionate liability on proof of damage from use of a drug, although a controversial and novel interpretation of negligence liability, properly captures the sense of justice implicit in the law. On the other hand, it can also be argued strongly that only someone who has caused damage ought to be held liable for it. If it cannot be proved who caused the damage, nobody can be held liable for it. This captures the sense of the long-established principle that there can be no liability without fault.[7]

The 'hardness' of this case in contemporary usage is not to do with the question whether the right decision constitutes hard luck for the drug companies, or hard luck for Mrs Sorenson, that is, whether the sympathetic pro-consumer judgment would be bad law. It concerns the difficulty involved in confronting the opposed, and strong, arguments of the two sides to this case, and coming to a view which is on the whole the better justified view, on which judgment for or judgment against Mrs Sorenson should be based. This is, in the classification proposed here, a grand

---

[5] Fernando Atria, *On Law and Legal Reasoning* (Oxford: Hart Publishing, 2002) at 178 takes the judge's comment as indicating that he thought judgment against the publican to be 'inappropriate', but this seems doubtful. Strict liability is well established in cases of sale of defective goods, even when (as must often be the case) the actual seller is 'perfectly innocent' concerning the defect.

[6] See Dworkin, 'Hard Cases', ch. 4 of *Taking Rights Seriously* (cited hereafter as *Taking Rights Seriously*) (London: Duckworth, 2nd edn, 1984). My own *Legal Reasoning and Legal Theory* also contributed to the change in usage, or at least joined in it without protest.

[7] This case is discussed in the opening sections of Dworkin, 'Hart's Postscript and the Character of Political Philosophy' *Oxford Journal of Legal Studies* 24 (2004) 1–37.

instance of the 'problem of relevancy'. Other hard cases can be figured concerning the problems of interpretation, of classification or evaluation, or of proof. These, I claim, exhaust the possibilities of problematizing a legal issue.

Whether a case is problematized or not is a pragmatic issue in the first place. A claim competently stated or a criminal charge competently laid exhibits the normal syllogistic form, or at least has that for its deep structure. In case of an admission of liability or a guilty plea, or (in civil matters) a failure to respond resulting in a default judgment, no problem arises. If (as in the *Lockerbie* example) the only problem raised concerns proof, the matter is not yet legally problematic, though perhaps what can be proved will turn out to be no more than doubtfully classifiable in terms of one of the crucial universals in the law. (For example, it is proven that a mountaineer fell to his death after his companion cut the rope holding him up. But the trial shows that what happened was that he fell, was roped to a colleague who made a belay and held on to him. After trying for an hour, she had found it impossible to pull him to safety but was then herself getting so weak that she was about to fall, with the result of almost certain death for both of them. Only then did she cut the rope. Was that murder, or a case of self-preservation that falls outside the forbidden necessity defence in relation to murder?[8]) Problems of classification can arise at any point in the legal process. On the other hand, problems of relevancy or of interpretation are likely to be raised from the beginning. If the claim is to be problematized, the right time to do it is as a defence from the outset—though different procedural systems will vary concerning the point in a process at which it is deemed too late to raise an objection of one kind or another.

Pragmatically, therefore, the answer to the question 'What is a problem case?' is simple: it is a case in which a problem has been raised—and, one must add, not dismissed summarily by the judge or judges involved, Let us therefore differentiate 'clear' from 'problematic' cases essentially on this pragmatic basis.[9] 'Clear' is much preferable to 'easy', since many areas of law are hugely complex—tax law, parts of property law, insurance law, and so forth. Even cases in which no problems of law are raised by anyone can be formidably complex in the concatenations of fact and law involved in them. It is almost insulting to call them 'easy' on the ground that the huge difficulties involved in handling them happen not to be topics of current controversy among legal theorists. Someone might object, however, to the hidden assumption involved even in calling the non-problematic cases 'clear'—what is the subtext here?

The question that arises is above all whether there is (or whether I am trading on the hidden implication that there is) a kind of 'ontological' clarity underlying

---

[8] For a more extended discussion of this problem, see Chapter 10 section 1(b), below.

[9] I owe this point to Joxerramon Bengoetxea, *The Legal Reasoning of the European Court of Justice* (Oxford: Clarendon Press 1993) 183–207 on the pragmatic versus semantic reading of 'clear' in the context of the '*acte clair*' doctrine in European Community law. The idea of 'pragmatic clarity' originated in discussions in Edinburgh involving Bengoetxea, the late Jerzy Wróblewski and several others in 1989.

at least some cases of pragmatic clarity. Nobody raised a problem because, in the circumstances, there existed no possible problem that anyone could have raised. Legal texts of whatever kind have open texture and greater or less vagueness, but this is not all-purpose uncertainty.[10] Considerations of justice or the like may sometimes suggest bold new interpretations or developments of old principles in new directions. But perhaps sometimes neither justice nor any other value pulls against the more obvious meaning of the statutes or precedents, and so no reason exists for problematizing the law. Proving the facts may or may not turn out to be a straightforward matter, and once they are proven there may emerge a new problem of classification—but also, there may not. It is again a question whether anyone sees reason to exploit argumentatively an element capable of being problematized. The final arguments for a conclusion on the point about ontological clarity must wait till the last chapter of the book. For the moment, it is enough to say that 'clear' cases are ones that no one has in fact problematized either in a concrete case or in some more theoretical juristic context. Probably, there are some cases that no one could problematize on any ground that would be useful to any interested party, but the fact that nobody has problematized a case gives no ground for assuming that no one could have. The noted lack of usefulness of problem-raising indicates that clarity is still being treated as a pragmatic concept.

1. Gapless Law?

William Lucy remarks that orthodox jurists such as myself are subject to the criticism (which he rejects himself) that we implausibly consider the law to be essentially complete and gapless.[11] Such a view would depict law as capable of generating certain and correct answers in nearly all cases, though sometimes only after difficult arguments and agonizing debates on what the law really says about some particular issue. Vincent Wellman[12] is one vigorous critic of the view that justification of decisions in clear cases is a matter of deductive logic, however long and complex chains of inference may be. According to his argument, this presupposes a belief that the legal system is a complete, gapless, and self-consistent (i.e. non-contradictory) set of norms or normative propositions. This, however, misreads the thesis I have put previously and wish to put here.

The legal syllogism applies case-by-case, and not on any supposition that the law in some way resembles an axiomatic system or even the kind of closed

---

[10] See B. Bix, *Law, Language, and Legal Determinacy* (Oxford: Oxford University Press, 1993) 7–35, 178–9.   [11] *Understanding and Explaining Adjudication* 194–201.

[12] See Vincent A. Wellman, 'Practical Reasoning and Judicial Justification: Toward an Adequate Theory', *University of Colorado Law Rev.* 57 (1985) 45–115 at 71–4. I must absolutely acquit Wellman of any misrepresentation of my position, to which he is eminently fair; but I take it that he thinks that only a rigorous theory of gapless and non-contradictory law could rigorously support a deductivist thesis. I do deny that this is of the essence of a sensible deductivist position.

rule-governed game that chess exemplifies, where all the moves that can ever be made are pre-defined in the rules.[13] In any given case, a party must produce as the basis of his/her argument a formulation of some rule or congeries of rules of the legal system in question, or a statement in reasonably concrete terms of a proposed governing principle, together with allegations of fact which he/she claims can be proven on the admissible evidence available. The opposing party is able and entitled to challenge such a case on any of its points. It is in the nature of legal systems, since the sources of law they recognize comprise sentences in natural languages, that they can give rise to sets of mutually contradictory norm-formulations. This follows from the truism about the 'open texture' of terms in ordinary languages.[14] It also illustrates the typically defeasible character of most formulations of legal rules or norms.[15] Unless a settlement is reached between the parties, each will in due course have to argue that its case is grounded in the more acceptable interpretation of the materials available in the sources. It is obvious that rival interpretations of statutory norms and of precedents abound, and rival readings of legal principles. Each of the parties to a dispute has to show some legal ground for the legal case argued, that is, has to produce a suitable formulation or interpretation of authoritative materials. Each case as initially stated is either syllogistic in form or in deep structure, or it attacks some element in the syllogism offered by the opposed party. The task of the judge is to uphold one or other, or, as it may be, a third view that is preferable to both. In so doing, the judge necessarily rejects one or another of the rival and partly contradictory interpretations of the law. The proposed solution of the case, and the legal interpretation which governs it, have to be constructed in a manner that shows its consistency with pre-established law according to the favoured interpretation of it.[16]

Despite the totality of judicial and legislative attempts to secure internal consistency, the existing authoritative sources of law in any legal system will almost certainly contain some explicitly contradictory elements, and many further

[13] See Fernando Atria, *On Law and Legal Reasoning* (Oxford: Hart Publishing, 2002), at 15, 31, 25–6, 45–7, differentiating 'autonomous institutions', which constitute certain activities such as games, and 'regulatory institutions', such as law, which regulate activities that would remain meaningful otherwise. Rules of the former (have to) apply absolutely. Rules of the latter are intrinsically defeasible.

[14] See N. MacCormick 'On Open Texture in Law' in P. Amselek and N. MacCormick (eds), *Controversies about Law's Ontology* (Edinburgh: Edinburgh University Press, 1991) 72–83.

[15] See Chapter 12 below, and compare R. H. S. Tur, 'Defeasibilism', *Oxford Journal of Legal Studies* 21 (2001) 355–68 and F. Atria, *On Law and Legal Reasoning* (n. 13 above) 121–40. Both Tur and Atria argue that defeasibility is a property built into legal rules, not only into the pragmatic process of interpreting and applying them.

[16] See MacCormick, *Legal Reasoning and Legal Theory*, ch. 8 on this interpretation of the requirement of consistency as it applies in legal reasoning. According to my way of looking at it, the requirement of consistency (like the related requirement of coherence in the legal system, op. cit., ch. 7) is a governing ideal of legal reasoning and interpretation, not a pre-accomplished fact of the legal system. For some reflections on the possibility of a formal representation of the legal system as a system of predicate logic, see Michael Sinclair 'The Semantics of Common Law Predicates' *Indiana Law Journal* 61 (1985–6) 373–99.

elements which can by rival interpretations yield contradictory pairs.[17] This is by no means completely soluble by reference to priority rules such as the rule that a later law derogates from an earlier one regulating the same subject matter in a contradictory sense, or a more particular law from a more general one. Judicial decision-making includes the task of seeking to resolve contradictions as they emerge. It cannot therefore presuppose that there already are none, or that they are merely apparent.

If anyone could frame a complete and wholly satisfactory theory or interpretation of an entire legal system—the task which Ronald Dworkin envisages as being carried out by 'Hercules'[18]—it would doubtless be fully self-consistent and free from contradictions. Then it could be the database, or indeed the knowledge base, for a complete deductive system such as that which Wellman suggests I envisage. But, while there is something to be said for this as a governing ideal for legal reasoning and legal interpretation, there is nothing to be said for representing actual legal systems as though they already had or will ever acquire this character. Nothing that I have said should be taken as meaning that they do.

What the confrontation with Wellman best teaches is how great a gap exists between logic as a specialist discipline and what might be called 'applied logic'. The latter is the kind of syllogistic reasoning that is at the kernel of legal reasoning in the view presented in this book, and that crops up in an analogous way in many departments of practical life. Embedded as legal deductions are in a web of other practical arguments, we can see that it would be a mistake to think of legal reasoning as having separate 'logical' and 'rhetorical' components. On the contrary, recourse to the legal syllogism is a necessary part of the rhetoric of legal justification, on the ground that respect for the Rule of Law requires respect for the rules of the law. The logicians' conception of formal proofs as strictly deductive inferences from axiomatic premises is indeed an idea at some remove from anything to be found in legal argumentation. The latter nevertheless has something to learn from its analogies as well as its disanalogies with the former. And when cases do turn out to be clear in the pragmatic sense defended here, an adequate justification of a decision disposing of them, however informally presented, is deductive in character.

This sets the context in which to assess the claim that there really is a syllogistic or deductive element in legal reasoning, and indeed that this is a central structural feature of legal argumentation. Even this rather guarded thesis is by no means uncontroversial, many jurists having on various grounds dismissed the idea that deductive logic can enter in any serious way into legal thought. The present chapter therefore plays an essentially defensive part, and defends the 'deductivist' position established in the last chapter against various objections. Much of what

---

[17] Compare N. Barber, 'Sovereignty Re-examined: Parliament and Statutes' *Oxford Journal of Legal Studies* 20 (2000) 131–53 at 134–9.

[18] See Ronald Dworkin, *Taking Rights Seriously* (London: Duckworth, 2nd edn, 1984) ch. 4, and cf. his *Law's Empire*.

follows in it is rather technical, and of specialist interest; a reader who does not wish to review objections to my previous position and replies thereto should proceed at once to Chapter 5.

2. The Kelsenian Objection

To speak of what makes a claim or a decision justifiable does not in itself entail that anyone actually poses a claim or hands down a decision with just such an appended justification; or indeed makes the claim or issues the decision at all. Claiming and deciding are acts of will, and acts of will are of course not logical conclusions from arguments. Decisions are made, not deduced. What is entailed by a set of premises is not decided by anybody, though one can indeed decide whether or not to state or to face up to a conclusion that is logically entailed by the premises one accepts. The thesis that decisions are acts of will, not inferences or acts of cognition, is both obviously true, and important in itself. It is a thesis of central importance in Hans Kelsen's 'Pure Theory of Law', especially stressed in the later versions of his theory. It reached its highest point in his final, posthumously published, work,[19] and led him to deny that there could be any kind of a logic of norms, or of normative thinking.

With great respect, we must hold Kelsen to be wrong about this. One can and one should accept his 'act of will' thesis. But equally one must emphatically reject a thesis that Kelsen mistakenly took to be its corollary. Certainly, an act of deciding, like any act, is not and cannot be logically entailed by certain premises, indeed by any premises whatsoever. But this does not mean that conclusions relevant to the question 'what decision is justifiable in a given case?' cannot be derived from relevant and appropriate premises. The premises *P1* 'Every person convicted of murder by a court ought to be sentenced to life imprisonment by the trial court', and *P2* 'Smith is a person convicted of murder before this court' do not entail the decision *D1*: 'Smith, I hereby sentence you to life imprisonment.' But they do entail the conclusion *C1*: 'This court ought to sentence this convicted person Smith to life imprisonment.'[20] That conclusion is not itself a decision. It is, however, a conclusion of law highly and directly material to the issue what this court can in this case now justifiably decide. If the court now formally orders that Smith be subjected to a sentence of life imprisonment, this is on the face of it a

[19] See Hans Kelsen, *Essays in Legal and Moral Philosophy* (Dordrecht: D. Reidel, 1973); chs 10–12, esp. ch. 10, and *Allgemeine Theorie der Normen* (Vienna: Mainzsche Verlags und Universitätsbuchhandlung, 1979), ch. 58, esp. pp. 188–9. Cf. Ota Weinberger, 'Logic and the Pure Theory of Law', in R. Tur and W. Twining (eds) *Essays on Kelsen* (Oxford University Press, 1986), 187–201.

[20] This example is based on Gidon Gottlieb, *The Logic of Choice* (London: Allen and Unwin 1968) 66–77 at 70. Gottlieb denies that the two premises entail a verdict 'Guilty', which is true in itself but not a proof that no conclusion relevant to reaching a verdict follows from the two premises stated.

justified decision, and if justifying reasons were sought, they could be given by repeating *P1* and *P2*, and the entailment of *C1* by these premises. Indeed, if the court were to pronounce, or openly to contemplate pronouncing, any decision other than the imposition of a life sentence, we would surely demand to know under what procedural dispensation and with what legal justification it could possibly do so. The nexus between reason and action can be expressed in the practical argument: 'This court ought to sentence this convicted person Smith to life imprisonment, therefore I hereby sentence you, Smith, to imprisonment for life.'

Here, the relation between justifying reason and action is not one of deduction or inference, but this does not mean that the justifying reason cannot itself be established by deduction or inference. There is every reason to suppose that deductive reasoning of such a kind forms a significant element in legal justification in any conception or system of law in which either the Rule of Law or the *Rechtsstaat* is accepted as the governing, or (more probably) a highly important, ideal. Where the duty of a tribunal is to uphold pre-established and pre-declared rules of law (whether of absolute or of strict application[21]), any form of reasoning will amount to at least a partial justification of a decision if it shows the derivability of a conclusion that would justify a certain decision from appropriate premises.

This can be reinforced by an argument from the principles of representative democracy, so far as concerns legislatively enacted rules in democratic states. Accordingly, reasoning of the kind envisaged really does justify decisions, at least where we presuppose a background commitment to a relevant ideology. To the extent that one considers the values and principles involved to be genuine and sound ones in their own right, not simply as elements in an ideology, one is thereby committed to accepting the decisions as justified in a yet stronger sense. In any event, to treat the reasoning as justifying the relevant decision is not in any way to confuse decision with deduction, or enactment with entailment.

Bernard Jackson, however, has an objection to deductivism based on the Rule of Law. In law, one often seeks to judge of the truth or falsity of averments of fact, or to decide whether they are proven or not. The averments of fact that interest us are in the pleadings of a case, or the indictment in a criminal trial. But these averments must always have been carefully constructed. They will have been constructed with an eye to their legal relevancy. By 'legal relevancy' we mean that they match an abstractly conceived legal basis, expressible in terms of what French lawyers call '*moyens*', or Scots lawyers 'pleas in law'. Where the (hopefully) relevant law is statute law, there is a statutory text (a section or sections of an act or code)

---

[21] Some rules are of absolute application, in the sense that they must always be applied without any exception or allowance for defeating circumstances. Others are of (more or less) strict application, accordingly as they may be overridden or defeated in unusual circumstances and for urgent reasons of principle. The former (following Atria) belong mainly in games like chess; the latter are more typical of legal systems. See F. Atria, loc. cit. n. 13 above, and N. MacCormick 'Ethical Positivism and the Practical Force of Legal Rules' in Tom Campbell and Jeff Goldsworthy (eds) *Judicial Power, Democracy and Legal Positivism* (Aldershot: Ashgate/Dartmouth, 2000) 37–57.

which has to be quite exactly matched by averments, if these are to be relevant. Where a matter of common law is in issue, the text to be matched will be one constructed in a process of common law argumentation from the texts of prior decisions and doctrinal explanations and statements of principles of law. In either case, a process of interpretation of the text relied upon will at some point be called for, to indicate why the law interpreted properly does match the facts averred so that these are relevant as averred.

Jackson argues[22] that this is a mistake, since facts legally averred, even if proven, cannot really 'match' the law. The reason for this is that laws expressed in universalistic and abstract terms do not refer to particular cases, but simply link universally stipulated legal conditions to universally prescribed legal consequences. By contrast, averments of fact in lawsuits or trials do refer to particular and concrete acts, events, and circumstances. This is, as I understand it, the gravamen of his critique of the 'traditional account' of legal decision-making as proceeding by way of a 'normative syllogism', such as deployed here. Jackson argues that this model of legal reasoning necessarily presupposes that the terms in the major premiss must refer in the same way as, and have the same reference as, the terms in the minor premiss. But this is not a sustainable thesis on any credible theory of reference, and cannot even be saved by recourse to the idea of denotation. Instead, Jackson proposes a looser, coherence-based account of the normative syllogism, where even the major premiss is understood in terms of its implicit stories. The touchstone of legal relevancy then becomes one of pattern-matching as between the hypothetical exemplary stories encapsulated in the major premiss and the actual concrete history narrated as the 'minor'.

Some points of great significance emerge from this narrativistic account of Jackson's.[23] Yet his critique of the traditional account does not seem convincing in itself. Nothing in the account which I (or other so-called traditionalists or supporters of orthodoxy) have offered of the possibility of normative syllogisms or about the deductive character of certain elements in legal justification requires the presupposition about reference which Jackson attacks (quite rightly) as unacceptable. General ('universal'[24]) propositions of law can be deployed as major premisses of a normative syllogism, or can be entertained in deliberation about the legal relevancy of particular averments of fact. In either such case, they are not (and, for reasons stated by Jackson cannot be) conceived as already referring to the particular cases which occur after their enactment and which are indeed so constructed as to match the provisions of these rules. At least they do not so 'refer' in the technical understanding of 'reference' used by Jackson in which reference is a speech act, the act of singling out some particular phenomenon in order to say something about it. Jackson's own example is that of the rule that makes those

---

[22] See B. S. Jackson, *Law, Fact and Narrative Coherence* (Merseyside: Deborah Charles Publications, 1988) ch. 2.   [23] Compare Chapter 11 below.
[24] It is important to stress 'universal', see Chapter 5 below.

who commit blasphemy against the gods be liable to the death penalty, as that rule was applied in the case of Socrates.

'All persons who have blasphemed the gods are liable to be executed;
Socrates (is a person and) has blasphemed the Gods;
therefore Socrates is liable to be executed.'

The major premiss here could be cast in a form suitable to predicate logic thus: 'for all persons, if a person blasphemes the gods then that person is liable to be executed'. To express this symbolically. Take 'p' as a person variable, and 'B' as a predicate constant signifying 'has blasphemed the gods', and 'L' as a predicate constant signifying 'is liable to be executed'. This would yield:

1. For all p, if Bp then Lp.

Such a formula does not (of course) single out, or refer to, any person, nor any person's act of blasphemy, nor any person's liability to execution. The sentence about Socrates stands in contrast on this point. For Socrates is (was) a particular person, and it is (was) averred of this very Socrates that he had blasphemed the gods. To put it formulaically, using 's' as a person constant referring to Socrates,

2. Bs.

Those who believe in the 'normative syllogism' hold that premisses 1 and 2 justify the following conclusion:

3. Ls (i.e. 'Socrates is liable to be executed').

Jackson's objection is to the postulated link between (1) and (2). If the universal proposition (1) does not refer to any particular case, but the 'minor premiss' (2) does so refer, how can the former authorize any conclusion at all as to the latter? If we are concerned about the Rule of Law, and hope that no case is decided save as provided for in a rule made and announced in advance, how can we understand rules as 'providing for' outcomes if enunciated without reference to any particular cases? How can we match the (referring) 'B' of the minor to the (non-referring, universal) 'B' of the major?

There is a real problem here, but it is a mistake to see the problem as one about reference.[25] The problem is one about sense. Is 'B' used in the same sense both in (1) and in (2)? If not, there is equivocation, and from a logical point of view this material fallacy would vitiate the reasoning. The problem, in logical parlance, is one of 'universal instantiation'. In premiss (2), it is stated that the universal 'B' is instantiated in the particular case of the individual 's'. The problem, in legal parlance, is either one of interpretation, or of classification (or 'qualification' or 'characterization'). The difference here is whether you focus primarily upon issues

[25] There is perhaps an echo here of Denis Patterson's reproof of the way 'reference came to dominate philosophical discourse' during the twentieth century. See *Law and Truth* (New York and Oxford: Oxford University Press, 1996) at 151.

about rival possible senses ascribable to the universalized major premiss (1), which is commonly taken to be a matter of interpretation, or focus primarily upon the facts, acts, and circumstances in evidence in the particular case. That involves asking whether or not they count as, or are properly classified as, instances of 'B' for the purpose of applying this rule—this is the legal problem of classification. The difference between questions of interpretation and questions of classification can be legally significant, particularly in the operation of a system of precedent, and for certain procedural regulations about appeals and other forms of judicial control of inferior decisions. In the latter, argument by analogy does play a particular part as discussed in the concluding part of Chapter 10.

The main point is clear. Any law-applying decision involves either or both of a decision of classification and an interpretative decision. Always, there has to be an at least implicit decision to treat the facts actually averred or proven as properly characterized by the predicate 'B' *in the sense in which this term is used in the relevant legal proposition.* That is the legal proposition stated or presupposed as legal ground of the decision (the major premiss of a normative syllogism). The specific case referred to by the decision maker then counts as an instantiation of the relevant legal universal, and this justifies the decision of the case, assuming it to be the duty of the decision maker to act according to the relevant rule. Often the process also explicitly involves (and some would say that it always implicitly involves) a deliberative interpretation of the terms of a relevant legal text. This is the process of selecting and deciding for one possible sense ascribable to 'B' (or whatever) as its legally appropriate meaning, giving reasons for that interpretative choice, and affirming that the particular facts averred or proven do qualify as instances of the given predicates in the sense fixed by the interpretative decision.

To exhibit this through our current example: the triers of fact come to a view of what it is that Socrates can be proven to have done within the scope of the allegedly blasphemous acts he is charged with committing. Then they must come to a view on this: does his proven conduct qualify as blasphemy under the relevant [Athenian] law? Is it blasphemy in the relevant sense? If the defence chose to raise a point of law, they might argue that a decision is needed as among three possible general interpretations of the law of blasphemy:

(a) as prohibiting expressions of strong disrespect for any divine beings seriously worshipped by any religious grouping, or

(b) as prohibiting expressions of strong disrespect for divine beings seriously worshipped in some official state religion, or

(c) as prohibiting expressions of strong disrespect for the one supreme divine being as s/he appears to a rational understanding.

In the historical case, (b) seems to have been the answer reached by the Athenian court, while Socrates in the *Apology* argued for (c), and argued that his conduct expressed no disrespect at all for the divine being rationally understood. In the controversy that blew up in 1988 concerning Salman Rushdie's *Satanic Verses*, some argued that blasphemy law in Scotland and England should be interpreted in sense (a). In that case, Salman Rushdie's book would count as blasphemy (against Islam). The prevailing view among lawyers favoured a version of (b), Christianity being the official religion that is alone protected by blasphemy law. Mr Rushdie himself seems originally to have argued for a version of (c), under which, in his then submission, there was no blasphemy.

Scarcely anybody thinks that the only correct, or the best, approach to interpretation of the sense of predicates like 'blaspheming the gods' in such controversial contexts requires us to ask what the historic legislator referred to when he/she/they/it used the term 'B' in framing this provision of criminal law. Some even doubt whether inquiry about the historical legislator's intentions about reference, sense, or anything else, could form any part at all of a rational approach to interpretation.[26] It is no wonder that Jackson can trash so effectively the theory of the normative syllogism after he has fixed it with the untenable presupposition about the supposedly referential character of the major premises of such syllogisms in the form of universal propositions of law. That presupposition is indeed untenable, but it is, as I have shown, no part of the theory of the normative syllogism.

In fact, as argued in Chapter 7, interpretative argumentation is highly complex and involves many types of potentially cumulating or conflicting arguments. These can indeed include arguments about objective or subjective intentions of historic or current legislators. These in turn may be intentions about ordinary or technical uses of language in a particular legal text, or intentions about the legal-systemic context of interpretation (e.g. intention to confirm or to overturn some set of legal precedents), or intentions about the purposes of legislation or about the conception of justice (or other legal value) the statute is to uphold. Equally, without any reference to intention either objectively or subjectively conceived, there can be arguments about the linguistic context of interpretation, and whether this supports a 'plain meaning' or a 'technical meaning'. There can be arguments about interpretation in its legal-systemic context, involving for example considerations of general legal principle, of precedent, of analogy, of legal history, and much else besides. There can be teleological arguments ascribing a purpose to the legislation as part of the context of interpretational problems, and axiological ones about the values the legislation ought to be seen as upholding, and these also can be relevant to a choice among possible interpretations.

In this context, Jackson's suggestion about the implicitly narrative or story-telling aspect of law is very fruitful. Others who have made this point may have tied it too exclusively to case law and precedents. Certainly one helpful and

---

[26] See R. Dworkin, 'On Gaps in the Law', in P. Amselek and N. MacCormick (eds), *Controversies about Law's Ontology* (Edinburgh: Edinburgh University Press, 1991) 84–90, at p. 87 arguing against any relevance of legislative history to good interpretation.

persuasive way of trying to tease out an interpretation of a statutory text must be to think of it in terms of possible or hypothetical cases, or characteristic situations which it fits. Legislative debate as well as interpretative deliberation can be made more vivid and meaningful in this way. Narrative illustrations might well help to cut out legislative cross purposes, just as they can help to clarify interpretative reasoning. Where *travaux préparatoires* are admissible as aids to interpretation, examples in them must be especially helpful, just as Jackson commends them for being in the appendix to the [English and Welsh] Law Commission's draft Criminal Code, published in 1985 as *Codification of the Criminal Law* (Law Comm. 143). This shows the interaction of sense and reference, for the sense of predicates is grasped by considering their potentialities for reference. Also, our grasp of an abstract principle may be achieved most vividly by a concrete case, by an arresting exemplary narrative. Biblical parables seem to be a *locus classicus* for this. In legal interpretation, narratives are not a substitute for argument from principles, more a way of making principles vivid even in cases where we are unsure how exactly to formulate the principle implicit in our reasoning. Like analogical arguments, they have a particular part to play in rational processes of discovery as well as in processes of justification.

All in all, I conclude that the problem of matching major and minor premises in a normative syllogism is the problem of securing sameness of sense of the predicates deployed in both. Narrative modes of argumentation can have real value here, but not to the exclusion of other modes. That it is only in minor premises that predicates are used referentially, with reference to particular features of particular concrete cases, while their use in major premises is non-referential, poses no difficulty for this theory.

The point, of course, is that interpretative and classificatory decisions have to be made so as to construct a syllogism (or a more informal deductive argument) in which all predicates are used unequivocally, that is, in the same sense throughout. Unless interpretative and classificatory decisions can themselves be based on sound arguments, not all of them deductive arguments, the deductive character of legal reasoning (the possibility of reconstructing it in terms of the normative syllogism) would be perfectly compatible with a substantial degree of arbitrariness in decision-making, and no very good guarantor of the Rule of Law. The same would be the case if there were no settled interpretative practice in a legal community. For then, even if each decision handed down were argued out on the basis of a perfect match of classificatory decision and interpretative decision, each in turn well-argued in itself, there would be no congruity or coherence in the reasoning process from case to case and decision maker to decision maker. Securing the Rule of Law as a desirable condition of a legal system requires not only that normative syllogisms be possible. It requires also the possibility that these can be encapsulated within an interpretative practice exhibiting coherence across decision makers and over time.

3. Truth-Value and Institutional Facts

Still, there may remain a related and fundamental objection to the deductivist thesis. For we start from the assumption that legal rules are norms of a particular kind. According to the view of Kelsen and of many like-minded thinkers, norms are themselves acts of will, or the contents of acts of will, and hence they lack truth-value, that is, they are not the kind of entity to which either truth or falsity can be intelligibly ascribed. On this ground, it is averred that rules cannot form premises for logical reasoning in any strict or strong sense. This Kelsenian argument has been restated both by Bernard Jackson[27] and by Vincent Wellman.[28] Wellman suggests that it is at best contestable and at worst false to ascribe truth-value to statements or formulations of rules, and that good methodology requires us to avoid contestable premises where weaker and less contestable ones can be found. So it is methodologically unsound to base a theory of legal reasoning on the assumption that truth-value can be ascribed to rule-statements. Bernard Jackson, on the other hand, argues that I fall into confusion between legal dogmatics as a semiotic system within which true-or-false statements may be made and the discourse of the judiciary in decision-making, this being a wholly different semiotic system, not admitting of truth-value. Yet this is where the notion of justification applies.

Ota Weinberger, with whom I have collaborated closely in relation to the 'Institutional Theory of Law', is a leading authority for the view that norm-logic is a special and non-truth-functional logic. Carlos Alchourrón and Eugenio Bulygin have shown in a series of distinguished and authoritative papers that it is a serious mistake to confuse the logic of norms on the one hand with the logic of (descriptive) normative statements on the other.[29] Only a logic of norms can establish crucial notions like that of contradiction (or conflict) between norms or can show the necessary relations which obtain between the obligatory and the permissible where these are conceived as normative terms, not norm-describing ones. These notions are crucial for, but not exactly or directly replicated in, the logic of (descriptive) normative statements. Alchourrón and Bulygin themselves hold that the logic of justification of judicial decisions must be the logic of norms, not of normative statements, hence it has to be different from the logic of a descriptive activity like that of legal dogmatics. In this, their critique is comparable with that of Jackson.

---

[27] B. S. Jackson, *Law, Fact and Narrative Coherence* (Liverpool: Deborah Charles, 1988) 37–60.

[28] See Vincent A. Wellman, 'Practical Reasoning and Judicial Justification: Toward an Adequate Theory', *University of Colorado Law Rev.* 57 (1985) 45–115; cf. A. Wilson, 'The Nature of Legal Reasoning: a Commentary with respect to Professor MacCormick's Theory', *Legal Studies* 2 (1982) 269–85.

[29] See Carlos Alchourrón 'Detachment and Defeasibility in Deontic logic' *Studia Logica* 57 (1996) 5–18; E. Bulygin, 'An Antinomy in Kelsen's Pure Theory of Law' *Ratio Juris* 3 (1990) 29–45.

Nevertheless, the Institutional Theory of Law gives a solid ground for rejecting the Kelsenian objection, and for responding to Wellman's methodological point, albeit this is subject to an important proviso. The proviso is that the logic of justification is seen as one which primarily has recourse to statements which make assertions about (what one understands to be) the content of a norm, rather than producing the very norm itself and working directly from that. To say this is to return to what was said earlier about the interpretative character of thought about norms and practices. We seek to capture, in what can even be called a 'descriptive' way, the sense of the norm that confronts us. Statements of this descriptive-interpretative kind can without the least absurdity be considered to be true or false (though by no means always uncontroversially true or uncontroversially false), that is, to have truth-value. Such statements are admittedly not very like statements of simple physical facts, what are sometimes called (or caricatured as) 'brute facts'. But this is quite unremarkable, for they are statements not of brute facts but of institutional facts. Such statements do have truth-value.

The strongest ground for doubting or denying this point is that speech acts like commanding or legislating lack truth-value. To the extent that they have any kind of propositional content, this is posed in a way that contrasts with assertive and descriptive ways of uttering a similar content. If I say that a certain door is locked, my words are supposed to fit the world, and to be corrected or withdrawn otherwise. So if, on inspection, we find that the tongue of the lock is engaged with the jamb in such a way that the key must be inserted and turned in order to open the door, we certify the statement as true; if not, as false. If I say, 'See to it that the door is locked', one who has to obey me must check whether the tongue of the lock is engaged, and, if not, engage it, otherwise, leave it alone. The point is to get the world to fit the word, not that words should fit the world as it already is. Assertive and descriptive (including interpretative-descriptive) ways of uttering produce sentences that have truth-value, and in this they contrast with imperative ways of uttering such as we find in acts either of legislating or of commanding.

When one drives past a thirty miles per hour speed limit sign, one is not supposed to think or to murmur, 'How true', but to adjust the speed of one's car accordingly. One is to derive from it (and to act on) an individual imperative. To think, 'Watch out! Keep your speed at or below thirty miles per hour until further notice!' and to decelerate accordingly is not to deal in the currency of true and false. Conforming to law is not the same as making true statements about it.

But there is a different point to be made. Acts of legislating are correctly said to 'establish' norms. But a norm thus 'established' constitutes valid law in the relevant system over a period of time. The conceptual structure of a legal system is one in which norms posed in statutes can be said to endure through time, from the moment of such enactment to a later moment of repeal, or a more drawn-out process of falling into disuse and eventual revocation by contrary custom ('desuetude'). Endurance through time, as distinct from occurrence at a moment of time, is the criterion of 'existence'.[30] Statements about something that exists (endures through time) are statements of fact. Since in an institutional normative order, norms exist, there can be statements of fact ('institutional fact') about these institutional norms. They are true or false in relation to the relevant order or system at any given point of time.

There is a quite general distinction between acts that are performed, or occur, at a moment in time, but are not themselves true or false, and the states of affairs that result from the acts, and endure over time, states of affairs about which true or false statements can be made. Putting a litre of petrol in a car is an act that lacks truth-value. Using it as intended, to fuel the car, is an act that lacks truth-value. But the petrol gauge in the car can still give true (or, alarmingly, false) information about the states of affairs resulting from such acts, and from the other acts and processes that result in depletion of the tank as fuel is used to propel the car. So too with the legal states of affairs which result from law-creating and conduct-guiding acts. These can be truly (or falsely) stated notwithstanding that the acts which brought them about cannot themselves be true or false, and are not acts which state true or false statements.

Bearing all this in mind, let us turn now to some concrete attempts to make normative statements of law. Suppose that I wish to try and state some proposition of law that will capture the point of a currently existent legal norm, and at the same time make it reasonably easy to use in drawing logical inferences. Let it be that I try to capture the sense of the common law concerning murder as this currently stands in Scotland, as relevant, for example, to the *Lockerbie* case discussed in the previous chapter. Here is such an attempt: 'For all x and for all y, if x is a legal person and y is a human being, then if y dies and if x so acted or deliberately refrained from acting as to cause y's death, and if x acted or refrained from acting with the intention to cause y's death, then x is guilty of the murder of y and x is liable to be sentenced to imprisonment for life.'

I do not present this as the whole truth about murder, having omitted for example provisos about self-defence and other forms of lawful killing, having overlooked mitigating or partially excusing circumstances such as provocation, and so forth. I have also left out killing through wicked recklessness and (if I were to extend my ambit to English law, cases of what English lawyers call 'transferred malice'). My statement involves an interpretation of murder as a crime that can be committed by legal persons, not necessarily individual human beings, but one that can only be committed on human beings. That again may leave somebody wondering about the status of the human foetus or (not so obviously a finally closed question just now) patients in an apparently irreversible persistent vegetative state. Nevertheless, if it is accepted that intentional killing is a crime in Scots

---

[30] Compare N. MacCormick and O. Weinberger, *An Institutional Theory of Law* (cited hereafter as *Institutional Theory*) (Dordrecht: D. Reidel, 1986) arguing that whatever can be envisaged as enduring in time can be counted as 'existing'.

(and English) law, namely the crime of murder, and that those who commit it are liable to be punished with life imprisonment, my interpretation is a reasonable one. Thus the statement can, with some confidence, be pronounced true. In fact, I doubt if anyone would be very likely to contest it strongly, or would seriously assert that a statement of this kind can quite properly be called true or false. Whether it is true exactly as stated or needs some shading or adjustment is indeed a question of opinion, depending partly on the current state of the law in the particular legal system in issue and partly on approaches to its interpretation.

That a certain question calls for the use of judgement and interpretation in forming an opinion is not incompatible with its being true or false. Medical diagnoses, mechanical investigations into persistent trouble with a car's transmission, judgements about personal character, and such like all have this same quality. Nobody thinks such diagnoses or judgements are incapable of ever being true or false. What makes us doubt this is some residue of a very naive correspondence theory of truth. By a 'naive correspondence theory' I mean one that holds that we can ascribe truth-value only to statements for which there could be some exactly corresponding state of affairs in the perceptible physical world. True statements are then those and only those with which this world does indeed correspond.

Such a theory is untenable for a whole variety of reasons, not least because its own statements cannot be true (or false) by its own criterion of truth. On this ground (and others) there is a temptation to abandon the very concept of 'correspondence' as supplying either a meaning of or a criterion for truth. Yet this in turn goes too far. There are indeed classes of statements within given forms of discourse for which 'correspondence' with perceptible events and states of affairs is a quite appropriate criterion of truth. Conversely, there is a perfectly acceptable (if somewhat different) sense of the term 'correspond' in which we can say that for every true statement in any veridical discourse there are corresponding facts. Correspondence in this latter sense, however, cannot be a criterion of truth, for the facts in question cannot be supposed to exist in some way independently of the grounds of truth of the sentences which state them. This is, indeed, a characteristic of all sorts of institutional fact.

'Institutional facts' are (to repeat a point) those facts that depend not only on some physical events and occurrences which are supposed to have taken place, but also on an interpretation of these (and/or other) events or occurrences in terms of some stable set of norms (either institutional or conventional norms) of conduct or of discourse. The fact that the sentence I have just written is a well-formed and grammatically correct sentence in English is an example of such a fact. Relevant occurrences in the world are the utterance by me of sounds or the production by me of marks on paper or on my computer screen. These amount to a sentence in the English language only given the complex but stable set of norms and conventions of discourse which constitute the grammar and semantics of English as a natural language. That the presentation of this and other sentences in an ordered declamation by me amounts to preparing a chapter for a jurisprudential book about rhetoric depends likewise on an interpretative understanding of the relevant occurrences in the light of a presupposed complex and stable set of rules about authorship and publication. If the truth of a true statement depends both upon the occurrence or non-occurrence of relevant events and upon the interpretation of these events by reference to the norms that make them count as relevant, then the statements in question state 'institutional facts'. That an interpretation of the norms in question is also involved does not defeat this conclusion.

In *The Opposite Mirrors*[31] Eerik Lagerspetz suggests that institutional facts can be conceptualized as a subclass of what he calls 'conventional facts', that is, that they are facts in virtue of the conventional (and mutual) beliefs of relevant populations or groups of people. The existence of at least some rules, for example, the ultimate rules of any given legal system, depends on convention rather than on yet higher-order rules (leading either to an infinite regress or to a Kelsenian arbitrary presupposition). Thus it is obvious that the present account of institutional facts has to be embedded in some account of custom or convention, and thus in something like Lagerspetz's conventional facts. Ota Weinberger's broader category of 'humanly conditioned' facts (*menschabhängige Tatsache*) probably plays the same role.[32] However that may be, it seems plain enough that our conventions are for us constitutive of facts, facts which hold good only because of our—or somebody's—observance of relevant conventions, or of institutional norms which themselves depend ultimately on some convention.

Further, if one can truly state that a certain (simplistically formulated) rule 'whenever *OF* then *NC*' is valid in a given legal system, then it seems equally unobjectionable to say that for this system, during the validity of that rule, *NC* is (truly) the legal consequence that follows in any given case where *OF* obtains. The truth that the rule is valid seems to entail the truth of the statement of its contents as a truth about the legal system as it now exists. It is murder in Scots law if one person deliberately kills another in the absence of any justifying or excusing conditions; and the legally mandatory penalty for murder is imprisonment for life. There seems to be something very odd indeed about denying that these statements can have truth-value, since no ordinary person would seriously doubt their truth. Moreover, if you wish to justify the fact that a certain person is serving a sentence of life imprisonment in a Scottish prison, it is surely at least the beginnings of a justification for this if he has been convicted of murder, and sentenced to life imprisonment on that account.

The final upshot of this section of the chapter is thus that there can be no serious objection to deductivism on the basis of the correct observation that legal norms lack truth-value. Norms indeed lack it, but interpretative-descriptive statements of law can possess it, and the case for deductivism in the form

---

[31] Lagerspetz, *The Opposite Mirrors* (Dordrecht: Kluwer Academic Publishers, 1995) ch. 1.
[32] MacCormick and Weinberger, *Institutional Theory*, ch. 3.3; in the original German, N. MacCormick and O. Weinberger, *Grundlagen des institutionalistischen Rechtspositivismus* (Berlin: Duncker & Humblot, 1985) pp. 114–15.

advocated here requires only that statements of that kind play a crucial and legitimate part in a reasonable practice of legal justification. The theory of institutional facts indicates that it is perfectly appropriate to ascribe truth-value both to statements of the validity of valid legal rules, and to interpretative-descriptive statements about the content of valid rules as statements about the existing law of a given jurisdiction or state.

This brings back to the forefront of attention Jackson's suggestion that there is a radical disjunction between the discourse of a judge who gives an opinion on the law in justifying a decision in a contested case, and a legal scholar who states an opinion about it in some discourse of legal dogmatics—say, writing a monograph or textbook or journal article about the law, or discussing it with fellow scholars or with students. It may be said, by way of contrast, that the scholar's statements are nothing more than mere opinion, carrying no authority from the mere fact of the scholar's uttering them, but the judge's carry judicial authority automatically with them. They become valid by being uttered by a judge in a judicial capacity, and the judge's act of saying something is a law-constituting act in the rather transparent guise of a descriptive-interpretative statement.

To answer this point is also to anticipate a conclusion argued more fully in Chapter 13. The judges' justifications of the decisions they make are effective as justifications only in so far as they offer genuine attempts to interpret the law, and it is the law so interpreted that justifies their decision. This does sometimes include an interpretation of existing law that holds it to be silent or not completely settled on a vital point. Then a decision must be made that settles the hitherto undetermined point, and that law-settling decision is a prerequisite of any law-applying decision. So indeed the law-settling decision is different from the interpretative discourse that leads into it. Moreover, especially where we deal with interpretation, with all its dependence on the formation of well-informed opinion, it is certainly reasonable to attach special weight in future interpretations to judicial opinions formed in decision-making after rigorous (or at least vigorous) argument by counsel. But plain mistakes will remain plain mistakes,[33] whether committed by judges or by scholars.

On the other hand, it is an important truth that judges who justify decisions have to be engaged in showing that the decisions they give fulfil the judicial obligation to respect the law. Hence the judge must, say Alchourrón and Bulygin, be concerned with deriving conclusions from binding norms, not from statements about them. They are right that it is indeed obligatory in the strong, normative, sense for a judge to decide according to law. He or she must show that the decision given does accord with law in order to discharge this obligation. But the task of showing that a decision does so accord is one that requires taking a descriptive-interpretative view of the norms of the system. Showing how one's decision squares with the system so considered is showing that the essential obligation of a judge is being honoured.

---

[33] See Chapter 13 below.

Jerome Bickenbach has suggested that this necessarily interpretative character of legal reasoning precludes its being in any nontrivial sense deductive reasoning.[34] This certainly does not displace or trivialize the conclusion established in the last chapter that syllogistic reasoning is structurally central to legal thought. Moreover, if the presence of interpretation were fatal to relying on logic so far as concerns the structure of one's arguments, it is not only legal logic that would be discountenanced. What would be precluded would be the application of logic to any empirical or practical realm.

The point to be gathered is not that applied logic is impossible, but that empirical truth is truth only of statements (and the like) that are considered as stating propositions to which a certain interpretation is ascribed. They are true given that interpretation of their meaning and of the world. Consider 'The cat is on the mat.' What cat? What mat? Where? When? What counts as a cat? Or a mat? And so on. On any occasion when somebody utters such a sentence, we have to interpret the sentence as referring to some particular cat, some particular mat, and the like. Only in the light of such an interpretation can we decide whether what the speaker said is true or false. And in order to decide this point after we have made our interpretation, we shall still need some form of truth-determining procedure.

4. What Logic for Legal Reasoners?

At this point it is appropriate to bring into the open what has been implicit up till now, at the same time acknowledging a deficiency in the way my earlier writings attempted to formalize the logic of deductive reasoning in legal justification. *Legal Reasoning and Legal Theory* (1978), attempted to show how part of the reasoning in one English case, that of *Daniels & Daniels v R. White & Sons Ltd and Tarbard*,[35] amounted to a deductive argument for the conclusion that the defendant was liable in damages to the plaintiff. This conclusion was worked out through recourse to a complex set of premises comprising various rules of British statute law (the Sale of Goods Act 1893) and of English common law, along with certain findings of fact. To account for this, I adapted the conventions of propositional logic to the task of representing the formal structure of the reasoning in the case and showed how the reasoning could be seen as a complex string of hypothetical arguments, syllogisms like the ones discussed in the last chapter. This was essentially correct, but not completely satisfactory as presented in 1978.

---

[34] See J. Bickenbach, 'Legal Hermeneutics and the Possibility of Legal Critique' in E. Simpson (ed.), *Antifoundationalism and Practical Reasoning* (Edmonton, Alberta: Academic Printing and Publishing, 1987) pp. 217–32, where a similar view is ascribed to R. Dworkin, *Law's Empire* (London: Fontana Books, 1986), probably correctly. A radically different version of the same objection is stated in the last chapter of Peter Goodrich's *Reading the Law* (Oxford: Basil Blackwell, 1986).

[35] [1938] 4 All ER 258.

Patricia White[36] vigorously criticized this on the ground that key elements in the reasoning fall out of sight if one restricts oneself to using propositional logic to give a formal representation or reconstruction of such arguments. A form of predicate logic is required here. The reason for this is that legal rules have the character of 'open hypotheticals',[37] that is, they deploy hypotheses that are realizable on any number of occasions. As was stressed in the preceding chapter and in earlier sections of this one, they deploy 'universals' or 'concepts' in stating what are the operative facts relative to given normative consequences. One part of the analysis of the *Daniels* case[38] helps to show this. I gave a representation of section 14(2) of the Sale of Goods Act 1893 (since amended) in the following terms: 'If goods are bought and sold by description, and if the seller of the goods is a person who deals in goods of that description, then there is an implied condition (which must be fulfilled by the seller) that the goods shall be of merchantable quality.'

Such a rule plainly purports to regulate any case in which the relevant conditions—the operative facts in question—are realized, and to ordain that in each such case the relevant normative consequence of an implied condition binding on the seller shall follow. Hence the application of the rule in any case requires that it be established in respect of that case that there exist particular instances of the universal predicates deployed as operative fact descriptions in the rule formulation. It must be established, of this and that person on a given occasion that this did sell and that did buy something, that the something was goods, that those goods were sold by description, and that this person does deal in goods of that description. Then it will be legally justifiable to read this contract as being subject to this implied condition that the goods in this case are of merchantable quality, and unjustifiable to hold otherwise without some very special reason being offered. It is the subsumption of observed particulars under universalized predicates which is decisive for the reasoning. Following earlier similar examples, it would thus be better to reformulate the premiss of the reasoning in terms such as:

'For all x and all y, if x and y are legal persons and if x sells to y and if y buys from x some thing g, and if g is a type of goods, and if x is a person who deals in goods of the type t, and if t is a type of goods to which g belongs, then the contract between x and y is subject to an implied term that g is of merchantable quality, and x is liable to compensate y if g is not of merchantable quality.'

---

[36] See Patricia White, book review, *Michigan Law Review* 78 (1979–80) 737–42.

[37] See D. Mitchell, *An Introduction to Logic* (Oxford: Oxford University Press, 2nd edn, 1964) p. 82.

[38] See MacCormick, *Legal Reasoning and Legal Theory* pp. 19–33 for my rational reconstruction of the *Daniels* case. Briefly to summarize the facts and point of the case so far as relevant for present purposes: Mr Daniels bought from Mrs Tarbard in her public house a bottle of R. White's lemonade. When he and his wife drank the lemonade, they suffered burning sensations and were hospitalized. The lemonade had a large admixture of carbolic acid in it. Since it was bought by description, the sale was subject to an implied term that the lemonade was of merchantable quality. Since lemonade with carbolic acid in it is not of merchantable quality, Mrs Tarbard was liable to Mr Daniels for damages for breach of contract.

The application of such a rule in the case of any actual humans *a* and *b*, or indeed Tarbard and Daniels, requires findings that they themselves in the relationships in which they stood at the material time do count as instances of the predicates (the universals, the concepts) stated in the rule-formulation. Each has to be found to be a legal person, they have to be found to have contracted between them a sale of something—a bottle of lemonade, it was—and the thing sold, the bottle in question, has to be found to belong to a type of goods, and *a*, or Tarbard, has to be found to be a dealer in goods of the type to which lemonade belongs. Then their sale of that bottle will rightly be held subject to that condition. And so on with the rest of the relevant argument. Decisive to the argument at every step, as Patricia White said, is that the universal predicate is held to be particularly instantiated in the particular case. The improvement she called for has already been incorporated into the argument of this and the preceding chapter. The point is that, once the requisite correction is made, the original argument stands up perfectly well.

5. An Objection: Classifying as Deciding

At this stage, however, several further objections arise, some of which have likewise been forcefully stated by critics of my work. First, it may be objected (as for example by the late Alida Wilson[39]) that events which occur in the world are not self-labelling. Therefore any classification of events which occur under some predicate-term as stated in a rule-formulation would necessarily involve a kind of decision, not a pure act of cognition. For example, in a case in which an actual individual, *a*, is accused of murdering a certain *b*, the issue may arise whether *b* is really a human being for the purposes of the rule—*b* is perhaps a foetus or unborn child,[40] and there can be controversy whether that counts as a human being. Or an issue could arise as to whether any act of *a*'s did cause *b*'s death—or even whether *b* has in fact died. If *b* has suffered brain damage from a blow struck by *a*, but has been kept breathing by artificial ventilation, while encephalography reveals a complete absence of brainstem activity, is *b* now dead? Or does death occur when doctors switch off the ventilator? What act is then the cause of death? With what intention did *a* act in striking the blow? How can we reliably ascribe intentions to agents in respect of their acts?

Such questions as these pose a very familiar legal problem, and they can be replicated for any rule-formulation that you care to mention. All are instances of what have here been called 'problems of classification'. It is obvious that their resolution in any given instance requires a determination, a decision whether that which has occurred can reasonably and properly be ascribed to the predicate

[39] See Alida Wilson, 'The Nature of Legal Reasoning: a Commentary with respect to Professor MacCormick's Theory' *Legal Studies* 2 (1982) 269–85.

[40] Or a 'conjoined twin' with no capability to breathe alone as discussed in relation to the *Conjoined Twins* case in Chapter 5.

that states one operative fact in a given rule-formulation. This depends on some kind of decision that has to be justified 'externally' to the deductive argument that applies once the classification is determined.[41] The presence of such ascriptive determinations leads the critics to the conclusion that there can be no question of logic or of deduction in the case. Ascriptive determinations are acts of will, and as such have no place in a chain of deduction. Certainly, this cannot be a realm of truth-functional logic, since what is in issue is not a simple question of true-or-false, but rather a matter for yes-or-no decision whether or not to ascribe this to that.

This objection, it can be seen, replicates the Kelsenian one considered earlier. My reply also replicates its predecessor, but here I shall add the point that the objection proves too much. For, if sound, it applies to all domains of applied logic, not just to legal or normative reasoning. What would become of the famous syllogism about Socrates if the objection were sound? 'For all x, if x is a man then x is mortal.' To apply this in the case of any individual being requires an ascription—'Socrates is a man'—before one can proceed to a conclusion—'therefore Socrates is mortal.' Only by deciding that Socrates is a man can we justify proceeding, under the warrant of that major premiss, to this conclusion. Was Jesus a man or God or both? Was He mortal? *A fortiori*, in any case of applied science where one seeks to apply a 'scientific law'. In building a bridge or an aeroplane, I may have information about the tensile strength of any piece of steel having a certain composition and dimensions. I may have calculated that a certain component has to have a certain tensile strength. But I am warranted in treating the piece of steel in my hand as fulfilling the required tensile strength only if I ascribe to it the relevant composition and dimensions. It is not only legal inferences that call for ascriptive determinations.

The conclusion to be drawn for all cases, the legal one included, is not that ascriptive decisions or determinations preclude or exclude deductive logic, but rather that they are a necessary precursor to any deductive reasoning whatsoever that is carried out with reference to the actual world. Every form of applied logic requires decisions as to the applicability of universals (predicate terms) to particular instances. The existence of decisions, and of the necessity for decisions, in the legal field is neither special to that field nor fatal to the possibility of deductive logic within it. If these require justification in given pragmatic circumstances, then certainly that 'external' justification has to be provided before any syllogistic representation of a conclusion can be convincing. But sometimes no serious objection is raised, and no serious answer by way of external justification is called for. That is what, in my view, occurred in *Daniels v White and Tarbard*. Notwithstanding objections from respected colleagues,[42] I therefore adhere to the view that this case shows how it can be possible to justify a decision in a purely

[41] See Fernando Atria, *On Law and Legal Reasoning* 174–84, first drawing attention to Robert Alexy's differentiation between 'external' and 'internal justification', then criticizing my view of *Daniels v White and Tarbard* on that ground.
[42] Especially Fernando Atria, *On Law and Legal Reasoning* 177–84.

deductive way (after rectifying the mode of logical presentation) when matters are pragmatically clear. This is so, whether or not they can ever be equally clear in a deeper, ontological, sense.

6. Truth and Truth-Determining Procedures

So far from being anomalous in this regard, the legal realm is in fact one that caters with particular thoroughness for the problem of truth-determination. Where determinations of fact are called for in any authoritative law-applying process, legal systems ordinarily make provision to endow determinate individuals with special fact-determining authority. Whether the fact-determining task be given to a jury, a judge, a minister, or some special tribunal, there are usually some legal dispositions giving some individual or group the power to make conclusive determinations of fact (or defeasible ones, that can be reversed on appeal, but only within some time-limit. After that, they become conclusive.)

Zenon Bankowski has, in another context, suggested that such processes of fact-determination carried out by authorized persons can be considered as 'truth-certifying procedures'.[43] This is a valuable insight. For certain purposes, that which an authorized fact-determiner determines to be true, or certifies as true, has to be deemed true or accepted as the conclusive truth of the matter. For legal purposes, the value 'true' is ascribed to that which is authoritatively so certified. Except in so far as processes of appeal or review can be utilized to reverse or correct certified truths, the legal system admits of no other truth of the relevant matter, whatever the relative strengths of the reasons for believing and for disbelieving *p* in the first place. Finality of decision requires this. But the law is not on its own in this. Albeit less formally, scientific communities have their own truth-certifying processes and their own procedures for rectifying previously certified truths which turn out to be unsound.

In effect, legal fact-finding processes transform brute facts into institutional facts. Whatever may have happened in the world, a jury's determination that *a* hit *b* on the head and caused *b*'s death makes that count as a legal truth, a proposition counted as true in a certain legal process. It is true given certain legal conventions of truth-ascription. That does not, of course, make it true for all purposes. Indeed one way of justifying or criticizing legal procedures is to try to form an estimate of the degree to which the things that are legally held true actually match the world as it really is, however one thinks it appropriate to judge of that. We return to the point that any process that is dependent on decisions is justifiable only in so far as the decisions on which it depends are justified ones.

---

[43] See Z. Bankowski, 'The Value of Truth: Fact-Skepticism Revisited' *Legal Studies* 1 (1981) 257–66.

In the light of contemporary discussions of the application of information technology in law, for example involving the use of expert systems in legal problem-solving, these reflections assume a certain significance. Our reflections on issues of truth, that is, of the certification or determination of what is to count as true, imply that there are fundamental elements in legal processes that should not be delegated to machines, however 'intelligent'. Determinations of fact require a capacity for evaluation of evidence, and determinations that certain brute facts count as instances of a rule's operative facts require a capacity for interpretation of rule-formulations in the light of human values. Such determinations can only be made by beings with intelligence and will, and with a capacity for evaluation of evidence and for understanding the values implicit in rules. It is therefore most likely that only a person, not a machine, can possibly answer them. In any event, it is better that they be determinations made by humans who can be directly held to account for the determinations they issue.

7. Evaluations in Legal Reasoning

Always, as I said, determinations of fact require evaluation of evidence. But this is not the only aspect of evaluation that enters into the fact-finding processes of the law. It is quite often the case that the law sets up a provision that is to be conditional on the satisfaction of a certain criterion or standard of value. For example, laws are often cast in terms of what is reasonable, or in similar terms. The common law concerning liability for accidental injury can be represented like this:

> 'For all x and all y, if x and y are legal persons, and if x commits an act or omission which causes harm to y and if it was reasonably foreseeable by x at the time of acting or omitting that harm of a type h could occur to persons in position p as a result of such acting or omitting unless reasonable care were taken, and if the harm suffered by y is of type h and if y was in position p and if x failed to take reasonable care in respect of y, then x is liable to make reasonable compensation to y for the harm suffered by y.'

Again, as was mentioned above, the Sale of Goods Act, before recent reforms, used to require certain goods to be of 'merchantable quality' (now replaced by a different value-criterion). The previous chapter's discussion of the *Microsoft* case adds a further illustration, as would the many legal requirements that allude to what is 'fair', as in the case of a landlord's entitlement to charge only a fair rent in the case of certain tenancies of houses.

All such criteria are obviously evaluative. It was noted in the preceding chapter that, to apply them, one must not only weigh up the evidence to reach a conclusion about what events occurred in the world. One must also judge of the events against standards of judgement, weighing a plurality of factors bearing on the question what ought to occur in such a case. So here, the task of determining whether the law's conditions are satisfied requires a double evaluation. It nevertheless remains the case that in common law, with its easy insouciance about the supposed gap between fact and value, such questions as that of what is reasonable or that of what is fair are classed as 'questions of fact'. Accordingly, their answers are determined by the determiners of legal facts, and their determinations here as elsewhere amount to certifications of what is true for legal purposes in this realm of value.

It is sometimes suggested[44] that there are special objections to ascribing deductive character to any reasoning process in which such values and evaluations play a part. Evaluations, say the critics, do not have truth-value, and it is always a question of opinion and judgement—of decision—whether or not a certain value is realized in given events. The objection is unsound. Of course, it is not a process of deduction but one of evaluation that enables one to reach the conclusion that the care a person took in driving a car was reasonable in the prevailing circumstances. And of course this is different from ascertaining the physical state of affairs existing at a given place and a given time. Justifying one's evaluations is not the same as deducing them, or giving a deductive proof of them. Such evaluations, however, are not here represented as conclusions of argument, but as premises.

The point, as already stated, is that legal truth-certification processes apply as much to them as to non-evaluative findings of fact. The question whether such evaluations can be true or false in themselves as a kind of moral facts is one which need not be resolved either way here. Within the law, and for the law's purposes, the truth about reasonableness is what it is found to be by authorized determiners of facts. This is not an arbitrary process, but one that can be justified by an appeal to reasons. Where it is carried on arbitrarily, and without adequate justifying reasons, it is susceptible to correction by appeal or review.

As will be discussed more fully in Chapter 9, the advantage for a legal system of the use of value-criteria in the way noted is that it enables all aspects of a case to be considered and evaluated against factors and standards derivable from common-sense morality and legal usage. Whereas rules formulated in terms of simpler operative facts may be easier to apply 'objectively', they necessarily exclude from consideration many factors which a commonsense judgement would hold to have a bearing on the right or fair outcome of a controversy. Even if all the relevant factors are always and universally relevant, their particular mix of presence and absence in a given case may well be quite unique. So the judgement of reasonableness or fairness or whatever is one which individualizes justice without abandoning regard for the universal in the particular. Thus the legal system can achieve individualized justice to some acceptable degree. It does so at a certain price, however. Necessarily, there has to be a judgement of what is reasonable in the given case before any rule for which this is an operative fact can be applied in the case, and that judgement has to be treated as a final certification of the truth of the matter. Therein lies also the drawback. For the rights of persons are made dependent on 'judgemental facts', to give them a name, and hence on the sound

---

[44] See Alida Wilson, cited above, n. 39, at 278–81.

discretion and sensitive evaluations of authorized triers of facts. This does not itself amount to arbitrariness, but it can lead to it.

A further aspect of such value-criteria is that they are open-ended. Even if there were present to our consciousness a knowledge of every prior case and every hitherto relevant factor with the weighting given to it every time it was considered, we might find new factors in new cases. There would be reasons why the new factors were relevant to the reasonableness of the matter in hand, reasons explicable by arguments of one kind or another. Applying these reasons is a matter of apprehending new information, not just of applying old information. Their open-ended character may supply a further reason for doubting whether machines could ever establish such 'judgemental facts' in a way that truly captures the point, in human terms, of their use. But machine-memories could most valuably store, and prompt human users about, the range of factors hitherto established as relevant to some given value in a certain context.

In any event, no one does suppose that deductive legal reasoning can supply all the information required for justifying legal claims or decisions. The present thesis holds no more than this: Once certain information is supplied, the process of reasoning with that information is a deductive one. That it is supplied by a process involving judgement does not entail that it lacks truth-value as supplied, or therefore that it cannot form a premiss or premisses of deductive reasoning. This is further discussed in Chapter 9 with particular reference to the concept of 'the reasonable' in law. Even information about 'brute facts' requires a process of determination or judgement to supply it. It does follow that the information-providing function requires its own justification, and that this justification cannot itself be wholly (or, in some cases, at all) deductive. But that is perfectly compatible with my thesis that legal reasoning can be and always is in part deductive.

8. Normative Predicates?

There could be a somewhat different though not unrelated objection to the present theory. It could be argued that the logic proper to norms is deontic logic, that is, a logic with the modality of obligation and permission (non-obligation) built into its set of predicates. Yet what I have argued for is treating legal reasoning, reasoning involving norms, as though it could be a form of ordinary predicate logic.[45] The notion of a predicate, it can be argued, belongs to the realms of that which is descriptively true or false, not to the consequences of norms. Take for example the notion of someone's being 'liable to be sentenced to imprisonment for life'. This notion, we may agree, is one that can be understood only in deontic

---

[45] I owe much in my attempt to grasp legal logic as predicate logic to Michael Sinclair. See his 'The Semantics of Common Law Predicates' *Indiana Law Journal* 61 (1985–6) 373–99. If the general idea is sound, there should be a link between the logic of normative predicates and deontic logic.

terms, that is, in terms of what ought to be the case, or of what it is right or obligatory to do or bring about. Very roughly, when one says in English that someone is liable to a certain penalty for a certain offence, one means that whoever does or is believed to have done that thing may be charged with it, that such a charge ought to be tried in a certain way, and that if at the trial it is held proven that the person committed the offence, then the person ought to be found guilty of the offence, and the judge ought then to pass a certain sentence (namely, a sentence of life imprisonment) upon that person. The notion of being liable, like many other cognate notions much used in legal discourse (e.g. having obligations or duties, having rights, being entitled, having authority or power) has normative import—it always implies some kind of a conditional or unconditional 'ought'.

Here let me call in aid the MacCormick–Weinberger 'Institutional Theory'. It is part of our argument that institutional facts have 'normative impact'.[46] Hence it can be true both that there are correctly ascribed predicates which state institutional facts and that these predicates, when categorically (i.e. unconditionally) applied, can be translated without loss or residue into deontic statements. In that form, they state, as was noted earlier, a kind of reason for action. The act of deciding that accords with the deontic statement is a justified one. The fact that such translation is possible does not, however, preclude using normative predicates in the untranslated form in which they so commonly appear in legislative and adjudicative speech and in legal discourse in all its modes. That statements about liability and obligation (and the like) are perfectly well-formed statements of institutional fact in many contexts elides the objection that they cannot be proper predicates.[47] To predicate something of something is to state a fact about it. Institutional facts are among those one can predicate of appropriate subjects. If this means that not all predicates are purely descriptive predicates, some being normative ones, this is hardly an objection in itself.

9. Conclusion

The message this chapter bears about legal deductive arguments is the unremarkable one that none can be more convincing in its conclusion than in its premises. Hence whoever makes such an argument has to stand ready to defend and justify the premises, using for this purpose the varieties of rhetorical or practical argument that are studied in the rest of this book. Legal dogmatics can never dare to be too dogmatical in style. All statements of institutional fact, and all statements of legal norms, have a certain defeasible quality. Norms and normative statements have to be open-ended. The 'institutive' rules of legal institutions have to be viewed as setting conditions which are 'ordinarily necessary and presumptively

---

[46] See MacCormick and Weinberger, *Institutional Theory* Introduction and chs 1–4.
[47] *Institutional Theory* pp. 99–104.

sufficient', not necessary and sufficient absolutely.[48] Every statement of law, both in judicial justifications and in doctrinal commentaries, rests at least on an implicit, and often on an explicit and articulated, interpretative argument. Such arguments presuppose, and often articulate value systems and value judgements. The values deployed in good legal reasoning are not merely idiosyncratic to judge or advocate or doctrinal lawyer; they derive from the system itself and from reflection on its inherent principles. The practice of interpretative reasoning with reference to values deemed implicit in the system interpreted is itself a heavily conventional one, and it contains (as we noted earlier) truth-determining processes.

Yet even with all these caveats the argumentation at this level cannot be properly conceived of in simply bivalent true-or-false terms. We enter here the realms of the better-or-worse, the arguable, the preferable, the more or less persuasive. The deeply controversial quality of interpretative argumentation confronts us here. That one can always cite grounds for preference of one good interpretation over another does not mean that such grounds are usually (even if they may sometimes be) conclusive. Such argumentation exercises and calls for virtues like wisdom, humanity, and common sense. It is practical reasoning, not deductive reasoning.

[48] See 'Law as Institutional Fact', ch. 2 of MacCormick and Weinberger, *Institutional Theory*.

5

Universals and Particulars

Introduction

There have been, and are, theories of practical judgement that represent reasons for decision and for judgement as fundamentally and intrinsically particular. Such theories tell us, quite correctly, that our decisions are always decisions to do particular things. Hence decision-making requires us to weigh the particular reasons for and against the one and the other particular course of conduct open to us. These particular reasons are found among the particular facts and circumstances of the case for decision. Universals—rules and principles—may be constructed by way of inductive generalization from particular reasons in particular cases. But such generalizations, though they may be useful by way of general guidance, are never in themselves adequate to justify a decision. For they cannot supplant the need in any particular dilemma for a full and careful review and evaluation of all the considerations that are relevant to making a choice between the one and the other horn of the dilemma.

This book does not endorse any purely particularistic theory. It presents universalization as essential to justification within practical reasoning. This is in line with that strand in thought about the Rule of Law that stresses its universalist, and thus egalitarian, character.[1] The considerations in favour of universalism will be expounded in the present chapter. It must be stated at the outset, however, that these considerations in no way entail a denial that particular reasons must always exist for particular decisions, justified ones anyway. Nor do they imply that inattention to the full particular detail of a case would be compatible with just or satisfactory decision-making. The issue concerns the significance of the justifying relationship between reason and decision, and whether or not this involves the universalizability of grounds of decision. To see how this issue arises, it is worthwhile attending closely to some of the particularists' arguments.

---

[1] Compare R. Dworkin, 'Hart's Postscript and the Character of Political Philosophy' *Oxford Journal of Legal Studies* 24 (2004) 1–37 at 30, for his discussion of Hayek on the Rule of Law and equality before the law.

1. Particularism

In the First Book of Kings, in the Old Testament, it is recorded how two women who shared a house had each given birth to a son within three days of each other. One night, one of the women rolled over in her sleep and suffocated her baby. But she exchanged the dead child for the living, and claimed it was the other that had died. They came before King Solomon each claiming the live baby as her own.

Then said the king, 'The one saith, "This is my son that liveth and thy son is the dead"; and the other saith, "Nay; but thy son is the dead, and my son is the living." '
 And the king said, 'Bring me a sword.' And they brought a sword before the king.
 And the king said, 'Divide the living child in two, and give half to the one and half to the other.'
 Then spake the woman whose the living child was unto the king, for her bowels yearned for her son, and she said, 'O my lord, give her the living child, and in no wise slay it.' But the other said, 'Let it be neither mine nor thine, but divide it.'
 Then the king answered and said, 'Give her the living child and in no wise slay it: she is the mother thereof.'
 And all Israel heard of the judgment which the king had judged; and they feared the king: for they saw that the wisdom of God was on him, to do judgment.

Across the centuries rings the sonorous wisdom of Solomon. He looks at the very particulars of the case, and the solution appears to him. By seeming instantly prepared to divide the child in two he creates the conditions for the right award. The divine wisdom penetrates to the heart of the matter and the decision is accepted as right in a way that both satisfies intuition and demonstrates its exercise.

Yet we cannot imagine a contemporary family court in any law-state acting in this way. Obviously not. No judge under the Rule of Law has power to order a child to be split in two, and everyone knows this. Even if judges could do so, and used Solomon's threat, the word would get about that this evidentiary device was in use, and litigants would be schooled in presenting the right demeanour to the court. It would become a routine procedure, and for that very reason it would not work. The biblical case is emphatically not part of a bureaucratic routine. Intrinsically, it is a one-off decision. It has to be so. The awful threat of the sword and the immediate reaction of the women there and then are of the essence of the Solomonic judgment. It works by its uniqueness—and that, above all, is what aroused the fear and wonder of 'all Israel', and perhaps of everyone to this very day when first confronting the tale in 1 Kings 3: 16–28. The fear, perhaps, is that a person who can see with such divine acuity into the heart of one ostensibly intractable matter can see into the heart of every other. If so, then, even though every decision will be based on a one-off flash of intuition, every one will display the same intuitive rightness. It will be as if God the searcher of hearts were an earthly judge available to stand over every single person at every moment.

The discussion in the previous chapters has taken it to be an important aspect of the Rule of Law that courts and judges take seriously the established rules of the institutional normative order that is a contemporary system of state law. Because of this, we can see that the justification of claims and decisions will contain and focus on a syllogistic element, showing what rule is being applied, and how. At the same time, however, it is clear that there is more to it than just this. Rules cannot solve everything by themselves, for problems of classification, of evaluation, of interpretation, of relevancy, and of proof can arise, and can be raised by parties to trials and to litigation of all sorts. Once the application of law becomes problematized, the problems that have been raised (whoever has raised them) must be solved. The question is how to do so.

King Solomon could be considered as one model to guide our thinking about this. We perhaps have as humans some instinct or intuition, some sixth sense—'a moral sense' some have called it—that points out to us the answer that the rules fail to yield. Such a sense could be supposed to 'lock on' to the particulars of the problem case, much as Solomon's might be said to have done. We can see what is right in the particular case, and of course that could give us a precedent for future cases. But the rightness would be intrinsic to the judgment, and only a right judgment would have any value as a precedent. Anyway, precedents can only be analogies for new decisions, since no set of events in the world can ever be exactly the same as another. Any incident involving two or more people must differ from every other, at least as to place or time, and often as to persons and as to other circumstances as well. So a precedent in one case might guide in another case to the extent of its rightness. It might alert us to aspects of the rights and wrongs of the new case, but the new judgment would have to be as right for this case in all its particularity as the precedent was in respect of its.[2]

In turn, this could warn us about too ready a reliance on rules even in an institutional normative order. If we are endowed with a capacity for practical judgement, or with intuition, or moral sense in a way that is relevant and appropriate to public decision-making, then this must be engaged also in the situation where we refer to a rule as applying in the decision of a case. We will judge that it is right to have a rule for such a case, and to follow it in this case. Product liability might be a good example. In contemporary societies, large-scale industrial manufacturing takes place, and goods are sold impersonally through great chain stores without any particular reliance by customers on the skill and judgement of those who sell what is sold. Here, there is an obvious case for having a rule that places the burden of insuring against risks of damage from goods that turn out as defective on the shoulders of manufacturers. Let us suppose that legislators have deliberated about this, have come to the conclusion that such a rule about product liability is best all things considered, and have enacted laws accordingly. It may then seem very

---

[2] Compare Steven J. Burton, *An Introduction to Law and Legal Reasoning* (Boston and Toronto: Little Brown, 1985) 21–4.

obviously right in almost every case of damage arising from defects in a product to hold the manufacturer liable to make good damage accruing to a consumer. The decision that applies the rule is right because it is right to treat the particular case as a 'rule-case' (to use the term suggested by Michael Detmold[3]). But anomalous cases will appear in which it will not seem right to hold in favour of the normative consequence that the rule ostensibly provides for. We will ask if the rule admits of some other interpretation than that which points to a result that makes us uneasy, or if all the facts before us are really appropriately classified as falling within the predicates that specify the rule's operative facts. Our sense of rightness will lead us to problematize the rule's applicability to the case in hand and thus to remove it from the category of 'rule-cases', treating it as a case of first impression that needs a fresh judgment directed at its very own particulars. Every judge, after all, to be up to the job, will have to be possessed of some small share of Solomon's wisdom.

Let us take King Solomon's problem and place it before a contemporary tribunal. Nowadays, we know that DNA profiling could give a no less accurate but much less drastic way of identifying which woman was the child's natural mother than Solomon's resort to the sword. We might be inclined also to establish a rule, namely that children should be under the custody of their natural mothers. In this simplistic conception, we have a rule to deal with child custody cases, and an evidentiary test to apply in any case of doubt. We have reason to believe that the evidence is 100 per cent reliable provided (an important proviso this) that the scientists and technicians who do the DNA testing are competent, careful, and honest, and have taken accurate readings in any particular case. Thus we would have transformed Solomon's brilliant feat of particularistic judgement into a routine practice in which most maternity disputes will be simple 'rule-cases'. Detmold's point is that it will remain the case that the complexity of the real world will always be capable of throwing up surprises. Take four possibilities:

1. *The undetected switching case.* In a maternity hospital babies **ba** and **bb** got accidentally mixed up, and mother **ma** went home with baby **bb**, while mother **mb** went home with baby **ba**, and for five years the children in question have been reared as members of the family to which the error had assigned them. The truth has now come to light in the context of routine genetic screening carried out in one or other family.

2. *The maternal deficiency case.* A natural mother has a severe and chronic addiction to prohibited drugs and appears completely incapable of providing a safe and stable home for her baby.

3. *The reluctant mother case.* The mother had become accidentally pregnant and has no wish to take responsibility for rearing the child, she lives in a society in which childless people are eager to adopt children at birth, and it seems probable that an adoptive home will provide at least as good an

[3] M. J. Detmold, *The Unity of Law and Morality* (London: Routledge and Kegan Paul, 1984).

environment for rearing the child as would the natural mother if she were forced to accept this responsibility herself.

4. *The surrogacy case.* The natural mother arranged to become pregnant by the husband of an intending adoptive mother and carried her pregnancy to term under a contract whereby she agreed to make over the child for adoption at birth, receiving substantial support payments during pregnancy and with contractual provision for a substantial fee on the completion of adoption formalities.

None of these is to a contemporary audience so very surprising, but let us suppose a legal system in which the simple natural mother rule is in force, and these other problems are not yet covered by legislation. A judge confronted by any of the four as a case of first impression has two choices. Either she must simply treat the case as a rule-case, and award the child into custody of the natural mother since that is what the law says. Or she must acknowledge that this is effectively a new problem that does not count in an uncomplicated way as an instance of the envisaged operative facts on a reasonable interpretation of the rule. For example, faced for the first time with the *maternal deficiency case*, she holds that the rule covers only those situations, in practice the vast majority, of an ordinarily competent mother. For she considers that the point of the rule is primarily to secure the well-being of the child. She awards the child into some other suitable custody, perhaps that of a grandparent.

If the next problem case to arise were the *undetected switching case*, the judge would face a different set of concerns, especially if one or both mothers wanted restitution of the birth-child instead of the nurture-child. The operative facts of the rule seem no worse satisfied than in King Solomon's case. It is known exactly who is whose natural mother. There seems to be no issue of incapability, certainly none of the kind of culpably acquired incapability that one may consider involved in a case of drug addiction. Everyone in the case is the innocent victim of some-body else's (possibly culpable) mistake, but still the question is what to do. It seems likely the judge will require the parties to bring forward expert evidence from child psychologists about the effect on each child of removing it from a home in which happy relationships have been built up with parents and siblings, and send it to live with perfect strangers who just happen to be its genetic parents (assume that **ma** lives with and is married to father **fa**, and they have other chil-dren of their own, and conversely with **mb** and **fb**). But the judge may also want to hear opinion on what happens to such relationships once they prove to have been based on a mistake. This case is even less easily tractable than the former one.

But once cases of this and the preceding kind have been dealt with, it will certainly seem relatively straightforward to authorize adoption by a suitable adopt-ive mother in the *unwilling mother case*. Then the *surrogacy case* may not seem so difficult in the case where all parties agree to go ahead with the bargain, at least if the court is satisfied that the adopting mother is fully competent and capable.

However, concern may be expressed about public policy aspects of 'womb-leasing', and it may be doubted if the contract for payment of a fee is enforceable under the law. Much more problematic will be the case of the surrogate mother who repents of her bargain and declines to deliver the child at birth to the agreed adopters— especially if it has already been held that a surrogacy contract is void as being in breach of public policy, *ordre public*, *bonnes moeurs*, or some like concept. Anyway, once the decision ceases to seem properly tractable as a rule-case, the judge is out on her own with King Solomon again.

Nobody will doubt or dispute that any one of these cases, especially as a case of first impression, would call for very great care. There would have to be a serious attempt to establish in full detail all the particulars of the case, including the character and circumstances of the parties, in these cases most particularly concerning the women involved, and also the children, though little in the way of information about character as distinct from potential would apply save in the case of the five-year-old children in the undetected switching case. The decision would be a particular one about a particular award of custody with all the consequences that must have for a particular child and his or her relationship with a mother, whether natural mother or adoptive mother, and with other family members. Such a decision is not about a class of persons. It is about particular persons, part of whose nature or circumstances enable us to state that they belong in certain classes, satisfy certain predicates, or instantiate certain universals (these being three ways to say the same thing). Therefore the reasons that can be stated to justify a decision will be reasons rooted in the particular case. The requirement that a decision be justified is met only if there are good reasons for deciding in the particular chosen way, and if these defeat in some way any reasons that can be offered for any alternative disposal of the case. Those rival reasons must be outweighed or cancelled or nullified by these ones.

Robert Summers suggests that substantive reasons for decisions come in two types, which he calls 'rightness reasons' and 'goal reasons'.[4] In a case like the one we are considering, you could take the goal of a child's well-being and say that the correct decision would be the one that gave the best probability of maximizing that well-being. This would not be to say that a mother's well-being is of no account, but only to consider that it is a secondary factor to the child's. It might also be relevant to reflect on general societal well-being. A decision that might be taken as an example could have implications for the kinds of ways people might behave in future, discouraging drug addiction among young women, for example, or giving a green light or a red light to commercial surrogacy arrangements, whichever is considered better to favour the general interest. The goal of sustaining family stability and security of long-term arrangements for the upbringing of children could also be considerations in such a case. In any event, whatever the

---

[4] R. S. Summers, 'Two Types of Material Reasons: The Core of a Theory of Common Law Justification' *Cornell L. Rev.* 63 (1978) 707, 716–22.

goals you consider to be relevant, there must be some ranking of the priority of goals relative to a particular case, and the particular decision that in its particular circumstances best favours achievement of the highest-ranking goal is the best justified decision so far as concerns goal-reasoning.

Rightness reasons available in the cases we are considering might well start with the rightness of ensuring that a mother has custody of the child to whom she gives birth, and be the person primarily charged with the care and nurture of the child until maturity. This could even be considered a right of the woman. It is right that she should have the child, because she has a right to the parenting of her own child. Perhaps also the child has a right to the care of his or her own mother, and would suffer a grave wrong if given to somebody else, unless some unusual circumstances dictated a different answer. Quite correctly, Summers does not equate rightness reasons and rights, for the latter are a subset of the former. The idea that it would be wrong to treat surrogacy contracts as legally binding is, for example, a rightness reason that is negative in character.

An intuitionist approach to decision-making would tell us that we have a capacity to discern (to 'intuit') the factors in situations of choice that make a decision right or not right. We also have a capacity to tell in context which rightness reason defeats which others, either on their own or cumulatively with other relevant reasons. We further have a capacity to discern when it is right to consider goals as justifying decisions, to rank different goals, and to see when an important goal overrides other aspects of a case, including rightness reasons that may be applicable. Each person who reflects carefully on any of the questions I have mentioned about child custody must be aware (particularists claim) that he or she has such a capacity. How, otherwise, could such cases ever come to be decided otherwise than by some random procedure like tossing a coin? The difference between a good judge and a bad one would turn on whether a person has sound intuition, or has developed practical wisdom through long experience of decision-making in problem cases of this kind. Even more would depend on the care she or he takes to look attentively at every aspect of any case for decision so as to be sure that every reason has been brought to light, considered carefully, and evaluated relative to all others. A good decision-making procedure would be one that maximized opportunities to give that kind of careful attention to all points of a problem situation, and that gave decision-making tasks to appropriate persons. These are persons of sound intuition and endowed both with adequate attentiveness to detail and with a fair-minded readiness to make no decision till in possession of all relevant reasons in any particular case. They are practically wise people, '*prudentes*'.

Does such intuition exist? Can such wisdom be cultivated? How could it come about that people are able to conduct themselves in the way this particularist approach asks us to envisage? The most promising answer of which I am aware comes out of Adam Smith's moral philosophy, or at least would start from some of

Smith's insights.[5] Morally significant cases, he tells us, are those interpersonal situations that arouse the emotion of resentment or of contentment or the like. This can happen directly, as in the case of the person who feels resentment over a blow inflicted by another. It can occur sympathetically, as in the case of a blow inflicted on another by a third party. During the UK General Election of 2001, in full view of television cameras, the Deputy Prime Minister Mr John Prescott, while passing through a knot of protesters against government policy, was hit by an egg thrown from close range. Straight away, in what appeared to be an automatic and unreflective response, he turned and directed a vigorous punch to the jaw of his assailant. The correspondence columns of the newspapers were filled for several succeeding days with letters from members of the public. Some expressed strong fellow feeling with Mr Prescott, others with the punched protestor. Mr Prescott's was a case of direct resentment; that of the letter-writers who had been televisual witnesses is an example of sympathetic resentment.

According to Smith, if the directly felt resentment of the injured party far exceeds the sympathetic resentment the spectators feel, so that they are unable to go along with it, the situation is disagreeable for the injured party. We prefer to enjoy the fellow feeling, or sympathy, of our neighbours. (Mr Prescott will have received some comfort, despite his loss of dignity, from many of the letters to newspapers and no doubt private messages of good will as well). The desire that others go along with us in our resentments teaches us a strategy of self-control. Each of us can, and most do, adjust our reactions down to the level at which spectators can go along with us in full sympathy. Spectators, however, can be biased; this is very obviously the case in relation to an example drawn from an election time. You get more sympathy from those who are on your own side than from those on the other side. If there is to be any possibility of finding a common standard that rules out bias, we must seek this in the sympathies of an impartial spectator who does not have any anterior ground to prefer either of the immediately involved parties. So the test of an appropriate reaction is in terms of the sympathies of the impartial spectator.

A further difficulty is that real spectators can be incompletely informed. On that account, Smith develops the model of an ideal, fully informed, impartial spectator. Each of us can seek to view our own relations with others and others' relations *inter se* through the eyes of this imaginary spectator, this ideal impartial spectator. In adjusting our actual or sympathetic resentments and affections to the level with which this 'man [*sic*] within the breast' can sympathize, we achieve a

[5] See Adam Smith, *The Theory of Moral Sentiments* (Glasgow edn, D. D. Raphael and A. L. Macfie (eds), Oxford: Oxford University Press, 1976; 1st edn, 1759), esp. at Pt II, s. III, ch. 1. See also T. D. Campbell, *Adam Smith's Science of Morals* (London: Allen & Unwin, 1971) and K. Haakonssen, *The Science of a Legislator: the Natural Jurisprudence of David Hume and Adam Smith* (Cambridge: Cambridge University Press, 1981), and N. MacCormick, *Legal Right and Social Democracy: Essays in Legal and Political Philosophy* (Oxford: Clarendon Press, 1982) ch. 6 at 106–8.

sense of propriety. This is a sense of rightness and wrongness, which can be at least inter-subjective and perhaps even thoroughly objective. But each judgement remains rooted in an appreciation of all the particulars of each occasion of judgement and of decision. For recurring cases—e.g. where a promise was made and is due to be acted on, to take the usual hackneyed example—we can inductively generalize from our previous approvals and disapprovals, thus establishing maxims and rules ('Always keep promises'). But always the particular judgement after full evaluation of the particular case has primacy.

Detmold is a sentimentalist like Adam Smith, a believer in moral sentiments, in 'the passions' as David Hume called them.[6] And his thesis is that moral reasons (including legal reasons) engage our will precisely because they represent a passionate or emotional involvement with the particulars of our world. People incapable of love and hatred, of anger and pleasure, would also be incapable of real moral commitments. The particulars of everyday life and of human relations as apprehended passionately by us are what constitute reasons. By contrast with this, Summers's position is somewhat more rationalistic, though it is not yet absolutely clear how his theory gets the length of showing how it is that we reason our way to a conclusion about relative weights of atomic reasons. In Detmold's view, however, it seems right to say that we more or less literally *feel* our way to a conclusion. For him this is an art not a science; it is learnable but not describable. And yet of course, since it is an obvious truth that different facts can have different emotional appeal, one can at least use this truth to make sense of the process much alluded to but little explained which is nowadays called the 'weighing' of reasons.

In his recent *Ethics without Principles*,[7] Jonathan Dancy puts a case for particularism that rejects both the idea of a 'moral sense' and the idea of 'weighing' reasons. Judgement is a practical skill, not a sense, he suggests.[8] The same faculty of judgement is involved in considering reasons for theoretical propositions as practical ones. You don't need a special sense to tell whether the arguments I put in this book are sound ones or not, he might say. Judging who ought to have custody of a child on the basis of the reasons for and against each of the alternatives is judgement in just the same sense. Reasons that are relevant to judgement are relevant in different ways—as favouring this decision, or as enabling or intensifying a reason that is already operative, or as disabling a reason that would otherwise be a reason in favour. 'Weight' is a bad metaphor to describe what is taken into account in a judging process, because it suggests, erroneously in Dancy's view, that

---

[6] See Detmold, op. cit., at p. 105: 'There is no escaping, in law or wider moral thought, the necessity or passionate commitment, for only passionate commitment can provide the weight of reasons and principles; and without that weight no hard judgement can be made.' The reference to David Hume is, of course, primarily to Book II of his *Treatise of Human Nature* (David Hume, *A Treatise of Human Nature* (cited hereafter as *Treatise*) L.A. Selby-Bigge and P. H. Nidditch (eds), (Oxford: Clarendon Press, 2nd edn, 1978).

[7] (Oxford: Clarendon Press, 2004). George Pavlakos drew to my attention the importance of this work for the present inquiry; and Victor Tadros drew to my attention the error of confusing epistemological and ontological issues.   [8] *Ethics without Principles* pp. 140–8.

a reason of a certain kind always makes exactly the same contribution in relation to every act for which it counts as a reason. Yet he persuasively argues that this is not so.[9] Having in a previous work expressed doubt about the application of the idea of weight in relation to choices among legal principles, I am glad to have Dancy's confirmation of my grounds for doubt. Less persuasive for the present context is his rejection of the Kantian idea of the universalizability of grounds for practical judgement,[10] a point to which we shall return.

As even a brief sketch shows, all three of Smith, Detmold, and Summers make powerful and interesting cases, and Dancy's recent work gives strong corroboration from the context of moral philosophy. Yet it remains worth inquiring how we do succeed in coming to an objective judgement of cases where there are conflicting reasons, as so often happens. Smith perhaps has the most complete and almost convincing view, because his device of the ideal impartial spectator supplies for us a common inter-subjective yardstick against which to adjust and objectify our particular passionate responses to cases. But how does this fare as a theory of how to *justify* decisions. What we do in justifying judgements, if Smith is right, is a matter of showing that we have gone beyond an immediate reaction to a situation seen at first glance. We will have sought to be fully informed and to have achieved an ideal impartiality in order to move from mere anger, sympathetic or direct, to settled moral concern and perhaps condemnation (or, in the converse case, approval in various degrees of warmth). In such a process of correction or adjustment of immediately felt sentiments, one literally rationalizes the passionate reaction, in seeking a view that can be common to all concerned persons. The whole balance of judgement concerns a rationalized response to the whole of a situation in all its particularity. Therefore the weight of one's final responses of disapproval and approval to a situation in all its aspects gives a common metric that makes intelligible how this sort of weighing might work.

It must further be said that a Smithian account would show how a fully developed moral agent would be capable of giving allegiance to moral rules, as settled guidelines derived from generalizing responses to recurring types of case. But of course, in a process of development the agent would be a member of a community whose members owe allegiance to such rules. The development of a fully refined moral capacity would be something that supervenes on a more unrefined attachment to rules of a heteronomous character. That in turn would no doubt belong among the conditions necessary to developing both the self-command that Smith takes to be essential to human maturity and the associated capacity for ideal spectator judgements. Again, we find no unbridgeable gap between judging according to rules and judging in a deeper way that confronts the whole complexity of real-life situations. A simple capacity to 'see' or 'intuit' rightness is then not

---

[9] Ibid, pp. 190–1.
[10] Ibid, pp. 67–70; it seems to me that the present account may actually not be Kantian in the way that Dancy wants to reject.

so much in issue as an accumulated wisdom from deciding and reflecting on decisions and their outcomes over a considerable period of time. What we need is not the intuition of Solomon, but indeed his wisdom.

2. Universalizing Particulars

None of the insights derived from particularistic theses such as those we have reviewed above should be overlooked or undervalued. But it would also be a mistake to overstate the particularistic quality of judgement, especially of the intuitive or passionate judgement once it is rationalized in the manner suggested by Smith. To show this, let us return to King Solomon's case and think further about it, to pick up a highly important aspect that has been disregarded so far. 'Then the king answered and said, "Give her the living child and in no wise slay it: she is the mother thereof."' What is the point here? The King has used a brilliant device to find out which of the women most deeply cares for the child. He infers that she is the mother, precisely because of the visceral depth of her love for it ('for her bowels yearned for her son', as the King James Bible so vividly and earthily expresses this). Then his judgment is, as to its substance, 'Give her the child . . . [because] she is the mother thereof.' The 'because' nexus is all-important. The terse and telling quality of the biblical story is due to the very fact that it strips the events down to their essentials: a dispute about the parenthood of a child. A patriarch's device for clarifying the critical fact *Which woman is truly the mother?* Then the unhesitating award. The sword-drama shows the judge and everyone else who is the true mother. It is being the true mother that is the reason for being awarded the child.

Surely, then, it would be just as much the reason, and the same reason, for restoring any disputed child to the natural mother once the facts were ascertained. Once you know who is a baby's mother, you know who ought to be looking after the baby, into whose care she or he should be restored if in some untoward way they have become parted. If that were not so, it would be difficult to see what the 'because' amounts to. For the motherhood relationship to be a justifying reason, a 'because-reason' in this case before Solomon, it must be understood to be equally a because-reason in any other case. In that sense, reasons are, and have to be, universalizable. To rationalize one's response by stating it as a reason in an objective sense, perhaps, as Smith suggests, through some kind of 'ideal spectator' type of reasoning, is explicitly or implicitly to state it in universal terms. 'X being the mother of Y' is a relationship that is a logical universal. It is instantiated in every case of this most basic process of animal life. If in any case one can with good reason say, 'Well, X ought to look after and nurture Y, because X is Y's mother' then one must be able to say so in every case.

This does not say, and it is vital immediately to stress this point, that such a normative universal ('every mother ought to have the care and nurture of every child of hers') has an absolute character. We already discussed problem cases involving a natural mother's self-induced incapacity to provide adequate care, or cases where she desires to give up her baby for adoption, or cases of long-undetected mixing up between two children so that each is with the 'wrong' mother, or problems posed by surrogacy deals. Each of these suggests the possibility of countervailing relevant factors, where we conclude that the principle of matching babies to natural mothers ceases to apply, because further relationships or circumstances (relationships and circumstances that are equally universal in the logical sense) have come into play in ways that make a difference to what seems the appropriate judgement.

Such problems inevitably challenge us to find reasons for our reasons. What is the rationale of the 'mother with child' principle. In a patriarchal society, it might be that both are in the same father's power (except for 'harlots' with illegitimate children, as happened in King Solomon's case[11]), and paternal power is considered both to be right in itself and a necessary basis for social cohesion. In more egalitarian circumstances, the matter may be viewed more as what is a woman's right, with any paternal rights being subordinated to the primary right of the female parent except in exceptional cases. Finally, what is typical of contemporary Western societies is that the child's own interest is the fundamental reason for preference between more immediate and detailed principles of decision.[12] The idea then must be that it is in all normal cases overwhelmingly in the interest of the child to be brought up by her/his own mother. There is in ordinary circumstances a coincidence between the interest of the mother, desirous to nurture her own child, and those of the child, and in fortunate family circumstances there may be a further coincidence with interests of the father, grandparents, and other relatives. But if the reason for the ruling is the interest of the child, then this in turn will provide a rationale for exceptional cases like some of the ones we have figured. In the *maternal deficiency case*, it seems that the normal interest of a child in receiving her/his own mother's care is defeated by circumstances where the mother is disabled or has disabled herself . In the *reluctant mother case*, on the other hand, the mother has disqualified herself, and the child's interest is (uncontroversially, in contemporary opinion) better favoured by making appropriate adoption arrangements.

What follows is that any universal proposition concerning what is right to do may prove to be subject to hitherto unstated exceptions or qualifications, resulting from an interaction between more than one relevant principle. It has been suggested[13] that all legal rules have an intrinsic defeasibility, and this is a theme that will be explored in Chapter 12 below. It is certainly true that any universalization

---

[11] 1 Kings 3: 16 'Then came there two women that were harlots unto the King, and stood before him.'

[12] Compare the UK Children's Act 1989 s (1) 'When a court determines any question with respect to—(a) the upbringing of a child . . . the child's welfare shall be the court's paramount consideration' (applicable in England and Wales).

[13] See Richard H. S. Tur, 'Defeasibilism', *Oxford Journal of Legal Studies* 21 (2001) pp. 355–68.

from a particular reason in a particular case has to be accepted with a certain caution, because different circumstances may suggest exceptions and qualifications that are not triggered in the circumstances of the case under consideration.

Contemporary judges do not—may not—use the Solomonic method in the ordinary case of deciding about the parenthood or custody of children. But the phenomenon of conjoined twins—'Siamese twins'—can pose issues quite as awful as the king's sword. For the issue may arise whether to perform an operation to divide a pair of conjoined twins, in circumstances where one has a fair chance of survival substantially unimpaired, but the other has no prospect of surviving the operation. This was exactly the situation before the English Court of Appeal in the case of *Re A (children) (conjoined twins)*.[14] The Court decided that, in the particular circumstances of the conjoined twins Jodie and Mary, an operation to sever them and let Jodie live was legally permissible and indeed obligatory, though its effect would also be to bring Mary's life to an end. For present purposes, the concluding words of the leading judgment by Ward LJ are instructive.[15]

Lest it be thought that this decision could become authority for wider propositions, such as that a doctor, once he has determined that a patient cannot survive, can kill the patient, it is important to restate the unique circumstances for which this case is authority. They are that it must be impossible to preserve the life of X without bringing about the death of Y, that Y by his or her very continued existence will inevitably bring about the death of X within a short period of time, and that X is capable of living an independent life but Y is incapable under any circumstances (including all forms of medical intervention) of viable independent existence. As I said at the beginning of this judgment, the case is a very unique one.

Uniqueness, one might respond, does not admit of degrees (how can anything be 'very unique'?). The judge's understandable stress on the case's 'very unique' character must be understood as meaning 'most unlikely to be repeated'. But the fact of the matter is that the judge's final ruling acknowledges that the case, however unusual, however unlikely to be repeated, has to be viewed in law as a type-case, as a universally stated situation. No doubt there are very few real-life examples of a relationship between any human being X and human being Y that will be exactly as described by Ward LJ. But the point is that if they recur, then a similar operation to save X at the cost of Y's accelerated death would be as justified in the later case as it was in the Jodie and Mary case. And if it would not be justified in the imagined later case, then it cannot be in the meticulously considered and described case that is now before the court. For it is not some ineffable particular feature of this Jodie interacting with this Mary that justifies the decision, but certain stabable aspects of the relationship between them in the context of a particular practical dilemma. These aspects are rightly presented by the judge as justifying his decision about the proper way to resolve the dilemma. The fact that Mary's

14   [2001] Fam. 147, [2000] 4 All ER 961.
15   [2001] Fam. at 204–205, [2000] 4 All ER at 1018.

continuing life will cause Jodie's death, because her lungs cannot sustain them both for many weeks longer, makes it impossible to preserve Jodie's life and to secure to her the chance of a normal existence unless the operation is performed. But it is also a fact that the operation will inevitably result in Mary's death. They both have a right to life, but Jodie's right can only be upheld by performing the operation that ends Mary's life. If you said nevertheless both that to perform the operation is right, and that this is the single occasion in the whole history of the world on which such an operation will be right, regardless of whether twins joined in materially the same way ever appear again, in effect you would be retreating into ineffability. If the relationship of just this sort is operation-justifying in any case, it has to be so in all cases, however infrequent we hope and pray such cases will turn out to be. The 'because' of justification is a universal nexus, in this sense: for a given act to be right because of a given feature, or set of features, of a situation, materially the same act must be right in all situations in which materially the same feature or features are present. This is subject to the exception that additional relevant features may be present that alter the right result, but the exception is a valid one only if it in turn has the same universal quality. We have to be dealing with some additional set of relations such that this in turn, if repeated, would be taken to justify the same exception in a similar future case.

This does not depend on any doctrine or practice of following precedents. On the contrary, the rationality of a system of precedents depends upon this fundamental property of normative justification, within any justificatory framework, its universalizability. Any commitment to impartiality between different individuals and different cases entails requiring that the grounds of judgment in this case be deemed repeatable in future cases. Of course, you have to add consistency over time as a further requirement, and in addition, within any normative system, the idea of an overall coherence of values and principles, enduring through time, before you have the basis for an actual system of precedent. This is further discussed in Chapter 8 below.

3. Universalization or Generalization?

The idea of universalizability, even as grounded in such a conception of rational impartiality, is, however, open to attack and has been attacked by Steven Burton.[16] In his view, the claim I make about the necessary universality or at least universalizability of justifying reasons is overstated and confuses universalization with generalization. The problem he poses is one that stems from the relative ignorance of fact and relative indeterminacy of aims and values under which any human decision maker must labour. How, asks Burton in effect, can a judge ever

---

[16] Steven J. Burton, 'Professor MacCormick's Claim Regarding Universalisation in Law', in C. Faralli and E. Pattaro (eds), *Reason in Law, Vol II* (Milan: Dottore A. Giuffré, 1988) 155–66.

be satisfied that he/she has exhaustively considered every possible relevant set of, or variant of, the facts of the given case, so as to decide exactly how to state some ruling on the matter in issue of the kind which we have formulated in the terms: 'Whenever *OF* then *NC*' (or in a more elaborated representation of the predicates in issue)? At best, surely, a real live judge can only hold that, *as a generalization*, it is right to give judgment *NC* when it is the case that *OF*. This makes properly prudent allowance for the fact that we cannot be sure we have thought of everything which on a complete (i.e. superhuman) view we might come to suppose relevant to giving any particular judgment in any particular case.

When things not naturally on land are brought on to a piece of land (for example, by constructing a reservoir for water), and when they escape from control and do damage to somebody, even without fault on the defendant's part, the mere facts that there has been an escape from control and that it has caused harm, even without any proof of fault, may be held to justify a judgment in favour of compensating the damaged party at the expense of the risk-creator. (See, for example, *Rylands v Fletcher*,[17] *Kerr v Earl of Orkney*.[18]) But giving and justifying a decision in those terms neither does nor should be supposed to conclude the question what it is right to do if an escape from control occurs without an escape over the perimeter of the piece of land being involved, the injury being suffered to a person who is present on the defendant's land. In *Read v J. Lyons and Co.*,[19] an explosion in an armaments factory injured an inspector lawfully visiting the factory. For the first time, it was decided that an escape over the perimeter of the land was required to make a judgment of liability without fault justifiable.

New cases need not always lead to closing off a line of legal development concerning liability in the way this occurred in *Read*'s case. The cautious growth of the doctrine of vicarious liability, making an employer liable for the faults of an employee, is a case in point. Should an employer be liable for fraudulent acts committed by an employee in the course of his/her employment? An early case involved the situation in which the employee's fraud brought a benefit to the employer, and it was held that in those circumstances the employer was vicariously liable. But then a case arose in which an employee committed a fraud in the course of employment to the damage of the employer's client, without any benefit to the employer. Clearly, the precedents did not require a decision in favour of liability in such a case—they showed that if an employer benefited, that employer should be liable. But equally, they did not have to be interpreted as holding that *only* if the employer benefited could there be vicarious liability. It was indeed held in *Lloyd v Grace, Smith, and Co.*[20] that the employer was properly to be made liable for the employee's fraud committed in the course of employment, even in the absence of a benefit to the employer. This decision was perfectly reasonable even though in *Barwick v Joint Stock Bank*[21] it had been treated as

---

[17] (1868) LR 3 HL 330.   [18] (1857) 20 D 298.   [19] [1947] AC 156.
[20] [1912] AC 716.   [21] (1886) LR 2 Ex. 259.

a material fact that the employee's frauds had been to the employer's benefit. What the later development reflected was (one may suppose) an extended understanding of the grounds for vicarious liability, that is, its underlying principles, in terms of the way in which a person's employment may create scope for injurious conduct that he/she would not otherwise be in a position to bring about, and assuming that it is more reasonable for the employer to insure against this or otherwise take steps aimed at protecting the interests of exposed third parties. Such lines of development of law would be severely inhibited if courts were expected at every point to try to sum up in conclusive terms all the necessary and sufficient conditions for some form of legal liability or the recognition of some legal right or another. The most a court should do is satisfy itself that there are *sufficiently* good reasons for the holding in the present case (we shall return to this in a later chapter discussing the place of precedent in legal reasoning). That reasons are sufficient implies sufficiency in the light of the facts and circumstances the parties have adduced to the court as material to the decision they have sought one way or the other. Such a tentative, step-by-step approach to decision-making is certainly very much a characteristic of the style of development of legal doctrines and principles in the common law. In his *Introduction to Law and Legal Reasoning*, Burton gives some vivid illustrations of this point, drawn from the law of sale of goods, on questions concerning a seller's liability for defects in the item sold.[22]

The point Burton makes is a most important one. It should be accepted, however, not as contradicting the present thesis about universalizability, but as underlining a useful and necessary qualification to it that was already briefly mentioned earlier in the present chapter. What he shows, I believe, is the always-tentative quality of commitment a wise and rational person will make in respect of any given universalized principle of decision. What he does not show is that the logical properties of a good justifying principle of or ground for decisions are other than those of universality. A universalized ground of judgement says 'Always if *c* do *v*', whereas a generalized one cannot ever say more than 'Very often if *c* do *v*' or perhaps 'Nearly always if *c* do *v*.' Compare 'Always if a child's mother claims custody of it, custody should be awarded to her' with 'Very often if a child's mother claims custody of it, custody should be awarded to her.' In any case that may occur, the latter totally fails to tell us what to do. For there is no way to tell if the case before us is one of the majority of instances, where custody is to be awarded, or one of the minority where it is not. Guidance is completely missing. The problem about the former is the opposite fault, for it does give guidance, but gives it in a too categorical way. A person's being the mother of a child is always a very strong reason indeed for her to have custody of it, but there can be circumstances in which that reason is defeated by other considerations such as those we noted in the case of maternal deficiency or of the reluctant mother, and quite a few others that might be thought of. Thus it makes better sense to postulate a kind of

---

[22] Boston and Toronto: Little Brown, 1985, 21–64.

qualified universalization. 'Always if a child's mother claims custody of it, custody should be awarded to her, *except when a sufficiently strong reason to make a different award is shown to be present.*' That does tell us what to do, while also alerting us to considering countervailing considerations if any are presented in a particular case. The point of a body of precedents concerning awards of custody will be that over time it teases out a basic universalization, qualified by a more or less exhaustive listing of such countervailing considerations—we may suppose, considerations grounded primarily in the welfare of children, taking account of their age and of the closeness of engagement with father and other relatives as well.

It is wise to say 'more or less exhaustive'. The variety of human circumstances is such that one can never be absolutely confident of having foreseen every possibility, and it is therefore a simple piece of practical wisdom to remain open to surprises, and be ready to respond intelligently to them. One should not rest content with an *ex ante* certainty that at last the perfect and complete rule for decision has been devised, stating every conceivable qualifying or defeating condition to which it is subject. A wise person's legal universalizability confines itself to defeasible universality—and the idea of 'defeasibility' will be explored more fully in a later chapter. Where defeasible universality obtains, it can of course give rise to descriptive generalizations about the law: 'In Brobdingnagian law, in custody disputes, custody is nearly always awarded to the mother'. But descriptive generalization, albeit useful in guiding prediction of decisions, is of itself very little help in making them. Defeasible universality is universality not generalization, and universalizability should be upheld as a condition of justification both in law and also in moral reasoning. This is so, even if one wisely allows for the ever-present possibility of unforeseen events and circumstances requiring one to revise hitherto accepted near-certainties. If 'particularism' is understood as no more than a position that insists on this openness to evaluate new cases and circumstances when these arise, then it is acceptable. But this is openness to new particulars within a justifying schema of defeasible universals, and each new exception once acknowledged becomes itself a universalized exception.[23]

If this captures what Burton means by 'generalization' as opposed to 'universalization', I agree with him in substance, but not in terminological preference. For it does remain valuable to contrast universality (even defeasible universality) with 'generalization' for a reason stated many years ago by R. M. Hare.[24] 'Universal' contrasts with 'particular' as 'general' contrasts with 'specific'. The latter pair of terms admits of differences of degree, but not the former. 'Universal' and 'particular' are logical properties, whereas generality and specificity are quantitative ones. In law, both rules and principles are universals—as are rulings on law that justify particular decisions. But some normative propositions are more general than

---

[23] Compare Klaus Günther, *The Sense of Appropriateness: Application Discourses in Morality and Law* (trans. J. Farrell) (Albany: NY SUNY Press, 1993) 224–6.
[24] R. M. Hare 'Principles', *Proceedings of the Aristotelian Society* (1972–3) 1.

others. Legal principles are very general norms, which often compete with other equally general norms in practical dilemmas. Legal rules are typically much more specific and immediately applicable. Contrasts drawn on the 'general–specific' axis make a different point from that which is made by reference to the mutually exclusive pair 'universal versus particular'. They are terms and concepts with a different part to play in the general theory of legal justification. Generalizations, in the sense of generalized statements of principle, have a special part to play in legal justification. Such statements of principle are very much more general in their terms than the kind of rulings on law we have been discussing up to now. Generality, as this very observation shows, is a matter of degree. Later chapters will show that at the broadest level of legal generalization, that of legal principles, we are concerned with overall coherence in law rather than with strict consistency, as when we test a possible ruling in law against pre-established rules and binding precedents. Sometimes, indeed, this very difference comes to the fore when judges deny that broad statements of principle are properly to be considered as 'universals'. A very clear illustration of this is to be found in *Home Office v Dorset Yacht Co. Ltd.*[25] All in all, to preserve a terminological distinction as between generalization and universalization seems highly desirable.

4. Universalization and Induction: Causal Thought

There is a possible analogy to be drawn between the view here taken about practical reasoning and justification and the inductive process of speculative judgement, or scientific judgement, so far as that deals with cause and effect. It is an arguable thesis that each particular event and state of affairs has some intrinsic causal potency such that by some explicable mechanism they generate further events or states of affairs. This has a certain credibility, since it is certain that causes and effects are always particular events, processes, or states, and that causal action is action by one event or process to bring about other particulars. It is each particular event that has its very own cause, if there are causes at all; not events in general that have causes in general. The thesis that things and states of affairs have in reality an intrinsic causal potency (let me call this view 'causal realism') fits perfectly well with this observation about the particularity of series of causes and effects. Whatever particular thing or combination of things it was that brought about the event in view—say, the eruption of Mount St. Helens or the Indian Ocean earthquake and tsunami of 26 December 2004—to identify the cause is to identify that thing or combination whose particular potency was so released as to yield just that and not any other direct result or effect.

[25] [1970] AC 1004, esp. at 1054, where Lord Pearson refers to the famous 'neighbour principle' as a 'basic and general but not universal principle'.

In so far as we can discover sets of like cause-and-effect series, we may be able to establish inductive generalizations from them. But on the causal realist view, no particular correct ascription of effect to cause would be correct in virtue of its fitting any such generalization. On the contrary, the generalization would only be as well founded as the number of confirming instances we could find, for causes are particulars and are known as such in and for themselves. We can be more certain that some particular *x* caused some particular *v* than that every member of the class of all *x*'s has the very same causal potency in respect of producing just one *v* for every *x*. That one particular has been shown to cause another particular would be no proof that anything else has ever caused, is now causing, or will ever again cause any other thing.

Just this was what David Hume classically showed to be the difficulty about causal realism.[26] We have in fact, he claimed, no sensory or any other evidence of any particular links of natural necessity between any pair of things, events, and states of affairs. At the level of mere particular observation of particulars, we never observe anything causing anything. We may see the snake biting, we may see the queen dying. But we do not see this bite causing this death. And even if we did see this bite causing this Cleopatra's death, that would be no ground at all for supposing that every such bite will be a cause of death (nor would it—very few forms of snake venom are inevitably fatal). The proposition that particular events cause particular effects is quite a different one from the proposition that there is a regular course of events in nature, and neither establishes the other. The same, it seems to me, would apply to ethical particularism. Even if I have some faculty for judging just exactly that these particular facts A, B, C are a reason for this decision *d*, a reason outweighing those rival facts E, F, G, nothing follows about future recurrences of similar facts. If reasons are particular, it is anyone's guess whether recurrences of the same, or similar, particulars have like weight the next time round.

In so far as Hume's critique of causal realism and of the claims of induction was a logical critique, it was a sound one. But the logical problem that Hume raised was not satisfactorily solved by himself, but only very much later by Karl Popper.[27] The relationship between particulars and generalizations is that of potential falsification. That there is regularity in our universe is a hypothesis tested in our every thinking moment, and corroborated so far over various ranges of events and phenomena. That there are particular recurrent regularities has also been tested and, for some, not yet disconfirmed.

So far as Hume raised an epistemological problem, he was correct. Causality is not an intrinsic part of the perceptible world. It is an explanatory category imposed by us on our phenomenal world—though here Kant's transcendental

---

[26] Hume, *Treatise*, Book I, Pt III.
[27] Karl R. Popper, *The Logic of Scientific Discovery* (London: Hutchinson, 1959); *Objective Knowledge* (Oxford: Clarendon Press, 1972), ch 1.

version of the argument is plainly more plausible than Hume's attempt to pull empiricism up on its own bootstraps.[28] The questions then remain when it is *justifiable* to apply this category in our explanations of events, and how we should apply it. My own answer is again Popperian: reasonable and justifiable ascriptions of effect to cause require recourse to unrefuted generalizations, and are the better justified the more thoroughly corroborated and the more greatly at risk of falsification any hypothesis is. Furthermore, any explanatory hypothesis one tests has also to be capable of forming a consistent part of a coherent general theory. Hypotheses come not as single spies, but in battalions.

This perhaps jejune taking of position on a vastly important and long-disputed question may perhaps suffice in a work whose focus is on other matters. The main present question anyway is that of how far the Popperian position as I have very crudely outlined it is a helpful analogy for practical reasoning. So let one concluding remark suffice on this: nothing in this position implies any denial that causes are always particulars. It is of course the snake bite, not the theory that snake bites can be fatal because of the properties of snake venom, that causes Cleopatra's death. But what enables us so to conceptualize the death of Cleopatra is that the particular fact of the biting snake belongs as minor premiss in an argument of which the major premiss is a hypothesis culled from the snake-venom theory and the conclusion is the death.

5. Universalization in Justification

The last point has certainly an analogical relevance in the practical sphere: it is indeed true, as the particularists maintain, Detmold most tenaciously,[29] that reasons for particular actions are both particular and factual. The fact that the snake is poised to bite the queen is the reason for my intervention. But this does not show, any more than in the case of causes, that the link between particular reason and particular act is not a relevant universal. It seems indeed quite obvious that the fact justifies the act only if both belong within some statable practical syllogism having as its major premiss something like: 'Anyone who is able to do so ought to rescue a queen from the imminent bite of a snake.' Of course, it is true that such a principle lacks applicability or immediate relevance to conduct on all these infinitely many occasions when one is not in the company of some particular queen and some particular about-to-bite snake. Of course it is true that

---

[28] Hume, in *Treatise* Book I, Pt. III, s. 15 prescribes 'Rules by which to judge of causes and effects'; there and elsewhere he gives as our reason for belief in cause and effect the operation of custom upon the imagination; clearly, it is circular to rest the theory of causality on a cause-and-effect hypothesis at the level of empirical psychology. For that reason, Kant's transcendental psychology—if so one may call it—is to be preferred. See I. Kant, *Critique of Pure Reason* (London: Macmillan, 1933) pp. 30–1 as discussed in W. D. Lamont, *Law and the Moral Order* (Aberdeen: Aberdeen University Press, 1981) ch. 5, 'causality and teleology'. [29] Detmold, op. cit., ch. 6.

nobody in the world has ever before thought of or formulated this principle—it has no place in any standing personal morality or positive social morality of which I have ever heard. But to say that the fact of the imminent snake bite would *justify* the intervention (and indeed unjustify non-intervention) entails acknowledging that some such principle holds good.

This follows, I believe, from the implications inherent in the very idea of 'justification'. To justify an act is to show that it is right. To show that it is right is to show that, upon any objective view of the matter, the act ought to have been done, or even had to be done, given the character of the act and the circumstances of the case. To say: 'it is right to do *this* in *these* circumstances because of what this is and what these are', however much one might expand on one's particular allusion by pointing and nodding, is to fail to show anything other than a purely subjective view of the matter. It is only once the 'this' and the 'these' are given some quantified value (not necessarily by verbal explanation, of course: I might get my meaning in the end clear enough by nodding and pointing as in a game of charades) that anything is available for objective scrutiny at all. Only once you show me that the 'this-ness' of the act is its being the act of saving Cleopatra— Cleopatra *the queen*, Cleopatra *the beautiful woman*, Cleopatra *the human being*— the circumstances being those of her endangerment by a snake, does an objectively discussable question arise at all.

Certainly, there may be disagreement: someone, myself for example, might deny that queens or beautiful women have special rights as such; and the same act might be deemed justified upon different grounds of judgement, even where such disagreement exists at the level of the principle in issue. But I do not believe that anything could be deemed a justifying reason which did not state or indicate the generic nature of the act and the generic circumstances of action. And the moment these are stated, an implicit principle, universal in terms, is revealed. To say: 'It was right to v, because it was a case of v-ing in circumstances C', is to imply that at least prima facie one ought to v whenever C obtains. Indeed it means the same as 'If C one ought to v; and C; so one ought to v.'

When one considers the matter steadily, there seems to be no way of making sense of the ideas of 'justification' and of 'justifying reasons' for action that does not lead to this conclusion. The point here lies in the thesis that justifying reasons for action are conceptually distinct from either explanatory or motivating reasons.[30] It is a point of fundamental importance. That I much want x and that v-ing is a way to get x is, for me, a reason now to v. That x was what I most wanted and that v seemed to me likely to bring about x will certainly be a good explanation of why I did v on some occasion. Such reasons are, of course, quite particular, though belonging under the explanatory principles that people are highly likely to

---

[30] William Lucy objects to the idea of 'explanatory reasons', and thinks one should speak only of 'explanatory causes'. Yet surely one can speak of the reason why Mount St. Helens erupted, or the reason why Cleopatra died. 'Rational explanation' is an important activity. See Lucy, *Understanding and Explaining Adjudication* 104.

do what they most want to do, and that strong desires are common causes of action. But exactly what motivating and explanatory reasons do *not* do is to *justify* an act. Much current discussion of reasons for actions and of practical reasoning seems to me to leave this crucial distinction wholly obscure. Why I want *x* and whether my desire is so strong that it will motivate me into *x*-seeking action are questions of some interest and importance. But whether it is right for me to seek or obtain *x* is another question again. Whether there is any *justifying* reason for me to seek or obtain *x* is a question quite different from that of whether there is any motivating reason for me to seek it.

There is, I submit, no justification without universalization; motivation needs no universalization; but explanation requires generalization. For particular facts—or particular motives—to be *justifying reasons* they have to be subsumable under a relevant principle of action universally stated, even if the universal is acknowledged to be defeasible. This applies to practical reasoning quite generally, and to legal reasoning as one department of practical reasoning.[31] Much of the argument in the present chapter has already concerned legal cases and legal reasons. This is not unimportant. Jonathan Dancy's thesis in *Ethics Without Principles* casts what seems to be well-grounded doubt about the idea that there is any kind of master rule-book of morality,[32] or that moral thought is aimed at trying to construct one. The principles that he urges us to do without are an imagined set of invariantly applicable universals, such that unless the maxim of a present action fits one of these, the action is wrong. I am disposed to accept this view, but to draw attention to the ways moral thinking differs from legal.[33] First, in law there is a kind of master rule book, the constitution, statute law, delegated legislation, codes, and the like; also, possibly precedents and (if precedents generate any such thing) 'common law rules'. Every contemporary legal system in any state has some of these, though perhaps none has all of them. Non-state legal systems like that of the European Union substitute foundation treaties for a 'constitution' in the formal sense, such as many states possess (and after 2006, the founding treaties may be superseded by a 'Treaty establishing a Constitution'). Hence legal reasoning always does include reflection on the bearing that relevant established rules have on particular situations. This happens when those who have private right or public competence to do so initiate civil or criminal legal processes, or take steps that are potentially preparatory to such processes. The Rule of Law requires that such interventions always be, and be shown to be,

[31] See Robert Alexy, *Theory of Legal Argumentation* (trans. R. Adler and N. MacCormick) (Oxford: Clarendon Press, 1989) 5–10, 212–20, and 294–5 on the thesis that legal reasoning is to be understood as a special case of general practical reasoning.

[32] See *Ethics Without Principles*, e.g., at pp 130–2.

[33] Dancy remarks (*Ethics Without Principles* p. 190) that 'To be rational, to think rationally, to be a competent assessor of reasons, need not be to be a competent rule-handler, nor is it necessary that one should be a competent assessor of the context-independent individual contributions of reasons present in the case, because there may be no such context-independent contributions to be assessed.' Lawyers do have to be competent rule-handlers, as well as having the more general capabilities noted.

grounded in the pre-established law in some appropriate way. Hence the universalization that goes on in law is in a context that is already law-defined in large part, and concerns the teasing out of issues where the purport of the established law is challenged or challengeable. Furthermore, by contrast with most moral deliberation, legal deliberation once matters come to court is (with a tiny handful of exceptions) a public process. In that public process, because of the public responsibility of judges, they are required (sometimes by law, sometimes simply by custom and usage) to state publicly what they are doing and why it is right to decide as they are deciding. That is what 'justification' means for present purposes. In the ways illustrated and argued above, this stating of reasons as public reasons by officials committed to even-handed justice in all cases, necessarily partakes of universality, albeit defeasibly so. In a certain carefully explained sense, one can perhaps conceive of 'ethics without principles'; the same does not go for law.[34]

   The thesis about universalizability is, however, not special to law, though it may have a more necessarily visible role there. To discover how this connects to other aspects of law, in particular a system of legal precedents, is a matter for a later chapter. First, however, it will be necessary to pursue a point concerning consequences. It seems to be a well-founded view that the justifying of a decision in the legal setting requires universalizing it (or showing that it would be acceptable if universalized). But this at once poses the question how the universalized proposition is itself justified. The answer I give is a controversial one: it is justified in view of its consequences—but only in a rather special sense of the term 'consequences'. To make good that thesis is the task of the next chapter.

---

[34] Emilios Christodoulidis pointedly observes that '[T]he complexity of the particular has (always-)already been reduced in law. Particularity could only be addressed by reverting to the domain of high complexity which would in fact undo law as an institutional achievement.' See 'The Irrationality of Merciful Legal Judgement: Exclusionary Reasoning and the Question of the Particular' *Law and Philosophy* 18 (1999) 215–41 at 237.

6

Judging by Consequences

Introduction

The *Terrorist Suspects* case was indeed a momentous one concerning the balance between basic democratic freedoms, and the right of a democratically elected Parliament to authorize the Government to exercise vigilance against the terrorist threat. Lord Hope of Craighead had this to say:[1]

> It is impossible ever to overstate the importance of the right to liberty in a democracy. In the words of Baron Hume,[2] 'As indeed it is obvious, that, by its very constitution, every court of criminal justice must have the power of correcting the greatest and most dangerous of all abuses of the forms of law—that of the protracted imprisonment of the accused, untried, perhaps not intended ever to be tried, nay, it may be, not informed of the nature of the charge against him, or the name of the accuser.' These were not idle words. When Hume published the first edition of his *Commentaries* in 1797 grave abuses of the kind he described were within living memory. He knew the dangers that might lie in store for democracy itself if the courts were to allow individuals to be deprived of their right to liberty indefinitely and without charge on grounds of public interest by the executive. The risks are as great now in our time of heightened tension as they were then.

Lord Hope, starting from an assertion of the importance of the right to liberty, ends with a warning against the risk of its loss through neglect by courts. These words serve as a challenging introduction to discussion of the question how far decisions—and not only legal decisions—can be justified or made right by their consequences. That is the question in this chapter. One can conceive of two extreme positions. On the one extreme, the only justification of a decision would be in terms of all its consequences, however remote—in terms, that is, of its productivity of the greatest net benefit, taking together all consequences and judging them by some suitable criterion of benefit and detriment. On the other extreme, the nature and quality of the decision, regardless of any of its consequences however proximate, would alone be allowed as relevant to its justification or its rightness. Neither extreme view is acceptable.

---

[1] *A (FX) and others v State for the Home Department* [2004] UKHL 56 at para. 100.
[2] Baron Hume, *Commentaries on the Law of Scotland Respecting Crimes*, (Edinburgh: Bell and Bradfute, 4th edn, 1844), vol. 2, p. 98.

The first one excludes the possibility of any rational justification of any decision, since the future is unknowable and chains of consequences stretch forward into infinity. It is also often understood as holding that there is some single ultimate criterion of value (pleasure, perhaps, or satisfaction of preferences) in terms of which we can do all the cost-benefit calculations. So far as consequentialism is taken to include this type of single-value reasoning, there are further grounds for doubting it. The second view, at the opposite extreme, ignores two crucial things. It ignores the extent to which the nature and quality of decisions and acts are themselves constituted by the consequences the decider intends, foresees, or hopes to bring about. Also, more seriously, it ignores the extent to which both prudence and responsibility to one's fellows require that one give serious thought to the foreseeable outcomes of one's acts and decisions before finally acting or deciding, the more so the more momentous the act or decision in view.

We must therefore reject both extremes. We should entertain only the middle view, that some kinds and some ranges of consequences must be relevant to the justification of decisions. To ignore 'risks' of the kind apprehended by Lord Hope would be extremely irresponsible, as it would also be irresponsible of a government to take lightly intelligence reports suggesting the imminence of some kind of large-scale terrorist action.

The purpose of this chapter is to argue that a certain kind of consequentialist reasoning is of decisive importance in justifying legal decisions. Reasoning about the problems of relevancy and of interpretation, and some aspects of reasoning about the problem of classification or evaluation, typically involve issues about the appropriate line of legal development through the particular case in hand. Should liability for some kind of harmful actions be extended into new fields, or restricted? Should a statutory right to compensation for unfair dismissal include a right to compensation for injury to feelings, or only for loss of a strictly financial kind caused by loss of a job? Should errors of law be assimilated to errors of fact in the law of restitution governing money paid in error by one person to another? These and many similar questions arise for discussion here and in later chapters. In all cases, we are dealing with legal problems, not with moral or political issues taken in the raw. So the answer always has to be capable of being framed in terms of the law, through interpretation of statutes or of precedents, or of legal principles developed through reflection on law as a practically coherent normative order. Problematic cases are, however, problematic just because there are rival possible interpretations, and the question becomes that of how it is rational to choose among legally supportable answers.

What seems most reasonable in such dilemmas is that judges, and others concerned, should look at the choice before them in terms of its consequences one way or the other, in relation to the law. This connects directly with the universalist theme developed in the preceding chapter, and also has implications for the later discussion of precedent (Chapter 8). To decide a case and to justify the decision requires that it be universalized, at least implicitly, and the merit of rival possible universal (even if universal but narrowly defined) propositions of law assessed qualitatively. Then reasons should be given for the preferred alternative, the preferred line of decision for this and like cases.

There is an analogy, but not an identity, here with 'rule consequentialism' in moral philosophy as recently expounded with great eloquence by Brad Hooker,[3] and with the 'ideal utilitarianism' espoused by the late R. M. Hare.[4] Decisions are not justified in terms of their direct immediate affects on the parties alone (that is when hard cases make bad law), but in terms of an acceptable proposition of law that covers the present case and is therefore available for other like cases (hence satisfying the demand of justice that like cases be treated alike). Moralists of the schools of Hooker or Hare contend likewise that we should make moral assessments through the prism of reflection on possible rules of conduct that would cover, and solve, the dilemma confronting the moral decision maker. The issue is not whether everyone else will in fact act on the basis of the rule contemplated, whether concerning what is permissible or what is obligatory. It is whether one could sincerely assent to this rule if it were a rule observed by everybody—or, in Hare's version, whether one would universally prescribe it (and live up to the prescription oneself, even if no one else did). What is distinctive about judicial decisions in actual cases is that, especially in appellate courts, and to whatever extent in a given legal system there is a practice of following precedent or even a rule requiring this, the universalized decision does become a kind of rule for everyone else. At least it becomes a rule that other judges should follow or overrule except where they can distinguish it.

1. Traps for Consequentialists

What is difficult about this concerns the extensiveness of the consequences that judges should consider, and the basis on which they should evaluate them. The social consequences, especially the long-term social consequences, of adopting one legal rule rather than another are notoriously difficult to calculate. Confidence about the accuracy of 'impact assessments' in relation to proposed new legislation can easily be misplaced, given the normal operation of the law of unintended consequences. (That is, the sociological generalization according to which projects aimed to bring about some desired and desirable state of affairs often fail because of unforeseen side effects of the project, partly determined by people's actions in response to it. The side effects can cancel out the intended ones.) Judges and lawyers, moreover, are very badly placed for that kind of assessment, by

---

[3] B. Hooker, *Ideal Rules, Real World—A Rule-consequentialist Theory of Morality* (Oxford: Oxford University Press, 2000).

[4] R. M. Hare, *Moral Thinking: its Levels, Method, and Point* (Oxford: Clarendon Press, 1981).

comparison with the executive branch of government, and the legislature itself. These latter can commission or carry out the kind of studies and surveys that would be required even to construct crude and approximate but defensible predictions about the outcomes of policy choices made by them. Apart from occasional, and very local, uses of the so-called 'Brandeis Brief', litigation involving individuals or even large corporations outside specialist areas like competition law (anti-trust law) is not well adapted to constructing or evaluating evidence of the kind required.

A further difficulty concerns evaluation itself. Even if you have established likely consequences of one decision rather than another, how do you evaluate these? Is there a single metric of evaluation available, such as that proposed by supporters of the 'economic analysis of law', or does this amount only to an arbitrary technique for subjecting incommensurable values to a single scale of measurement?

The challenge to be faced in this chapter is to see if it is possible to establish a satisfactory version of legal consequentialism that will evade the traps just identified.

2. Consequences as Implications: 'Juridical Consequences'

If we are to find how consequences may be relevant to justifying decisions, we must look beyond and away from particular causal consequences and outcomes. In fact, the very activity of justifying decisions by giving reasons for them will prove to be the source of the kinds of consequences that count. Because of the institutional nature and setting of the practice of adjudication and because such a practice is properly governed at least by the principle of formal justice, to treat like cases alike, justified judicial decisions presuppose universalizable reasons or rulings in law that 'cover' the particular decision justified. And only well-justified rulings can in turn justify decisions.[5]

A necessary part of the justification of such a ruling is to show that it does not contradict validly established rules of law.[6] A further necessary part is to show that it is supported by established legal principles or by reasonably close analogy with established rules of law where some statable principle sustains the relevancy of the analogy.[7] But such grounds of justification, although always necessary, are by no means always sufficient or conclusive in favour of but one possible ruling in a case. The conclusive or clinching point of argument when a case still stands open after such testing for consistency and coherence is an argument about consequences in a somewhat different sense than any we have yet considered.

[5] G. Hughes (ed.), *Law, Reason and Justice Essays in Legal Philosophy* (New York, 1969) at 117.
[6] MacCormick, *Legal Reasoning* at 126–28, 195–228.
[7] Id. at 119–26, 152–94. The principles of law explicated and deployed in this type of argument seem to me to comprehend a good deal of what Summers, supra note 10, treats as 'rightness reasons'.

The remarkable nineteenth century English case of *R v Dudley and Stephens*[8] furnishes an example. Two shipwrecked mariners faced prosecution for murder because they had saved their own lives by killing the cabin boy and eating him after they had been adrift in the lifeboat eight days beyond the end of their food supply and six since they had finished their last drinking water. The defence tried to set up a principle of necessity as a justification for killing in order to save one's own life. But said Lord Chief Justice Coleridge:[9]

It is not needful to point out the awful danger of admitting the principle which has been contended for. Who is to be the judge of this sort of necessity? By what measure is the comparative value of lives to be measured? ... It is plain that the principle leaves to him who is to profit by it to determine the necessity which will justify him in deliberately taking another's life to save his own ... [I]t is quite plain that such a principle once admitted might be made the legal cloak for unbridled passion and atrocious crime.

Notice that the 'awful danger' apprehended here is an awful danger concerning what will follow *logically* from the principle if adopted. The only statable way of framing a suitable exception for necessity in the law of murder will be a ruling in law, or in Lord Coleridge's term a principle, which authorizes people whose lives are in pressing danger to judge whether they should kill another innocent victim of the same danger in order to save themselves. The alarming or unacceptable quality of the principle is exhibited by attending to its practical implications as a possible governing norm for future cases. In a similar way, in the *Conjoined Twins* case, Ward LJ, having come to the conclusion that the doctors owed a duty to each of Mary and Jodie to respect their lives, posed a dilemma and a way out of it:[10]

What are the doctors to do if the law imposes upon them a duty which they cannot perform without being in breach of Mary's right to life if at the same time the respecting of her right puts them in breach of the equally serious duty of respecting Jodie's right to life? A resort to a sanctity of life argument does not enable both rights to receive the equal protection the doctrine is supposed to provide each of them equally. In those circumstances it seems to me that the law must allow an escape through choosing the lesser of the two evils.

The problem is that the implications of the law are that a pair of incompatible duties exists. If that is so, there must be some legal way out. In fact, the element of 'necessity' links this case to *Dudley and Stephens*, and there was considerable discussion of the relevancy of the problem posed by that case to the very different case of Jodie and Mary. Brooke LJ remarked:[11]

If a sacrificial separation operation on conjoined twins were to be permitted in circumstances like these, there need be no room for the concern felt by Sir James Stephen [in parallel to the concerns of Coleridge LCJ about the risk of people judging their own case] that people would be too ready to avail themselves of exceptions to the law which they might suppose

8 [1884] 14 QBD 273.   9 Id. at 287–8.
10 [2001] Fam. 147 at 202–3, [2000] 4 All ER 961 at 1016.
11 [2001] Fam. 147 at 240, [2000] 4 All ER at 1051–2.

to apply to their cases (at the risk of other people's lives). Such an operation is, and is always likely to be, an exceptionally rare event, and because the medical literature shows that it is an operation to be avoided at all costs in the neonatal stage, there will be in practically every case the opportunity for the doctors to place the relevant facts before a court for approval (or otherwise) before the operation is attempted.

That is, of course, a matter of negating a possible adverse implication of the ruling in favour of carrying out the operation. Even greater difficulties appeared to Brooke LJ in the event of holding that the operation was unlawful:[12]

We pointed out repeatedly to Dr Taylor and Mr Harris during the course of argument that if their contentions were correct, no separation surgery which would inevitably involve the sacrifice of one conjoined twin could ever lawfully take place, however ardently their parents wished one of their children to survive, and however severely compromised the condition of the other twin. It would also follow, if their arguments based on the effect of Article 2 of the European Convention on Human Rights...are well-founded, that no separation surgery involving the sacrifice of a conjoined twin could take place in any of the member states of the Council of Europe. Mr Taylor and Mr Harris accepted, realistically, that this was indeed the effect of their submissions.

To Brooke LJ by contrast, this was a reduction to absurdity of the argument advanced by Dr Taylor and Mr Harris.

Arguments such as those the three excerpts exemplify have in view consequences in the sense of logical implications. Why they matter depends on the context in which they arise. In *Dudley and Stephens*, the court would not have been able to justify putting the defence of necessity to the jury unless it had been able to commit itself to a ruling in law that in any similar extreme case necessity of a similar extreme kind should there also be allowed as a defence. Likewise, with conjoined twins, the operation to separate these twins cannot be justified without a ruling that there is a context in which, in very rare and unfortunate circumstances, an operation that saves one life may be performed although it is at the cost of another life.

Bernard Rudden, in a masterly and helpful critique of *Legal Reasoning and Legal Theory*, suggested that we should call such consequences as implications 'juridical consequences'.[13] The name is well chosen, for to declare a particular right (*jus dicere*) is necessarily, in the role of an impartial judge, to declare it as available in every like case. Hence, as a person of prudence and forethought any judge must look across the range of possible situations which will have to be covered by a proposed ruling in point of right. Such consideration of a range of possible cases cannot but be necessary to adequate assessment of the acceptability of the decision entertained in the present case.

---

[12] [2001] Fam. 147 at 219, [2000] 4 All ER1031–2.

[13] Rudden, 'Consequences', *Juridical Review* 24 (1979) 193, 197–9. It seems to me that what Rudden distinguishes as 'inbuilt consequences', id. at 199–201, are simply a special case of 'consequences as implications'.

John Dewey, in one of the classical texts of legal pragmatism, argued that the law should be developed on the footing of '*a logic relative to consequences rather than antecedents*, a logic of prediction of probabilities rather than one of deduction of certainties'.[14] Contrary to this notion of Dewey's, the example of *Dudley and Stephens* exhibits all the certainty and necessity that is involved in any case of logical implication. Questions of doubt or probability focus only on whether the proposed necessity defence requires a statement of principle in the form envisaged by the judge. Must the relevant principle be stated in such a form as to have those implications for hypothetical test cases? Have we exhausted all the reasonable possibilities in the way of propositions that can at present be formulated with appropriate bearing on the case in question?

It remains uncertain whether the hypothetical test cases will arise at all, whether passing judgment with reference to them will alter or affect behaviour patterns in the community. Such questions about the outcomes consequent on adoption of a given ruling, questions about what Rudden has called 'behavioural consequences',[15] are indeed open only to conjectural answers. This is a point that Peter Cane has made forcefully in an essay in which he casts doubt on the genuine objectivity of 'consequence-based reasoning' in the judicial setting.[16] He is certainly right about the problems he poses, for there are plenty of studies, although many more in respect of statute law than case law, of past legal changes that indicate how difficult and disputable it is to establish what have been consequences and outcomes of, or responses to, any given change in the general rules of law. All the more conjectural must be forecasts about the likely impact of novel rules or rulings on the way people will conduct themselves.[17] No wonder, then, if judges rest but lightly on such predictions.

Twice over is this noticeable in Lord Coleridge's opinion in *Dudley and Stephens*. Recall his objection to admitting the so-called necessity defence into the law of murder. Recall his description of it as a potential 'cloak' for 'unbridled passions and atrocious crime'. There is here a hint of a prediction that the

---

[14] loc. cit. (emphasis in original).   [15] Id. at 194–7.

[16] P. Cane, 'Consequences in Judicial Reasoning', in J. Horder (ed.) *Oxford Essays in Jurisprudence* (4th Series) (Oxford: Oxford University Press, 2000) 41–59.

[17] See, e.g., David Nelken's, *The Limits of the Legal Process: A Study of Landlords, Law and Crime* (1983). At pages 36–7, there is a brief discussion of the unresolved controversy over the question whether exploitation of tenants by landlords was a consequence of the Rent Act of 1957 (enacted under a Conservative government), or was a consequence not of the 1957 Act but of a housing shortage. The main burden of Nelken's book is an attempt to establish what were the consequences and outcomes of the enactment of the Rent Act of 1965, from which may be gathered how difficult it is to answer such questions with reasonable certainty at any point in time, much less through a continuity of changing times and consequences. Moreover, the study certainly shows that, as is now officially admitted, the Act did not bring about the consequences that were predicted at the time of legislation as being likely to flow from it. By contrast with the case of the 1957 Act, this failure of prediction cannot be ascribed to a lack of care in investigating the problem and in attempting to make well-grounded predictions. The 1965 Act was preceded by the Milner Holland Report (Report of the Committee on Housing in Greater London, Cmnd. 2605 (1964–5), a report that might be considered perhaps the most thoroughgoing British social policy report of the twentieth century.

consequence of such a general exception to prohibitions on killing will actually be more passions less bridled and more crimes more atrocious. But I doubt if such probabilistic prediction is much at issue. The point seems rather to be that there will be a legal cloak for certain such things if they occur, and hence whatever the influence of the law as a disincentive, which we do not know, the disincentive will be diminished. The second caveat against too probabilistic an interpretation of the opinion arises from Chief Judge Coleridge's candid admission that the defendants' temptation is one to which he himself might likely have given way in their position:[18]

> It must not be supposed that in refusing to admit temptation to be an excuse for crime it is forgotten how terrible the temptation was; how awful the suffering; how hard in such trials to keep the judgement straight and the conduct pure. We are often compelled to set up standards we cannot reach ourselves, and to lay down rules which we could not ourselves satisfy. But a man has no right to declare temptation to be an excuse, though he might himself have yielded to it.

There could scarcely be a more candid admission of the uncertainty that in extreme cases a rule one way or the other affects behaviour at all. Yet again, the judgment is obviously that if the law can have an influence, then in so far as it does, it ought to be on the side of not yielding even to extreme temptation. By contrast, in the *Conjoined Twins* case, the idea that the decision gives an incentive to disregard sanctity of life is negated by the relatively small number of such situations that can arise, and by the way in which the decision has to be taken some time after the birth of such twins. In this kind of case, moreover, in doubtful instances it is always likely that the courts, at least of first instance, will be involved in authorizing or refusing to give authority for an operation to separate twins. Advisory committees on medial ethics and medico-legal questions are always likely to be well-informed about significant court rulings on matters of this kind. So the present decision is likely to have, and in a legal perspective ought to have, a significant role in guiding future decisions by medical people and others in relation to such operations.

One can view great constitutional decisions in a similar perspective. *Marbury v Madison*[19] was a decisive—*the* decisive—case that shaped the evolution of the United States Constitution and laid the basis for judicial review of legislation as well as of executive action. There, Chief Justice Marshall backed his ruling that the Supreme Court has power to refuse implementation of unconstitutional acts of Congress by explicit reference to the unacceptable consequences of the alternative ruling:[20]

> Those . . . who controvert the principle that the constitution is to be considered, in court, as a permanent law, are reduced to the necessity of maintaining that courts must close their eyes to the constitution, and see only the law.

---

[18] (1884) 14 QBD at 288.   [19] 5 US (1 Cranch) 137 (1803).   [20] Id. at 178.

This doctrine would subvert the very foundation of all written constitutions. It would declare that an act which, according to the principles and theory of our government, is entirely void, is yet, in practice completely obligatory.

Not quite two centuries later, in *Costa v ENEL*, a similar question arose in what was then the European Economic Community. How were the Community Treaty and legal norms validly made under it to relate to legislation of the Community's Member States? The question received a similar answer to that in *Marbury*, for similar reasons:[21]

The integration into the laws of the Member State of provisions which derive from the Community, and more generally the terms and the spirit of the Treaty, make it imposs-ible for the states, as a corollary, to accord precedence to a unilateral and subsequent measure over a legal system accepted by them on the basis of reciprocity ... The executive force of Community law cannot vary from one State to another in deference to subsequent domestic laws, without jeopardizing the attainment of the objectives of the Treaty ...

The obligations undertaken under the Treaty ... would not be unconditional, but merely contingent if they could be called into question by subsequent legislative acts of the signatories ...

In cases of this kind, there is always an element of begging the question. There are two open possibilities at the inception of such polities. It could have been that the federal legislature was left to be self-policing about its powers and their exercise, rather than that the judges acquired oversight of legislative constitutionality. It could have been that the Community Treaty was left to function simply on a basis of inter-national law, rather than being 'constitutionalized', and it is an open question what the upshot of that would have been. But within the legal order that emerges from *Marbury* or from *Costa*, the original decision is in a way self-authenticating. The legal order that would have been subverted by the alternative approach becomes the legal order that exists as a result of the relevant decision and of its acceptance and (sometimes grudging) respect by other political and constitutional actors. From within the emergent legal order, the subversive implications of the alternat-ive are obvious, and unacceptable.

One way or the other, it seems almost always to be in this somewhat hypothet-ical way that courts examine possible behavioural consequences or outcomes of rulings one way or the other on a difficult point. Even in the cases that Bernard Rudden cites as relatively clear examples of 'behavioural consequences', this is so. He alludes to a number of admiralty cases involving rescues and salvage at sea, such as the case of *Scaramanga v Stamp*[22] in which Chief Justice Cockburn makes the following point:

The impulsive desire to save human life when in peril is one of the most beneficial instincts of humanity, and is nowhere more salutary in its results than in bringing help to those who,

---

21 Case 6/64, *Costa v ENEL* [1964] ECR 585, [1964] CMLR 425 at p. 593.
22 [1880] 5 CPD 295, 304.

exposed to destruction from the fury of winds and waves, would perish if left without assistance. To all who have to trust themselves to the sea, it is of the utmost importance that the promptings of humanity in this respect should not be checked or interfered with by prudential considerations as to injurious consequences, which may result to a ship or cargo from the rendering of the needed aid. It would be against the common good, and shocking to the sentiments of mankind, that the shipowner should be deterred from endeavouring to save life by the fear, lest any disaster to ship or cargo, consequent on doing so, should fall on himself.

Yes, indeed. But we notice that Chief Justice Cockburn does not commit himself to a view on the probable effects of such a deterrent. It is enough that it would be bad if the law constituted such a deterrent, however people might actually respond to it.

Common experience suggests that the greatest weight should be given to outcomes in the way of probable behavioural changes in respect to novel rulings when these are really likely. That means, in those areas where it is particularly likely that people will explicitly ground their actions in the law as it is laid down (*inter alia*) by courts. Tax law, insurance law, and conveyancing are such fields. In such fields people and companies are expected to act after informing themselves, or being professionally advised, about the law. It is therefore highly probable that the outcome of rulings on the law will be behaviour that either conforms to it or takes advantage of opportunities offered by it or otherwise adjusts affairs and practices to allow for it. And in such fields indeed rather more account is, quite properly, taken of probable outcomes in the way of future responses to legal rulings. But even here it is worth remembering that the law and rulings in law are not causes of behaviour. Rather, they are grounds for choice by people, and how people will choose to respond is always in some degree an open question. Probably the only conduct one can see as actually necessitated by a ruling in law, and here the necessity is that of obligation rather than causation, is the conduct of a judge who adheres faithfully to prior rulings and seeks to act in their spirit. And that sort of 'behavioural consequence', if such it be, is already covered by our discussion of consequences as implications. So, in the main, what I call consequentialist reasoning law is focused not so much on estimating the probability of behavioural changes, as on possible conduct and its certain normative status in the light of the ruling under scrutiny.

It can also happen that a decision or a line of decisions may be found to have given rise to problems experienced by judges themselves. A notorious example from European Community law is the case of *Keck and Mithouard*,[23] in which the issue concerned violation of a provision of French law against the selling of goods at a price lower than their cost price to the seller. The parties contended that this article of French law was a measure that could actually or potentially, directly or indirectly, hinder intra-EC trade across the boundaries of Member States. On that

---

[23] Cases C-267 and 268/91 [1993] ECR I-6097, [1995] CMLR 101.

account, it should be struck down as a violation of Article 30 of the Treaty, being a measure having 'equivalent effect' to a quantitative restriction on imports from one Member State to another. The ECJ held that Article 30 should not be interpreted as applying to legislation by Member States prohibiting resale at a loss, in the course of its reasoning making this observation: 'In view of the increasing tendency of traders to invoke Article 30 of the Treaty as a means of challenging rules whose effect is to limit their commercial freedom even where such rules are not aimed at products from other Member States, the Court considers it necessary to re-examine and clarify its case law on this matter.' It cannot be said that this attempt to close an open floodgate has yet achieved either the praise of commentators or a new and satisfactory realignment of the jurisprudence affecting Article 30. It is nevertheless an interesting example of judicial appreciation of the response by citizens (and, of course, their legal advisers) to the juridical consequences of earlier rulings.

Not dissimilar has been the steady retreat by the UK House of Lords from its decision in *Pepper v Hart*.[24] That case abandoned the long-standing rule of interpretative practice according to which citations of Parliamentary debates were inadmissible as bases for elucidating the sense of a provision in an Act of Parliament whose meaning proved problematic at the point of applying the law. Dissenting at the time, Lord MacKay of Clashfern cited both reasons of constitutional principle and reasons of expediency—greatly increased costs of preparing litigation in higher courts, with no real gain in clarity—against using such materials. Later decisions of the House of Lords suggest he was right on both points, and the use of such material is now confined to contributing to an understanding of the legislative context.[25]

3. Evaluation of Consequences

Cases of the kind we have considered indicate the real but limited extent to which behavioural consequences and outcomes matter in legal decision-making. Responsibility generally attaches to persons for the foreseen and foreseeable consequences and outcomes of their actions, and judges are no exception. We cannot conceivably speculate on all the things that will or might possibly happen if people react in some way or another to a new ruling in law. We can, however, at least realize that they are entitled to take the law to be as a court has ruled it to be. People are supposed to act conformably to the law, and when they do act on the law as the court has ruled, the judges at least would be debarred from saying that they hoped it would not be so. This is really just to come back yet again in another

---

[24] [1993] AC 593.
[25] See Aileen Kavanagh, '*Pepper v Hart* and Matters of Constitutional Principle' *Law Quarterly Review* 121 (2005) 98–122.

Behavioural consequences matter

way to the kind of thing that Chief Justice Coleridge meant when he spoke about not creating a cloak for unbridled passions or atrocious crimes. Likewise, when Chief Justice Marshall apprehended the subversion of the written Constitution as an outcome of holding acts of Congress to be above judicial review, or the ECJ envisaged the subversion of the common market absent a rule in favour of supremacy of Community law, or the House of Lords considered the risks to erosion of the right to liberty in the *Terrorist Suspects* case.

But to see this is to see how we proceed from scrutiny of juridical consequences to their evaluation. What is at issue is whether the conduct that the law would tolerate or permit is acceptable when or if, in reliance on the law's permission, people engage in it. The test is whether it is acceptable[26] that the law stigmatize as wrongful or invalid deeds that citizens may have contemplated committing even in the face of such a ruling as is in view. But what grounds this notion of acceptability? What is it that reflection on juridical consequences via such hypothetical test cases enables us to evaluate, and how does this help us to reach fairly confident conclusions about what is or is not acceptable? By what standards of value do we do this?

As a matter of fact, judges often allude to justice, to public policy and/or the common good of the community, to legal expediency or convenience, and to common sense as ostensibly different grounds or criteria of evaluation which they apply to the juridical consequences and possible ulterior outcomes of possible rulings in contested cases. To observe this is to be alerted to the probability that legal evaluation operates on a plurality of values, rather than on some single standard such as so-called 'pleasure' or 'preference satisfaction' or 'utility', and that is important for a start. What is more, to take but one of the concepts mentioned, 'justice' hardly seems to be the name of a simple and unitary standard of evaluation. Justice itself has many aspects, and the problem is under which of its aspects it bears upon particular problems. When a judge tells us, as for example did Chief Justice Vanderbilt in the New Jersey case of *Greenspan v Slate*,[27] that the implications of a particular ruling are contrary to justice—the rejected ruling would have allowed parents of an infant child to refuse payment to a doctor for urgently needed medical treatment given to the child without the parents' prior consent—the appeal to justice seems conclusory rather than argumentative. It states the result of an evaluation without showing the working of it.

[26] See John Bell, 'On the Acceptability of legal Arguments' in N. MacCormick and P. B. H. Birks (eds), *The Legal Mind* (Oxford: Clarendon Press, 1986) 45–66. Compare Ch. Perelman, *L'Empire Rhétorique: rhétorique et Argumentation* (Paris: Librairie Philosophique J. Vrin, 1977) 80–4. See also Eveline T. Feteris, 'A Pragma-Dialectical Approach of the Analysis and Evaluation of Pragmatic Argumentation in a Legal Context' *Argumentation* 14 (2000) 1–19. Feteris argues that values must be made explicit to establish what is 'acceptable'.

[27] 12 NJ 426, 97 A. 2d 390 (1953) (Vanderbilt, C. J.): '[A]ny such artificial basis for a fundamental doctrine as "inferences from slight evidence" is not only unsound in principle but ineffective in operation, because it does not reach the cases where no express promise exists and where there is no "slight evidence" from which to infer a promise, and the cases not so reached are the ones where in simple justice a legal right and an adequate remedy are most needed.'

problem with the minority torture ev

Sometimes also judges differ on whether or not some apprehended adverse consequence is to be considered a matter of 'expediency' or of 'justice'. In deciding to assimilate errors of law and errors of fact in the law of restitution concerning money paid under error, the House of Lords acknowledged that this might give rise to undesirable uncertainty. For businesses would never be sure when they could close their books on certain transactions, in case new legal doctrines emerged with retrospective effect in relation to payments received on some legal ground or another. Lord Hope of Craighead acknowledged that this might 'give rise to widespread injustice'[28] while other judges dealt with the same fear as one concerning 'policy' or 'expediency'. All concurred that, one way or another, the legislature might have to intervene (while the two dissenters thought that the whole task of changing the 'mistake of law' rule and attending to related issues about prescription and limitation of actions should be left to the legislature). There is room to try and make clearer what is involved in evaluations of this kind.

Just as there are many virtues, so there are many values: things or states of affairs or qualities in life and interpersonal dealings on which we set value. Our notion of rightness and wrongness in action maps onto these values in the sense that conduct is reprobated as wrong when it falls below some minimal degree of, say, humanity or good faith or honesty or carefulness. It is all the more wrong when it manifests an active disregard for them or their like. One acts rightly, though not perhaps excellently or even well, provided one exhibits the minimum required regard for such values. Individuals and groups may vary, of course, in where they draw the line, and even in the things on which they draw lines at all. But legal orders are in central part authoritative orders of line drawing between right and wrong, the lines so drawn having application in common to all persons within a jurisdiction. Justice, or at least justice according to law, is a rather complex function of the lines between rightness and wrongness, and responses to actions that cross them, and it ranges across the whole set of relevant values. It is also concerned to ensure that, with respect to such values, essentially similar cases of deficiency in regard to them are treated in essentially the same way.

Different branches of law focus on different values or clusters of values. For example, tort law focuses mainly on respect for the integrity of persons and their possessions. Contract law focuses on the liberty of persons to pursue their own ends, balanced against fidelity to undertakings, and mutual trust and good faith. All criminal law to some extent and some parts of criminal law exclusively focus on public peace and order as a context of personal security and integrity. The law of trusts focuses obviously enough on trust, and so on. These examples are of course all too gross and crude, but they point in the right direction. The justice at which legal systems aim includes centrally the preservation of adequate respect for these values in dealings between persons and the enforcing of due remedies and penalties when they are breached.

---

[28] *Kleinwort Benson v Lincoln City Council* [1999] 2 AC at 417; [1998] 4 All ER at 569; full-scale discussion of this case is deferred to Chapter 13.

To see this is to take a little further an answer to the question about grounds of evaluation of juridical consequences. For legal problems arise in legal settings and new rulings in problematic cases build out from established bodies of law. Established bodies of law focus on given values or complexes of value. It is against those very values that we test and eliminate rival rulings in problematic cases. In considering the juridical consequences of a ruling by way of its implications for hypothetical cases, we discover whether a ruling commits us to universally treating as right deeds that subvert or fail of sufficient respect for the values at stake, or to treating as wrong forms of conduct which include no such subversion or failure. Either consequence is unacceptable because it wreaks injustice, that is, fails of the proper virtue of legal institutions; but the present analysis perhaps shows why and how such a conclusion of injustice would hold, rather than merely asserting it.

If I am right about that, the question about the particular values proper to legal deliberation almost answers itself. The values against which it is proper to test juridical consequences are those which the branch of law in question makes relevant. And if that is too abstract an answer, recall the place that constitutionalism or respect for a constitution as the written foundation of the body politic had in *Marbury v Madison*;[29] that which respect for liberty and non-discrimination had in the *Terrorist Suspects* case,[30] or respect for life had both in *Dudley and Stephens*[31] and in the maritime rescue case that I quoted;[32] that which proper parental care for children and reciprocation of benefits conferred played in *Greenspan v Slate*.[33] The same goes very strongly for the various reflections on family law and the paramount duty to have regard for children's well-being in decision-making about them, and the near absolute value accorded to the principle of the sanctity of life in respect of medical law and criminal law so far as concerns the duty to respect human life, and on criminal law in relation to the termination of life in *Re A (children) (conjoined twins)*.[34]

4. The Law's Values

It seems desirable to take a little further the idea of values implicit in law, taking note that each branch of law has, when studied in detail, a set of value orientations. Can one say anything of a more comprehensive character about legal systems in their entirety? Certainly, such an effort will be schematic at best, but seems worth trying. In doing so, one finds guidance in the wisdom of the past and of other scholars.

---

[29] 5 US (1 Cranch) 137 (1803); see text accompanying nn. 19–20 above.
[30] [2004] UKHL 56.   [31] [1884] 14 QBD 273; see text accompanying nn. 8, 9, 18 above.
[32] See text accompanying n. 22 above.   [33] 12 NJ 426, 97 A. 2d 390 (1953).
[34] [2001] Fam. 147, [2000] 4 All ER 961.

The fundamental precepts of law according to high but ancient authority are these three:[35]

- Live honestly
- Harm nobody
- Treat all persons with the respect due to them.

The value of honesty attaches to basic commandments against deceiving, breaking promises, or acting in breach of trust or of good faith. Criminal law focuses on this where fraud is involved, that is, dishonesty deliberately applied to the pursuit of unjust gains. The civil law restricts itself to remedying financial or economic damage caused by dishonest conduct and breaches of contract or of trust.

The value of freedom from harm starts with protecting life itself, and physical security from bodily injury or bodily confinement, and from harms to reputation, emotional security, and environmental quality. Criminal law dealing with offences against the person looks to these values, with particular concentration on killing, battering and assaulting, violent abduction, and the like. The civil law in modern times acknowledges a general duty of care to avoid damaging people in body or in respect of their possessions, and in various more restricted ways protects economic, emotional, and reputational goods. Environmental goods (apart from issues of private nuisance) tend to be protected primarily through public law.

The value of respect for persons goes now well beyond what the ancient Romans could have envisaged under the heading of their '*suum cuique tribuere*', giving to each his/her own. That all persons have as their due certain basic elements of respect is now particularly, but by no means only, the subject matter of human rights law. This can be tracked through instruments like the United Nations Universal Declaration on Human Rights, the European Convention for the Protection of Human Rights and Fundamental Freedoms, and now most recently and with elegant economy of language by the Charter of Fundamental Rights of the European Union. The Charter covers, through various particular concretizations of each of them, the values of individual dignity, personal liberty, interpersonal equality, social solidarity, political citizenship, and proper administration of justice under law.

Any such listing contains overlaps and possible repetitions. Not harming people is no doubt a part of what respect for persons requires, and honesty includes respect for people's property rights, but so does abstaining from harm and acting with due respect. In contemporary understanding, many of the requirements of respect require systems of state-administered social security—solidarity rights, in the parlance of the Charter. Citizenship rights and rights to

---

[35] Justinian, *Institutes* I.1.3, *Digest* I.1.10.1, attributed to Ulpian. This is a somewhat free translation of the Latin 'honeste vivere, alterum non laedere, suum cuique tribuere'. Compare my slightly different version in A. Watson (ed.) *English Translation of the Digest of Justinian*, T. Mommsen & P. J. Krueger (eds), (Philadelphia: University of Pennsylvania Press, 1985).

fair administration of justice ('natural justice', in one use of that phrase) require institutions of democratic political participation, and well-organized and properly staffed tribunals, courts, and legal professions. All of this entails a large body of public law, including taxation law, to establish and sustain the necessary public institutions.

Ronald Dworkin contends that the most basic legal right of human beings is to be treated with equal concern and respect by the agencies of the state. We can certainly agree that concern (or 'care') and respect are fundamental to law, as is honesty, and that equality matters most in relation to the fundamentals of care and respect. John Finnis has argued persuasively in the context of his masterly restatement of Thomistic natural law theory that the good for human beings can be summed up under seven or eight headings (life, knowledge, practical reasonableness, religion, friendship, play, and aesthetic experience;[36] also possibly fulfilling work). He then tracks the way the basic values show up in human rights instruments in a new form. My suggestion about the values specific to legal order is compatible with what he says though not entailed by it. It is also compatible with though not derived from the way in which he relates the case for sustaining an established order of law-and-government to the practically reasonable realization of the good, including the common good, in human communities. But it is not necessary for present purposes to take a stand on the deeper ontological issues about the nature of things, people, and law raised by Finnis.

Positivists as much as natural lawyers can acknowledge that law expresses and aims to uphold a plurality of values: Joseph Raz is an important case in point.[37] They can also accept, what seems to me true, that these values are imperfectly commensurable. That is to say, they are not globally commensurable—it makes no sense to ask whether life is better than liberty or solidarity or dignity, or less good. Nor does it appear that there is any master value like 'happiness' (for example) to which the acknowledged values contribute a measurable share, such that they could be measured against each other by their relative contribution to attaining it. It does not follow, and seems to me false, however, to deny that basic goods are situationally commensurable. That is to say, such questions as the following often have to be asked and answered in particular situations: Whether some sacrifice of liberty is acceptable where there are pressing and present dangers to life and limb, and if so how much and in what way.[38] Whether some degree of 'economy with the truth' is justified by regard to individual reputation or privacy (as with data protection law). Whether considerations of cost (impacting via taxation on the pursuit of other goods) justify tolerating some imperfections in the administration of justice, and, if so, how much imperfection? The judgement

---

[36] J. Finnis, *Natural Law and Natural Rights* (Oxford: Clarendon Press, 1980) IV.2.

[37] See J. Raz, *Ethics in the Public Domain* (Oxford: Oxford University Press, 1995).

[38] The *Terrorist Suspects* case says that it is deeply incompatible with the law's values enshrined in international human rights law to set the balance in such a way that non-nationals are treated as less worthy of liberty than nationals. Respect excludes unwarranted discrimination.

in such cases should be in terms of whether or not it is acceptable to sacrifice one value to some degree, and, if so, to this degree, for the sake of a more thorough upholding of the other in the given situation of judgement. The situation is, by the hypothesis, one in which the sacrifice is in favour of a value that is itself in some way threatened or endangered. So something has to give. The judgement in question may be by a legislature or a court or (so far as applicable) by citizens individually or in groups (e.g. political parties, trade unions, religious associations).

Needless to say, such judgements are difficult and contentious ones, and it seems often to be the case that reasonable persons can find themselves in irresolvable disagreement while acknowledging that the other side also has a reasonable view.[39] In that situation, where reasonable opinions differ, it is also reasonable to have a decision procedure, such as voting by some relevant majority (of legislators, of citizens in a referendum, of judges on the bench of an appeal court) to settle arbitrarily but reasonably what the decision shall be. This is the inevitable logic of dealing with values that are imperfectly commensurable, even situationally. The reflections on reasonableness in Chapter 9 will perhaps clarify this a bit further.

Other instances of consequentialist reasoning will also be highlighted in other contexts. In the interpretation of statutes, for example, there is an overlap between this way of arguing and what is sometimes called 'purposive' or 'functional' interpretation. It has to be noted though that deference to the particular ends of particular legislation—which is always proper—has also to be constrained by the need for continuing respect for fundamental values. This may arise, for example, in relation to the interpretation of penal statutes in which a regime of strict liability may be considered useful to the end of inhibiting drug trafficking, but where principles of justice create a strong presumption in favour of requiring *mens rea* as a precondition of guilt in the case of grave and stigmatizing offences.[40]

As noted in the previous chapter, Robert Summers has argued[41] that, over and above the appeal to formally established authorities in law, there are at least two[42] types of substantive reason that can be advanced in justification of judicial decisions. On the one hand, there may indeed be 'goal reasons' for giving decision *D*. *D* is good because by so deciding we will secure or promote state of affairs *S*, and *S* is a good goal to pursue. Here we could imagine a case where a court holds

---

[39] I am inclined to hope that the condition on which disagreement is reasonable is stringent enough to limit the number of such irresolvable disagreements there can be. However, I note that in *In Re A (children) (conjoined twins)*, Ward LJ refers to the 'generous ambit within which reasonable disagreement is possible'. See [2001] Fam. 147 at 182, [2000] 4 All ER 961 at p. 996.

[40] Consider the discussion of *Sweet v Parsley* ([1968] 2 All ER 337 (CCA); [1970] AC 132, [1969] 1 All ER 347 (HL)) in Chapter 10 below.

[41] R. S. Summers, 'Two Types of Material Reasons: The Core of a Theory of Common Law Justification', *Cornell L. Rev.* 63 (1978) 707, 716–22; cf., R. S. Summers and L. Kelley, "Economists" Reasons for Common Law Decisions—A Preliminary Inquiry', *Oxford Journal of Legal Studies* 1 (1981) 213.

[42] Summers introduces a third type of 'substantive reason', namely 'institutional reasons', 'Two Types', at 722–7. I pass over this third type here, not out of disrespect, but because the distinction between 'rightness' reasons and 'goal' reasons, if well made, is sufficient for the present case.

that, since bussing pupils from one elementary school catchment area to another will promote educational equality, there must be bussing. But on the other hand, there may be 'rightness reasons' for *D*, reasons which are backward-looking rather than forward-looking in contradistinction to 'goal reasons'. Given all that has occurred between the parties, and having regard to some standing 'sociomoral norm' about right conduct in such cases, the right decision as between these parties, in the relationship which has come about between them, is *D*. Here we could imagine a case where defendant has acted in breach of good faith to plaintiff, and simply on account of that ought to be held liable. For it is, in itself, right to insist on observance of good faith in contractual relationships.

Summers's contentions about the bifurcation of types of substantive reason poses an apparent dilemma for the present thesis that consequentialist arguments are the most fundamental justificatory reasons available for judicial decisions in problem cases. The dilemma is this: either we interpret consequentialist reasoning as coextensive with the advancing of goal reasons for decisions, in which case the possibility of rightness reasons as equally fundamental is overlooked. Alternatively, we have to interpret consequentialist reasoning as including both appeal-to-goal reasons and appeal-to-rightness reasons, in which case the category of consequentialist reasoning may appear a confused and ambiguous one. This conclusion should be resisted. For example, if anything is a rightness reason, the right to liberty must surely count. Yet taking decisions guided by one's sense of the need to forestall erosion of that right in times of heightened tension looks like a goal reason too. Lines of distinction may be difficult to sustain here. The goals that lawyers should properly set themselves are, perhaps, goals of ensuring that the right prevails. The rightness they pursue is in terms of the consequences of some universalistic proposition of law considered as the basis for resolving a particular problem case and any materially similar others that may occur.

In Ronald Dworkin's[43] work we find a different though not utterly dissimilar critique of some contemporary ideas about consequentialism in the law. At the heart of Dworkin's original anti-positivist thesis about law, his 'rights thesis', lies an objection not so much to the view that good legal decisions must be oriented to the achievement of political aims as to the view that political aims are all identical in kind. Some of the aims that we think it good for our political community to pursue may be envisaged as collective goals or advantages, like an adequate defensive capability or an efficient postal service or an increase in Gross National Product. But others are envisaged as goods realizable only through the participation of individuals in them, like free speech or the enjoyment of private property or of some tolerable minimum standard of personal welfare. Most fundamental among this latter class of goods is, in Dworkin's view, the good for any individual of being treated with the same degree of concern and respect as any and every

---

[43] See R. Dworkin, *Taking Rights Seriously* (rev. edn, 1977) (chs 2–4 and the App. are especially useful).

other individual. The only morally acceptable form of human community is one in which every individual member receives from every other and from collective institutions of government the same equal degree of concern and respect, indeed that full concern and respect which is properly due to moral agents as such.

Dworkin has stipulated that we recognize a distinction between 'policies' and 'principles'. This stipulated distinction gives a mirror image of the distinction between the two types of social aim to which we have drawn attention.[44] Arguments of policy, says Dworkin, support a decision calculated to further some intrinsically collective good or advantage. By contrast, arguments of principle support a decision on the ground of the rights secured both to individuals at large—and thus to each and every qualifying individual. The proper task of the distinctively law-bound agencies of government, and in particular of courts of law, is to ascertain and vindicate rights. The rights they must vindicate are not every imaginable 'background right' we might think of lying in the moral hinterland beyond positive law. They are the rights that are grounded in the political principles best geared to justifying the community's institutions, whether or not these principles happen to be at any given moment concretized in explicitly formulated rules of statute or case law. It is not a proper task of courts to pursue or implement policies, except where decisions of policy have been duly enacted into legislation by authorized legislators in a manner consistent with fundamental constitutional principles of individual right.

One criticism of Dworkin's thesis, offered by Kent Greenawalt,[45] is that Dworkin's insistence on a radical differentiation between questions of policy and matters of right is refuted by the prevalence of consequentialist arguments in justifications of legal decisions. If consequentialist reasons for decisions are good reasons, policy must have a fundamental role in legal decision-making; and hence the rights thesis fails as a description of the legal system we actually have. To this, Dworkin's reply[46] is that it all depends on the kinds of consequences the courts take into account, and the grounds on which they evaluate them. The securing of rights is one kind of aim of a political community; hence the argument that *D* ought to be the decision in this case in order to secure or promote aim *A* may refer to some aspect of the aim of protecting rights. In this case, the consequentialist argument is an argument of principle, not one of policy. The argument by Lord Hope at the outset of this chapter, on the importance of the right to liberty, and the risk of letting it be eroded, is a case much in point. Dworkin effectively claims, in perhaps like vein, that legal consequentialist arguments are characteristically, and ought characteristically to be, arguments that test decisions and their consequences against principles rather than against pure policies. Thus the debate between Dworkin and Greenawalt draws fresh attention to the possibility of some hidden ambiguities in the very notion of a consequentialist argument. One can

---

[44] Id. at 90. For criticism of the stipulation, see N. MacCormick, *Legal Reasoning* at 259–64.
[45] K. Greenawalt, 'Policy, Rights and Judicial Decision' *Georgia Law Rev.* 11 (1977) 991.
[46] See R. Dworkin, supra n. 43, at 294–330.

indeed make a battery of useful points of differentiation, but the important one is the difference between 'juridical consequences' and others.[47]

What I finally derive from these reflections is a confession and avoidance concerning the risky conflation of Bob Summers's rightness reasons and goal reasons. There is indeed a certain conflation, but not one that causes confusion. The values pursued through and upheld by legal rules are properly considered to be standing aims of and for the law. It must then count in favour of a ruling in law that it promotes or supports a certain value, and this can be expressed in a sort of goal reasoning. But since judicial reasoning proceeds under the constraint of universalizability, the matter is also one of setting norms of rightness, thus yielding rightness reasons. In this context and at this level rightness and goal orientation are two sides of the same coin.

That recognition puts me in something like the same camp as Ronald Dworkin after all, but not to the point of accepting his stipulative distinction of policy and principle. Are not the values of the law capable of being considered a kind of standing policy? That judges pursue them under the constraint of universalizability entails indeed that their decisions must always be decisions of principle. But this does not mean that such decisions require pre-identification of rights as a route to finding principles. I should rather say that legal rights are consequential upon than presupposed by the decisions of principle we make in law. That some of the deepest values of the law are now enshrined in documents like the Charter of Fundamental Rights of the European Union does not undercut this point. The introductory quotation from Lord Hope can be read in counterpoint to the following from Lord Hoffmann, eloquently pointing out that many of the rights and values enshrined therein have a very long history in the legal systems of the United Kingdom:[48]

The technical issue in this appeal is whether such a power [to detain without charge or trial] can be justified on the ground that there exists a 'war or other public emergency threatening the life of the nation' within the meaning of article 15 of the European Convention on Human Rights. But I would not like anyone to think that we are concerned with some special doctrine of European law. Freedom from arbitrary arrest and detention is a quintessentially British liberty, enjoyed by the inhabitants of this country when most of the population of Europe could be thrown into prison at the whim of their rulers. It was incorporated into the European Convention in order to entrench the same liberty in countries which had recently been under Nazi occupation. The United Kingdom subscribed to the Convention because it set out the rights which British subjects enjoyed under the common law.

---

[47] Consider the discussion of 'results', 'causal consequences', and 'outcomes', as well as juridical consequences, in MacCormick 'On Legal Decisions and their Consequences: from Dewey to Dworkin', *New York University Law Review* 58 (1983) 239–58, which paper can be read as a precursor to the present chapter.   [48] See *Terrorist Suspects* case [2004] UKHL para 88.

7

Arguing about Interpretation

Introduction

Applying the law always involves interpreting it. Any norm posed in an authoritative legal text has to be understood before it can be applied. Accordingly, in a wide sense of the term 'interpretation', every application of law requires some act of interpretation, since one has to form an understanding of what the text says in order to apply it, and any act of apprehension of meaning can be said to involve interpretation. This applies even in mundane settings. If I see a 'No Smoking' sign in the room I am entering and put out my cigarette in response, I evince simple understanding of the sign, and compliance with it. Without any element of doubt or resolution of doubt, I immediately apprehend what is required. This immediate apprehension of meaning can be called 'interpretation', but only in a very broad sense of that term.[1]

A narrower or stricter conception of interpretation is more useful and relevant to the study of legal reasoning. This is the sense according to which we 'interpret' only when facing some occasion of doubt about meaning, followed by a resolution of that doubt by reference to some reason(s) supporting the preferred way of resolving it. This reflective elimination of doubt is to be distinguished from simple unmediated understanding of a text. For example, there might be a particular occasion at a multilingual gathering when I see a 'No Smoking' sign while wearing a formal dinner jacket ('*un smoking*', as they call it in French). I might then pause for a moment to ask myself whether the notice requires me to change into less formal attire, rather than to abstain from tobacco.[2] To think over this doubtful point and to resolve one's doubt by opting in a reasoned way for one rather than another view of what the text requires is to 'interpret' it in this more strict sense of the term. By 'interpretation in the strict sense', I thus mean entertaining some doubt about the meaning or proper application of some information, and

---

[1] Compare J. Bjarup, 'Kripke's Case: Some Remarks on Rules, their Interpretation and Application' *Rechtstheorie* (1988) 39–49 at 46; not all rule-apprehension and application is mediated through any conscious act of interpretation.

[2] This light-hearted example derives from a remark made to me at a conference by a colleague whose name I now forget. I had appealed to the 'No Smoking' sign on the wall as an example of an unambiguous text whose meaning we apprehend—and can act on—in an unmediated way. The ingenious counter-example of course requires to be supplemented by some sort of special context.

forming a judgement to resolve the doubt by deciding upon some meaning which seems most reasonable in the context. Here, I shall be dealing only with interpretation so understood.[3]

Issues of interpretation in the defined sense are endemic to law, because differences of legal relationships can turn on differences of the understanding of a statutory or other binding text. People have reason to seek out doubtful points and have them resolved one way rather than another. Hence arguments aimed at upholding one or another of rival interpretations of the same text are omnipresent. Written constitutions and treaties constituting international organizations or supranational unions have a special status as written instruments adopted by some constituent act. In turn, they make provision whereby denominated legislative authorities can make laws binding throughout the state or other entity. Executive authorities may exercise delegated regulatory power under constitutional provisions or other legislation. Private citizens can make legally binding instruments such as contracts, trust deeds, wills, or documents constituting corporate entities. All such texts are normative in import—by virtue of them persons may acquire duties, claim rights, purport to exercise powers, assert liabilities of others, prosecute crimes, and so on.

Every invocation of any such legal text as a basis for a specific claim in a concrete situation can be expressed in the type of legal syllogism discussed in Chapter 3, though much more informal representations of such a structure of reasoning are what is common in ordinary usage. But disputes may always arise concerning the proper meaning to be ascribed to the text, both in general terms and with particular regard to a particular situation. It is a well-recognized truism that even the most carefully drafted and detailed text can never convey a fully determinate meaning for all possible purposes.[4] All the more is this so when texts that embody legal norms (rules, principles, standards, individual decisions, and other individual norms) are brought into play in ways that critically affect human interests, hence being susceptible to keenly argued practical disputes concerning the impact of variant possible meanings.

Legislation that regulates employment relationships may, for example, establish special industrial tribunals to provide simple and relatively informal adjudication of employment disputes, including, for example, disputes concerning an employee's alleged unfair dismissal from a job by an employer. The current UK legislation (Employment Rights Act 1996) provides in section 123(1) for the

---

[3] See J. Wróblewski, 'Legal Language and Legal Interpretation' *Law and Philosophy* 4 (1985) 239–55; also D. N. MacCormick and R. S. Summers (eds), *Interpreting Statutes: a Comparative Study* (cited hereafter as *Interpreting Statutes*)(Aldershot: Dartmouth Publishing Co., 1991) chs 2 and 8.

[4] See H. L. A. Hart on interpretation and 'open texture', *The Concept of Law*, P. A. Bulloch and J. Raz (eds), (Oxford: Clarendon Press, 2nd edn, 1994) pp. 125–9, 204–5, deploying ideas derived from Wittgenstein mediated through Friedrich Waisman. Many writers since Hart have restated the theme of law's indeterminacy, some indeed asserting a deep and radical indeterminacy, though this in turn should not be overstated—see Duncan Kennedy, *A Critique of Adjudication* (Cambridge Mass.: Harvard University Press, 1997) pp. 59–63, acknowledging the potential for a degree of determinacy in rules that helps to define what is ideologically at stake in conflicting interpretations of them.

making of a compensatory award to an unfairly dismissed employee: 'Subject to the provisions of this section and sections [124, 126, 127 and 127A (1), (3), and (4)], the amount of the compensatory award shall be such amount as the tribunal considers just and equitable in all the circumstances having regard to the loss sustained by the complainant in consequence of the dismissal in so far as that loss is attributable to action taken by the employer.' Often, dismissal of an employee takes place in highly stressful and distressing circumstances. Sometimes, employees can suffer bullying and harassment by superiors, and have to give up their job to escape this, and such situations amount to 'constructive dismissal'. Can compensation be given to cover injury to feelings and self-respect, or can it only cover the loss of money necessarily involved in losing one's job (cessation of wages or salary, etc)? Naturally, aggrieved former employees would welcome compensation for injured feelings, and in common law this can be obtained. But what about the statutory remedy? Does 'loss' in section 123(1) mean pecuniary loss only, or has it a more extended meaning? Employers for their part have been determined to argue that it has only the restricted, pecuniary, meaning in the context of the Employment Rights Act. This has been a disputed point, but was settled by a decision on final appeal to the House of Lords in July 2004.

This dispute about the meaning of a statutory provision illustrates well what I mean by 'problems of interpretation' in law. The doubt for resolution is framed in terms of two (or sometimes more) rival possible meanings to be ascribed to a word or words in a legal text, where the determination of the meaning one way or the other affects the legal position of the disputants—that is, their rights or duties or powers or liabilities or the like. Arguments are presented to the court why one reading should be preferred to another or others. The court's conclusion on the issue which reasons are the stronger for one interpretation or the other leads to the decision on the concrete matter in dispute—for example, how much compensation shall be paid by former employee to former employer.

There is another kind of interpretational issue that seems not to turn on interpreting the text in order to justify a decision on the matters of fact before the court. This other kind of issue, which I earlier called the 'problem of classification' (or you might say 'characterization' or 'qualification'), seems more to involve interpreting the facts in the light of a rule rather than the other way round. To give another example in the domain of employment law, it is practically tautologous to remark that only an employee can be entitled to rights conferred by statutes on employees. But who then counts as an employee? Often the matter is too obvious to require much or any reasoning. But there can be problematic cases. What about a company in which one person holds all the shares, and that same person enters into a purported contract of employment with the company to act as its managing director for set remuneration and with set hours of work? Is the managing director in such a case genuinely an employee?[5] One can see reason to doubt it, but so

---

[5] This was the problem in *Secretary of State for Trade and Industry v Bottrill* [2000] 1 All ER 915, discussed below in the last section of the present chapter.

posed the question is really too abstract. Only by looking in greater detail at the facts and circumstances of a given case could we judge whether the relationships involved satisfy the conditions the law recognizes as necessary to establish the relationship of employer and employee. Any full account of legal reasoning and interpretation has to reflect on the quality of reasoning in such 'classification' issues as well as on the more restricted set that I am specifically calling 'problems of interpretation'. So the concluding part of the present chapter will give a brief account of reasoning involved in resolving problems of classification, leaving further reflection to later chapters on reasonableness and on argument by analogy. The task of the whole chapter is to establish, with close reference to actual instances of judicial interpretation, what should be acknowledged as good arguments for interpretative conclusions.

1. Categories of Interpretative Argument

The next logical stage is therefore to examine what are the kinds of arguments, interpretative arguments, that judges and lawyers can deploy in the justification of interpretations where these are themselves reasons for decisions. As a member of a group of scholars who slightly jocularly called themselves the '*bielefelder Kreis*', I participated during the 1980s and 1990s in a project dedicated to the comparative study of legal interpretation—interpretation both of statutes and of precedents—across a considerable range of different legal systems. Despite well-known systemic differences between codified and non-codified systems, European and American ones, common law and civil law, this group found a remarkable common-ness in the types of arguments that are acknowledged as persuasive as grounding a favoured interpretation of a legal text in a situation of dispute or doubt. This applies particularly to judges' justifications of their decisions about interpretation. In summary of these findings, we suggested a typology and systematization of the interpretative argumentation characteristic of a wide range of contemporary systems and traditions of law. According to this, there are three main categories of interpretative argument, and within each of these several different types of interpretative argument.[6]

The categories of interpretative argument are, first, those that appeal to the linguistic context itself as a source of reasons for favouring one interpretation or another ('linguistic' arguments); secondly, those that look at the legal system as the special context of the authoritative text to see how best to make sense of it in that context ('systemic' arguments); thirdly, those that look to the end or aim of the authoritative text to see how best to make sense of it given that end or aim ('teleological-evaluative' arguments).[7] Not covered by any of these headings is a

---

[6] MacCormick and Summers, *Interpreting Statutes* chs 12 and 13.

[7] Compare Tony Honoré, 'The Necessary Connection between Law and Morality' *Oxford Journal of Legal Studies* 3 (2002) 489–95 at 494, 'The interpreter has to take account not only of moral but of linguistic, systematic and teleological arguments.'

common further element in interpretative argument, namely appeal to an author's (the lawmaker's) intention as a guide to elucidating the meaning of the authoritative text. The problem about 'intention' is its ambiguity, for sometimes it means an objective intention imputed to an author, sometimes a subjective intention gathered from statements by the author. There can also be differences concerning the reference of the intention in question. Sometimes it may involve reference to the author's intention about the use of language simply. Sometimes it may involve reference to author's intention about a term's or a sentence's use in the legal-system context. Sometimes it may involve reference to author's intentions about the ends and values to be realized through legislation. For that reason, this rather indeterminate element of interpretative argumentation is best considered as one that can range across all of the other categories and their types. On that ground, it should be deemed (if rather grandly) a 'transcategorical' type of argument relative to the other categories here identified.

In discussing this I shall largely rely on a single running example, dealing with the earlier-mentioned point about the meaning to be ascribed to 'loss' for the purpose of compensation awards under section 123(1) of the Employment Rights Act 1996 to unfairly dismissed employees. As Lord Steyn stated the issue in *Dunnachie v Kingston-upon-Hull City Council*,[8] 'An employee, who claims to have suffered humiliation, injury to feelings and distress, as a result of constructive dismissal, argues that properly construed section 123(1) allows for the recovery of non-pecuniary heads of loss. The employer argues that section 123(1) only permits recovery of pecuniary loss. This is the central dispute of statutory construction before the House.'

(a) Linguistic arguments

The principal type of what the *bielefelder* typology classifies as 'linguistic arguments' concerns the appeal frequently made by lawyers to the 'plain meaning' of words used in 'ordinary language'. Sometimes critics deride this as depending on naïve and false assumptions about language and semiotics, but perhaps this is because too little attention has been paid to whether and how this kind of argument can be convincing in context. In *Dunnachie* Lord Steyn considered that[9] 'A statute does not always yield . . . a plain meaning. Sometimes arguments of principle must be considered and a balance of consequential arguments must be struck. But in the present case . . . [r]ead in context the word "loss" has a plain meaning which excludes economic loss.' After scrutinizing the whole context provided by the 1996 Act, and even allowing that '[it] can readily be accepted that the word "loss" in varying contexts may have wider and narrower meanings' he concluded by holding 'that the plain meaning of the word loss in section 123(1) excludes non-economic loss'.

---

[8] [2004] UKHL 36 at para. 2, [2004] 3 All ER 1011 at 1015.
[9] [2004] UKHL 36 at para. 16, 17, and 22; [2004] 3 All ER 1011 at 1021–2.

We must reflect on the words 'read in context'. The basic context of any utterance is the language to which it belongs, and the register of language involved in a particular utterance. British statutes are (nowadays) written in the English language, in the rather formal (non-colloquial) register used by parliamentary draftsmen as appropriate to legislation enacted by 'The Queen in Parliament' or 'The Scottish Parliament'. It is very obvious that the use of words in ordinary (natural) languages to construct sentences relies on the 'compositional' character of the contribution each word makes to the whole sense of what is said or written. The competent language user gathers the meaning of a whole sentence from the contribution all the words taken together in that setting make to it, each word contributing from an available repertoire of possible meanings.[10] Meaning is in this way always contextual, words in the context of phrases and sentences, sentences in the context of larger texts, texts in the light of the kind or genre of writing to which they belong and their practical aims and applications if any. Dictionaries can account to us for the typical repertoire of contributions particular words typically make when used in their 'literal', that is, non-metaphorical, sense. Lord Steyn's conclusion that 'loss' is to be understood in the Act as bearing its 'ordinary meaning' has to be understood as 'ordinary in this context'. The point is that even if we were not dealing with a statutory text, a sentence about compensation for loss would not ordinarily be interpreted as one about compensation for injury to feelings.

Why does such an argument carry weight? It may be said that this is just a necessary part of respecting authority. If someone in authority issues a norm of some kind, necessarily using some language or another to do so, one does not respect that authority unless one reads the norm text in the language and register in which it is issued. To treat a linguistically formulated text as authoritative, one must also ascribe a kind of normative authority to the 'compositional' meaning of the wording used by the authority. This has obviously to be taken in the light of the syntactic and semantic conventions of the language (whether 'ordinary' or 'technical') in which the text has been formulated.

Behind this can be detected an appeal to ulterior value-considerations. The reception of the 'ordinary language' argument can be justified on an appeal to principle; for example, the principle that language ought to be used by the legislator, and therefore readily understood by the citizen, in as straightforward and immediately comprehensible a way as possible. Observing this principle will prevent legislative texts being in effect given new meanings retrospectively by judges to the disadvantage of citizens and hence will uphold a more fundamental principle of justice.

An alternative though not greatly dissimilar line of argumentation would look to the cumulative effect of a practice of relying on linguistic arguments in

---

[10] The account of 'compositionality' of meaning deployed here is substantially borrowed from Jonathan Dancy, *Ethics Without Principles* pp. 193–8, where he calls it 'weak compositionality'.

interpretation. By upholding 'ordinary', or 'plain', meanings in disputes about the meaning of legislation, even in cases in which this brings about non-ideal outcomes, one creates a situation in which legislatures (and their draftsmen) have to take care to draft statutes in ordinarily intelligible terms. Then citizens can with confidence read them in terms of plain meaning, hence the possibility of effective and trouble-free communication between legislature and citizen is maximized, and the trouble and expense of litigation about proper interpretation minimized.[11] In this light, it has to be recognized that behind what are often described somewhat disapprovingly as 'formalistic' or 'legalistic' approaches to interpretation there do lie evaluative reasons of a highly respectable kind.

'Ordinary meaning' is sometimes contrasted with 'technical meaning' where laws deal with specialist subject matter. A text may be concerned with some technical subject matter with a specialized vocabulary of its own, and in that setting terms which have a technical as well as an ordinary meaning are better understood in the technical sense. For example, the word 'diligence' in 'ordinary' English means praiseworthy and careful application by a person to a task. But in Scots law, it has a technical usage, meaning a legal process for enforcing pecuniary judgments; and at one time, in the terminology of transport, it meant a particular kind of horse-drawn vehicle. So in Scottish legislation about legal procedures, it should be read in its technical legal sense, and in an ancient piece of English transport legislation, it should be read as signifying the relevant sort of carriage. But in the rules of a school or university offering students prizes for special diligence, the 'ordinary' meaning should prevail. Likewise in the phrase 'due diligence' used in reference to full scrutiny of the accounts of a company or such like. That it is proper and reasonable to ascertain whether a word is being used in a technical rather than an ordinary sense, or vice versa, is pretty obvious.

(b) Systemic arguments

I have shown that even taken in isolation, one can make sense of, and ascribe value to, the use of simple arguments from ordinary meaning or technical meaning. Nevertheless, the stress is on 'ordinary in context', and in fact there is always a relevant legal context for every piece of statute law, indeed for every authoritative legal text. The part makes sense in the context of a whole, and the whole is the statute as an element in a whole legal system. In the *bielefelder* typology, 'systemic arguments' are ones that work towards an acceptable understanding of a legal text seen particularly in its context as part of a legal system. No list of types of such argument could be complete, since it is the whole context that is significant

---

[11] Consider, in this light, Lord Steyn's reference in *Dunnachie* (p. 8) to MacCormick, *Legal Reasoning and Legal Theory* (Oxford: Clarendon Press, 2nd edn, 1994) at p. 204, endorsing the argument that judicial respect for plain meaning enhances democratic accountability by ensuring that legislation is drafted in reasonably clear and explicit terms.

and may have a different bearing in different cases. But the following six give varied and vivid examples.

(i) Contextual harmonization

The argument from contextual harmonization looks to the way in which any statutory provision is to be found nested in a larger legal scheme, at least that of the single whole statute, often that of a set of related statutes. To argue from legal-contextual harmonization is to contend that any problematic terms ought to be interpreted in the light of the whole statute[12] or set of related statutes. This makes particularly relevant concentration on closely related provisions of the statute or other statutes[13] in *pari materia*, and shows that what is a more or less obvious 'ordinary', or respectively 'technical', meaning ought to be interpreted in that light. In *Dunnachie*, section 123(2) cast light on the sense of 123(1), because it deals only with aspects of pecuniary loss. The setting of the section 123(1) provision in the context of earlier legislation and other parts of that earlier legislation dealing with compensation also made the pecuniary interpretation of 'loss' much more plausible. 'Read in context, the word "loss" has a plain meaning which excludes non-economic loss. It does not cover *injury* to feelings. It is to be contrasted with section 66(4) of the Sex Discrimination Act 1975, section 57(4) of the Race Relations Act 1976 and section 8(4) of the Disability Discrimination Act 1995 which all expressly provide for compensation for injury to feelings.'[14]

(ii) Argument from precedent

The argument from precedent says that if a statutory provision has previously been subjected to judicial interpretation, it ought to be interpreted in conformity with the interpretation given to it by other courts. *Dunnachie* again affords a relevant example. The argument on Mr Dunnachie's behalf in favour of extending the concept of loss to include injury to feelings and psychological damage was partly based on a statement by Lord Hoffmann in the earlier case of *Johnson v Unisys Ltd*[15] suggesting that an extension could be appropriate. On due consideration, however,

---

[12] In the running example of *Dunnachie*, for example, the use of the word 'loss' in section 123(1) of the 1996 Act has to be understood in light of the fact that section 123(2) lists matters which subsection (1) is 'taken to include', and all these are items of possible pecuniary loss consequential on losing one's job: [2004] UKHL 36 at para. 2, [2004] 3 All ER 1011 at 1015.

[13] In *Dunnachie* it was of importance that section 123(1) of the Employment Relations Act 1996 had its 'ultimate genesis [in] . . . section 116(1) of the Industrial relations Act 1971', where for the first time tribunals were set up with power to award 'such amount as the Court or tribunal thinks just and equitable in all the circumstances, having regard to the loss sustained by the aggrieved party in consequence of matters to which the complaint relates . . .' [2004] UKHL 36 at para. 3, [2004] 3 All ER 1011 at 1015.

[14] Lord Steyn in *Dunnachie* [2004] UKHL 36 at para. 16, [2004] 3 All ER at 1021.

[15] [2003] 1 AC 518: 'It was said that the word "loss" can mean only financial loss. But I think that is too narrow a construction. The emphasis is upon the tribunal awarding such compensation as it thinks just and equitable. So I see no reason why in an appropriate case it should not include compensation for distress, humiliation, damage to reputation in the community or family life' (para. 55).

the House of Lords concluded that these remarks were *obiter dicta* going beyond what had been fully considered in the case, and not necessary to the decision reached in *Johnson*. Moreover, there was a long-standing precedent, *Norton Tool Co Ltd v Tewson*,[16] in which the President of the Industrial Relations Court had held that section 116(1) of the Industrial Relations Act 1971 in using the word 'loss' was to be interpreted as signifying only pecuniary loss. This precedent had been followed and approved many times, and in fact contained an acceptable rationale for the pecuniary reading of 'loss'. It was a better guide for the future than Lord Hoffmann's remarks in *Johnson*. (As always, reference to precedent depends on particular systemic doctrines about when precedents are binding, when persuasive, and in respect of what elements either binding or persuasive. In this line of cases, it was open to the House of Lords to have overruled *Norton Tool* and established a new ruling on the issue of 'loss'. If Lord Hoffmann had actually authoritatively done that in *Johnson*, this would have been binding unless an enlarged Bench had been convened in the House of Lords to reconsider the matter. As it was, *Norton Tool* was only persuasive, but its *ratio decidendi* had been followed for many years and was based on sound reasons. In other legal systems precedents are handled differently, and in France, for example, what carries particular weight is a *jurisprudence constante*, a standing body of similarly oriented decisions, of the higher courts. Single cases are not deemed decisive doctrinally, though quite frequently they prove to be so in practice.)

(iii) Argument from analogy

The argument from analogy says that if a statutory provision is significantly analogous with similar provisions of other statutes, or a code, or another part of the code in which it appears, this is a good ground for supporting an interpretation that follows the analogy. What has been said about *Dunnachie* could be rephrased to stress the material analogy between the 1971 Act and the 1996 Act. Indeed, this was particularly important when it came to considering the bearing of the phrase 'just and equitable' as qualifying a tribunal's discretion to award compensation for loss. In *Norton Tool*, Sir John Donaldson had explained the discretionary nature of the statutory award of compensation as follows:[17]

The discretionary element is introduced by the words 'having regard to the loss'. This does not mean that the court or tribunal can have regard to other matters, but rather that the amount of compensation is not precisely and arithmetically related to the proved loss. Such a provision will be seen to be natural and possibly essential, when it is remembered that the claims with which the court and tribunals are concerned are more often than not presented by claimants in person or in conditions of informality. It is not therefore to be expected that precise and detailed proof of every item of loss will be presented.

In that case, the argument from analogy shows the rationale for sticking with the 'plain meaning' of 'loss' in the later statute, because the same feature of relative

---

[16] [1973] 1 WLR 45.   [17] [1972] ICR 501 at p. 504.

informality of adjudication continues to characterize the new statutory system of industrial tribunals.

In other situations, there may be a significant extension of or departure from a term's ordinary meaning. In appropriate contexts this can be justified with a view to securing similarity of sense with the analogous provisions *either* considered in themselves *or* considered in the light of prior judicial interpretations of them. (The argument from analogy appears to be stronger on the second hypothesis, where it incorporates a version of the argument from precedent, as *Dunnachie* also exemplifies.)

(iv) Conceptual argument

The conceptual argument (known as 'logical' argument in those legal systems particularly influenced by Savigny) says that if any recognized and doctrinally elaborated general legal concept is used in the formulation of a statutory provision, it ought to be interpreted so as to maintain a consistent use of the concept throughout the system as a whole. At least, there should be particular regard to conceptual consistency within any particular branch of the law, such as property law, or employment law, or criminal law, for example. The case of 'loss' in employment law is one current example, and need not be further laboured here.

(v) Argument from general principles

The argument from general principles of law says that if any general principle or principles of law are applicable to the subject matter of a statutory provision, one ought to favour that interpretation of the statutory provision which is most in conformity with the general principle or principles. Where they conflict or tend toward different decisions, the typical problem has to be faced and resolved of seeking reasons why one takes priority over another, or outweighs it for the context of the type of case in view. In the *Terrorist Suspects* case, many appeals to basic constitutional principle were made, notable among them this by Baroness Hale:[18] 'It is not for the executive to decide who should be locked up for any length of time, let alone indefinitely. Only the courts can do that and, except as a preliminary step before trial, only after the grounds for detaining someone have been proved. Executive detention is the antithesis of the right to liberty and security of person.'

(vi) Argument from history

The argument from history takes note that a statute or group of statutes can over time come to be interpreted in accordance with a historically evolved understanding of the point and purpose of the statute, or of the group of statutes taken together as a whole. Where that is so, then any provision of the statute or group of statutes

---

[18] *A (FC) and others v Secretary of State for the Home Department* [2004] UKHL 56 at para. 222.

ought to be interpreted so that its application in concrete cases is compatible with this historically evolved understanding of the point and purpose involved. *Dunnachie* can again be cited as one rather obvious example of this point, but of course this has nothing special to do with employment law.

Arguments of any of these six types expand on the idea of the contextual character of meaning and interpretation, but take it beyond simple (and of course contestable) assumptions about 'ordinary language' considered in abstraction from the legal system.

Obviously, the legal system is a necessary part of the context in which each particular authoritative legal text is first issued and subsequently applied, occasionally in a context of controversy about how to apply it properly. The legal system has therefore a particularly strong relevance, even beyond that supplied by simple reflection on the semantics of 'ordinary language' as explained above. This indicates why such arguments carry the weight they obviously do in contemporary legal systems. No linguistic communication is fully comprehensible save in an entire presupposed context of utterance. All legal materials are uttered in the context of the legal system in general, and in the light no doubt of a whole complex of concrete legal, political, and factual circumstances. So interpretation cannot be satisfactorily carried through even in a purely 'linguistic' sense unless the whole systemic context is kept in mind. Moreover, as any real life example along the lines of *Dunnachie* shows, the argument for a particular interpretation rarely depends on just one single factor singled out here in terms of argument type. There can be a cumulation of severally inconclusive arguments that taken together constitute a highly persuasive albeit not logically demonstrative case for the interpretative judgment finally reached.

Still, that is not the whole story, for it fails to say just why the legal context gives special appropriateness to arguments stressing features like the six I have mentioned. As to that, I think it is necessary to draw attention to an ideal of overall *coherence* which governs our view of the legal system as a system and hence gives weight to the interpretative approach favoured by our various types of systemic argument. This theme is further explored in Chapter 10 below. The point is that legal systems do not contain single or isolated commitments of principle or determinations of policy. Rather, they comprise a multiplicity of interacting norms of many kinds, and these may be taken to express a plurality of principles and policy choices. As such, they are capable of being handled in a way that tries to make as much sense as possible of the whole taken together and taken as a whole.[19]

If one were to reject the attempt to view law holistically as a coherent system, each decision would presumably have to be considered as taken on its own merits with regard to any attractive interpretation of norms relevant to the instant case.

---

[19] See Chapter 10 below and compare R. Dworkin, *Law's Empire* (London: Fontana Books, 1986) pp. 176–86.

In an extreme, the law would then approximate to the poet's wilderness of single instances. By contrast, a practice of construing the law so as to give it coherence in form and content is one that actually constructs and reconstructs law into an ordered scheme of intelligibly differentiated cases and situations.

In interpretative dilemmas, recourse to systemic argumentation exhibits a special regard for this overall quality of rational coherence and intelligibility in law. It involves superimposing a principle of rationality on the institutional actuality of law. As such, the argument from coherence is a necessary supplement to arguments about the particular values considered implicit in a specific piece of legislation and the particular politico-legal goals or objectives which are considered to have motivated the legislature to enact it.

(c) Teleological–Evaluative arguments: Consequentialism by another name

Coherence is of significant value for law, and is indeed an essential element of the Rule of Law. But other values can be significant in interpretation. Statutes do not come into being by accident. They are the product of legislative decisions, promoted by governments and enacted by parliamentarians. They are promoted and enacted, usually, with a view to reforming the law. The idea of reform presupposes identification of some pre-existing defect in the law which the reform is designed to cure—a 'mischief' as an old expression has it. An obvious reason for preferring one possible interpretation to another is if its practical implications tend towards achieving the postulated reform, by removing the defect or suppressing the mischief.

In a broader way, legislation may be considered as embodying some socially relevant value or values. One spectacular case of this is provided in the UK by the Human Rights Act 1998, which made most of the human rights enshrined in the European Convention for the Protection of Human Rights and Fundamental Freedoms directly enforceable in the UK as part of domestic law. One of the protected rights is that of respect for private life; does this include protection of familial rights for homosexual partners? Speaking of this, Baroness Hale said:[20]

[Making a] distinction between heterosexual and homosexual couples might be aimed at discouraging homosexual relationships generally. But that cannot now be regarded as a legitimate aim. It is inconsistent with the right to respect for private life accorded to 'everyone', including homosexuals, by article 8 [of the Convention] since [the ruling handed down by the European Court of Human Rights] in *Dudgeon v UK* (1981) 4 EHRR 149. If it is not legitimate to discourage homosexual relationships, it cannot be legitimate to discourage stable, committed, marriage-like homosexual relationships of the sort which qualify the survivor to succeed to the home. Society wants its intimate relationships, particularly but not only if there are children involved, to be stable, responsible and secure. It is the transient, irresponsible and insecure relationships which cause us so much concern.

---

[20] *Ghaidan v Mendoza* [2004] 2 AC 557 at 608, [2004] 3 All ER 411 at 461.

The context of these remarks was a decision of the House of Lords concerning the proper implementation of the provisions of the Rent Act 1977 concerning tenancies protected under the Act. In the case of a protected tenancy, a surviving spouse of a person who has a protected tenancy, if residing in the house at the time of the death of the other spouse, becomes her- or himself a protected tenant in place of the deceased. The statute further provides that 'For [this] purpose...a person who was living with the original tenant as his or her wife or husband shall be treated as a spouse of the original tenant.' In *Ghaidan v Mendoza*,[21] the question arose whether or not the survivor of a long-term stable homosexual partnership was entitled to that protection. Under the Human Rights Act, 'So far as it is possible to do so, primary legislation and subordinate legislation must be read and given effect in a way which is compatible with the Convention rights.' Partly by analogy with the way in which the courts have considered it right to adjust the terms of domestic legislation to secure conformity with European Community law, it has been held, and the point was further reinforced in *Ghaidan*, that 'so far as is possible' does not restrict the courts to 'reading and giving effect to legislation' only within the limits of a possible but strained reading of the words in the legislation under view. As Lord Rodger of Earlsferry has explained, the reading of such an Act as the 1977 Act to secure compatibility may properly involve ignoring some words in it, or effectively adding some. This is legally proper, provided that doing so does not violate the fundamental principles of the Act, or deprive it of its 'pith and substance'. In relation to the very point in the case:[22]

[S]ociety has moved on since 1988. In this particular context, even if there once was, there is no longer any reason in principle for not including within the concept of 'spouse' someone who had lived with the original tenant in a long-term, but homosexual, relationship. To interpret para 2 so as to include such a person would, of course, involve extending the reach of para 2(2), but it would not infringe any cardinal principle of the 1977 Act.

This shows how the societal values that the interpreter conceives to be implicit in legislation such as the Human Rights Act can guide the interpretation not only of the Act itself, but also interpretation of other legislation which falls to be read under the guidance of the Act.

Similarly, if even more broadly, satisfying the demands of justice may sometimes push in the direction of favouring one interpretation of a provision than another. Even where the kind of *contra legem* interpretation required by the Human Rights Act is not applicable, relatively less 'plain' or 'obvious' interpretations of terms can be supported by reference to the injustice entailed by practical implications of an alternative interpretation.. The gist of the argumentation we are here considering entails a view of legislating as a rational and teleological activity. Those who participate in enacting a statute, or who support

---

[21] [2004] 2 AC 557, [2004] 3 All ER 411.
[22] [2004] 2 AC at 603–4, [2004] 3 All ER at 457.

its enactment, must be presumed to suppose that value of some kind will be achieved through implementation of the enactment. Employees will be more fairly protected if certain rights in the workplace are recognized, and the same cause of fairness will be pursued through setting up an efficient and inexpensive because relatively informal system for adjudicating on statutory employment rights. Tenants can be protected from exploitation of local housing shortages through the device of protected tenancies under the Rent Acts. Respect for persons is fostered by outlawing discrimination on grounds such as gender or sexual orientation.

Deployment of values such as these to justify choosing one interpretation rather than another of a contested expression or phrase in a statute is simply a local manifestation of the kind of consequentialist argumentation discussed in the preceding chapter (also sometimes called 'purposive' or 'functional' interpretation). In the context of interpreting statutes or other authoritative texts, its value-based and teleological character prompts an inquiry as to who should say what values or ends and aims should be postulated as the *telos* or end imputed to legislation. The seemingly obvious answer to this is that the chief actor in the activity to which a *telos* is imputed must presumably be the person who has the say about what values are aimed at. So the legislature's intention is the proper guide to the imputation of values as ends of legislation—certainly, in applying the law, the judge must do the imputing of intention, and the choosing of interpretations that tend to fulfil the values in question. But the presuppositions that make teleology relevant here at all have to do with the assumption that law-making is a rational and purposive activity guided by political programmes structured by some sense of justice and the common good.

Postmodernist approaches to interpretation cast doubt on this apparently commonsensical thesis. The 'death of the author' leaves the text a semi-autonomous source of meaning dependent on the common opinion or variant opinions about the text held within an interpretative community. This thesis can be somewhat fortified by reflection on the fact that interpreters very often use the text itself to infer what its author must have meant by it, and then read that intention back in as a ground for supporting a particular interpretation. Another remark of Lord Rodger's in *Ghaidan* is instructive:[23]

What matters is not so much the phraseology chosen by the draftsman as the substance of the measure which Parliament has enacted in those words. Equally, it cannot have been the intention of Parliament to place a premium on the skill of those called upon to find a neat way round the draftsman's language. Parliament was not out to devise an entertaining parlour game for lawyers, but, so far as possible, to make legislation operate compatibly with convention rights. This means concentrating on matters of substance, rather than on matters of mere language.

[23] [2004] 2 AC at 601–2, [2004] 3 All ER at 455.

We might compare some words of Lord Steyn's in *Dunnachie*:[24]

Counsel for the employer made a telling point about the consequences of adopting the reasoning of Evans-Lombe J on the meaning of the word 'loss' in section 123 [suggesting it could here include non-economic loss]. He asked: what in the language of section 123 would then rule out an award of aggravated or exemplary compensation by way of penalisation of the conduct of the employer? The answer is that only if the word 'loss' in section 123 is restricted to financial loss are such awards ruled out on the face of the legislation. And nobody could seriously suggest that Parliament intended to allow such awards.

In each of these instances, Lords Rodger and Steyn are respectively teasing out implications of views about the proper interpretation of the provision under scrutiny and suggesting that these amount to absurd consequences of the reading in question. Read in the whole context of the legislation, they do not make sense. Parliament could therefore not have intended them. It could not, that is to say, if we postulate a Parliament that approaches law-making as a rational teleological activity whereby to change law and improve it in some way by a coherent reforming measure that fits intelligibly into the legal system as altered by it.

This being so, one has here an example of what one might call the ascription of an 'objective' intention to Parliament. It is gathered from a reading of the legislation as a whole, guided by the assumption of Parliamentary rationality in a teleological enterprise guided by some—perhaps contestable, perhaps even contested—conception of justice and the common good. This is not then an 'intention' discovered as a historical fact from outside the materials for interpretation and the common assumptions of the interpretative community about rational law-making. It is a heuristic device internal to juridical interpretation, not a fresh datum added to it from the outside, as it were.[25]

Sometimes, however, legal systems authorize their judiciary to engage in further heuristics aimed at ascertaining a certain kind of 'subjective' intention: what did some identifiable person or persons engaged in the process of making a particular law actually say they were trying to do while they were doing it? The admissibility of so called '*travaux préparatoires*'—various sorts of pre-legislative materials, including possibly reports of legislative debates in a parliament—has been a controversial topic in many legal systems. Since the decision of the House of Lords in *Pepper v Hart*[26] the courts of the United Kingdom have relaxed their former practice of excluding recourse to reports of parliamentary debates as materials to guide interpretation. A particularly relevant use is in the case of a

[24] [2004] UKHL 36 at para. 19, [2004] 3 All ER at 1021.

[25] Ronald Dworkin in chapter 9 of *Law's Empire* offers a vigorous critique of all sorts of reference to 'author's intention' in interpreting statutes. He denies legitimacy to the use of 'legislative history' as offering a special insight into the intention of the lawmakers and thus guiding interpretation. Apart from the special type of case covered by the narrow construction of *Pepper v Hart* [1993] 1 All ER 835, [1993] AC 593 discussed immediately below, I accept much of what he says. But this should not blind us to the acceptability of appeals to objective intention as I describe these.

[26] [1993] AC 593, [1993] 1 All ER 835.

dispute concerning how widely or narrowly to construe a power that some piece of legislation confers on the Executive, for example by way of delegated legislation made by a Minister under an enabling provision. In *R. v Secretary of State for the Environment ex p Spath Holme Ltd*,[27] the Court of Appeal had to decide whether an order made by a Minister to cap rent increases affecting protected tenancies was valid. The order was made under section 31 of the Landlord and Tenant Act 1985, which contained powers derived originally from Counter-inflation legislation enacted in the previous decade. The Court accepted arguments showing that Ministers had repeatedly assured both Houses of Parliament in 1974 and 1975 that the powers were exclusively for the control of general inflation and were 'reserve' powers.[28] On that account, and on the basis of other interpretative arguments, the Court held that Ministers having asked Parliament to legislate conferring certain powers for certain purposes, later governments could not subsequently use these powers for different purposes not related to the control of general inflation but aimed at protecting a particular subset of tenants of private rented housing from hardship through rapid rent increases. Such an argument seems to carry particular force in suggesting that Parliamentarians engaged in the debates really did intend to confer a power only of a limited kind for limited purposes. So the 'subjective' intention of legislators can be called in aid in the process of ascribing an 'objective' intention to the legislature as a whole. As a means to ensure that Acts are not interpreted to the illegitimate advantage of the Executive branch of government, this is very proper and legitimate.

Even the guarded use to which the Court of Appeal put the *Pepper v Hart* ruling in *Spath Holme* was speedily restrained yet further by the House of Lords on appeal.[29] They held that no sufficient ambiguity existed to require reference to Hansard, and that the case was not one in which the Executive was conducting itself towards citizens in a sense contrary to assurances given to Parliament during the presentation of a Bill. In general, therefore, it remains the case that law-making power rests with the legislature as a corporate entity, not with any party or faction in it, nor even a government that has a solid majority in the principal legislative chamber.[30] A parliament can act only by way of Act (or other resolution according to its own rules of procedure), not via statements made by particular members during debates. It is not, however, true that corporate entities cannot have intentions—most intentional human activity involves one kind or another of group action. But intention can only be inferred from acts, together with a

[27] [2001] 2 AC 349, [2000] 1 All ER 884.

[28] [2001] 2 AC at 359, [2000] 1 All ER at 889–90.

[29] [2001] 2 AC 349; per Lord Hope at 407–8: 'The limited exception to the general rule that Hansard is inadmissible which was recognized in *Pepper v Hart*...is available to prevent the executive seeking to place a meaning on words in legislation which is different from that which ministers attributed to these words when presenting the legislation in Parliament. ... No such issue arises here.'

[30] See Aileen Kavanagh, '*Pepper v Hart* and Matters of Constitutional Principle' *Law Quarterly Review* 121 (2005) 98–122.

presumption of rationality and a sufficiency of information about circumstances surrounding the act.

Where a parliament's intention is in issue, these include commission reports, committee papers, and the like which identify a mischief and propose possible remedies for it. The 'intention of parliament' plays a proper role in legislative interpretation, but not because there is a discoverable state of somebody's mind that can with special authenticity explain the words used as bearing the meaning attested by that mental state. On the contrary, it is because the legislature makes a practice of legislating in English of a particular register; because rational acts of legislation hang together in a coherent way internally and in relation to the rest of the legal system; and because reforms aim to remedy sensibly some identified deficiency; that one can finally impute to the legislature an intention that certain words be understood with a certain meaning rather than another one that they might bear. 'Intention' is a rhetorically effective and legitimate way to frame a conclusion about what is the most reasonable interpretation in context, not a further argument to that effect.

2. Conflicting Arguments and Conflict Resolution

From all the above, it is only too clear that interpretative argument in law presents considerable complexity, since there may be arguments of many types available, and each is capable of generating an interpretation of a given text at variance with that generated by some other possible argument. This is a variant on Duncan Kennedy's point that 'argument bites' hunt in pairs.[31] Indeed for any set of rival interpretations, $I1, I2, \ldots, In$, if these were seriously viable rivals at all, there would be some arguments of one or another of these types (or perhaps others similar) to support one or another of the rival interpretations. Nor is there any reason to suppose that arguments of different types within the same category must all tell in the same direction. Of course this is not the case. Ordinary meaning can be at variance with technical meaning, precedent may conflict with conceptual logic, and indeed an argument of one type may be found to conflict with one of another type, regardless of categories identified. In legal disputes, arguments of all these types are materials available for those who wish to contest the meaning of a text. Finally, it is for the judge or court to reach a conclusion by deciding in the whole context which interpretation ought to prevail (and thus which shall prevail) on the basis of what such reasons. Hence there must be a stage of argumentation which sums up their relative persuasiveness in the given context and accounts for the appropriateness of the conclusion to be reached; as noted, this may be expressed as a conclusion about legislative intention.

---

[31] See Chapter 2 above, at n. 15.

As for this, one can certainly suggest relatively simple models for ordering and perhaps ranking possible arguments. It is tempting to suggest that in all systems there is a tendency to start out with the linguistic arguments, then to proceed to systemic, and only to have recourse to teleological–evaluative argumentation when arguments of the other sorts remain problematic. A relevant doctrine of positive law in this context is provided by what Scottish and English lawyers call 'The Golden Rule'. Here is a classical formulation:

[W]e are to take the whole statute together and construe it altogether, giving the words their ordinary signification, unless when so applied they produce an inconsistency, or an absurdity, or inconvenience so great as to convince the court that the intention could not have been to use them in their ordinary signification, and to justify the court in putting on them some other signification which, though less proper, is one which the court thinks that the words will bear.[32]

And here is a relatively more recent formulation:

[O]ne is to apply statutory words and phrases according to their natural and ordinary meaning without addition or subtraction, unless that meaning produces injustice, absurdity, anomaly, contradiction, in which case one may modify the natural and ordinary meaning so as to obviate such injustice etc. but no further. (Nowadays we should add to 'natural and ordinary meaning' the words 'in their context and according to the appropriate linguistic register'.)[33]

As these dicta suggest, if there is one interpretation that is clearly favoured by a reading of the text in the light of syntactic and semantic conventions of ordinary language (or special registers in special settings), and if this is confirmed by a reading of the text in its whole systemic context, there is no need for recourse to further evaluative or teleological arguments. But if there remains uncertainty in the light of all the linguistic and systemic arguments, further grounds of interpretation are required, or if there is an 'absurdity' of some sort, that should be resolved. A valuable study by Dr Yizhar Tal[34] shows, contrary to much that has been said in the doctrinal literature, that, both in practice and in authoritative rulings about interpretation, 'absurdity' for the purpose of the Golden Rule includes conflict either with justice or some other legal value, or with other aspects of what is deemed good policy. The present chapter is in debt to Tal's work. It is in the relevant sense 'absurd' to read a statute either in such a way as to generate injustice by reference to some legally recognized principle of justice or in such a way as to be self-defeating in terms of presumed objectives of public policy pursued through legislation. So it would not be correct to say that the category of teleological–evaluative argument comes into play only if the other two categories fail to yield an unequivocal result. Consideration of arguments in that category

---

[32] Lord Blackburn in *River Wear Commissioners v Adamson* (1887) 2 App Cas 743 at 764–5.
[33] Lord Simon of Glaisdale in *Stock v Frank Jones (Tipton) Ltd.* [1978] 1 All ER 948 at 952.
[34] Y. Tal, *Statutory Interpretation and Expressed Reference to Justice: A Study of Cases in English Law and Implications for Interpretative Approach*, D. Phil. Thesis (Oxford University, 1992).

may show up such an absurdity as will displace a prima facie binding conclusion about the meaning of the legislative words in their (fully contextualized) 'ordinary signification'.

Interesting and suggestive though the Golden Rule is, however, it is not really a rule. It is better considered as a maxim of practical interpretative wisdom, indicating how the various types of argument may be handled in cases of real interpretative difficulty arising from conflicts among relevant arguments. It does not provide any simple binary directive about right and wrong interpretations in the difficult cases. It indicates an approach to the resolution of difficulty, rather than a rule about rule interpretation.

3. Interpretation within Practical Argumentation

In understanding such difficulty and solutions for it, we need to reflect further on the values and principles I have suggested as underlying each of the categories of argument. Behind linguistic interpretation lies an aim of preserving clarity and accuracy in legislative language and a principle of justice that forbids retrospective judicial rewriting of the legislature's chosen words. Behind systemic interpretation lies a principle of rationality grounded in the value of coherence and integrity in a legal system. Behind teleological–evaluative interpretation lies respect for the demand of practical reason that human activity be guided by some sense of values to be realized by action and by principles to be observed in it. But in the case of this last most fundamental level of practical argumentation, the perennial problem of the human situation is the interpersonal disputability of the values and principles that should guide us.

As is commonly held, a strong justifying reason for the maintenance of legal and other common social institutions among humans is to diminish the scope for disputes about governing values and principles in the social arena. And this is what in turn justifies giving considerable weight to linguistic and systemic argumentation in law. These are genuine and generally operative legal values connected with the ideal of the Rule of Law.[35] They therefore compete on equal terms with other values and objectives ascribed or ascribable to particular texts in particular legal contexts, and suggest that reference to more particular values has to be the exception rather than the norm. In the end, which should prevail is an issue engaging practical wisdom and the sense of justice in the particular circumstances of particular disputes concerning specific legislation. The legislative text itself is, of course, universal in its formulation, always applying to a whole class,

---

[35] 'In a society living by the rule of law, citizens are entitled to regulate their conduct according to what a statute has said, rather than by what it was meant to say or by what it would otherwise have said if a newly considered situation had been envisaged.' *Stock v Frank Jones (Tipton) Ltd.* [1978] ICR 347 at 354, per Lord Simon of Glaisdale.

and any ruling as between rival interpretative possibilities is likewise universal or universalizable for reasons discussed earlier. The conclusion reached has to be a conclusion about what is right for any such case, not just right *ad hoc*.

The assumption implicit in this chapter hitherto has been that interpretation and interpretative argumentation dealing with authoritative legal texts can be taken as one topic within a wider theme of legal reasoning and argumentation. This follows a well-known tradition in accordance with which 'statutory interpretation' has been considered a topic in its own right within a broader approach to jurisprudential questions. It has specialities of its own different from a discussion, for example, of precedent, such as will occupy the next following chapter. Of course, precedent is a topic also concerned with a kind of authoritative text, namely, the authorized reports of the decisions of the superior courts of a given legal system in a given state or a given supranational entity. But the texts in this case differ importantly from legislative texts, in which each sentence has the force of a law or a part of the law, exactly as the lawmaker finally resolved to enact it. That is why interpreting legislative texts differs so markedly from interpreting precedent texts.

This is a point upon which one may wish to dwell a little for its bearing on contemporary debate in the philosophy of law. Ronald Dworkin proposes that law is itself an 'interpretive' enterprise. This means that every venture into a discussion of what law requires concerning employment or contractual or tortious liability or intellectual property or the validity or reasonableness of an act of a public authority or anything else at all that is legal calls for an effort of 'interpretation'. Moreover, it engages us in an interpretation of 'law' as a concept, at any rate in respect of the conception of law that prevails within the polity in question. This he proposes in the context of a thesis about 'constructive interpretation', according to which interpretation regards a whole activity within a certain genre, and seeks to understand it in such a way as to make it the best of its own kind that it can be.

This approach risks oversimplification. There are different objects of interpretation in law, and differences of interpretative approach and interpretative arguments appropriate to different objects—obviously, interpreting statutes is not the same as interpreting precedents, nor is either the same as interpreting a constitution or a treaty. Interpreting a whole practice, 'law', say, is not the same as interpreting any of its parts. Ascribing sense and value to law as such, or to the law of Scotland or of England or of the United States or the European Community, is not the same as solving a litigated dispute about the impact of a particular section of a statute, nor about the binding element in a particular precedent, nor about a provision in the US Constitution or the European Community Treaty. Certainly, if no sense and value could be found in or reasonably ascribed to a certain body of law, the interpretation of any text belonging to it might be highly problematic. Moreover, it has already been suggested that the idea of 'coherence' has a particular part to play in underpinning interpretative practice, alongside of other values considered implicit in law and relevant to its proper exegesis. In Chapter 10 this will be considered in greater depth. Here, suffice it to say that the specific task of interpreting authoritative legal texts and the specific appropriateness of a range of types of argument cannot themselves be derived deductively or inferentially from any concept of 'constructive interpretation'. Rather, such a concept would at best be a way of concluding upon and summing up wherein lies the grander unity of all the more specific interpretative argumentative elements identifiable by close reflection on the practice of legal reasoning, revealed by a process of 'rationally reconstructing' it.

4. Classification

There is much overlap between interpretation as so far discussed, and arguments directed at what have been called problems of 'classification' (alternatively, of 'characterization', or 'of qualification', *qualification* being the relevant French term). These deal with the question whether a given situation counts as belonging in a relevant category for the purposes of applying a legislative text. Sticking for the moment with issues concerning employment, a simple example is afforded by the question whether a given person counts as an employee for the purpose of entitlement to a redundancy payment. In *Secretary of State for Trade and Industry v Bottrill*[36] Mr Bottrill had been sole shareholder of a company Magnatech which had been set up with a view to a relatively early takeover by an American company. As Managing Director of the company, he entered into a contract of employment with it, paying tax and national insurance contributions as appropriate. Before the intended takeover took place, Magnatech became insolvent, and Mr Bottrill lost his job.

As an ex-employee in such circumstances, he would be entitled to redundancy payments from the Secretary of State—but was he truly an ex-employee? Could an arrangement whereby a sole shareholder authorized the making of a contract by himself with the company as its employee suffice to constitute a genuine employment relationship within the meaning of the Act? In the specific case of Mr Bottrill, the Court of Appeal upheld the decision of the tribunal that, in the particular circumstances of himself and his company, there was a genuine contract of employment and Bottrill qualified as an employee for the purposes of the Act. 'We agree with the Employment Appeal Tribunal that the industrial tribunal was entitled to conclude that there was a genuine contractual relationship between Mr Bottrill and his company, and that the industrial tribunal, having carefully and properly weighed the competing factors, had arrived at a conclusion which was unimpeachable on the facts.'[37] Here, what is in issue is not so much an

[36] [2000] 1 All ER 915.
[37] Per Lord Woolf, MR, at p. 927. It should be noted that the ground for this is that 'whether or not an employer or employee relationship exists can only be decided by having regard to all the

interpretation of the Act as an interpretation of the facts and circumstances of the case to see whether they fit within the concept or category specified in the Act. There may be reasons for and against such a holding, but in the end the decision must be whether those that favour one conclusion cumulatively outweigh those tending the other way. Typically, such questions are in turn themselves classified by lawyers among 'questions of fact'. This means that they have to be decided by the judge of facts, and reconsidered on appeal only if the judge of facts has misdirected him/herself in law or has reached a conclusion that cannot reasonably be supported in the light of the findings of fact.

In other cases, it can happen that sometimes the problem presents itself as one calling for interpretation of a statutory or other rule. Should same-sex harassment be counted as a possible breach of the anti-discrimination provisions in Title VII of the (US) Civil Rights Act 1964? In *Oncale v Sundowner Offshore Services Inc,*[38] the Supreme Court held that this was the proper interpretation of the Act. For the legislative intent to prevent unfair discrimination on sexual grounds applied as much to same-sex bullying of a gay person on account of his sexual orientation as to bullying a person of the opposite sex. Hence the complaint in the case was relevant to the issue of breach of the Act. In this situation, the resources of interpretative argument are no different from the general types of interpretative argument discussed above.

In the other type of case exemplified here by *Bottrill*, the concept in issue is taken (by the parties and thus by the Court) to need no clarification, but the fact-situation revealed by the case gives rise to dispute whether or not it fits the concept. In this latter case, there is a very particular part to be played by arguments from analogy. For that reason, further discussion is postponed till Chapter 11 below. Problems of classification in either guise also overlap largely with problems of evaluation. Often the legislature introduces into a legal text terms that import a standard of judgement—'fair', 'just', 'proportionate', 'adequate', 'unconscionable', for example. Naturally, the decision of problem cases often then turns on the issue what counts as being reasonable (or whatever) in the given context. Here, there is an obvious element of evaluation, not merely of classification. To allow for that difference, reasonableness is separately considered in Chapter 9 to assess the kinds of arguments appropriate to applying standards of that kind.

---

relevant facts. If an individual has a controlling shareholding that is certainly a fact which is likely to be significant in all situations and in some cases may prove to be decisive. However, it is only one of the factors which are relevant, and certainly is not to be taken as determinative without considering all the relevant circumstances.' Lord Woolf gave further, more discursive, guidance about the factors tribunals should take into account and weigh up at the end of his judgment (pp. 927–8).

[38]   (1998) 523 US 140, L. Ed 2d 201, 118 S. Ct. 998.

8

Using Precedents

Introduction

Why do lawyers argue so much about precedents? Why do they read the records of decisions in prior cases and seek to apply them to present problems? Why do judges think they can justify decisions by showing they square with precedent, or think they cannot justify a decision that contradicts established precedent? A part of the answer to this is a reason of justice: if you ought to treat like cases alike and different cases differently, then new cases that are relevantly like ones previously decided ought (prima facie, anyway) to be decided in the same or an analogous way to the previously decided ones. Connected to this is the idea of an impartial legal system that does the same justice to everyone, regardless of who are the parties to a case and who is judging it. In a modern state with many judges in many courts, and a structured hierarchy of appeals, the same rules and rulings should be acted on without regard to which judge is deciding the case. Faithfulness to the Rule of Law calls for avoiding any frivolous variation in the pattern of decision-making from one judge or court to another. This is a consideration that reappears in Chapter 10 in the discussion of consistency and coherence as systemic virtues of the law. A third reason for sticking to precedents is economy of effort—judges and lawyers should not have to keep on going over the same ground. So once something has been settled after careful argument it ought to be treated as settled finally, except if some very special occasion for reconsideration can be shown to have arisen.

The practice that has grown up almost universally in contemporary legal systems bears witness to the power of these arguments in favour of having regard to precedent. Decisions of the superior courts are recorded in officially and unofficially published series of law reports. These we might call 'precedent texts', having an authority of their own, but different from that of the texts of statute law, whose every word is itself a part of enacted law. Legal commentators base their explanations of the law as much on these precedent texts as on the statute book itself, or on the code, in countries with codified law. In one way or another, the reported decisions of the superior courts have become an essential element in the argumentative weaponry of lawyers. They play a crucial part in the construction of judicial opinions in which judges state what they consider the best justifying reasons for the decisions they hand down.

In some legal systems and traditions, precedents are recognized only as pointers to the best way of interpreting codified law or law otherwise enshrined in statutes. This view depends on a strict understanding of the separation of powers as an element in sustaining the Rule of Law. Since judges are not legislators, their decisions and opinions cannot be accepted as though they were themselves a source of law as distinct from being a persuasive guide to the proper interpretation of the law and laws made by the legislator.[1] In other systems and traditions, a different view prevails. Precedents are acknowledged as a source from which a certain kind of law is derived, namely case law. For present times, at least, the caveat must be added that, even in the countries of the 'common law', pure case law is quite rare. Much case law now takes the form of glosses upon statute law.

What kind of texts are precedent texts, and how are they to be interpreted? As noted, the law reports give an account of judicial decisions supported by judicial reasons and reasoning as stated in explicitly presented judicial opinions. It is in the statement of opinions upon cases by way of justifications of decisions that judges lay down precedents and build up case law (or, perhaps, provide the materials out of which scholars and practitioners can build up an articulate body of case law). To make the point that the judicial opinion which sets or constitutes a precedent is a judge's opinion *considered as stating a justification of a decision* matters a great deal. For it is as *justificatory* reasoning that judicial opinions are normative, and it is only as being normative that they can go toward the construction of normative law or towards guiding its interpretation. Accordingly, it must seem doubtful whether any adequate understanding of precedent (its source) could proceed in the absence of an adequate theory of legal justification. Only by knowing the kinds of justifying reasons which are proper to judicial decisions can we know the possible elements of judicial precedents. Surprisingly, a great deal of writing about precedent has proceeded without full regard to the prerequisites of an articulate theory of legal justification. Everyone, of course, must have had some implicit or partially explicit theory of justification. But without a fully articulated one, a satisfactory analysis of case law must be difficult. The importance of this will appear in due course.

In any legal system that records precedent texts, we can expect to find some current doctrine as to the way in which precedents are to be conceived and used as argumentative sources. Different doctrines of precedent may prevail in different legal systems and/or at different times. For example a doctrine of strictly binding precedent may prescribe that each decision of every tribunal is strictly binding on every other tribunal of the same (or of coordinate) or of inferior level in the hierarchy of tribunals. A doctrine of persuasive precedent will prescribe that tribunals ascribe a greater or less persuasive weight to decisions or to lines of decision of the same, or coordinate, or superior tribunals.

---

[1] See D. N. MacCormick and R. S. Summers (eds), *Interpreting Precedents: A Comparative Study* (Aldershot: Ashgate/Dartmouth, 1999). This work, by members of the '*bielefelder Kreis*' surveys practice concerning precedents in eleven national legal systems and in the European Union.

To be fully intelligible, any such doctrine must indicate in some way the element in precedents which is supposed to be binding (if any is) or persuasive in the strongest degree of persuasiveness admitted. Many current legal systems in the world of the common law and of mixed systems such as that of Scotland have mixed doctrines of binding and of persuasive precedent—all precedent being persuasive at a given level of hierarchy, but binding for tribunals or courts lower in a given hierarchy. Thus the identification of the binding or the specifically persuasive element in decision is a matter of some importance.

Verbally, it is easy. It is well known that it is the *ratio decidendi* of a decision which is (if anything is) the specifically binding or, under the other doctrine, the strongly persuasive element, in a precedent. The *ratio decidendi* is the rule or principle of decision for which a given precedent is the authoritative source, whether that rule or principle of decision is then to be treated as binding or only as persuasive in some degree for other later deciders of similar questions. It is, of course, the rule or principle of decision which is supposed to have in some sense governed or grounded the deciding of the case whose *ratio* it is. As a *ratio decidendi*, it may be contrasted with the *obiter dicta* to be found in the judicial opinion. These are other statements of opinion upon the law and its values and principles in their bearing on the instant decision, statements which in some way go beyond the point or points necessary to be settled in deciding the case. The contrast commonly drawn between *ratio decidendi* and *obiter dicta* is most comprehensible if it is supposed that the *ratio*, like the *dicta*, is identifiable as some kind of *saying* by a judge stated in the course of giving an opinion in justification of a decision.

The greatest difficulty in the way of a clear understanding of any doctrine of precedent and thus of any kind of case law is the controversial quality of the *ratio decidendi*. It is a disputed question whether there is any such thing as *a* or *the ratio* in a given case. It is disputed whether or not there is a *ratio* to be found authoritatively within a given opinion, or whether the so-called *ratio* is simply some proposition of law which a later court or courts find it expedient to ascribe to an earlier decision as the ground of that decision. This may then be used to help justify some later decision—perhaps even under the guise of its being that which necessitates the granting of the given later decision. An extreme version of this view would presumably be that the *ratio* of a case is whatever it is at any time authoritatively said to be authority for, and thus no one single proposition over time. Although the term *ratio* seems in ordinary legal usage to refer to some single proposition or principle of law, this apparent referentiality of the term is an illusion, and the category *ratio* is no more than one of what Julius Stone called 'categories of illusory reference'.[2] These are systematically misleading forms of expression which convey an illusion of reference and thus of legal stability and certainty while the legal reality is one of change.

---

[2] See Julius Stone, *Legal System and Lawyers' Reasonings* (cited hereafter as *Legal System*) (London: Stevens, 1964), ch. 7, esp. pp. 263–80, on the *ratio* as a 'category of indeterminate reference'.

What this indicates is that in addition to doctrines of precedent, that is, doctrines of positive law telling us what authority is to be ascribed to judicial precedents, we also have to have theories of precedent. For without some theoretical understanding of precedents and of such key concepts as that of *ratio decidendi* we cannot in fact implement any legal doctrine of precedent. As usual, the question is not whether to have or to do without a theory; it is only whether or not to have an articulate, well thought out and, preferably, correct theory or to rest content with an implicit, inarticulate, and quite probably incorrect one.

We can consider theories of precedent as tending from the more or less strict or formalistic to the more or less sceptical end of a spectrum.[3] At the formalistic end are those which represent the *ratio* as relatively fixed and determinate or at least determinable; at the sceptical end are those which treat the term as having only illusory reference and thus as signifying whatever its current user wishes. The theory for which I argue here is a relatively strict or formalistic one. There is no great difficulty in showing why and how the sound and justifiable decisions of a legal dispute must proceed on the basis of a reasonably firm and determinate ruling as to the applicable law. Such a ruling is, in my view, properly to be understood as the *ratio* of the decision.

Such a formalistic view of the *ratio* does not necessitate adherence to or advocacy of a strict or strong doctrine of binding precedent. For reasons which will also appear, it seems wise to me to treat precedents, and especially single precedents, as revisable rather than fixed and binding for all purposes. Case law ought to be somewhat flexible and open-ended over time. So precedents are best treated as more or less highly persuasive rather than absolutely binding. But that is not to say that there are no determinate propositions in respect of which they are well treated as persuasive, and can in appropriate situations be held binding. There are; and these are what (I submit) have been given the technical name of *rationes decidendi*. Working towards establishing that conclusion, I shall first recapitulate on the present theory of legal justification so far as relevant to binding precedents. I shall then consider an objection that this account is objectionably legalistic. Then I shall offer a model of the *ratio decidendi*, and finally shall discuss whether this is the best that can be done by way of 'rational reconstruction'.

1. Justification in Legal Decision-Making

To recapitulate some points made in earlier chapters: Legal decisions presuppose legal disputes. That is, they presuppose cases in which one party makes some kind of a claim about or from another person: the claim that he or she is guilty of an offence, the claim that he or she should pay damages or desist from some course of action or such like, this claim being at least formally denied or contested by the

---

[3] Compare Raimo Siltala, *A Theory of Precedent* (Oxford: Hart Publishing, 2000) 65–108.

other party. In this wide sense of 'dispute' and 'claim', legal decisions are to be understood as decisions about claims in the context of disputes; further, however, they are to be understood as decisions about claims advanced as *legal claims*. A claim is advanced as a legal claim only if its maker shows or purports to show that it can be justified by reference to some legal ground and that it is relevant to facts which have occurred and which implicate the party against whom the claim is made. The maker of a legal claim has to be willing to enter into some sort of specifically legal argumentation by way of justifying it. Likewise, for there to be a real contest or dispute at law, the party denying or resisting the claim must be ready to do so in legal terms. It may be sufficient simply to deny allegations of fact; but being bothered to deny them normally implies an acknowledgement that facts such as those alleged would be legally relevant if true (or if proven). And direct denial of the legal relevance of facts alleged (even setting aside any disputes as to the truth of the allegation) is always a possibility. All this presupposes an objectively and commonly acknowledged way of identifying some normative propositions—rules and principles and the like—as being legal in character. Further, it presupposes some institutionalized process of identifying or asserting the special character of these propositions as bases of argumentation; that is, it presupposes some common ground between parties and tribunal as to legitimate sources of propositions upon which claim-justification can be effected.

For reasons already stated at considerable length, this has as its deep structure and often as its surface structure, a kind of deductive argumentation. The claimant, C, is in effect saying that: because, according to law, whenever a person p engages in activity a in circumstances c, the judgment j ought to be pronounced against that person, and because D (the defendant) is a person p and because D has engaged in activity a and because D's activity a took place in circumstances c, *therefore* the judgment j ought to be pronounced against D; (and therefore, according to law, D ought to do or suffer whatever is required in order to satisfy the judgment j). Such an argument is the only plain and watertight way of showing why a claim made by C against D ought to be upheld and indeed implemented as a legal claim. That is not to say that claims made in this way are always, often, or even ever, conclusive as stated. At least it is always possible that D may challenge the asserted major premiss of the argument, or challenge the interpretation of terms involved in any of the minor premisses, or the assertion that a particular being or activity or set of circumstances properly amount to those envisaged in any proposition of law properly understood. And it is never possible that C can in advance foresee and forestall each and every possible ground of challenge or of quibbling that D might dream up. All this is quite apart from the risk of D's simply denying some one or more of the crucial allegations of primary fact.

Not merely is it the case that claims and defences to claims ideal-typically take or tend towards this form. All the more is it the case that a justified legal decision as between any C and D who are parties to any such dispute must also aspire towards this ideal type. For J the judge in the case to be justified in deciding for

C or D, in such a dispute, J must surely be willing to make a ruling on the law upholding not merely *ad hoc* and *ad hominem* C's claim so advanced or D's defence so presented. J must be willing to do so on terms that hold good for any persons who satisfy the same qualifications and engage in the same acts in the same circumstances. As between rival propositions of law, or interpretations of propositions of law, put forward by C and by D, J must make some choice; or J must substitute an alternative possibility and uphold *that* as the soundest view, or the soundest that it seems possible at present to formulate. Only by getting the argument to such a point will J have given an adequate ground for upholding or rejecting C's claim or D's defence.

All this repeats in effect the theses concerning universalizability established in Chapter 5. The requirement of formal justice, to treat like cases alike, has a forward-looking as well as a backward-looking application.[4] That is why a justifiable judicial decision where disputes of law arise must be founded on a ruling about the law which is neither *ad hoc* nor *ad hominem*. No doubt such a justification is relativistic in a sense: it is a justification in the face of C and D and in respect of their arguments which is sought. Their arguments and dispute must be resolved by J as they have brought it before J. J is not superhuman and cannot think of everything. Others may devise new doubts and qualifications about what is said today so that what seemed right as between C and D will later seem at best only qualifiedly right. In the future, we may wish to consider what has been decided as fixing no more than ordinarily necessary or presumptively sufficient conditions for a given legal consequence. But today it is as between C and D that matters must be decided and it is upon their dispute as they have disputed it that a decision must issue.

So J, to decide that issue, must decide how to rule upon the points disputed by C and D. Furthermore, J will have to justify that ruling, that is, show why it is right in law. As was urged in Chapter 6, this justification has to have regard to consequences, at least 'juridical consequences' and sometimes causal or behavioural consequences as well, evaluated by reference to relevant legal values. Consistency with established law and coherence in the legal system as a whole have a particular value already discussed in relation to statutory interpretation, and awaiting further discussion in Chapter 10.

The present conception of justification takes universalizability to be essential to justification. This holds as much for the justification of claims and defences as for

---

[4] This argument is more fully stated in MacCormick, *Legal Reasoning and Legal Theory*, 75–6; Michael Moore's discussion of that argument of mine in his 'A Natural Law Theory of Interpretation' (*Southern California Law Review* 58 (1985) 277) seems to me, with respect, to miss the point that formal justice is forward- as well as backward-looking, and that its forward-looking aspect is what governs the duty to decide today's case in a way one would stick to for the future. Thus the question how to universalize past decisions is not, for me, the crucial point. If judges in prior cases have not then universalized, there may well be no good ground for even attempting to follow them by inventing now some relevant universalization on their behalf. If they have, we should now have regard to their universalizations on the very ground of the forward-looking reference of those earlier decisions as universalized.

that of judicial decisions of disputed claims and defences. To justify requires one to put one's claim, defence, or decisions on the footing that *because* the facts are F1, F2,...Fn, the judgment *j* ought to be pronounced. But such a '*because*...' requires a commitment to the universal, 'whenever $f1, f2,..., fn$, then *j*', coupled with: 'and in this case, F1, F2,..., Fn, which are instances of $f1$, $f2..., fn$'. No doubt one must have and give some ulterior reasons for the 'whenever...' clause, but the 'whenever...' clause is essential to justify the actual decision. That justification requires universalization or universalizability in this sense follows from the idea that justifying involves propounding good rational grounds for what one does, and thus depends on a conception of rationality and a commitment to rationality so conceived.

2. Legalism in Justification

The whole argument hitherto assumes that it is possible to find or to formulate some commonly agreed or persuasively proposable propositions as propositions of law that have a bearing upon facts in issue between the parties to a case. Only given such an assumption, indeed, would it be possible for them to focus sufficiently on some fact for there to be any defined issue between them at all. But such propositions and their proper formulation and/or interpretation can be highly disputable, and their disputability can be exploited in order to try out far-fetched claims or dubious defences—or in order to try to expound equitable reformulations of, or adventurous new interpretations of, legal rules or principles.

Despite that, this puts significant limits on the strength of Steven Burton's argument about generalization as preferable to universalization[5] (see Chapter 5). The hazards of trying to formulate reasonable and universalizable rulings in law are less troubling than the potential infinity of fact-descriptions may suggest. For in law, we do not formulate our universals in a vacuum, but in the context of rules previously enacted by legislators and discussed, propounded, or proposed by jurists and judges. Particular rulings will have to take their place under constraints of consistency, coherence, and a reasonable evaluation of consequences in an existing even if incomplete corpus of law. So the parties and the judges have only quite restricted freedom of manoeuvre as they try to work through to a reasonably justifiable conclusion *justified as a conclusion of law* in the case seen as a *legal case*.

The concept of universalizability, which I propound as essential to that of justi-fication in law, albeit a concept shared with moral philosophers in the schools of Kant and R. M. Hare, is a concept limited by the requirements of legality and the Rule of Law. Judges have to universalize rulings as best they can within the context of an existing and established legal order. The existence of this context of

---

[5] Steven J. Burton, 'Professor MacCormick's Claim Regarding Universalisation in Law', in C. Faralli and E. Pattaro (eds), *Reason in Law, Vol II* (Milan: Dottore A. Giuffré, 1988) 155–66.

argumentation makes reasonable and indeed possible a task that might seem even supra-Herculean were it contemplated entirely in a vacuum. So one may acknowledge (in partial agreement with Burton) that there has to be a certain relativism, open-endedness, and tentativeness or revisability in the commitment a judge should make to the rulings he or she hands down in deciding cases (see Chapter 12 on defeasibility). Nevertheless the grounds and materials of decision already exist in profusion and already have been often and anxiously worked over. The fact that the justification sought for decisions is justification within an established and thoroughly institutionalized legal order, not justification at large and without limits, is a fact which encourages some optimism as to the reasonable possibility of settling disputes in reasonably determinate and final terms. Even where precedents are treated as persuasive rather than absolutely binding, there must be a rather strong presumption against departing from what has already been decided. It would require to be shown that some new departure would cohere better with the main line of legal development, as well as being fairer or preferable in its consequences than the relevant precedent(s), before there would be sufficient reason for not standing by decisions.

This very line of argument has, however, attracted sharp criticism from David Lyons. He considers that my approach, and (rather surprisingly) that of Ronald Dworkin as well, adopts an excessively legalistic, or legal-positivistic, conception of justification.[6] Lyons attacks the idea that one can conceive of 'justifying' a decision in law where the reasoning process does not also evaluate the moral quality of the decision at stake, and indeed gives priority to that moral evaluation if it proves to be at odds with the legal reasons that have been adduced.[7] Justification in Lyons's view is an essentially moral concept. Any legal component in the argument for a decision can be accepted as an element in 'justification' only to the extent that it is capable of being endorsed from a moral point of view as well. A decision has to be justifiable in moral terms before it can (also) be justifiable in legal or any other terms.

The problem as I see it about Lyons's view is that it seems to leave the problem of justification—and of finding rulings or Kantian 'maxims' to universalize—far too wide open. The very fact that justifications have to focus themselves on rulings about disputed points of law narrows the field of argumentation as between parties and of judicial deliberation on the questions they put in issue. This is what makes it practicable to use legal institutions as dispute-*resolving* agencies; for their use requires disputants to focus their dispute in terms of manageable issues of

---

[6] David Lyons, 'Justification and Judicial Responsibility' *California Law Review* 72 (1984), 178–99 at 196–9; also 'Derivability, Defensibility, and the Justification of Judicial Decisions' *The Monist* 68 (1985) or D. Lyons, *Ethics and the Rule of Law* (Cambridge: Cambridge University Press, 1984) 92–109.

[7] For similar reasons, Richard Tur suggests that all legal provisions are subject to potentially being overridden by moral considerations in particular contexts, as an aspect of what he considers to be the built-in defeasibility of legal norms. See R. H. S. Tur, 'Defeasibilism' *Oxford Journal of Legal Studies* 21 (2001) 355–68, at 367; and compare Chapter 12 below.

dispute, and at least restricts the range of legally justifiable resolutions that can conceivably be advanced. This opinion of mine is by no means a novelty; for it simply repeats Kant's view that the first thing a rational universalizer of maxims of action would do would be to subject him- or herself to a legal system in common with others.[8] Or again, it borrows Robert Alexy's (also Kantian) point that the omnipresent indeterminacy of general practical reason makes it necessary for us to procure more determinate modes of interpersonal reasoning on practical issues, namely by resort to law and to the specialized concerns of legal argumentation.[9]

In a more mundane way, this squares also with the thought that what legal counsel have to sell is skill in law and in legal argumentation, as distinct from any purported special skill in moral theory or moral argument. Lawyers are hired to argue cases at law, and judges are appointed to resolve legal cases. Neither would welcome (or, one would suppose, be much good at fulfilling) a duty to deal in terms of raw moral argumentation as part of their professional or official role. This limitation of lawyerly and judicial skills and tasks is not however a morally disgraceful one if what has already been said indicates that there is moral justification for a specialized practice of legal decision-making that involves justification of claims, defences, and decisions. The practical human need for definability of interpersonal issues and determinability of human disputes by reference to interpersonally pre-established (albeit never fully determinate) norms of decision and of conduct seems to me to supply just such a moral justification for recourse to a specialized practice of legal justification. And it indicates precisely why it is a moral responsibility of a lawyer to acquire and exercise legal skill in the interest of clients, not to refer all their questions to the tribunal of his or her own personal ethic.

This is the basis on which to rebut Lyons's critique. It is certainly true that legal justification would be justification only in a very Pickwickian sense if it lacked any moral foundation. But the moral foundation that it has is one that justifies a specialized and distinctive recourse to legal norms and legal justifications for the resolution of disputes under the coercive power of agencies of state. This cannot guarantee that always the best legally justified decision of a given case or type of case is the best justified decision there is of that matter from a moral point of view. So legal justification, albeit itself a morally justified practice, is not the same as, and does not necessarily yield the same conclusions as, pure moral argumentation on the same matters.

To this legalistic or positivistic view an important corrective or qualification must be adopted in the light of Lyons's critique. It is true within limits that we can morally justify a legal justification practice whose conclusions diverge from those derivable from the very principles we use to justify having the legal practice. But it

---

[8] I. Kant, *The Metaphysical Elements of Justice* (trans. J. Ladd) (Indianapolis: Hackett, 2nd edn, 1999), pp. 71–2.

[9] R. Alexy, *Theorie der Juristischen Argumentation* (Frankfurt am Main: Suhrkamp, 1978), pp. 349–51.

can only be within limits that this is true. For example, a legal justification practice that generated conclusions directly contradictory to fundamental principles of respect for persons or of fair argumentation would be a practice that strayed beyond the bounds of the very justification offered for having such a special practice.[10] Such 'legal justification' would never be better than purported justification. And, of course, the perennial risk arising from the existence of positive legal institutions is that they will generate purported justifications of actually unjustifiable actions. Some protection against this can be achieved through international charters of human rights, especially when these (or other catalogues of fundamental rights) are given domestic legal efficacy, or are constitutionally entrenched.[11] Fully to discuss that risk and the conceptual problems it reveals about the nature of law is a theme for a different book from the present one. Here, it is enough to have shown how the requirement of universalizability, with its implicit reference to an evaluation of that which is universalized, is what links justification at law with justification at large.

3. A Model of the *Ratio*

What I have tried to reinforce here is a certain model of the making and rejecting of claims-at-law and of decision of cases between claimants and disputants of their claims. The model is a model of this as a justifiable practice of dispute resolution under special canons of legal justification. In such a practice claims have to be founded on propositions of law justifying certain judgments in the light of acts, facts, and surrounding circumstances, and on particular assertions of relevant acts, facts, and circumstances. Defences to such claims have to dispute the general proposition or its interpretation, or deny the facts alleged. A justifiable decision of the legal dispute has to make a ruling on the issues in contention between the parties as to the relevancy of any proposition adduced as a proposition of law by either party or as to the interpretation of such a proposition, or as to the proper classification or evaluation of facts in the light of the descriptive or evaluative concepts or categories involved in the given proposition. A ruling of this kind must be logically universal or at least must be in terms which are reasonably

---

[10] The *Terrorist Suspects* case exhibits this problem, as witnessed by the House of Lords issuance of a 'declaration of incompatibility' concerning the provisions of Part 4 of the Anti-terrorism, Crime and Security Act 2001 that permit the Home Secretary to order indefinite detention without trial or even formal charge of foreign nationals reasonably suspected of being involved in terrorist organizations. (*A(FC) and others v Secretary of State for the Home Department*, 16 December 2004, [2004] UKHL 56). Prime Minister Blair announced in Parliament on Monday 20 December 2004 that he nevertheless considered it necessary in the public interest to continue such detention.

[11] Compare the discussion of human rights in the *Terrorist Suspects* case in Chapters 1 and 6, and the UK Human Rights Act (Chapter 7 above at n. 20) and its impact on statutory interpretation as considered in relation to *Ghaidan v Mendoza* [2004] 3 All ER 411.

universalizable; and it must be open to ulterior justification in terms of arguments about consequences, and about consistency and coherence.

It is not necessary for judges to reach conclusions on everything the parties have disputed. But they have to enunciate some conclusion sufficient to justify acceptance or rejection of all the particular claims, counter-claims, defences, and so on, which have been advanced by either party. This is so except in so far as a decision on any one or another may close off others as live claims, counter-claims, and so on. In different legal systems, different views prevail on the extent to which a judgment can properly or fairly be given about factors in a case that the parties have not had an opportunity to argue in full. Some final appellate tribunals make a practice of recalling counsel to let them make submissions on points that seem relevant but have not been fully argued. At least, justice between the parties requires the giving of full and fair attention to the points they have argued. The further a judgment goes beyond the points actually argued, the greater the risk there is of arguments being adopted without fully adequate consideration of all relevant circumstances and of possible counter-arguments. Also, a point that will be noted again later, it is possible that a party to a case may expressly concede a point in the context of that case, the concession being in fact erroneous. But the judge in the instant case is not called upon to go into the question of the correctness of such concessions. In this situation, what is perfectly fair between those parties may not turn out good law the next time round when different parties are in dispute. Within such a model one can give a clear and satisfactory definition of *ratio decidendi*; it will be in the following terms: '[A] *ratio decidendi* is [a] ruling expressly or impliedly given by a judge which is sufficient to settle a point of law put in issue by the parties' arguments in a case, being a point on which a ruling was necessary to his/her justification (or one of his/her alternative justifications) of the decision in the case.'[12] Arguments of legal principle and arguments evaluating other authorities or evaluating the consequences of the favoured ruling and its rivals will then belong to the class of *obiter dicta*. This is so even though some such arguments are necessary to justify a ruling given, and even where only the very arguments actually advanced could justify the ruling.

It must be noticed that the *ratio* on this view is a function of a judge's decision and of the justification offered by that judge in the opinion he/she states supporting it. Thus there can be multiple *rationes*. A single judge may find it necessary to make a ruling on more than one point in issue. Moreover, in an appellate court of several judges there may be several *rationes*, and if the practice is for judges to issue concurring or dissenting opinions, different judges may take different lines even in favour of the same concrete decision between the parties to the case. In some cases several judges may concur in a single majority opinion. In others it may be

---

[12] This formula derives from MacCormick, *Legal Reasoning* p. 215, but amending 'the' to read 'a' as the first and fifth words of the definition; the amendment was first adopted in my contribution to Laurence Goldstein's *Precedent in Law* (Oxford: Clarendon Press, 1987).

possible to construct a single composite ruling as some kind of logical product of the several *rationes* of the judges. But in yet others, there will be no single *ratio* of a case decided by a multi-judge court as an appellate court. There will be a range of possible rulings on the issue in hand, each with a justifying argument supporting it as the best for this and like cases. It might be said that, if all those offered are mutually consistent, all should be followed at least in the sense of not being contradicted in the future. But this is not likely to yield much coherence over time, so surely all should be deemed persuasive, future courts being left free to develop whichever in the light of later considerations seem soundest all things considered.

For this reason, as well as to reinforce the wisdom learnt from Burton's critique of universalizability, reflection on this model tells in favour of a relatively weak doctrine of binding precedent. We can take *rationes* for what they are—rulings on law stated as necessary parts of justifications of decisions *relatively to the cases and the arguments put by given parties*. But in taking them as that, we should acknowledge the unwisdom of any doctrine under which they are ever treated as absolutely binding on the basis of a single case. (Anyway, where the single case is an appeal case with more than one opinion given in favour of the decision, it may be quite rarely that one single univocal *ratio of the case* as such will be statable.) By contrast, however, a doctrine of persuasive precedent coupled with a fairly strict theory about the definition and identification of the *ratio* will be possible. Moreover, considerations of justice, of consistency of decision, and of the public interest in discouraging perpetual controversy on particular legal questions will argue strongly in favour of such a doctrine of persuasive precedent. Such a doctrine will help, moreover, in the essential business of rendering as determinate as possible the available grounds of legal argument. The debate with Lyons led us to identify the importance of that.

All that remains to be shown is that the model proposed here is not merely a model for intelligible and acceptable practices of justification and doctrines of precedent, from which emerges a clear and satisfying theory of precedent, but also a good rational reconstruction of actual practice and doctrine. That is what I shall try to show, or at least suggest, in the final section of this chapter, to which I now turn.

4. The Most Rational Reconstruction?

It would be too much to claim that the theory presented here perfectly represents the full complex reality or rather the multitudinous realities of actual systems of common law or mixed common-and-civil law. The fact is that there is no such perfect consistency of usages or practices that any one theoretical view of precedents, *rationes*, and the rest could be faithful to the entirety of the evidence. For any theory one advances there will be some contrary evidence. In the face of such evidence, one has either to revise the theory or to re-evaluate the evidence.

It cannot be dismissed as non-existent, or as irrelevant. But it is quite reasonable to put forward arguments why it should be deemed relevant as exemplifying an abuse or ill-use of concepts rather than as a proper or standard use. In this case it ceases to be counter-example that undermines the overall account.

This brings back in to focus the idea that theory in this domain aims at 'rational reconstruction' of the practice of lawyers and courts in the decisions of cases and in all recourse they make to argument from precedent in that process.[13] The pretension of work such as the present is not merely to propose *a* rational reconstruction, but to advance the best one currently available. To succeed in that, one has to examine the justificatory practices of courts, to examine prior theories, that is, prior attempts at rational reconstructions, and to show that the theory offered transcends previous efforts. It will do so, if at all, by incorporating their best features while also penetrating more closely to the point of the system and thus encapsulating the essence of good practice.

A starting point in reviewing practice might well be the case of the conjoined twins, Jodie and Mary, that occupied much attention in Chapter 5. Let us recall the concluding words of Ward LJ[14]

> In my judgement the appeal must be dismissed. Lest it be thought that this decision could become authority for wider propositions, such as that a doctor, once he has determined that a patient cannot survive, can kill the patient, it is important to restate the unique circumstances for which this case is authority. They are that it must be impossible to preserve the life of X without bringing about the death of Y, that Y by his or her very continued existence will inevitably bring about the death of X within a short period of time, and that X is capable of living an independent life but Y is incapable under any circumstances (including all forms of medical intervention) of viable independent existence.

It would be difficult to envisage a more complete and careful attempt to give a ruling on the key point of law in issue. It is helpful also to note the express words used to exclude any future reading of the case as authorizing any kind of mercy killing by a doctor. The 'restatement' of the 'unique circumstances for which this case is authority'. But 'unique' is here an exaggeration. Such circumstances will be very rare indeed (at least, any humane-minded person will hope so). But the proposition is deliberately framed in universal terms and would be capable of being applied in any future case of this rare and distressing situation.

The consideration of *Johnson v Unisys Ltd*[15] in *Dunnachie v Kingston-upon-Hull*[16] (discussed also in Chapter 7) is instructive. The issue was whether the Employment Rights Act in providing for 'just and equitable' awards in compensation for 'loss' suffered by employees in cases of unfair dismissal covered only pecuniary loss, or could include also injury to feelings. In *Johnson v Unisys*, Lord Hoffmann, giving the leading opinion of the House of Lords, noted that in the circumstances of the

---

[13] See Chapter 2 above, at note 47.
[14] [2001] Fam. 147 at 204–5, [2000] 4 All ER 961 at 1018.
[15] [2001] 2 All ER 801, [2003] 1 AC 518.   [16] [2004] UKHL 36, [2004] 3 All ER 1011.

case it was unnecessary to consider an additional element 'by way of compensation for . . . distress, damage to family life and such matters', since even without that the upper financial limit for compensation under the act had been reached. In that sense,[17]

the point [about non pecuniary loss] would have been academic. But perhaps I may be allowed a comment all the same . . .

It was said that the word 'loss' can mean only financial loss. But I think that is too narrow a construction. The emphasis is upon the tribunal awarding such compensation as it thinks just and equitable. So I see no reason why in an appropriate case it should not include compensation for distress, humiliation, damage to reputation in the community or to family life.

At issue in *Dunnachie* was the question whether these words were to be considered as part of the *ratio decidendi* of *Johnson*, and thus binding on courts lower in the judicial hierarchy, except if formally overruled by the House of Lords itself. The conclusion of the House as stated emphatically by Lord Steyn was that the statement quoted was an *obiter dictum*. If it had been part of the *ratio*, it would have involved overruling a long-standing precedent in industrial law.[18]

But the House heard no adversarial argument exploring the correctness or otherwise of that decision. In these circumstances a definitive overruling of a decision which had stood for nearly 30 years would have been surprising.
. . . Lord Hoffmann's language clearly excludes the view that [his statement was part of the *ratio decidendi*]. He described it as a 'doubtful question'. He described it as 'academic'. Then he introduced his comments by the words 'But perhaps I may be allowed a comment all the same.' This is not the language of a Law Lord inviting the House to overrule a longstanding decision on a point of statutory construction that was not in issue and not explored in opposing arguments.

Here, it is worth recalling the point I made in defining '*ratio*'. It is a ruling 'on a point on which a ruling was necessary to her/his justification (or one of her/his alternative justifications) of the decision in the case'. It is exactly this question of necessity that comes in focus in *Dunnachie*. In *Johnson*, no ruling had been necessary on the possible extended meaning of 'loss', and as a consequence no adversarial argument on that was heard, nor was the soundness of the thirty-year old precedent exposed to critical scrutiny. Just for that reason, the remarks about loss, however suggestive for future possible development of the law, were not a part of the *ratio*, hence had no binding quality. In *Dunnachie*, by contrast, the House considered the arguments in favour of overruling the *Norton Tool* case and extending the boundaries of 'loss' in the manner suggested by Lord Hoffmann in *Johnson*. But it decided that the better reasons were in favour of affirming it, not overruling it, once the point had been fully argued. By contrast, in *Re A* Ward LJ's

---

[17] [2003] 1 AC 518 at 547 ([2001] 2 All ER 801 at 821), cited in [2004] 3 All ER at 1017, [2004] UKHL at para. 5.   [18] [2004] UKHL at paras 11–12, [2004] 3 All ER at 1019.

focus is very clearly on enunciating exactly what is sufficient, and not a bit more than sufficient, to settle a point (the point, indeed) that was necessary for the decision and on which argument from many quarters had been heard.

A further instance of such beside-the-pointness is supplied by the practice sometimes used by the House of Lords, of giving guidelines for future cases while deciding appeals upon present ones. Thus when the Lords had to decide an appeal against misdirection in a criminal case involving intention implied on the ground of an actor's foresight, they found it proper, through Lord Bridge of Harwich, to lay down some guidelines on the imputation of intention.[19] But such were not necessary to justifying the decision to uphold the appeal in the given case. Hence they were neither *ratio* nor, in the strictest sense, binding for the future. So in the case of the Welsh miners and the taxi-driver who was killed during the miners' strike in 1985, the miners' conviction for murder was quashed because the trial judge had misdirected the jury in reliance on one of Lord Bridge's guidelines.[20] The Court of Appeal distinguished the precedent on the ground that the guidelines, being acknowledgedly unnecessary in the original decision, were therefore *obiter dicta* in it.

However that may be, the examples given above all seem instances of *sound* or *adequate* justification precisely because of the clarity of the rulings made by the judges and because of the care taken to show their coherence and consistency with relevant law. If there were to be any rational doctrine of precedent, it should surely be one based on the admission of such rulings on law as binding or (preferably) persuasive for future cases. Consistency through time and across cases matters for the sake of law and matters for the sake of justice. A system which expects reasonable clarity of ruling by judges may also expect them to test rulings for their acceptability across the range of cases actually present and hypothetically to come which, as rulings, they will cover. Only in this case can rational consistency be reasonably pursued, and no doubt with due allowance for revising precedents. But to allow that a present ruling may be revisable for the future is not at all the same as supposing that no present ruling need be made, or, once made, can exist.

Apart from such appeals to the reason of things we may take note of the general state of juristic opinion, assuming this to be in general addressed to the project of rational reconstruction. Does the present thesis capture what is best in prior reconstructions, while successfully reaching the parts other theories do not reach? I immodestly think so. To show why, I shall start from the late Sir Rupert Cross's deservedly famous 'description' of what a *ratio* is. He says: 'The *ratio decidendi* of a case is any rule of law expressly or impliedly treated by the judge as a necessary step

---

[19] *R v Moloney* [1985] AC 905, [1985] 1 All ER 1025; Lord Bridge made it perfectly clear that the guidelines he stated as to imputation of intention went beyond what it was necessary to decide in the case.

[20] *R v Hancock and another* [1986] AC 455 at 473–4, [1986] 1 All ER 641 at 644 and 651.

in reaching his conclusion, having regard to the line of reasoning adopted by him, or a necessary part of his direction to the jury.'[21]

In doubly stressing the importance of judicial lines of reasoning, as indicating what is necessary to a conclusion, this is admirable. But the trouble is that it clearly extends too wide. In any case in which a statute is being interpreted and applied, the statute itself, or a section of it, will constitute a rule without which the same conclusion could not be reached (so far as we mean by the 'conclusion' a conclusion of, e.g. liability *under that statute*). But nobody supposes the statute to be the *ratio*; rather, it will be what the court holds to be the correct interpretation of the statute that is the *ratio*. On this account it is surely preferable to describe or define *ratio* in terms of its being a *ruling* by the judge rather than 'any rule' on which his conclusion depends.

Further, as to 'necessity', it is indeed true that unnecessary rulings make no precedents. But unnecessary to what? Cross's conception, like other conceptions of necessariness to a conclusion, runs much too wide, as Brian Simpson has in effect shown,[22] and as follows from the argument in the last paragraph above. We must shift our focus to necessariness in the justificatory and argumentative context, that is, to the idea of what necessarily has to be decided between these parties; the necessity here is the necessity of obligation, not causal or logical necessity. If P seeks decision *d* against D, and D denies that *d* ought to be granted, this dispute between P and D must be referable to some difference over facts in issue or over pleas-in-law (as they are called in Scots law, and also in EC law, where the Scots term has been received as satisfactorily translating the French '*moyens*'), or both. So far as the parties dispute a certain point of law as decisive for *d* or *not-d*, it is the judge's duty to rule upon that point, or to show some other ground for making a determination as between *d* and *not-d* even if the parties' point be left open.

This worry about the implications of what is 'necessary' was first raised by Brian Simpson in his paper in *Oxford Essays in Jurisprudence*. There, he showed that, in Cross's form, and perhaps in certain judicial formulations, 'necessary' lets in far too much. Accordingly, Simpson proposed substituting for the idea of that which is necessary to a decision, that which is sufficient for the decision. Even so, in Simpson's formulation, this point seems to let in quite as much too much as does Cross's 'necessary'. The Simpsonian idea of sufficiency is accordingly amended in my presentation. A ruling which is a *ratio* has indeed to be sufficient for the purpose of settling a point of law put in issue by the parties' arguments. But that is subject to the point's being, in the above-stated sense, a point on which a decision is necessary for justification of the decision in the case.

Where a ruling is expressly stated, all is no doubt plain enough sailing; and the fact that most applications of precedent in most cases are straightforward and

---

[21] R. Cross, *Precedent in English Law* (Oxford: Clarendon Press, 3rd edn, 1977), p. 76.
[22] A. W. B. Simpson, 'The *Ratio Decidendi* of a Case', in A. G. Guest (ed.), *Oxford Essays in Jurisprudence*, (Oxford: Oxford University Press, 1961), ch. 6.

uncontroversial may well help to confirm that clear and express rulings are by no means as infrequent as some sceptical reasoners say. In extreme cases, judges may do no more than indicate that it is because the facts of the case are certain facts viewed under certain fact-descriptions that the decision ought to be as it is. When this is how things are, what we come down to is the famous 'Goodhart method'[23] for determining a *ratio*—the method also favoured by Glanville Williams in respect of English law and by D. M. Walker in respect of Scots law.[24]

That is to say, we can only treat such a process of justification as implying rather than stating a universalized proposition of law: If facts *F* occur then decision *D* ought to be given. Why we have to suppose that justification does presuppose universalizability is the point considered in Chapter 5 above. What makes some facts rather than others be material facts, in the sense of being material to justification of a decision, will be the judge's representing them as facts *because of which* he/she comes to his decision. It is, so to say, that maxim of *his* or *her* decision which is universalized, not any old maxim that could be addressed to the given evidentiary facts. So the Goodhart method becomes an important corollary of the present theory.

This in turn deals with certain forms of scepticism according to which *rationes decidendi* have such infinite flexibility as to be to all intents and purposes indeterminate, or at least whatever any subsequent judge chooses to formulate as the real point of some earlier case. A classical formulation of such scepticism is that of Julius Stone in *Legal System and Lawyers' Reasonings*.[25] There the category *ratio decidendi* is said to belong among Stone's 'Categories of Illusory Reference', and more specifically to be 'a legal category of indeterminate or concealed multiple reference'. Stone's chief point, addressed to Goodhart, is that facts can be material under an infinite range of fact-descriptions, broad or narrow; and that for any given decision a succession of subsequent judicial reformulations of that prior decision is possible.

Nothing here said should be taken as denying the possibility (or even, in some few cases, the probability) of judicial incompetence. Judges can in fact and sometimes do decide cases without satisfactorily resolving or ruling upon disputed points of law; or they can categorize and recategorize facts under a multiplicity of descriptions and bumble through to a decision. And in any such case a *ratio* could only be indeterminate or multifarious, even if not concealedly so. But this should not blind us to the fact that judges are often capable of giving clear and crisp rulings, either explicit or unambiguously implicit in their justifications; rulings, that is, on points of law in issue.

[23] See A. L Goodhart, *Essays in Jurisprudence and the Common Law* (Cambridge: Cambridge University Press, 1931), ch. 1 ('Determining the *Ratio Decidendi* of a Case').

[24] G. L. Williams, *Learning the Law* (London: Stevens, 9th edn, 1973), ch. 6; D. M. Walker, *The Scottish Legal System* (Edinburgh: W. Green and Son, 5th edn, 1981), pp. 390–3.

[25] Stone, *Legal System* pp. 263–80. There is perhaps a hint of a similar view in A. A. Paterson and T. St. J. N. Bates, *The Legal System of Scotland: Cases and Materials* (Edinburgh: W. Green and Son, 1983), pp. 301–4.

Whether clarity ought to entail non-revisability under subsequent reflection is a quite different point. As was earlier said, non-revisability appears to be an unwise idea. Even binding precedents may rightly provoke new reflections in new circumstances. Certain doctrines of precedent may then force judges to say on each occasion of revision that it is the latest revision which *is* the *ratio* of the earlier case. Under such an impolitic doctrine of precedent, *ratio* may acquire what Stone calls 'concealed multiple reference'. Surely, however, this should lead us to reject so impolitic a doctrine of precedent rather than to abandon the present theses as to what *rationes decidendi* are. It is on this and other like grounds that I claim only to be in the business of rational reconstruction. What follows about the interpretation of precedents is that they can be construed in several ways. What can be binding or highly persuasive is the *ratio* as explained here, the ruling that is carefully made after full argument on a point that has to be settled, and that is sufficient—but not more than sufficient—to settle that point. For the rest, *obiter dicta* are not to be dismissed merely because they are not binding. These after all include judges' discussion of the inherent values of the law, their weighing of principles, and indeed their attempts to formulate principles hitherto more implicit than explicit in the law. Much legal argument concerns matters such as these, and the absence of strictly binding force in such dicta is irrelevant to their broader value as an element in legal discourse. Moreover, it is not only as binding precedents that lawyers read cases. Precedents play a great part in argument by analogy in law, and argument by analogy is an important form of argument in the law.

One last point to be made about the theory of precedent concerns the so-called 'declaratory theory'. Historically in the common law countries and still in civilian systems, precedents were or are considered as doing no more than declaring the true import of the existing law, whether this is law as laid down in statute or code, or law as contained in case law. In that case, they necessarily declare the law as it is now and has been always, or at least since the coming into force of the law that is being interpreted with a view to establishing its true import. This declaring of law comes, inevitably, after the acts and events that are subject to controversy in the case. So the true import of the law may only become clear to the parties *ex post facto*, once the court has stated its opinion and decided the case.

It is nowadays recognized by judges and others that there is an element of the myth, even the 'fairy tale', about this theory, so far at least as concerns the common law. In common law and mixed systems, judges at the very least have the function of 'developing the law', and thus in a sense 'making' it (though in a different sense, and within different parameters, from those applicable to the legislative process in a Parliament). This gives rise to a concern, vital from the point of view of the Rule of Law, that judge-made law is retrospective in its application, and open to all the objections concerning uncertainty and unfairness that afflict any form of retrospection. One response is to suggest the introduction of a practice of 'prospective overruling', when a court decides to depart from an established precedent or line of precedents.[26] That in turn poses the question by what means it would be appropriate, if indeed it would be wise at all, to make such a change—by judicial decision, or by legislative enactment? Recent case law[27] in the United Kingdom has given heightened salience to this issue, discussion of which is postponed to Chapter 13.

[26] See R. H. S. Tur 'Time and Law' *Oxford Journal of Legal Studies* 22 (2002) 463–88, esp. at 474 for a critical discussion of *Kleinwort Benson v Lincoln City Council* [1999] 2 AC 349, [1998] 4 All ER 513 at 552 and compare his 'Varieties of Overruling and Judicial Law Making: Prospective Overruling in a Comparative Perspective' *Juridical Review* (1978); also Lord Rodger of Earlsferry 'A Time for Everything under Law: Some Reflections on Retrospectivity' *Law Quarterly Review* 121 (2005) 57–79 at 77–8.

[27] Particularly *Kleinwort Benson v Lincoln City Council* [1999] 2 AC 349 at 377–9, [1998] 4 All ER 513 at 552.

9

Being Reasonable

Introduction: Subjectivity and Objectivity

Chapters five and six established that the justification of legal decisions in problematic cases[1] calls for universalization of the proposed grounds of judgement and evaluation of the universalized proposition by reference to consequences. Such consequentialist judging looks mainly at what we called 'consequences as implications' or 'juridical consequences', but also, in some contexts at least, at consequences as practical or behavioural outcomes of decision-making. This in turn raises the question of the role of values in legal reasoning. To what values can legal reasoners make appeal to show that one possible line of judgement is better than another? Can this be an objective judgement, or is evaluation a purely or substantially subjective matter? To test further some of the suggestions made at the conclusion of Chapter 6, this chapter will focus on one value concept which plays a particularly omnipresent part in legal discourse in the anglophone traditions, namely that of 'reasonableness'.

The concept of the 'reasonable' is used frequently and in very diverse contexts by lawyers and legislators in these legal traditions. In the spectrum from purely descriptive to purely evaluative, 'reasonable' seems to belong more toward the evaluative than the descriptive pole, not that there is no element of the descriptive in it. Indeed, it can properly be ranked among what philosophers have classed as 'thick' evaluative terms, by contrast with thin terms such as 'right' or 'good'.[2] If I say that the care manufacturers took in manufacturing some article fell short of the care it would have been reasonable for them to take in the given setting, I am not describing the care they took or failed to take, I am evaluating the care they

---

[1] That is, cases where somebody has credibly raised any of the problems we identified as arising from doubt or contestation about legal claims, namely problems of interpretation, or of classification or of evaluation, or of relevancy. See Chapter 3 above.

[2] See J. Dancy, *Ethics Without Principles* pp. 84–5. 'Thin' concepts express conclusions about what to do. Thick ones state reasons relevant to what it is right to do. If to act reasonably is normally to act rightly, because being reasonable tends to make an action, 'reasonable' is a 'thick concept'. It will follow that it is not always and necessarily right to act reasonably (rather than imaginatively, or passionately, for example). Dancy expresses doubt whether by this test 'justice' is thick or thin; the reasonable and the just have much in common, I shall argue in due course. See also J. Raz, 'Notes on Value and Objectivity', in B. Leiter (ed.), *Objectivity in Law and Morals* (Cambridge: Cambridge University Press, 2001), 194–233 at pp. 215–16.

took. I am comparing what was done with what could have been done. I am assessing whether a proper consideration of the value of the activity undertaken, balanced against the risks inherent in the activity and the possibility (and cost) of guarding effectively against more obvious or graver risks, would have shown that there was better reason to discontinue the activity pending installation of further effective safeguards than to continue with it. In this sense, I am asking whether a reasonable evaluation of the risks would have left an actor in that situation satisfied with the degree of care that was taken, or not so satisfied.

Evaluation of this kind has an obviously subjective aspect. Different evaluators will form different opinions about the benefits of the activity, the likelihood of the risks, the seriousness of the risks, the costs of the safeguards, and their probable efficacy. Notoriously, reasonable people attending fairly to a complex question can reasonably disagree about the reasonable answer. In that case everything may turn on the question who is the most authoritative judge, for that person's opinion will prevail. That suggests a degree of subjectivity, since different subjects considering the same question can inveterately disagree (not that they always or invariably disagree) on what is the correct answer. Where subjectivity in that sense prevails, majority voting, or hierarchical authorities of decision-making, or a combination of these two devices, as with majority voting in appellate courts, may be the only practicable solution to deal with conflicting opinions.

Lawyers, however, have not characterized the 'reasonable' as involving a subjective test. In law, what is reasonable is commonly deemed an 'objective' matter. Kent Greenawalt's *Objectivity in Law*[3] gives one account of the elements of objectivity and of subjectivity in legal thought, whether in relation to the elements required by the law for liability, civil or criminal, or in relation to the objectivity, inter-subjectivity, or even pure subjectivity found in the weighing of legal arguments. In relation to the former topic, Greenawalt points out that liability judged by the foresight of the reasonable person is objective, by contrast with liability grounded in the actual intentions of an acting person.[4] In relation to the latter, while he acknowledges a measure of objective rightness and wrongness, and a considerable degree of inter-subjective checkability in the weighing and balancing of arguments, he nevertheless concludes that, on any fine point of balancing, reasonable people can differ. These differences are not objectively corrigible. To that extent, there remains an element of apparently irreducible subjectivity in the inevitable leeways of legal judgment.[5] But the fact that persons disagree, and acknowledge that they do, does not entail that any one of them thinks there is nothing that is really reasonable. What they differ about is exactly the answer to the question which really is reasonable.

It may be helpful to pick up the former of Greenawalt's points, concerning the difference between liability judged by the foresight of the reasonable person, and

[3] Kent Greenawalt, *Objectivity in Law* (cited hereafter as *Objectivity*) (New York and Oxford: Oxford University Press, 1992). [4] *Objectivity* pp. 100–8.
[5] *Objectivity* 216–28. I hope this is a reasonable summary of a careful and sensitive argument.

liability grounded in the actual intentions of an acting person. A person can be held liable in law for failing to take the care a reasonable person would have taken to avoid a misadventure that has occurred, in circumstances where such a mis-adventure was foreseeable. Such a person need have had no real guilty intention or even any conscious advertence to the misadventure that occurred, certainly no wilful intention to bring it about. We are even ready to acknowledge that there need not have been any moral fault on the agent's part, for he/she may have been striving to the best of weak abilities to prevent the accident that happened. Where the law deals thus with liability for causing mishaps, its point is that a common standard is set for all persons and all must meet that standard or be held liable in the event of mishaps occurring. This may well be fairer from the point of view of accident victims, so far as concerns compensation, than any attempt to grade fault according to the different capabilities of different actors.[6] So in this case the potentially liable party can be said to bear a duty to take reasonable care towards her/his neighbours. The duty set is, from the duty-bearer's point of view, some-thing other than a subjective standard of achievement. The law's exhortation is not simply to do your best, or to avoid acting with evil intentions toward others; it is to act according to the common standard of the community, as a 'reasonable person' would—or to refrain from acting in the area of risk altogether.

That standard is objective with regard to the state of mind of the acting subject, and yet it has to be applied only as mediated through the subjectivity of whoever has to decide after the fact whether reasonable care was shown. There is nothing a bit surprising in the thought that objective standards are applicable only through adjudicative subjectivity. It is an objective question who crossed the line first, but before a winner of the race can be declared this has to be judged by the line judge, or the photo finish adjudicator, or the like. But by reference to the second point of Greenawalt's cited above, it seems that it is not just the necessary subjectivity of appreciation that is engaged here, but something in the very idea of the reasonable that calls for attending to more than one factor, more than one variable. The issue is how to reach a final valuation taking due account of all such factors. There may then only be limited inter-subjective controllability in evaluation, even when everyone acts in the best of good faith trying to judge the matter fairly and correctly. Is there really an 'objective' answer to the question when this 'objective' criterion of liability is satisfied? This is a question to which we shall return.

Before getting to that point, I want at once to warn against an undue narrowness of concern, as though reasonableness were in issue only in relation to civil liability for negligence, important though that is as one context for legal deployment of 'the reasonable'. For there are many legal settings in which the question arises what it is reasonable to do, to say, to conclude, or to doubt in a given context. A value like 'reasonable' may be very context-sensitive, and always the judgement is going

---

[6] Compare 'The Obligation of Reparation', in N. MacCormick, *Legal Right and Social Democracy* (Oxford: Clarendon Press, 1982) pp. 212–31.

to be a concrete one in a concrete context, as Chaim Perelman was wont to stress.[7] As we shall see, there may be many factors which in any given situation have to be considered and assessed in judging of the reasonableness of an act or an omission to act or a decision in its concrete context. For this reason and in this sense 'reasonableness' taken out of context is what Julius Stone called a 'legal category of indeterminate reference'.[8] Whether or not it remains indeterminate in context is less clear. Anyway, when we think of legal reasoning in the common law systems or in mixed systems such as Scots law, the category of the reasonable has great importance and many uses. The same, no doubt, is true of civilian legal systems also. In German law, for example, the concept of 'proportionality' plays a not dissimilar role, one that has in turn influenced the law of the European Union. In many branches of the law, 'reasonableness' is the standard set by the operative principles and rules of conduct and of judgement, as we may see from the following illustrations.

Within public law, it is a general principle that the powers of public authorities must not be exercised unreasonably.[9] Within the criminal law, the standard required in trials for the proof of an accused person's guilt is proof 'beyond reasonable doubt', this being a more exacting standard of proof than the proof 'on balance of probabilities' required in most issues of civil litigation.[10] In the private law of reparation of injuries, the standard of care which each person owes to every other is the care which a 'reasonable man [sic]' would take for the safety of his neighbours in the given circumstances.[11] The extent of liability for negligent wrongdoing is likewise limited by the consequences of a course of conduct so far as, at the time of action, these would have been foreseeable by a reasonable person.[12] This duty of reasonable care although originally elaborated in the jurisprudence of the higher

[7] Compare Ch. Perelman, *L'Empire Rhétorique: Rhétorique et Argumentation* (Paris: Librairie Philiosophique J. Vrin, 1977) p. 40, 'En fait, ces valeurs font l'objet d'un accord universel dans la mesure où elles restent indeterminées; dès qu'on tente de les préciser, en les appliquant à une situation ou à une action concrete, les desaccords...ne tardent pas à se manifester' English translation, *The Realm of Rhetoric*, (Paris: Notre Dame University Press, 1982) 26.

[8] Julius Stone, *Legal System* ch 7 and 8.

[9] See *Westminster Corporation v London and North Western Railway Co* [1905] AC 426 at 430, per Lord Macnaughten. 'A public body invested with statutory powers...must take care not to exceed or abuse its powers. It must keep within the limits of the authority committed to it. It must act in good faith. And it must act reasonably. The last proposition is involved in the second, if not in the first.' Some commentators have doubted the utility of this wide sense of reasonableness. See S. A. De Smith, *Judicial Review of Administrative Action* (4th edn, London: J. M. Evans, 1980) pp. 346–54.

[10] See C. Tapper, *Cross and Tapper on Evidence* (8th edn, London: Butterworth, 1995) pp. 1162–3; some English judges have tended to discourage the 'reasonable doubt' formula, but the Scots have held to it. See A. G. Walker and N. M. L. Walker, *The Law of Evidence in Scotland* (Edinburgh and Glasgow: W. Hodge & Co., 1964) ch 7 and 8, esp. at p. 76: 'It is for the Crown to prove the accused's guilt beyond reasonable doubt...The doubt must be reasonable in that it must not be a strained or fanciful acceptance of remote possibilities.' See also *Shaw v H.M. Advocate* 1953 JC 51, and the quotation from Lord Justice General Cullen in the *Lockerbie* case in Chapter 3 above, n.19.

[11] See, e.g., *Donoghue v Stevenson* [1932] AC 562, 1932 SC (HL) 31; 'reasonable man' is gradually giving way to 'reasonable person', and this is much to be welcomed. See Greenawalt's wise words in *Objectivity* at pp. 145–6.   [12] See, e.g., *The Wagon Mound* [1967] AC 388.

courts is now also confirmed in certain more particular instances by statute law.[13] In the law of contract, there is a general common law principle under which contracts in restraint of trade are invalid if they set restraints which go beyond what is reasonable in the interest of the parties and in the public interest.[14] Damages for breach of contract are restricted to losses reasonably foreseeable as of the date of contracting, and there are other instances where rules of statute law enable courts to set aside contractual provisions which are unreasonable.[15] In relatively recent divorce law, we find provisions whereby unreasonable conduct by one spouse towards another may be a ground for judicial dissolution of marriage.[16]

These are merely illustrations of a very general (and much remarked) tendency in the law to rely upon the standard of reasonableness as a criterion of right decision-making, of right action, and of fair interpersonal relationships within the law of evidence, the law of property, the law of obligations, family law, and public law. Even as a few illustrative examples, they suffice to ground the thesis that reasoning about reasonableness is a matter of great moment within the operations of the law. If we did not understand how to work with such a notion, we would fail to understand an essential and central feature of contemporary legal reasoning. How then are we to understand it?

The first point to make is that the 'reasonableness' the law has in view must be practical reasonableness,[17] not an abstract capacity for reason upon theoretical issues. The reasonable person has the virtue of *prudentia* and uses this in action. It is a virtue that is incompatible with fanaticism or apathy, but holds a mean between these, as it does between excessive caution and excessive indifference to risk. Reasonable people take account of foreseeable risks, but with regard to serious possibilities or probabilities, not remote or fanciful chances. They do not jump to conclusions, but consider the evidence and take account of different points of view. They are aware that any practical dilemma may involve a meeting point of different values and interests. They take the competing and converging values and other reasons for action seriously, seeking a reconciliation of them or, in cases of inevitable conflict, acting for whatever are, all in all, the more cogent reasons or the greater or overriding values.

Reasonable persons resemble Adam Smith's 'impartial spectator'[18] (indeed, it might be better to say that they themselves exhibit recourse to 'spectator' reasoning).

---

[13] e.g. Occupiers' Liability Act 1957; Occupiers' Liability (Scotland) Act 1960.

[14] See J. D. Heydon, *The Restraint of Trade Doctrine* (London: Butterworths, 1971).

[15] e.g., Unfair Contract Terms Act 1977.

[16] See Matrimonial Causes Act 1973, section 1(2)(b); Divorce (Scotland) Act 1976 section l(2)(b).

[17] In what follows, I am profoundly indebted, not only to Greenawalt's *Objectivity*, but also, and even more, to John Finnis's, *Natural Law and Natural Rights* (Oxford: Clarendon Press, 1980) ch. 5; though in relying as I do on Smith and Alexy, I fall well short of Thomistic value-realism.

[18] See Adam Smith, *The Theory of Moral Sentiments* D. D. Raphael and A. L. MacFie (eds), (Oxford: 1976) pp. 129–37; and cf. K. Haakonssen, *The Science of a Legislator: the Natural*

For they seek to abstract from their own position to see and feel the situation as it looks and feels to others involved, and they weigh impartially their own interests and commitments in comparison with those of others. They are aware that there are different ways in which things, activities, and relationships can have value to people, and that all values ought to be given some attention, even though it is not possible to bring all to realization in any one life, or project, or context of action. Hence they seek to strike a balance that takes account of this apparently irreducible plurality of values. In this way reasonable people are objective: they are not so consumed with passion for their own interest or project (though they may indeed be very committed to it) as to be unable to stand back momentarily and see the situation from other persons' points of view. Having done that, they are able to judge their own interest in competition with others' with at least a fair degree of impartiality. They will recognize that a greater interest or deeper value of another can properly take priority over the interest they pursue and the values they seek to realize, so far as conflict is inevitable. Reasonable people cultivate the Smithian virtue of self-command, and apply it in self-restraint when others have legitimate priority over them.

Perfectly reasonable people would doubtless be unreal paragons of virtue. There are few to be found. Ordinary people are not; but most are reasonable some of the time and some are reasonable most of the time. And on all of us the law imposes the requirement that we act reasonably, or, at any rate, whether by luck or by judgement, keep up to the standard of the reasonable when we act in any one or another of a variety of settings such as those noted. But contexts do differ. As a juror in a criminal trial, I must look at the prosecution evidence with a critical eye, especially having regard to any competing evidence offered by the defence, and considering whatever grounds of doubt have been put before me by the defence. Certainty is impossible in relation to contingent assertions about the past, such as are involved in every criminal trial. Some doubt (or possibility of doubt) must always be present, but not all doubt rises above that threshold at which a person has reason to treat the doubt as a serious one, even without further considerations to support it. Some points of doubt are properly ignored or treated as remote and unrealistic, fanciful, even, set against a powerful body of credible evidence tending to a certain conclusion. As an administrative decision maker, I must be careful to review the whole scheme within which I exercise discretion, and be sure to ground my decision on a review only of the factors relevant to the scheme and their relative importance singly or in combination, taking no note of irrelevant matters.

Jurisprudence of David Hume and Adam Smith (Cambridge: Cambridge University Press, 1981) pp. 47–52. I have never found myself persuaded by the 'rational choice' version of reasonableness that prevails in the contemporary 'economic analysis of law', and commend economists to other aspects of Adam Smith's thought. I gratefully endorse the argument of Heidi Li Feldman in her 'Science, Reason, and Tort law: Looking for the Reasonable Person' *Current Legal Issues* 1 (1998) ('Law and Science'), H. Reece (ed.) pp. 35–54 at 39–43. Joseph Raz has also recently drawn attention to impartiality as one strand in the idea of objectivity. See J. Raz, 'Notes on Value and Objectivity', in B. Leiter (ed.) *Objectivity in Law and Morals* (Cambridge: Cambridge University Press, 2001), pp. 195–6.

As a driver, I must always bear in mind that, however pressing my reasons for haste may be, and whatever burdens of worry and concern beset me, there are other road users whose safety in life and limb ranks higher on a just scale of value than my urgent need to keep an appointment. And so on. Reasonable doubt is not the same as reasonable decision-making nor is either the same as reasonable care in driving. But there is a common thread that links the appellation 'reasonable' in these and other instances of its use. That common thread lies in the style of deliberation a person would ideally engage in, and the impartial attention she/he would give to competing values and items of evidence, in the given concrete setting. The 'reasonable person' is an ideal deliberator, and actual human agents achieve reasonableness to the extent that their decisions or actions or conclusions match those that would result from ideal deliberation. Naturally, where issues arise for decision in a court after the fact that gives rise to criminal charge or asserted civil liability, the court's deliberation, the heat of the moment being long past, can more probably replicate the ideal deliberation than can the individual human response to the heated moment.

It is a common saying that there are many questions on which reasonable people can reasonably differ. Some of these are simple differences of personal taste—baseball is for one person a more exciting game than cricket, but another prefers cricket for the long slow build up of expectation and tension by contrast with the more explosive action in the baseball game. *De gustibus non est disputandum*, it is foolish to treat differences of taste as occasions for disputation. But this is not the only kind of difference there is. In any question that involves weighing much evidence or many interests and values, and coming to a conclusion on what may seem a relatively fine balance, it does not surprise us to find others reaching a conclusion different from our own. There can here be a real difference of judgement about what is right and what ought accordingly to be done.

Such a difference of judgement is no mere difference of taste. And it matters to us, because a decision must be made according to one or the other view, whereas in most differences of taste it is sufficient for different persons each to go their own way. Such differences of judgement, as Greenawalt notes, are typical of so-called 'hard cases' (here, 'problem cases' is the preferred terminology) as these have been discussed in the jurisprudence of the last half century.[19]

The problem may have to do with the 'procedural'[20] character of reasonable deliberation. In the light of human values, interests, and purposes, one must consider all that is relevant, and assume an impartial stance in assigning relative weight or importance to different contextually relevant values or interests. But

[19] *Objectivity*, ch. 11 esp. at p. 228.
[20] Compare Robert Alexy, *A Theory of Legal Argumentation* (trans. R. Adler and N. MacCormick), (Oxford: Clarendon Press, 1988) pp. 177–209; Alexy's proceduralist approach follows, but refines, that of J. Habermas, as discussed in Chapter 2 above.

different people may differ in how exactly they assign such weights, and carry out balancing. There may be obvious errors of partiality, or gross anomalies in differential weighting, but, beyond that, it is difficult or impossible to show that one approach is superior to another. Provided people avoid fickleness or capriciousness, and observe a decent constancy in judgement over time, while remaining open to revision of their opinion in the light of reasoned arguments, they are not unreasonable just because they take a view different from mine, or from yours.

It follows that on some questions or in relation to some decisions there may be more than one reasonable answer, or, at least, a range of answers that cannot be shown to be, or dismissed as, unreasonable. That is compatible with the fact that those who hold to any of the reasonable answers can readily dismiss other approaches, on good grounds, as unreasonable ones. The absence of a single reasonable answer is not a proof that there is no such thing as an unreasonable one. This is itself strongly persuasive in favour of establishing authorities charged with decision-making. Provided those holding authority are experienced and wise persons, and provided there is some way of controlling or checking their decisions (e.g. by appeal, or by answerability before some representative body, or the like), there seems to be no better way than this of dealing with the problem of the non-univocal character of the reasonable.[21] It is not surprising that law-states are marked by the practice of appointing decision makers to exercise discretion within the domain of a defined jurisdiction by the use of proper procedures. Sometimes, moreover, to ensure the discursive and deliberative quality of the search for final decision or answer, authority is granted to a group, committee, assembly, or bench of several persons. In that case, there have to be voting procedures to make possible final decisions on finely balanced questions. Again, this is an unsurprising feature of contemporary constitutional landscapes.

These reflections may suffice by way of an introductory attempt to analyse and to flesh out in general terms an understanding of the idea of the reasonable. Next, I wish to pursue this in relation to positive law, to check how far the ideas put forward here find illustration, if not proof, in the materials of the law. I shall do this in three stages, considering first the reasons that might be advanced to justify use of the standard of reasonableness in law, and secondly the ways there are of interpreting the factors relevant to reasonableness in different branches of the law. Finally, I shall review concrete decisions about reasonableness, where what is reasonable is (sometimes, at least) said to be a 'question of fact'.

---

[21] This seems to be the best way to answer Scott Veitch's doubt about the question whether, in a competition between two reasonable opinions on the same question, it is right to establish institutional decision-making arrangements that can 'break ties' by voting or the like. But see Scott Veitch, *Moral Conflict and Legal Reasoning* (Oxford: Hart Publishing, 1999) 169–71; but compare also Veitch's critique of the 'reasonable man', 171–81.

1. Why 'Reasonableness'?

There has been a fair amount of writing on what justifies the law's resort to prescribing 'reasonableness' as a guiding standard in a given general context. Early in the field was H. L. A. Hart's discussion of the reasons that sometimes militate against a legislative strategy of laying down specific and detailed rules of conduct. 'Sometimes', he says,[22] 'the sphere to be legally controlled is recognised . . . as one in which the features of individual cases will vary so much in socially important but unpredictable respects, that uniform rules to be applied from case to case without further official direction cannot usefully be framed by the legislature in advance.'

In such a case, suggests Hart, a legislature may prescribe general principles and set up a subordinate rule-making authority to issue by way of delegated legislation more specific rules for the guidance of the general public or some section thereof. Alternatively, it may resort to the 'similar technique' of requiring persons in general 'to conform to a variable standard before it has been officially defined'. In this case 'they may learn from a court only ex post facto when they have violated it, what, in terms of specific actions or forbearances, is the standard required of them.'[23] The prime example in Hart's view of such a 'variable standard' in Anglo-American law is the standard of reasonable care as it applies in the civil and criminal law for defining actionable or punishable forms of negligence.

This way of depicting recourse to the 'reasonable' as an operative standard in law assimilates it to delegated legislation. The law as it leaves the legislator's hand is incomplete, and it falls to the judge who applies the law to supply a more detailed rule within the partially incomplete framework laid down. Hence the judge participates in the legislative process in a subordinate way, exercising the kind of strong discretion legislatures have in liberal democracies. In the light of the discussion so far, this seems to exaggerate the purely decisionist element in judgement concerning the reasonable. There must indeed be a decision after a critical evaluation of relevant considerations, but this really is a kind of judging, not a kind of legislating. A scintilla of evidence in favour of the present view against Hart's is that his view clashes with the lawyers' view (discussed further below) that what is reasonable in any case is a 'question of fact'.

Moreover, it fails to square with the possibility that lay persons and businesses can perfectly well guide their own conduct with some confidence by reference to such guidelines as 'reasonable care', 'reasonable notice', 'reasonable conformity of goods to sample'. They can do so without waiting for decisions to be laid down by the authorities. But that is what must usually be done when delegated legislation is awaited to complete a statutory scheme which lays down only a normative

---

[22] H. L. A. Hart, *The Concept of Law* (cited herafter as *Concept*) (Oxford: Clarendon Press, 1961) p. 127.   [23] *Concept* p. 129.

framework whose details have to be supplied before it becomes fully operational. 'Directives' in European Community law are a striking example of such framework laws requiring further rule-making activity to complete their normative effect.[24]

To say this is to pick up a point from Ronald Dworkin's critique of the theory of 'strong discretion' to which he considers Hart committed.[25] Dworkin considers Hart's whole approach to be vitiated through ignoring the role principles play in interaction with rules. This, he says, has the upshot that concrete legal questions always involve appraisal of the overall balance in a constellation of principles as one interprets a legal problem involving the contested application of rules to facts. Rules that incorporate standards, says Dworkin, function much as do principles, in that they call for a measure of balancing.

As will be seen in what follows, I agree with Dworkin in rejecting the 'delegated legislation' model, though I do not accept all the implications Dworkin derives from his interpretivist approach. Nevertheless, we can take up some of what Hart says. As he points out, we face a standing possibility of conflicts of interests or of values, and the case of negligence in the law of torts or delict is a case in point. On the one hand we set value upon the security of persons and their property and their economic interests from damage resulting from others' acts. On this account, we think it right and proper that each person take care to avoid inflicting bodily harm on others or damaging their property or economic well-being. On the other hand, we set value upon the freedom of individuals to pursue their own activities and way of life without having to undertake an intolerable burden of precautions against the risks of damage to others. The law has to express a balance between these values in general terms, and it expresses this balance by prescribing that such care has to be taken as would be taken by a reasonable and prudent person. But just as this implies in general terms the striking of a balance between the two values of relative security from harm and relative liberty to do as you like, so it points in particular situations to a critical ranking of relevant values in their particular manifestations.

Judicial dicta are readily available to back this up. In *Read v J. Lyons & Co. Ltd.*[26] the plaintiff, a government inspector working in a munitions factory in wartime, was injured by an explosion in the shell-filling shop of the factory. She sued for damages, arguing that the factory proprietor was subject to *Rylands v Fletcher* strict liability, and accordingly that she was entitled to compensation without proof of any fault in the conduct of the operations of manufacturing

---

[24] Even so, it has been held that Directives can themselves have direct effect. See Case 41/74 *Van Duyn v Home Office* [1974] ECR 1337 and Case 148/78 *Ratti* [1979] ECR 1629, the arguments in which are lucidly analysed by Sionaidh Douglas-Scott in her *Constitutional Law of the European Union* (Harlow: Longman/Pearson Education, 2002) 288–91.

[25] R. Dworkin, *Taking Rights Seriously* (London: Duckworth, 2nd impression, 1978) ch. 2; also now *Law's Empire* (Cambridge, Mass.: Harvard University. Press, 1986) pp. 280–2.

[26] [1947] AC 156.

shells. The House of Lords rejected this argument. Lord Macmillan stressed that:[27] 'the process of evolution [of the law] has been from the principle that every man acts at his peril and is liable for all the consequences of his acts to the principle that a man's freedom of action is subject only to the obligation not to infringe any duty of care he owes to others'. In the particular case, indeed, it was argued that an exception to the modern principle existed in the case of 'things and operations dangerous in themselves', but as to this Lord Macmillan observed that:[28]

[I]n the case of dangerous things and operations the law has recognised that a special responsibility exists to take care. But I do not think that it has ever been laid down that there is absolute liability apart from negligence where persons are injured in consequence of the use of such things or the conduct of such operations. In truth it is a matter of degree. Every activity in which man engages is fraught with some possible element of danger to others. Experience shows that even from acts apparently innocuous injury to others may result. The more dangerous the act the greater is the care that must be taken in performing it.

Here is a pretty straightforward judicial exposition both of the standard argument in favour of upholding a requirement of 'reasonable care' rather than 'strict liability' and of the argument acknowledging that the degree of care required as 'reasonable' must vary according to the risks at stake. This is indeed 'a matter of degree'. Since no legislature either can or should try to foresee all particular situations of risk, it neither can nor should seek to make for all purposes detailed rules about precautions to be taken. It is sufficient that the law prescribe the standard of care as that which is reasonable, and defer the evaluation of particular risks to particular cases.

Still, the question of reasonableness as a matter of due care in the law of civil liability for harm negligently caused is merely one illustration of the general point. It can be made no less vividly with regard to the use of 'reasonableness' in public law as a criterion for good decision-making by public authorities. One can summarize, and inevitably oversimplify, the relevant body of law,[29] as follows. Every public power of decision-making, whether judicial, quasi-judicial, or administrative must be exercised reasonably, that is, with proper regard to relevant considerations, and without any regard to irrelevant considerations.[30] The test of relevance in this case is governed by the terms in which and the objects for which the power of decision-making is granted by law.[31] Provided that the decision maker has grounded his/her decision upon a general appraisal of all the relevant factors, and has not acted upon any irrelevant considerations, the decision cannot be quashed by the courts merely on the ground that it is erroneous 'upon the merits'. Only if the decision is one that no reasonable person could have reached

---

[27] At 171.   [28] At 172.

[29] See Lord Irvine of Lairg, 'Judges as Decision-makers: the Theory and Practice of *Wednesbury* Review' [1996] *Public Law* pp. 59–78.

[30] See, e.g., *Anisminic v Foreign Compensation Commission* [1969] 2 AC 197.

[31] See, e.g., *Padfield v Minister of Agriculture* [1968] AC 997.

upon any reasonable evaluation of the relevant factors, may the decision be reviewed and quashed in a court.[32]

Again, what justifies resort to the requirement of reasonableness is the existence of a plurality of factors requiring to be evaluated in respect of their relevance to a common focus of concern (in this case a decision to be made by a public body for public purposes). Unreasonableness consists in ignoring some relevant factor or factors, or in treating as relevant what ought to be ignored. Alternatively, it may involve some gross distortion of the relative values of different factors. Even though different people can come to different evaluations in such questions of balance, and a variety of evaluations could be accepted as falling within the range of reasonable opinions about that balance, the range has some limits. Some opinions are so eccentric or idiosyncratic that they are not accepted as valid judgements at all.

As Kent Greenawalt and Duncan Kennedy have shown,[33] what is presupposed in any resort to reasonableness as a standard is that there is some topic or focus of concern to which, in accordance with variable circumstances, various factors are relevant. These then have to be set in an overall balance of values one way or the other. Kennedy observes that legal standards typically embody a relatively specific subset of social values, and one would be inclined to concur for values like 'fairness', 'due care', 'due process', 'natural justice', or the like. But in the case of the 'reasonable', there is not the same degree of localization of values. What is reasonable in the particular circumstances depends upon an evaluation of the competing factors of decision, and what factors of decision are relevant (and thus in competition) is highly context-dependent. The very thing that justifies the law's recourse to such a complex standard as reasonableness in the formulation of principles or rules for the guidance of officials or citizens is the existence of topics or focuses of concern to which a plurality of value-laden factors is relevant in a context-dependent way.

2. Interpreting 'Reasonableness'

There must be at least two ranges of variation within the variables to which any question of reasonableness relates. The topics to which reasonableness connects are variable, and the factors relevant to judgement vary according to the topic. The topic, as noted several times already, may be decisions by public authorities, or decisions about guilt in criminal trials, or activities of persons which are potentially harmful to other individuals, or contractual relationships, or marital relationships, or any of many others determined by legislators or judges.

---

[32] See, e.g., *Associated Provincial Picture Houses Ltd. v Wednesbury Corporation* [1948] 1 KB 223; *Secretary of State for Education and Science v Tameside M.B.C.* [1977] AC 1014; *Malloch v Aberdeen Corporation (No. 2)* 1974 SLT 253.

[33] See *Objectivity* pp. 144–5, quoting D. Kennedy, 'Form and Substance in Private Law Adjudication', *Harvard Law Rev.* 103 (1976) 1685 at 1700–1; and see D. Kennedy, *A Critique of Adjudication: Fin de Siècle* (Cambridge, Mass.: Harvard University Press, 1997) p. 139.

Given this variability of topic, there are necessarily certain questions about reasonableness which are pure questions of law, that is, of the proper interpretation of the law. What are properly to be treated as the factors and values relevant to a given topic? That is a question of the correct interpretation of the law as it bears upon the topic. It is quite common that statutes prescribing a standard of reasonableness explicitly indicate relevant factors. Thus, for example, in relation to England and Wales, the Occupiers' Liability Act 1957 requires that every occupier of premises 'take such care as in all the circumstances of the case is reasonable to see that the visitor will be reasonably safe in using the premises for the purposes for which he is invited or permitted by the occupier to be there'.[34] Then the Act further provides as follows:[35]

The circumstances relevant for the present purpose include the degree of care, and want of care, which would ordinarily be looked for in such a visitor, so that (for example) in proper cases—

    (a) an occupier must be prepared for children to be less careful than adults and

    (b) an occupier may expect that a person, in the exercise of his calling, will appreciate and guard against any special risks ordinarily incident to it, so far as the occupier leaves him free to do so.

Again, the Unfair Contract Terms Act 1977 makes provision whereby the courts can control exemption clauses in contracts between suppliers and consumers of goods and services. Any contractual term which seeks to exempt a party from his normal legal liabilities may be struck down if it is not reasonable, as to which the Act makes the following further provision:[36]

In determining whether . . . a contract term satisfies the requirement of reasonableness, regard shall be had in particular to . . . any of the following [matters] which appear to be relevant

    (a) the strength of the bargaining positions of the parties relative to each other, taking into account (among other things) alternative means by which the customer's requirements could be met;

    (b) whether the customer received an inducement to agree to the term, or, in accepting it, had an opportunity of entering into a similar contract with other persons, but without having to accept a similar term;

    (c) whether the customer knew or ought reasonably to have known of the existence and extent of the term (having regard, among other things, to any custom of the trade and any previous course of dealing between the parties)

    (d) where the term excludes or restricts any relevant liability if some condition is not complied with, whether it was reasonable at the time to expect that compliance with that condition would be practicable;

---

[34] Occupiers' Liability Act 1957, section 2(1).   [35] Id. section 2(3).
[36] Unfair Contract Terms Act 1977, section 11(2) and Schedule 2.

(e) whether the goods were manufactured, processed or adapted to the special order of the customer.

In both the instances quoted, the legislature has given explicit but non-exclusive guidance as to factors which are relevant to a judgement of reasonableness in respect of the topic in question. Similar attempts to give a partial definition of factors relevant to judgements about reasonableness in particular contexts are commonly and regularly to be found in judicial dicta. The High Court of Australia has attempted to clarify the extent of the duty to take reasonable care in giving information or advice, the following being a useful dictum by Gibbs CJ:[37]

[I]t would appear to accord with general principle that a person should be under no duty to take reasonable care that advice or information which he gives to another is correct, unless he knows, or ought to know, that the other relies on him to take such reasonable care and may act on the information which he is given, and unless it would be reasonable for that person so to rely and act. It would not be reasonable to act in reliance on advice or information given casually on some social or informal occasion, or, generally speaking, unless the advice or information concerned 'a business or professional transaction whose nature makes clear the gravity of the inquiry and the importance and influence attached to the answer'.

In this case of *Shaddock v Parramatta City Council*, the High Court was, *inter alia*, deciding to override a restriction upon the range of liability for negligent misstatements established by the Judicial Committee of the Privy Council in an earlier Australian case,[38] in which the class of persons subjected to a duty of care was those persons who have, or hold themselves out to the public as having, professional skill upon some matter upon which they choose to give advice. As Mason J observed in *Shaddock*'s case,[39] the justifying ground for such a restriction is some such policy ground as that indicated in the second edition of the *American Restatement of the Law of Torts*, namely that: 'When the harm that is caused is only pecuniary loss, the courts have found it necessary to adopt a more restricted rule of liability, because of the extent to which misinformation may be, and may be expected to be, circulated, and the magnitude of the losses which may follow from reliance on it.'[40] But Mason J rejected this as sufficient justification for the restriction envisaged, because[41]

In the first place, it denies a remedy to those who sustain serious loss at the hands of those who are not members of the class and whose conduct is negligent. Secondly, it ignores the availability of insurance as a protection against liability. Thirdly, there is no logic in

---

[37] *Shaddock v Paramatta City Council* [198 l] 55 ALJR 713, at p. 715, quoting from *Hedley Byrne & Co Ltd v Heller & Partners Ltd* [1964] AC 465, at 539, per Lord Pearce; and compare now *Caparo Industries v Dickman* [1990] 2 AC 605, [1990] 1 All ER 568 at p. 574, per Lord Bridge of Harwich.

[38] *Mutual Life and Citizens' Assurance Co Ltd v Evatt* [1971] AC 793.

[39] *Shaddock's* case [1981] 55 ALJR 713 at 723.

[40] American Law Institute, *Restatement of the Law, seconds: torts, 2d* (St. paul, minn.: American Law Institute Publishers, 1965–) para. 552.

[41] *Shaddock's* case [1981] 55 ALJR 713 at 723.

excluding from the class of persons liable for negligent misstatement persons who, though they may not exercise skill and competence, assume a responsibility to give advice or information to others on serious matters which may occasion loss or damage. Finally, the rule, recently established by *Caltex Oil (Australia) Pty. Ltd. v The Dredge 'Willemstad'* (1976)136 C.L.R. 529, is that economic loss not consequential upon property damage, may be recoverable from those whose negligence occasions it.

One might here remark, almost parenthetically, that we have here yet another not uncharacteristic example of consequentialist reasoning by a judge. In arguing in favour both of the more extended interpretation of 'reasonable reliance' and thus of the more extensive view of liability for negligent misstatement, Mason J is advancing in his first and second points consequentialist grounds for favouring the given interpretation. He deplores the juridical consequence of leaving without any remedy a class of persons likely to suffer damage through negligence, even though liability for this is potentially insurable. Typically, he backs these considerations up with arguments showing how the more generous liability rule coheres with related parts of the law, albeit not required for strict consistency with them.

Nor is this an unusual feature of such arguments concerning the interpretation of what is reasonable. Consider the New York case of *American Book Co. v Yeshiva University Development Foundation Inc.*,[42] concerning the interpretation of a covenant in a lease under which the tenant of commercial premises was restricted from sub-letting the premises without the written consent of the landlord, such consent not to be 'unreasonably withheld'. The Book Company wished to sub-let to an organization called 'Planned Parenthood—World Population'. The Yeshiva University, as successor in title to the landlord with whom the lease had originally been made, withheld consent on the ground of 'philosophical and ideological "inconsistencies" between itself and the proposed subtenant, [and] the "controversial" nature of the subtenant'. (The controversial nature in question was Planned Parenthood's character as a propagandist for contraception.) Greenfield J ruled that only 'objective' grounds for refusal of consent were acceptable as grounds for 'reasonable' refusal, that is:

standards which are readily measurable criteria of proposed subtenant's or assignee's acceptability from the point of view of any landlord:
(a) financial responsibility; (b) the 'identity' or 'business character' of the subtenant— i.e. his suitability for the particular building; (c) the legality of the proposed use; (d) the nature of the occupancy—i.e. office, factory, clinic or whatever.

This denied recourse to 'subjective' grounds of objection based on the particular likes and dislikes or philosophical, religious, or ideological convictions of the landlord. For the learned judge's ruling on the interpretation of 'reasonableness' as here implying an objective standard, we find very characteristic reasoning pointing to the inexpedient and unjust consequences of adopting the subjective

---

[42] 297 NYS 2d 156 (1969).

standard: 'if indeed the potentiality for controversy were a serviceable standard for measuring the acceptability of a subtenancy, many of our most socially useful institutions would be homeless vagrants on the streets, and our buildings would be tenanted by bland, unexceptionable models of propriety and dullness. Even proponents of unpopular ideas are entitled to a roof over their heads.' The point just considered deals with one of the most important general aspects of the interpretation of 'reasonableness' as a standard, namely its typically objective character, to which we have already alluded. Even here, though, the question can sometimes be an open one whether, for a given topic, the reasonable has to be construed as that which is objectively reasonable, without regard to personal peculiarities or predilections of individuals in a particular relationship. Cannot 'reasonable' signify what is subjectively reasonable, reasonable for a particular individual in a particular setting?

On grounds that were classically expressed by Holmes J[43] and by Lord Reid,[44] the ordinary presumption is that the test of reasonableness is, in the sense indicated, an objective test. The rights of persons against others in society ought to be fixed by common inter-subjective criteria, not by reference to particular peculiarities of individuals. At least in all matters affecting the rights of persons in civil law or in public law, there should normally be an objective grounding of the rights established. On the other hand, as Lord Reid once pointed out,[45] in matters of criminal liability, at least for serious crimes, we should always apply a very strong presumption in favour of subjective *mens rea* or at least subjective culpability on the part of the person accused.

Once we see the matter in this light, we can, however, see ground for a different judgement in such an area as family law, given the intensely personal quality of relationships (for example) between spouses. Lord Reid himself once remarked that 'In matrimonial cases we are not concerned with the reasonable man, as we are in cases of negligence. We are dealing with this man and this woman and the fewer a priori assumptions we make about them the better.' This statement was in turn adopted by the Court of Appeal in England in ruling on the proper interpretation of the 'reasonable' in the context of divorce law. The statute provided that divorce might be granted if a marriage had irretrievably broken down on the ground that (*inter alia*) one spouse behaved toward the other in such a way that that other 'cannot reasonably be expected' to go on living with this spouse. The test to be applied must take account of the subjective propensities and characters of the two individuals in the relationship of marriage: 'would any right thinking person come to the conclusion that this husband has behaved in such a way that this wife cannot reasonably be expected to live with him, taking into account the

[43] O. W. Holmes Jr., *The Common Law* (Boston, Mass.: 1887) pp. 110–111.

[44] Lord Reid, 'The Law and the Reasonable Man' *Proceedings of the British Academy* 54 (1968) 189–205, pp. 200–201.

[45] Ibid., and see Lord Reid's dicta in *Warner v Metropolitan Police Commissioner* [1969] 2 AC 256, [1968] 2 All ER 356.

whole of the circumstances and the characters and personalities of the parties?'[46] This stress on the subjectivity of the spouses, and the related subjectivity of the test for reasonableness as between them appears at first sight to go against the general requirement of universality or universalizability in rulings upon the law and its interpretation.[47] Obviously, there must between each set of marriage partners be a different 'personal equation', so that what is reasonable as between any one pair may not be reasonable for any other, and we shall lose all view of the universal in a thicket of particulars. But on reflection, this doubt is groundless. We may make it a universal rule always to apply an objective test of reasonableness, for example in negligence cases (and we may have good justifications for so doing), and yet make it an equally universal rule always to apply a subjective test of what is reasonable for any particular spouse in relation to his/her partner in matrimonial cases, having here a sound justification for applying the subjective test, precisely because of the type of relationship in view in any such case.

What would be objectionable would be to vary the interpretation of 'reasonable' as between subjective and objective within a single type of case having a single common topic. In public law, the much criticized wartime case of *Liversidge v Anderson*[48] ruled that a Minister might be held to have 'reasonable cause to believe' that a person had hostile origins or associations, and therefore to be acting lawfully in causing him to be detained under the Defence (General) Regulations, 1939, provided only that he honestly believed that he had reasonable cause for his belief. In this branch of law, there are the most powerful reasons for treating criteria of reasonableness as being objective, not subjective. Hence even the special exigencies of wartime can hardly be pled in aid to justify giving a special subjective interpretation to that criterion. In fact, the decision in *Liversidge v Anderson* has been so generally disapproved as to be of practically no weight as a precedent. It is an unjustified exception to a well-justified general rule for the interpretation of reasonableness as an objective standard in public law.[49]

Let it be remarked again that the legitimate variability as between objective and subjective grounds of reasonableness, dependent in turn on variations of topic or of focus of concern, is only one of the elements of variability in the interpretations which may properly be given of the criterion or standard of 'reasonableness'. What the present discussion has shown is that 'reasonableness' is not itself a first order value, but a higher-order value which we exemplify in considering a balance of

[46] Per Dunn, J. in *Livingstone-Stallard v Livingstone-Stallard* [1974] Fam. 47 at 54, cited with approval by Roskill LJ in *O'Neill v O'Neill* [1975] 3 All ER 289 at 295; emphasis added.

[47] For a discussion of the requirements of universality in legal rulings, see Chapter 5 above. On the point of present difficulty, it is worth remembering that, as R. M. Hare argues, a principle may be universal even though it contains reference to 'bound variables', as if we were to say that 'Every married person ought to treat his or her spouse in a way that his or her spouse finds reasonable.' See R. M. Hare, *Moral Thinking* (Oxford: Clarendon Press, 1981). Compare Greenawalt on 'generality', *Objectivity* pp. 141–62.   [48] [1942] AC 206.

[49] See *Nakkuda Ali v Jayaratne* [1951] AC 66 at 76–7 and compare the robust views of the present House of Lords as expressed in the *Terrorist Suspects* case.

first order, or anyway lower-order values and coming to a conclusion about their application. The task of interpretation of 'reasonable' in a given context is that of identifying the values, interests, and the like that are relevant to the given focus of attention. This in turn depends on the types of situation or relationship that are in issue, and on a view of the governing principle or rationale of the branch of law concerned.

3. What is Reasonable, and is this a Question of Fact?

It is worth observing at the outset of this section how strange it appears on the face of things to call questions of reasonableness questions of 'fact' at all. To conclude in a given case that a person has acted or decided reasonably or unreasonably is surely to make a value judgement rather than a judgement of fact. Yet 'questions of fact' are what Scots lawyers and common lawyers call such judgements. Lord Denning once said the following about the analogous case of judicial determination of an employer's duty to take reasonable care for the safety of their employees:[50] 'What is "a proper system of work" is a matter for evidence, not for the law books. It changes as the conditions of work change. The standard goes up as men become wiser. It does not stand still as the law sometimes does.' It is important that we appreciate Lord Denning's point about the mutability-through-time of judgments concerning what is proper or reasonable given changing facts and circumstances. Precautions at work which were once treated as unusual or extravagant may come to be accepted as normal and proper.[51] Advances in medical knowledge may reveal risks in simple procedures such as the administration of injections, risks avoidable by the taking of new precautions; then the reasonableness of taking such precautions changes and is governed by the new state of available knowledge in the profession.[52] What can reasonably be expected of a marriage partner may change with changes in the social milieu—what husband in the present day could think unreasonable an expectation that he participate in domestic chores which even forty years ago were firmly identified as women's work? As Lord Rodger of Earlsferry has remarked, human rights law likewise exhibits a readiness to adjust the standards of protection in accordance with changing social conditions and attitudes.[53]

But that is not the only point to be taken from Lord Denning's remark. For it reminds us also of two particular features of decision-making in the common law context. First, we must remember that there is a division of legal labour whereby judges are masters of the law but juries are masters of the facts. It is for the judge to

---

[50] See *Qualcast (Wolverhampton) Ltd v Haynes* [1959] AC 743 at 762.
[51] Ibid. Cf. *General Cleaning Contractors Ltd v Christmas* [1953] AC 180.
[52] See, e.g., *Roe v Minister of Health* [1954] 2 QB 66.
[53] Lord Rodger of Earlsferry, 'A Time for Everything under the Law: Some Reflections on Retrospectivity' *Law Quarterly Review* 121 (2005) 57–79 at 75–7.

give authoritative guidance on questions of law and of its interpretation, including interpretations of the criteria of reasonableness such as were discussed above in Section 2 of this chapter. It is for the jury to decide whether these criteria are satisfied by the facts of the given case. Most obviously, in a criminal trial, it is for the judge to explain to the jury that the prosecution must prove its case 'beyond reasonable doubt', and what that means. But it is for the jury to decide whether that standard of proof has been satisfied in the case before it.

Secondly, even though (outside the sphere of criminal law) resort to jury trial is on the decline, the distinction remains between questions of law and questions of fact on the basis of how these would be apportioned between judges and juries, even where a professional judge or judges are deciders of both sorts of question. This has an obvious bearing on the doctrine of precedent. Later courts and lower courts are obliged to respect decisions by earlier courts or higher ones on questions of law (including therefore questions as to the proper interpretation of, e.g. criteria of reasonableness). The same obligatory force, however, does not attach to decisions on the facts of particular cases, including the question whether, in a given case, a person acted reasonably. The latter point was the one most at issue in the case from which Lord Denning's remarks above were quoted. His argument was aimed at stressing that a court's judgment as to what is (for example) a 'proper system of work' in all the circumstances of one case does not constitute a binding precedent of direct applicability to other cases. Hence the importance of his stress on the possibility that social standards may change, and with them conclusions as to 'proper system of work', 'reasonable care', and such like.

These considerations are of importance in understanding why lawyers include questions about reasonableness as falling within what they classify as 'questions of fact', even although they are also in part at least questions of value. Certainly, on any view, they are, as Lord Denning put it, 'matters for evidence'. We must know in any case what was done and what was not done, and for what reasons, and what might otherwise have been done or omitted, and what is normal practice in such matters, before we can judge of the reasonableness of the actings and omissions in view. Analytically, at least, the process of judgement is one which has two phases—the phase of discovering what happened and why, and the phase of appreciating that which happened in the light of the relevant value-factors.

In a famous essay, John Wisdom[54] once drew attention to what he took to be a special peculiarity of legal reasoning, in the light of which it could not be classified either as deductive or as inductive reasoning in the ordinary sense of these terms, but was in effect *sui generis*. He pointed out that the reasoning process in law is not like a chain of mathematical reasoning, where each step follows from the preceding one, and where any error at any step invalidates all which follows. Rather, legal

---

[54] J. Wisdom, 'Gods' in *Proceedings of the Aristotelian Society* 56 (1944), esp. at pp. 157–8; the essay is reprinted in Wisdom's *Philosophy and Psychoanalysis* (Oxford: Basil Blackwell, 1953) pp. 249–54, sensitively criticized and expanded by William Twining and David Miers, in their *How to Do Things with Rules* (London: Butterworths, 4th edn, 1999), 361–64.

reasoning is a matter of weighing and considering all the factors which 'severally co-operate' in favour of a particular conclusion, and balancing them against the factors which tell against that conclusion. In the end, the conclusion is to be reached rather on a balance of reasons than by inference from premises to conclusions or from known to unknown facts. The reasons for a conclusion are commonly mutually independent, offering a set of supports for the conclusion, so that failure in one of them does not leave the conclusion unsupported; such reasons are, in Wisdom's vivid phrase, 'like the legs of a chair, not the links of a chain'.

To accept Wisdom's thesis as a complete account or description of legal reasoning would be to mistake the part for the whole. But the part to which it applies, and with which his essay explicitly dealt, is the very part that is under review at the moment. As to that, Wisdom captures exactly and vividly the way in which we must bring a plurality of factors together into consideration when, as a 'matter for evidence', we seek to pass judgement upon the reasonableness of some decision, or action, or omission, or choice to rely upon advice, or contractual provision, or matrimonial expectation, or whatever. What is necessary now is, however, to move beyond general description of the process to the scrutiny of particular cases in a variety of fields to see if we can establish how exactly to understand the process so often, but perhaps misleadingly, called 'weighing' or 'balancing' the various factors of judgement that are in play.[55]

We may start with problems of public law. How do we find judges evaluating the 'reasonableness' of public authorities' decisions? The answer here seems to be that the grounds for the decision made have to be evaluated for their relevancy to the making of the decision in the light of the aims and purposes of a statutory power of decision-making. Thus in *Padfield v Minister of Agriculture*[56] the Minister had refused to exercise his statutory power to appoint a committee to investigate complaints made by members of the Milk Marketing Board about the scheme established for fixing the price of milk. Each of the reasons stated by the Minister was reviewed in terms of its relevance to the statutory Milk Marketing scheme. The House of Lords concluded that the Minister's stated reasons showed his refusal to have been motivated by irrelevant reasons and thus to have been calculated to frustrate rather than promote the purposes of the legislation. On that ground, the Minister was ordered 'to consider the complaint of the appellants

---

[55] Twining and Miers, in their *How to Do Things with Rules*, accepting some doubts I have expressed about too ready recourse to the metaphor of 'weight' in this context, have this to say: 'In the dialectical process which typifies legal argumentation, preferences are expressed in terms of one argument being more or less convincing, or stronger, than another; and such preferences are defensible notwithstanding that no exact and objective measurement of them is possible, so long as some criteria exist which are recognized by the disputants. The process of making and expressing choices may be conveniently described as one of balancing or weighing arguments; but we should also recognize the limits of such metaphors . . .'. (p. 364). Jonathan Dancy's objection to the idea of 'weight' in the context of a holistic conception of moral reasoning was already noted in Chapter 4 above.

[56] [1968] AC 997.

according to law'. Such a case has to be distinguished from one in which a public authority's decision is based on a genuine review of relevant grounds for decision, and is not motivated by any irrelevant grounds, but is complained against on the ground of having come to a false judgement on the relative merits of relevant reasons for and against a particular course of action. Within this area, the public authority's conclusion as to what is right or reasonable must be taken as conclusive.[57]

In such cases on the relevancy of grounds of decision, it obviously makes sense to say that among the plurality of grounds offered, each may 'severally co-operate' with every other in favour of the decision made and as showing it to be relevantly grounded. Yet the attack made upon the decision will seek to isolate some one or more of the grounds as having been both irrelevant and determinative of the decision. If a dominant motive for a decision is a wrong one, that may be fatal to it even though there are, or might be, perfectly acceptable other reasons for the same decision.[58] While 'reasonableness' may arise from a plurality of grounds, it may be that the presence of a single improper or irrelevant consideration is sufficient to 'tilt the balance' the other way.

The same may apply in relation to other legal topics of 'reasonableness'. For example, in the law of delict or torts, the central question is commonly whether some harm suffered by the plaintiff resulted from a want of 'reasonable care' on the defendant's part. It is worth remembering that in such cases the burden rests upon the plaintiff to show that the defendant did not take reasonable care. So for example, it must be proved both that harm was suffered by the plaintiff as a result of some act or event or state of affairs within the defendant's control and that it was open to the defendant to have taken some precaution which would have prevented the occurrence of the harm. In one case, a bus passenger fell out of the open door of a bus while making his way towards the door with a view to alighting at the next stop.[59] It was argued that this accident need not have happened if either the door had been kept closed or a central pillar (in addition to nine other existing handholds) had been provided as a handhold on the bus platform. Failure to take one or other such precaution, it was contended, amounted to a failure to take reasonable care. As against this, it was shown that (a) buses of this type had been run for several years without such accident occurring and (b) that either of the possible precautions would have required great expense and caused great inconvenience in the use of the buses. So the House of Lords held that the precaution lack of which was alleged to be unreasonable was one which it was reasonable not to take. This involved comparing the value to be set on general convenience in

---

[57] See *Secretary of State for Education and Science v Tameside M.B.C* [1977] AC 1014.

[58] As *Padfield's* case itself indicates.

[59] *Wyngrove's C. B. v Scottish Omnibuses Ltd* 1966 SC(HL) 47; nowadays, buses have automatically opening and closing doors, and the standard of 'reasonable precautions' for passengers' safety has surely risen, in the manner mentioned in connection with Lord Denning's opinion—see n. 50 above and referring text.

the use of the buses, taken in contrast with the low degree of risk established by the evidence in relation to the type of accident involved in the case. By contrast, where window cleaning employers failed to require employees to take any precautions in cleaning windows while balancing on window ledges, this was held to be unreasonable even although it had been shown that two of the possible safety systems would be impracticable, in some cases, and prohibitively costly in others. Provided there was some precaution that could practicably be taken to diminish the obviously high risk of falling from window ledges, it was unreasonable not to take it. Avoiding obvious risks to the life and limb of one's employees is of high value.[60]

That in such cases there is necessarily a comparative evaluation of factors for and against is very obvious, and well illustrated by *Bolton v Stone*.[61] A woman walking along a street outside a cricket ground was injured by a cricket ball struck out of the ground by a batsman. Such mighty hits of the ball were naturally rare, but did happen from time to time. To guard against the risk of injury to pedestrians, it would have been necessary to erect a fence of some height all round the ground. It was argued that failure to take this precaution amounted to a breach of duty on the part of the cricket club.

Those being the facts, a breach of duty has taken place if they show the appellants guilty of a failure to take reasonable care to prevent the accident. One may phrase it as 'reasonable care' or 'ordinary care' or 'proper care' but the fact remains that, unless there has been something which a reasonable man would blame as falling beneath the standard of conduct that he would set for himself or require of his neighbour, there has been no breach of legal duty. And here, I think, the respondent's case breaks down. It seems to me that a reasonable man, taking account of the chances against an accident happening, would not have felt himself called upon either to abandon the use of the ground for cricket or to increase the height of his surrounding fences. He would have done what the appellants did; in other words, he would have done nothing.[62]

Here we have to set on the one hand the (implicit) value to be attached to the traditional English game of cricket, the cost of fencing the ground, and the low risk of pedestrians actually being hit against on the other hand the value of

---

[60] *General Cleaning Co v Christmas* [1953] AC 180. A more up-to-date example, this one concerning duties of disclosure in an insurance context is the following holding of Potter J.: 'It was the duty of PUM as prudent managing agents seeking unlimited protection . . . to consider with care what required to be disclosed to a prospective reinsurer; in particular, the mounting claims for asbestosis and DES which were the reason why reinsurance was sought in the first place. Further, that duty extended to disclosure of facts which were arguably material *so as to avoid unnecessary risk of avoidance' Aiken v Stewart Wrightson* [1995] 3 All ER 449 at 481.   [61] [1951] AC 850.

[62] Ibid. at p. 903. For a criticism of this line of reasoning, on the ground that in fact the cricket club and other cricket clubs would have had to pay for insurance, not pay for new fencing, had the decision gone the other way, see P. S. Atiyah, *Accidents Compensation and the Law* (London: Butterworths, 1970) pp. 467–9; the most recent edition of this work, P. Cane's *Atiyah's Accidents Compensation and the Law* (London: Butterworths, 5th edn, 1993) drops this point, but see p. 35 for a valuable discussion of the weighing of rival values, and p. 150 for a suggestion that there might be liability here without negligence.

personal security from bodily injury. The House of Lords concluded that the former values in this case counted for more than the latter. The plaintiff had pointed to a failure of precautions—but this failure was not evaluated as unreasonable set against the other values at stake. Likewise, in cases where risks are taken in situations of emergency, the degree of risk which it is held reasonable to take is greater than in ordinary circumstances. If you are trying to save lives, you may reasonably have to take some quite serious risks in doing so.

In all such cases, it is up to one party to show a failure of reasonableness, to identify the alleged lack of reasonable care; but then the other party counters this by showing the difficulty or impracticality or excessive costliness in terms of relevant values of that which it is alleged he should have done. It is in that process of countering an allegation of failure to do what is reasonable that we find recourse to Wisdom's plurality of grounds severally cooperating to cancel out the allegation.

The same applies in other spheres, for example the contractual or proprietary. We saw earlier how in the *Yeshiva University* case[63] Greenfield J ruled that relevant criteria for reasonable objection to a subtenant of leased property must be 'objective' ones. That being so, on the facts of the particular case it was fatal to the landlord's objection that the proposed subtenant of the premises did satisfy all the objective criteria under scrutiny. The substantial ground of objection being the subjective hostility of the landlord to the subtenant's activities as an advocate of contraception, that fell to be dismissed as an unreasonable objection.

We can find similar reasoning in the cases on contracts in restraint of trade; at common law contractual provisions which fetter a person's freedom to trade as he wishes are illegal except where they constitute a reasonable protection for the other party and are reasonable in the public interest. In *Dumbarton Steamboat Co Ltd, v MacFarlane*,[64] the pursuers had bought over the carriers' business of the defender and his partner, who were to be employed by the pursuer company and who undertook to procure for the company the benefit of their own previous business and also not to 'carry on or be concerned in any business of a like or similar kind in the United Kingdom' for a period of ten years. Three years after the agreement had been made, the defender was dismissed by the company and then recommenced business as a carrier in the Dumbarton area. It was established that in his new business he had been actively canvassing former customers of himself and of the company, in breach of his agreement. Upon this point, the pursuers were granted an interdict to prevent him from infringing a provision perfectly reasonable in the context of the sale of a business and its goodwill. By contrast, on the other point, as Lord Moncrieff said:[65] 'As the business which was sold by the defender to the pursuers was of a very limited character, the restriction which would prevent him from carrying on the business of carrier in any part of the United Kingdom, however remote from Dumbarton and unconnected with the Dumbarton trade, is excessive, and should not receive effect.'

---

[63] 297 NYS 2d 156 (1969).   [64] (1899)1 F 993.   [65] Ibid. at p. 998.

In the matrimonial cases, where one of the modern grounds for divorce as following from irretrievable breakdown of marriage is 'that the respondent has behaved in such a way that the petitioner cannot reasonably be expected to live with the respondent'[66] the criteria of what is reasonable, as we saw earlier, are subjective rather than objective. But it remains a matter of weighing the evidence, and of seeing whether things have been done by one to another which go beyond what that person with his or her character can reasonably accept. For this purpose, the petitioner must establish something seriously objectionable to him or her about the other spouse's behaviour. Hence the case put by the petitioner husband in *Pheasant v Pheasant* was necessarily an insufficient one, as appears from Ormrod J's summary of it:[67]

The husband was unable to establish anything which could be regarded as a serious criticism of the wife's conduct or behaviour. His case, quite simply is that she has not been able to give him the spontaneous, demonstrative attention which he says that his nature demands and for which he craves. In these circumstances he says that it is impossible for him to live with the wife any longer and that in consequence he cannot reasonably be expected to live with her.

There is a sharp contrast between such a case and that of *O'Neill v O'Neill*.[68] After eighteen years of somewhat mobile married life, the husband having been an airline pilot and having been forced to retire for medical reasons, the O'Neills bought an apartment in which to settle down. For two years the husband worked single-handed on trying to renovate the flat, a process which involved the removal of the lavatory door and the lifting of most of the floorboards in the house. His wife found this intolerable due to the loss of privacy and the impossibility of having guests at home in the circumstances. Eventually she left with the two children of the marriage. The husband responded by writing her a letter casting doubt on the legitimacy of the children. She petitioned for divorce on the ground of his behaviour having been such that she could not reasonably be expected to live with him. The husband argued that her objection was in effect to his character rather than to his behaviour. But the Court of Appeal rejected this. As a woman who had for long desired a settled home with neighbours and friends, Mrs O'Neill had much to object to in her husband's conduct in trying to renovate the house, on top of which there was the unacceptable act of suggesting that the children were illegitimate. What is at issue is whether in the behaviour or conduct of one spouse there has been something objectionable to the other, which can be alleged to go beyond what it is reasonable for him or her to tolerate. Whether it does go beyond that limit is to be assessed in the light of allegedly counteracting considerations advanced by that other.

That is, in sum, the dialectic of debate upon the reasonable. Starting from a view, most probably an open-ended or non-exclusive view as to the criteria or

---

[66] Matrimonial Causes Act 1973 section 1(2)(b); Divorce (Scotland) Act 1976 section 1 (2)(b).
[67] [1972] 1 All ER 587 at 588.   [68] [1975] 3 All ER 289.

factors relevant to a given topic, an allegation must be made as to one or more failures under one or more criteria or factors. It is then for the other side to counter this alleged failure by reference to positive values under the same or other criteria or factors. In this sense the final judgment is one attained by a relative evaluation of the considerations offered on each side, taking them both separately and also in the light of any cumulative relevance two or more factors may have when taken together. The relative values of the factors brought into consideration may themselves be sensitive to the particular context rather than invariant in any case in which they occur (consider the matrimonial cases, in contrast to those involving negligence liability). For that reason, 'weighing' and 'balancing' may express too crudely the process of deciding whether, all things considered, they constitute not merely good and relevant reasons in themselves for what was done, but adequate or sufficient reasons for so doing even in the presence of the identified adverse factors.

It may, however, be impossibly self-denying to avoid completely the metaphor of 'weighing'. This is all right, as Twining and Miers stress,[69] provided we recognize that it is a metaphor. Reasons do not have weights as material objects do. To say that some reasons for action or value-factors bearing on action 'outweigh' others is almost to restate the initial problem rather than to solve it. For at best we *ascribe* greater or less weight to some reasons or factors than others, and the question is what are the grounds of such ascription.

Perhaps the answer to this question is best given by referring back to the 'procedural' aspect of reasoning. What is required is attention to, and deliberation over, the relative human importance of the different factors that enter judgment in any given case. Wherein lies relative importance? One important thing is how much people care about one thing rather than another, and surely there is no reason to leave out sense and sentiment, nor the actual psychological make-up of real people.[70] But bringing one's reflections beyond raw feeling and into the realm of the reasonable calls for something like Adam Smith's 'impartial spectator' procedure considered above.[71] A measure of weight is found in the sympathetic or empathetic response of the deliberator to the feelings of persons involved, after making adjustments for impartiality and adequate information. If this is so, there is bound to be for each of us an element of the subjective in every one of our best efforts at pure objectivity.

Many readers will consider that this chapter has ignored the obvious merits of applying an economic analysis to the task of giving an objective account of all the

---

[69] See the passage from *How to Do Things with Rules*, cited in this Chapter at n. 55 above.

[70] Heidi Li Feldman's 'Science, Reason, and Tort law: Looking for the Reasonable Person', cited above, n. 18, is an important and path-breaking work. She brings to our attention the empirical psychological work of Daniel Kahneman and others to show how far the construct of the 'reasonable man' can be rooted in ordinary people's attitudes to risk and risk-taking, and why this differs from the hypotheses built into rational choice theory. Feldman is now embarked on an 'Ethico-Psychological' project, aimed at further fleshing out the evaluative as well as descriptive components of 'reasonableness'. The present work is confessedly longer on ethics and shorter on psychology, but I am sure Feldman is right concerning the need to incorporate findings such as Kahneman's.

[71] See n. 18 above.

troublesome issues of relative evaluation that the discussion of reasonableness has thrown up. If preferences, or wealth conceived as aggregate satisfaction of preferences, can be counted and if different lots of them are fully commensurable, surely the best way to handle the dilemmas discussed in this chapter as issues of reasonableness is to translate them into these other terms. To satisfy most preferences, or to achieve the greatest overall wealth for the community is the best approach, and appeals to what is reasonable should be so understood. Responding to this, I have to say that it seems very doubtful whether full commensurability can be established in the same terms across the many topics in relation to which 'reasonableness' is in play. Is 'reasonable doubt' in matters of criminal evidence calculable by the same economic calculus as 'reasonable care' in negligence, 'unreasonable conduct' in divorce cases, or 'reasonableness' of an administrative decision? This is intuitively implausible. This does not mean that there are different concepts of reasonableness in issue, only that the conception in question is based on practical reasoning not purely on economic calculation. Evaluating different reasons and values in different settings does not require us to work through a different conceptual prism.

Supposing these doubts about economic analysis to be unfounded, the theoretical upshot of the error will be obvious. In effect, a kind of far-reaching consequent-ialism enters legal thought through recourse to 'reasonableness' and other similar concepts. For the use of the test of what is reasonable acts as a filter to permit calculation (perhaps rather crudely carried out) of what resolution of legal disputes, especially legal disputes universalized as type-cases, will yield in terms of maximum societal preference-satisfaction. This conclusion, if sound, will suggest that the conclusion of Chapter 6 was unnecessarily timid. To justify a legal decision on a problem case will involve applying tests that look to optimal societal consequences demonstrable by reference to economic argumentation. This would put in the shade the conclusions hitherto stated about the predominance in legal consequentialist reasoning of 'consequences as implications', alias 'juridical consequences'.

It is no part of the purpose of the present work to adjudicate about the much-contested issue of the validity of the 'economic analysis of law'. If it is valid, the present arguments will amount to a rather wordy (but possibly useful) prolego-menon to that analysis. If it is either invalid, or (as I suspect) more local than its proponents believe in the jurisprudential illumination it yields, there remains a different task for the present style of more rhetorical and discursive study of the elements of argumentation. In that case, a concern about 'juridical consequences' of contemplated legal decisions is of more general value. We might return to a theme introduced in Chapter 2. There, it was noted how T. M. Scanlon[72] suggests

---

[72] See T. M. Scanlon, 'Contractualism and Utilitarianism', in A. Sen and B. Williams (eds), *Utilitarianism and Beyond* (Cambridge: Cambridge University Press, 1982) pp. 103–28; and *What We Owe to Each Other* (Cambridge, Mass: Harvard University Press, 1998). Since no actual agreement or contract is involved in such reasoning, and obligations generated by or under it are not in fact contractual in character, it seems to me regrettable that this style of procedural testing of practical

that an action is wrong if any principle that permitted it would be one that, just by reason of its permitting such an action, could be reasonably rejected by any person whose aim was to find principles for the general regulation of behaviour that others, similarly motivated, could not reasonably reject.[73] Scanlon presents that as a test for the acceptability of moral principles. In that context, we may note that the stress is not on what people would do, or would object to other people doing. Rather it looks to the issue of what would be permissible and what people could object to being made permissible. That is, it concerns the morally normative implications of a decision, where the legal reasoning we have in mind concerns the legal-normative implications of possible rulings. The legal context is also one in which any prevailing doctrine of precedent is likely to make these normative implications binding or at least persuasive for future decision makers.

How, then, do we evaluate what one can object to making permissible, or obligatory, or an offence, or somebody's property or other right, or a valid exercise of power in law? These are the kinds of normative implications that universalized legal decisions point to. One possible answer is that one should review the reasonableness of the provision and of the possible objections to it. This utilizes the kind of multi-factorial reasoning we have analysed at such length in the present chapter. Sometimes, factors that will emerge will include likely behavioural consequences, and sometimes perhaps a full-scale application of economic analysis may even prove useful. But this is not likely to be the case every time.

In any event, one does not make decisions as to what there is best reason to do in a vacuum, certainly not where legal decisions are at stake. The values and other factors relevant to legal decisions are themselves woven into the fabric of the law. To understand this requires reflection on different problems of interpretation of legal materials—and related issues of classification. These in turn lead to a review of coherence and consistency as components of justice according to law.

principles has been dubbed 'contractualist'. But its value as a mode of reasoning is unaffected by the name it bears. Compare MacCormick, 'Justice as Impartiality: Assenting with Anti-contractualist Reservations' *Political Studies* 44 (1996) 305–10.

[73] Quoted from T. M. Scanlon, 'Promises and Contracts', in P. Benson (ed.), *The Theory of Contract Law* (Cambridge: Cambridge University Press, 2001) ch. 3.

10

Coherence, Principles, and Analogies

Introduction

That a piece of reasoning be coherent as a whole is one commonly accepted criterion of its soundness as reasoning.[1] Our problem is to make intelligible the nature of the criterion so set, and to show its place within a canon of rational justification. This chapter and the next will suggest that, in legal justification, there are two distinct sorts of test for coherence. The first, which we may call the *normative coherence* test, has to do with the justification of legal rulings or normative propositions more generally in the context of a legal system conceived as a normative order. The second, which we may call the *narrative coherence* test, has to do with the justification of findings of fact and the drawing of reasonable inferences from evidence. Apart from a few preliminary remarks, narrative coherence is the subject of the next chapter, normative coherence of this.

It remains to be seen how much normative coherence and narrative coherence have in common beyond name and assonance. Yet perhaps even from the outset we may allow this as a common feature of the two cases: either in normative or in narrative contexts, a lack of coherence in what is said involves a failure to make sense. An incoherent set of norms might be such that each could be fulfilled without infringing any other, yet the whole seems to make no sense as constituting or mapping out a reasonable order of conduct—imagine a house within which all inhabitants are to make their rooms as untidy as possible on Mondays, Wednesdays, and Fridays, then tidy them up to the highest perfection on Tuesdays, Thursdays, and Saturdays, Sundays being strictly observed as a day of rest. To have, and to observe, such house-rules is possible—but what sense does it make? Likewise an incoherent story, though it may contain no proposition which directly contradicts or logically entails a contradiction of any other proposition in the story, yet in some way fails to make sense. That a perfect stranger entered the

---

[1] Leonor Moral rightly points out that one should distinguish the issue of coherence in a legal system from that of coherence in an argument about applying the law. What I am driving at here is the way in which establishing that a particular ruling or interpretation helps to secure the coherence of the system, at any rate of the branch of law in issue, works as a (partial) justification of the interpretation or ruling in question. See L. Moral Soriano 'A Modest Notion of Coherence in Legal Reasoning: A Model for the European Court of Justice' *Ratio Juris* 16 (2003) 296–323. As for overall argumentative coherence, that is of concern throughout the present work.

house, that he therein committed a crime, and that the watchdog failed to bark, is a story which contains no contradictions; but once Sherlock Holmes has drawn our attention to it, we see that it does not make sense—it does not 'hang together'—no more than our crazy house rules hang together. But what do we mean by 'make sense', 'hanging together', 'coherence'?

Here as in previous writing,[2] I assume that 'coherence' can usefully be distinguished from consistency. This is partly a matter of fidelity to the nuance of ordinary language but more a matter of prejudice in favour of letting different words serve different purposes. So I interpret consistency as being satisfied by non-contradiction. A set of propositions is mutually consistent if each can without contradiction be asserted in conjunction with every other and with their conjunction. By contrast, coherence, as I said, is the property of a set of propositions which, taken together, 'makes sense' in its entirety. Complete consistency is not a necessary condition of coherence, since unlike consistency, coherence can be a matter of degree. A story can be coherent on the whole and as a whole, though it contains some internal inconsistencies—and in this case, the sense of the overall coherence of the story may be decisive for us in deciding which among pairs of inconsistent propositions to disregard as anomalies in an overall coherent account or opinion.[3] (Sometimes exact consistency in a story can be a ground of suspicion. For in trying to recall the past, people usually make some mistakes or have some inexactness in memories, or two witnesses have a different perspective and do not quite coincide in what they say. Perfect consistency may therefore arouse suspicion that a concocted but untruthful story is being told.) Obviously enough, as earlier examples showed, the mere consistency of a set of propositions is no guarantee of their coherence as a story.

These preliminaries settled, I turn to considering normative coherence.

1. Normative Coherence

(a) The meaning of coherence

Why is it that a set of legal norms might sometimes appear incoherent, even when as a set they are not inconsistent? An example of such a set, which I once suggested, was if a statute laid down different speed limits for different cars according to the

---

[2] On normative coherence, chiefly N. MacCormick *Legal Reasoning and Legal Theory* chs 7 and 8; on narrative coherence, id. ch. 4, pp. 89–92, and also 'The Coherence of a Case and the Reasonableness of Doubt', *Liverpool Law Rev.* 2 (1980) 45–50.

[3] Lambèr M. M. Royakkers criticizes me for 'den[ying] the connection between consistency and coherence', see *Extending Deontic Logic for the Formalisation of Legal Rules* (Dordrecht: Kluwer Academic Publishers, 1998) at 43. For avoidance of doubt, I should confirm that perfect coherence would require an elimination of all inconsistency, but some inconsistency is compatible with relative coherence, and it is one's grasp of relative coherence that in turn furnishes the ability to detect the inconsistencies that can and should be eliminated.

colour they were painted. Little did I realize when I figured that fanciful case that there was a real case rather like it. Subsequently I became indebted to Ruggero Aldisert for producing a real case more or less to the same effect. For some time ago the legislature in Italy determined that there should be differential speed limits for different types and makes of car.[4] Do such laws fail to make sense? And if they so fail, why do they so fail? My answer to that is that they fail to make sense if there is no common value or value-cluster which the enactment of such laws serves. In our examples, is there no common value at issue?

At least at first sight, it appears that there is not. Consider: there are three ends which statutes limiting driving speeds may promote, all of which we may suppose to be of serious social value: the safety of road users; economy in the use of fuel; and prevention of excessive wear and tear of road surfaces. (Relating this back to the discussion of general legal values in Chapter 6, care for life and limb, and care for the environment are in issue.) If the colour of cars is purely a matter of taste, and many colours are available, it seems doubtful whether any speed limit differential between differently coloured cars could possibly serve effectively any such end as those envisaged above. Moreover, if people have bought cars prior to the colour laws, it seems unfair that they should *ex post facto* be treated differently according to the colour choice they made. So without serving any value special to road safety laws, the colour laws would in fact conflict with or subvert another value of importance in a very general way to legal systems.

It is doubtless possible to imagine circumstances in which the colour laws would be coherent. If all cars had to be repainted according to their weight and fuel consumption, and if all inexperienced drivers had to acquire or drive only cars of a low-speed colour, we would begin to discern a value-scheme behind the apparently arbitrary colour laws. They could turn out to be part of a scheme which after all does rationally relate to the endeavour to minimize fuel consumption and damage to roads while tending to improve road safety. Perhaps the Italian law was designed according to some such principles. Perhaps there was a legislative intent rationally to relate differential speed limits to such objectives as economy and safety. Aldisert reports, however, that the car drivers of Italy did not see it that way.[5] They treated the differential speed limits as incoherent nonsense, and ignored them entirely. Desuetude overruled the act. Maybe the car drivers judged wrongly. Maybe the lawmakers failed in persuasion rather than in coherent thought. But we need not

---

[4] Ruggero J. Aldisert, book review of *Legal Reasoning and Legal Theory*, in *Duquesne Law Rev.* 20 (1982), 383–98 and, in general, cf. Aldisert J's opinion in *Pfeiffer v Jones and Laughlin Steel Corp.* 678 F 2 d (1982) 453, esp. at 461. Ruggero Aldisert was at the time of these writings Justice of the US Court of Appeals, 3rd Circuit.

[5] Op. cit., p. 395 'A few years ago Italian officials could not agree upon a speed limit for Italy's superhighway, the *autostrada*. They compromised on regulations that set speed limits according to automobile engine size. Thus a small Fiat was limited to 80 k.p.h., a larger car to 100 k.p.h., and so on. Each car owner was required to post on the rear of his vehicle a decal showing the car's assigned speed limit. If the desired goal was road safety, the regulations seem absurd. Though internally consistent, they had no coherence. In practice no problems have resulted, however, because neither car owners nor police have paid any attention to the regulations.'

go into that. Sufficient has been said to ground the suggestion that at least one aspect of normative coherence is a matter of the common subservience by a set of laws to a relevant value or values. Additionally, it involves an absence of avoidable conflict with other relevant values (e. g. with justice, as in the above case).

Are there then other aspects of coherence? One candidate that comes to mind has to do with principles. We might say that a set of rules are coherent if they all satisfy or are instances of a single more general principle. If it is a principle that human life ought not to be unduly endangered by motor traffic on the roads, this will (help to) make sense of speed limit laws and many other parts of road traffic law taken together. But it will not work for all possible speed limit laws—judged by reference to that principle, car colour differential speed limits will be arbitrary unless in some such expanded context as was imagined above.

The very fact that we can re-express in terms of common principles the coherence of a set of laws (road traffic laws) that we previously expressed in terms of common values raises an obvious question. Is appeal to 'values' different in substance from appealing to principles, or only different in grammatical form? 'Safety on the roads' is a noun phrase; 'safety on the roads' conceived as a *value* is the state of affairs signified by the noun phrase conceived as being a state of affairs which is a good or worthy purpose of human endeavour. 'That human life ought not to be unduly endangered by motor traffic on the roads' is a normative sentence which in virtue of its very general scope can be considered as a possible principle. It is actually somebody's principle or a principle of some normative system if some person assents to it as a practical norm for his/her own and others' conduct or, respectively, if it is an accepted or acceptable justifying norm for more particular and specific norms ('rules') within that system.

'Values' are not merely the *de facto* purposes, aims, goals, or ends actually pursued from time to time by individual persons or institutional agencies. They are actually pursued or possibly pursued states of being or of affairs which are conceived to be legitimate, desirable, worthy, or even (the scale ascends by degrees) mandatory for pursuit as standing purposes, aims, goals, or ends. If these two propositions are accepted, then there appears to be considerable overlap as between 'values' and 'principles'. For any value V there is a principle according to which V either may be, or ought in the absence of countervailing considerations to be, or ought normally to be, or must in the absence of overriding considerations be, pursued or realized. Observance of such principles is not an instrumental, but an intrinsic, means of realizing values. That V is genuinely a value does not, of course, mean that it is enshrined in any established principle of a particular legal system. Legal principles concern values locally operationalized within a state's legal system or some other analogous normative order.[6]

---

[6] Andrew Halpin, *Definition in the Criminal Law* (Oxford: Hart Publishing, 2004) follows up a suggestion by Lord Goff in distinguishing four kinds of (argument from) principle. I rather think, however, that these are differences of degree in the strength of a principle-based argument, affected by the quality one ascribes to a principle, rather than differences of kind.

Where, as in the law of a state, or in the organization of a club, a school, or a college, it proves necessary to regulate common affairs by the adoption of quite specific and detailed rules of conduct, it is also necessary to have in view the values which having these rules and living by them is supposed to realize. Reflection on the way the rules are supposed to realize value can lead to the formulation of broad normative generalizations such as that staff ought to have time and resources available for research (in pursuit of knowledge) and also for teaching (for the transmission of acquired knowledge and understanding). Opportunities for access to the resources ought to be non-discriminatory on such grounds as ethnicity or gender (for the sake of justice). However, since resources are scarce there ought to be discrimination on the basis of the quality and likely fruitfulness of particular research proposals (for the sake of efficiency in pursuit of more fundamental values). Principles provide broad guidance about the pursuit of value in a context of rule-regulated activity. We have already noted how, in the legal context, they can thus function as guides in the interpretation of statutory texts in problem cases

Forming an explicit view about values (or virtues) like 'knowledge', 'safety', 'health', 'humanity', or 'justice', or others can be very useful in critically reviewing a system of rules and of recognized or established principles as these have hitherto been formulated. By reflecting on what it is that we suppose to be, or are committed to treating as, good to bring about, we may be led to better or more general expressions of the principles of our practical systems or (yet more likely) to see new areas for their application.

Thus the coherence of norms (considered as some kind of a set) is a matter of their 'making sense' by being rationally related as a set, instrumentally or intrinsically, to the realization of some common value or values. This is also expressible as a matter of fulfilling some more or less clearly articulated common principle or principles. For the principles and values themselves to be coherent requires that in their totality they can be conceived as expressing a satisfactory form of life.[7] That is, one by which it would be possible for human beings, as human beings are, to live together in reasonable harmony and with some perception of a common good in which all participate. In short, the coherence of a set of norms is a function of its justifiability under higher-order principles and values, provided that the higher-or highest-order principles and values seem acceptable as delineating a satisfactory form of life, when taken together.

---

[7] Cf. Aulis Aarnio, *On Legal Reasoning* (Turku: Turun Yliopisto, 1977) pp. 126–9. There is a case for introducing the idea of 'Aarnio-optimality' as the aspirational point at which a fully satisfactory 'form of life' is achieved. One should note again Leonor Moral's argument ('A Modest Notion of Coherence in Legal Reasoning') that the idea of coherence in a legal system overall is different from, and prior to, the application of a test for coherence in argumentation on a case-by-case basis. Andrew Halpin has expressed interesting doubt concerning the possibility of system-wide coherence, however. *Reasoning with Law* (Oxford: Hart Publishing, 2001) 177–80.

(b) Principles and coherence in justification: some examples

At this point, it will be helpful to return to the discussion of the problem in the case of the *Conjoined Twins*.[8] Hitherto, the case has been used to illustrate the ideas of universality and universalizability in legal reasoning, and the element of consequentialism (particularly in respect of juridical consequences) that enters into legal justification. A third element in the reasoning of the Court of Appeal, explored differently by each of three very senior judges, is the element of legal principle. The case was a problem case precisely because there was no precedent or statutory rule precisely in point concerning the issue whether it was lawful to authorize an operation one of whose direct effects would be the death of the weaker conjoined twin, Mary. The other principal effect would be the prevention of Jodie's death from coming about through Mary's sharing of her cardiovascular system, and thus the creation of an opportunity for Jodie to enjoy a relatively normal life (though only after further quite major surgery).

It fell to be considered whether this would involve violating Mary's right to life, or whether failure to perform the operation to separate the twins would violate Jodie's. It fell to be considered how the duty to treat as paramount the welfare of a child bears upon such a case. It also fell to be considered whether a decision to authorize the operation involved introducing an exception to the principle enunciated in *R v Dudley and Stephens*, that necessity can never be a defence to a charge of murder—for who should be the judge of the necessity that somebody else die to save another person? Ward LJ, commenting on the extreme difficulty of the case (though far from doubting that he had found the right answer) remarked that this was so 'because the search for settled legal principle has been especially arduous and conducted under real pressure of time'.[9] That search ranged across three extensive judgments by three very senior judges in the Court of Appeal. It involved reviewing aspects of family law, considering the principle of the sanctity of life as that had evolved in decisions concerning (for example) cessation of treatment to avoid prolonging the life of patients in a persistent vegetative state. It involved considering how far (if at all) the principles of criminal law can ever acknowledge a 'necessity' defence in cases involving the killing of a human being. The researches of the judges ranged far in time and space, from medieval legal authorities to judgments of the Canadian Supreme Court. Brooke LJ concluded that:[10]

According to Sir James Stephen, there are three necessary requirements for the application of the doctrine of necessity:

    (i) the act is needed to avoid inevitable and irreparable evil;

    (ii) no more should be done than is reasonably necessary for the purpose to be achieved;

---

[8] [2001] Fam. 147, [2000] 4 All ER 961.
[9] [2001] Fam. at 155, [2000] 4 All ER 961 at 969.
[10] [2001] Fam. at 240, [2000] 4 All ER at 1052.

(iii) the evil inflicted must not be disproportionate to the evil avoided.

Given that the principles of modern family law point irresistibly to the conclusion that the interests of Jodie must be preferred to the conflicting interests of Mary, I consider that all three of these requirements are satisfied in this case.

This view of the case puts the necessity doctrine in line with the family law principle, and in effect introduces a new qualification to the *Dudley and Stephens* ruling. In working to this conclusion, Brooke LJ gave countenance to the idea that there are some contexts in which a person may be 'designated for death', because the situation is such that nothing (further) can be done to prevent early death. In that case, there is no invidious choice involved in preferring one person to another in the situation where one can perhaps but the other can certainly not survive. (In considering the use of argument by analogy, we shall review this point further.)

Another instance of a search for principle was provided by the Scottish High Court of Justiciary in its consideration of the appeal in the *Lockerbie* murder case.[11] Inevitably, where a plane has been blown up at high altitude and there are no survivors, the evidence available against anyone charged with planting the bomb will be largely circumstantial—there having been no admission of guilt nor any eyewitnesses claiming to have seen someone plant the bomb. In the appeal, it became material to establish the principles of Scots law relating to evidence in criminal trials. A particular issue concerns the use of circumstantial evidence in the context of the principle of law that requires corroboration of evidence. Scots law precludes convicting a person on the uncorroborated evidence of a single witness, or single-sourced circumstantial evidence. So what constitutes sufficient support for circumstantial evidence from different sources? Is circumstantial evidence corroborative only if it is more consistent with the direct evidence than with a competing account given by the accused? A recent authoritative dismissal of this was provided by Lord Justice-General Rodger[12]

[I]t is of the very nature of circumstantial evidence that it may be open to more than one interpretation and that it is precisely the role of the jury to decide which interpretation to adopt. If the jury choose an interpretation which fits with the direct evidence, then in their view—which is the one that matters—the circumstantial evidence confirms or supports the direct evidence so that the requirements of legal proof are met. If on the other hand they choose a different interpretation, which does not fit with the direct evidence, the circumstantial evidence will not confirm or support the direct evidence and the jury will conclude that the Crown have not proved their case to the required standard.

Approving this, Lord Justice-General Cullen continued:

This passage is, in our view, equally applicable where there is no direct evidence and the evidence is wholly circumstantial. In the same case Lord Coulsfield said . . . :[13] [I]t seems to me to be wrong to try to divide cases into different categories by reference to the nature of the evidence which is relied on, and if there were a rule that each piece of evidence must

---

[11] *Megrahi v HM Advocate* 2002 JC 99.   [12] *Fox v HM Advocate* 1998 JC 94 at 100–1.
[13] *Megrahi v HM Advocate* 2002 JC at 112, Lord Coulsfield in *Fox* 1998 JC at 118.

be incriminating, I would find it difficult to see why that should not apply in every case. I do not, however, think that it is necessary that each piece of evidence, of whatever kind, should be incriminating in that sense. The proper approach, it respectfully appears to me, is already given by Hume, that is, that what matters is the concurrence of testimonies. Whether a single piece of evidence, or a number of pieces of evidence, are incriminating or not is a matter which can only be judged in the whole circumstances taking all the evidence together.

These are lines of reasoning that might be considered to dilute the protection to accused persons afforded by a strong requirement of corroboration. On the other hand, they involve ascribing a reasonable cognitive competence to juries (or judges, where, as in the *Lockerbie* trial, they are the triers of the facts as well as judges of the law) to assess the evidence either as incriminating or too equivocal to count. Another issue in such a case as the *Lockerbie* trial concerns the role of an appeal court: has it more, or different, powers of reviewing evidence where the trial court has comprised three judges who gave a reasoned verdict on the basis of the evidence? Or is their privileged access to the evidence as originally presented in Court such as to privilege their verdict in ways similar to that of a jury's unreasoned verdict? On the principle of the finitude of any reasonable trial process, the Court held that it was competent only to correct the trial judges for misdirection, not for the weight they had ascribed to various elements of the evidence before them. In all respects, the effort is clearly to try and ensure that a trial that was exceptional in every way—the first ever case of a Scottish criminal trial held outside Scotland, by judges alone without a jury—was conducted in a manner coherent with the general principles of evidence and procedure normally operative in Scots law. This is a domain in which case law has been the main vehicle of legal development over the years.

By way of a contrasting example, I turn to a decision in English criminal law, that of *Sweet v Parsley*,[14] concerning the problem of interpreting a statute[15] which provided: 'If a person—(a) being the occupier of any premises, permits those premises to be used for the purposes of smoking cannabis or cannabis resin or of dealing in cannabis or cannabis resin . . . ; or (b) is concerned in the management of any premises used for any such purpose as aforesaid; he shall be guilty of an offence against this Act.' The particular problem in the case focused on paragraph (b), to be precise, whether the offence of 'being concerned in the management of any premises used for any such purpose' requires or does not require guilty knowledge or intention or participation in the 'purpose' in question. Miss Sweet, a schoolteacher in Oxford, was tenant of a farmhouse outside Oxford. She sub-let rooms in the house to other persons. After a certain time, her car broke down, and she had to take rooms in Oxford. Thereafter she kept only one room in the farmhouse as her own and sub-let all the other rooms, with a kitchen and so on

---

[14] [1968] 2 All ER 337 (CCA); [1970] AC 132, [1969] 1 All ER 347 (HL).
[15] Dangerous Drugs Act 1965, section 5.

retained for common use. She was able to visit the house only occasionally to stay over a night, collect rent, and check that the house was in reasonable condition.

In due course, the police discovered that residents in the house were smoking cannabis. They charged Miss Sweet, who was indubitably managing the premises, with 'managing premises used for [the purpose of smoking cannabis]', contrary to section 5(b) of the Act. The trial court found as a fact that 'she had no knowledge whatever that the house was being used for the purpose of smoking cannabis or cannabis resin'. Nevertheless, the court convicted her, being of the opinion that the Act was in terms which implied absolute liability, that is, liability without regard to a person's intention or knowledge as to the purpose in question, provided she or he was actually concerned in the management of the relevant premises. At the first level of appeal, this view was upheld: 'paragraph (b) in dealing with somebody concerned with the management of premises where cannabis is smoked contains an absolute liability; it does not depend on know-ledge at all',[16] this being in contrast with paragraph (a), under which 'permitting' necessarily involves knowledge of what is going on.

On the final appeal to the House of Lords, this interpretation of the Act was rejected. There can be discerned at least three elements in the reasoning in favour of allowing the appeal and quashing the conviction: first, there is ambiguity in the Act: 'Is the "purpose" the purpose of the smoker or the purpose of the manage-ment?'[17] Either possible answer to that question being *consistent* with the express terms of the Act, either answer is permissible in law, given the requirement that rulings in law and particular decisions must not contradict established rules of law. Secondly, however, the consequences ('consequences as implications') of holding that the smoker's purpose suffices are unacceptable:[18]

The implications are astonishing. Parliament would not only be indirectly imposing a duty[19] on persons concerned in the management of any premises requiring them to exercise complete supervision over all persons who enter the premises to ensure that no one of them should smoke cannabis, but Parliament would be enacting that the persons concerned in the management would be guilty of an offence if, unknown to them, some-one by surreptitiously smoking cannabis eluded the most elaborately devised measures of supervision.

Such reasons—and many such points were taken by the five Law Lords—indicate the extreme undesirability, in their view, of imputing to Parliament the intention

---

[16] [1968] 2 All ER 337 at 339, per Lord Parker CJ; the magistrates' finding of fact quoted above has the same source.　　　　[17] [1970] AC at 151, [1969] 1 All ER 347 at 352, per Lord Reid.
[18] Id. at 155 (All ER 355), per Lord Morris of Borth-y-Gest. On 'consequences as implications', see Chapter 6 above.
[19] A duty which, as Lord Pearce pointed out, [1970] AC at 157, [1969] 1 All ER 356, would necessarily extend to 'the innocent hotel keeper, the lady who takes in paying guests, the manager of a cinema, the warden of a hostel, the matron of a hospital, the housemaster and matron of a board-ing school' though 'the most that vigilance can attain is knowledge of their own guilt. If a smell of cannabis comes from a sitting room, they know that they have committed the offence. Should they then go at once to the police and confess their guilt in the hope that they will not be prosecuted?'

that the word 'purpose' be read as referring to anything other than the purpose *of the person concerned in management*. What is said, of course, is that Parliament 'cannot' have intended so unjust a result. But the grounds for the imputation of intention are the evaluations of the implications of the rejected interpretation. As noted above in Chapter 7, the imputation of intention does not involve searching out somebody's actual psychological state at some point in history. It is justified by a conception of an ideal rationality on the part of the legislature as a corporate entity.[20]

Thirdly, and also apparently essential to the justification of the ruling in law is what I call the argument from 'coherence':[21] 'A consideration of previous and analogous legislation removes any doubt that these words are intended to refer to such a special and limited class as I have described, one which quite clearly excludes such persons as the appellant. This legislation deals with other "anti-social" activities, such as the keeping of brothels, opium "dens" and gaming houses.' Thus for example:[22] 'The Dangerous Drugs Act, 1920 dealt with opium. The relevant sections are reproduced in the Act of 1965 (s. 8), and it is obvious that the provisions regarding cannabis are based on them. In dealing with the management of premises it seems clear enough that what is in mind is not the lessor of premises on which opium may come to be smoked, but a manager of what, if a noun is required, might be called "opium dens".' So, if a coherent view is to be taken of the legislation controlling such 'anti-social activities', it must be the view that none creates offences of strict or absolute liability. Reference was also made to the earlier decision of *Warner v Metropolitan Police Commissioner*[23] from which, especially from the leading opinion of Lord Reid, there can be extracted a general principle as to the differentiation of offences of absolute liability from those requiring *mens rea*. As he restated that principle in *Sweet*'s case, it is to the effect that there is a class of 'quasi-criminal acts', acts which 'in the public interest are prohibited under a penalty'. Being penalized in such matters involves no real moral stigma. By contrast, in the case of 'acts of a truly criminal character', 'a stigma . . . attaches to any person convicted . . . and the more serious or more disgraceful the offence, the greater the stigma'. It has then to be asked whether 'in a case of this gravity, the public interest really requires that an innocent person should be prevented from proving his innocence in order that fewer guilty men may escape'. That is: where an offence is created to regulate in the public interest a potentially dangerous activity of a specialized kind, and where conviction does not carry moral stigma, liability may be strict or absolute; where offences properly carry some stigma, *mens rea* ought to be required. This Lord Reid took to be the

---

[20] But see id. at 151 (All ER at 351), per Lord Reid, 'Speaking from rather long experience of membership of both Houses, I assert with confidence that no Parliament within my recollection would have agreed to make an offence of this kind an absolute offence if the matter had been fully aired before it.' Does the counterfactual at the end support or confute my suggestion in the text?

[21] Id. at 160 (All ER 359) per Lord Wilberforce.   [22] Ibid.

[23] [1969] 2 AC 256, [1968] 2 All ER 356 (HL).

best—though not a perfect—rationalization of the previous decisions on the question of absolute liability versus *mens rea*. In the former class of cases, in his view, the value of public safety is promoted without grave injustice. In the latter class of cases the injustice of a stigmatizing conviction of a morally innocent person is normally and properly taken to outweigh any competing public interest in general safety and good conduct.[24]

These considerations, together with the principle of interpretation that 'if a penal provision is reasonably capable of two interpretations, that interpretation which is most favourable to the accused must be adopted,[25] completed the justification of the decision.

This reading of the reasoning in *Sweet v Parsley* conforms to and illustrates what I said earlier by way of explaining my conception of 'coherence'. So far as concerns the coherence argument, the task the judges undertake is a twofold one. First, the inquiry is as to the principles or values which as far as possible make sense of a relevant set of legal norms: statutes and precedents dealing with similar subject matter in the same field of law. These are partly found in the existing materials, partly constructed afresh so as to establish a coherent view of the branch of the law, by showing it to be compendiously supportable by reference to some 'underlying' principle or value or coherent set of principles and values. The rules are taken to be determinations or concretizations of these principles, thus to be the vehicle of giving them legal effect. New rulings and decisions that can also be subsumed within the same schema are thus properly considered coherent with prior law. Accordingly the principles form part of the justification of decision and ruling in the instant case. Where, as in *Sweet v Parsley* (and as is almost invariably the case in codified systems of law), the problem concerns the interpretation of a statutory text, the rhetoric of such justification is to pose it as the intention of the legislator to legislate coherently. A legislature that respects the Rule of Law cannot be one that chooses arbitrarily to exercise legislative power without regard to the way in which new laws hang together with the legal system as a whole.

What, however, is the balance required in respect for the Rule of Law when considering the respective roles of courts, legislature, and the executive in promoting or protecting the public good? This question was, necessarily, much to the fore in the *Terrorist Suspects* case.[26] By an Order made under the Human Rights Act 1998, the Home Secretary had made a derogation from the UK's obligations under the European Convention for the Protection of Human Rights and Fundamental Freedoms. This derogated from Article 5(1)(f) of the Convention (on personal liberty) so far as necessary to permit the detention of suspected terrorists at a time of emergency threatening the life of the nation. At the same time, Parliament moved swiftly to adopt the Government's legislative proposals for detaining certain terrorist suspects in ways that would otherwise have been unlawful, enacting the Anti-terrorism, Crime and Security Act 2001, of which Part 4 dealt

---

[24] See [1970] AC 149, [1969] 1 All ER 350.   [25] Ibid.   [26] [2004] UKHL 56.

with the terrorist emergency following on the massive terrorist attacks in New York, Washington, and Pennsylvania of 11 September 2001. In particular, the Act authorized detention of certain terrorist suspects certified by the Home Secretary, specifically terrorist suspects who were not UK citizens but who could not be deported from the UK on the ground of a well-founded fear of death or torture were they to be returned to their country of origin. Other non-UK suspects could be deported or permitted to leave to a country of their choice; UK suspects could not be detained indefinitely on suspicion and without trial.

The appellants had moved for an order to quash the Derogation Order, on the ground that it did not satisfy the test of proportionality imported into UK law from Article 15(1) of the European Convention. They had also sought a 'declaration of incompatibility' holding that section 23 of the 2001 Act was incompatible with the fundamental rights laid down in the European Convention that were incorporated into domestic law by the Human Rights Act 1998. Reversing the Court of Appeal's decision, a nine-judge House of Lords acting by an eight-to-one majority granted both the quashing order and the declaration of incompatibility. It thereby threw the ball back into the Government's court, for it now has a duty either to bring before Parliament proposals to make the legislation compatible with binding Human Rights requirements, or to state grounds why it considers such a course inappropriate.

The leading speech in the case, by the Senior Law Lord, Lord Bingham of Cornhill, is a remarkable exercise in lucid scrutiny of all the arguments advanced to justify the derogation and the detentions. He pursues this by elucidating both common law principles concerning individual liberty and, all the more, the currently prevailing body of international law at European and global level. His speech puts together a masterful exposition of cumulatively marshalled points of principle, both those restricting the right of derogation from human rights obligations to what is proportional to the situation objectively present and those debarring unfair discrimination (e.g. on grounds of nationality or citizenship) in measures aimed at averting a public danger by detention of suspects without trial. Given globalization[27] both of terrorist activity and of responses to it, and the steadily accumulating international consensus on human rights and their effective protection, Lord Bingham's speech ranges widely both in its references to different jurisdictions worldwide and in its careful attention to persuasive statements from many sources of the current international standards applying to such matters. It shows that the basis for recognizing established principles, certainly in domains affecting human rights, is by no means confined to the domestic jurisdiction—for governments and parliaments have themselves subjected the UK to international Conventions and the standards of conduct they uphold.

---

[27] See, on this otherwise much neglected topic, William Twining, *Globalisation and Legal Theory* (London: Butterworths, 2000).

Is the intervention by judges in such sensitive matters not, however, subversive of democratic accountability (judges not being elected officials) and thus also the Rule of Law? The reply to this is devastatingly direct:[28]

It is of course true that the judges in this country are not elected and are not answerable to Parliament. It is also of course true . . . that Parliament, the executive and the courts have different functions. But the function of independent judges charged to interpret and apply the law is universally recognised as a cardinal feature of the modern democratic state, a cornerstone of the rule of law itself. The Attorney General is fully entitled to insist on the proper limits of judicial authority, but he is wrong to stigmatise judicial decision-making as in some way undemocratic. It is particularly inappropriate in a case such as the present in which Parliament has expressly legislated in section 6 of the 1998 Act to render unlawful any act of a public authority, including a court, incompatible with a Convention right, has required courts (in section 2) to take account of relevant Strasbourg jurisprudence, has (in section 3) required courts, so far as possible, to give effect to Convention rights and has conferred a right of appeal on derogation issues. . . . The 1998 Act gives the courts a very specific, wholly democratic, mandate.

It would be difficult to bring forward a more powerfully persuasive example of coherentist reasoning, setting the judicial function in its context of constitutional principle and the checks and controls among different branches of government required for realizing the Rule of Law.

(c) Why coherence justifies

It may not be necessary in this light to say much more about why coherence is material to justification, but perhaps a few further remarks are in order. Why, and in what sense, does coherence justify? Is the theory that legislators ought to legislate for a coherent body of law a sound theory, such as to justify judges also in seeking a coherent overall view of the law it is their duty to uphold and enforce? More generally, is coherence a quality which legal norms ought to exhibit?

To sketch a few considerations in virtue of which 'coherence' may be esteemed relevant to justification: first, it is agreeable to a certain conception of rationality in practical life, that which requires both universality and also the greatest possible degree of generality in practical principles. There are also reasons (fair notice to persons affected by the law, relative clarity in the law, and reasonable predictability in its application) why the law should be expounded at the level of relatively detailed rules. But these relatively detailed rules will be arbitrary if they are not also instances of more general principles, fewer in number than the number of the detailed rules, and more general in their terms. Further, since few people can know much of the detail of the law, they are more likely to find it intelligible in its effects and predictable in its application if it does instantiate a reasonably small range of general principles that can be regarded as part of the common sense of the

---

[28] [2004] UKHL 56 at para 42.

community. This further point amounts to an element of justice in the dealings between citizen and state. Finally, to borrow from Jaakko Hintikka and Georg-Henrik von Wright,[29] a legal order can be conceived as an ideal order in the sense of a possible ordering of human affairs which is taken to set a pattern at least for aspiration in the actual conduct of affairs. On that ground, it seems not enough that it should constitute merely an aggregate of non-contradictory but apparently arbitrary propositions of a relatively detailed sort, the whole having subjoined to it a single general norm that this order is to be realized in social practice. Judged by the standards of extra-legal practical reason, such an order could not be a satisfactory form of 'ideal order' for rational human agents.

All this implies a somewhat relativistic approach to justification. Whatever the actual content of a legal system may be, such considerations as the above imply that it is preferable that application and interpretation of the system be guided by the supposition that its more detailed provisions are treated as deriving from or instantiating some general principles. (That is, treated as being together supportable by reference to those principles, and hanging together because of this relationship of common support.) It also has to be supposed that the principles themselves as a set, making allowance for priorities and for different justificatory levels, are capable of being thought coherent in the ultimate sense suggested above in reliance on Aulis Aarnio's idea of a satisfactory form of life.[30] Put in the alternative, the detailed provisions of the system ought to be interpretable as serving a possible set of mutually compatible values. 'Coherence' can then be at least partially satisfied by a system that relates rationally to what those responsible for determining its content regard as values. Unfortunately, this does not in itself exclude a distorted sense of values. 'Racial purity' was pursued as a value under the National Socialist government in Germany 1933–45, and in a different version under South African apartheid laws more recently. Cases like *Dred Scott v Sandford*[31] remind us, unhappily, that there have been times and places in which slavery was a legally recognized institution, and one that had its own rationalizing principles.

It is true that the critique of those principles by reference to more fundamental ones concerning respect for the dignity of human beings eventually led to their being cast aside. The same has happened over the long run, not yet fully exhausted, of overcoming inequalities in the treatment of men and women. No doubt future generations, like present-day critical scholars, will detect much in the present bodies of law even of the most self-satisfiedly civilized countries that is unworthy of the pretension to justice and good order. The thesis that the law's

---

[29] G. H. von Wright, 'Is and Ought', in E. Bulygin (ed.), *Man, Law and Modern Forms of Life* (Dordrecht: D. Reidel, 1985) 263–81 at 372–3: 'In order to be rational to entertain, the ideal must be a picture of a *possible world* which is, to use a phrase coined by Jaakko Hintikka, *deontically perfect*.' See also J. Hintikka, 'Deontic Logic and its Philosophical Morals' in J. Hintikka (ed.), *Models for Modalities* (Dordrecht: D. Reidel, 1969) 184–214.   [30] See n. 7 and accompanying text, in this chapter.

[31] *Dred Scott v Sandford* 1857, US Supreme Court; Chief Justice Taney's judgment, repellent now to read, explains the 'principles' on which it is proper to treat members of the 'African race' as perpetually inferior under the US Constitution.

values and principles of a more local kind must be grounded in some schen...
expressive of a satisfactory form of life poses a perpetual challenge. Coherence as a
purely internal value of the law, the current, actual positive law of a given jurisdiction, is not enough in itself a sufficient guarantee of justice.

Considerations of 'coherence' are nevertheless justifying reasons on the ground
stated. With whatever blemishes, coherent law is preferable to incoherent, and
interpretations of potentially incoherent law that restore it as far as possible to a
coherent self-conception are on that ground to be preferred. But this can only
guarantee that decisions made in the light of such argument are genuinely
derivable from, albeit not dictated by, the existing body of law—and thus do not
constitute unacceptable versions of judicial law-making, imposing new liabilities
in a purely retrospective way. It is thus true, as David Lyons contends in his
'Justification and Easy Cases',[32] that coherence concerns the 'derivability' of a
novel decision or ruling in law from the pre-existing body of law, not the ultimate
'defensibility' of the decision or ruling from a moral point of view. Moreover, the
constraint of coherence determines only what we might call the 'weak derivability'
of a ruling or decision from the pre-existing law. This contrasts with 'strong
derivability' where some ruling or decision is deductively derivable from binding
rules of the system, in the sense that any other decision would be directly inconsistent with (or contradictory of) some such binding rule, even in the light of all
reasonable interpretative arguments applied to the rule. If the rules are themselves
wicked rules, strong derivability by no means entails defensibility. But in so far as
the adjudicative role is a role determined by positive law, it is clear that the legal
duty of the judge is to decide only in ways that are consistent with the established
rules of law. The moral duty of the person who holds the judicial office can and
should override the legal duty, if necessary by resorting to obfuscation.

The reason why coherence determines only weak derivability of a ruling or
decision from established law is dependent on the fact that coherence is a desirable
ideal feature of a system of law. As such, however, it may compete with other ideal
features of law, like substantive justice (judged by appropriate criteria) and so
forth. It does impose a real and important constraint on judges if we interpret it in
a negative sense. Unless, by the coherence test, some ruling or decision is at least
'weakly derivable' from existing law, it is not permissible for judges in their judicial
capacity to make such a ruling or decision, however desirable on other grounds it
may be.

This finally enables me to contrast 'consequentialist' reasoning in the special
sense explained in Chapter 6. In evaluating the implications of rival rulings in a
contested case judges and lawyers raise questions of justification in Lyons' sense of
defensibility. Certainly, this is defensibility within narrow constraints posed on the
one hand by the requirement of consistency and on the other hand by the negative
requirement of coherence. The most 'defensible' decision may be one outside the

---

[32] D. Lyons, 'Justification and Easy Cases' *ARSP-Beiheft* 25 (1985) 162–7.

dges. There are sound principles of political morality under
ould not except in extreme cases opt for the best purely moral
se in defiance of their legal duty as officers of the (positive) legal
nly, the values by which judges evaluate the defensibility of
their consequences are for good reasons noticeably legal values. Yet
dgements made in the course of consequentialist reasoning in law
are—   ought to be—value judgements of the kind engaging the genuine
commitment of the judge. The question is: which decision seems genuinely best
among the legally admissible ones? The judgement here is a judgement of substance,
not a 'formal' one in the way that judgements of coherence are. The issue is: 'what
is in principle the best way in which to decide the case in hand?' It is not: 'what is
the principle which best explains the law as heretofore established by those
responsible for establishing it?' But the latter is the issue when we are concerned
simply with coherentist argument.

Beyond that, judges can acknowledge that decisions supported by the principles they discern in the law so far nevertheless involve 'developing' the law. In the
Conjoined Twins case, Brooke LJ noted that the court was in a position in which
'we should explore the possibility of developing the law'. Similarly, Robert Walker
LJ said:[33]

> In truth there is no helpful analogy or parallel to the situation which the court has to con-
> sider in this case. It is unprecedented and paradoxical in that in law each twin has the right
> to life, but Mary's dependence on Jodie is severely detrimental to Jodie, and is expected to
> lead to the death of both twins within a few months.
>
> In the absence of Parliamentary intervention the law as to the defence of necessity is
> going to have to develop on a case by case basis, as Rose LJ said in *R v Abdul-Hussain*.
> I would extend it, if it needs to be extended, to cover this case.

This acknowledges both that in a sense new law is being made yet that it is being
made with support from the existing body of law, because fully coherent with it
and hence already inside its present frame of reference. For it is being made under
the guidance of what seem to the court to be the most relevant guiding principles
that can be constructed out of the established law dealing with killing and the
sanctity of life.

Such a case-by-case approach suggests the possibility of a body of law growing
more dense over time. A material example concerns the development in European
Community law of the doctrines of direct effect and supremacy of that law in
respect of the law of the Member States of the Community (now 'Union'). It is
difficult to argue that the original decisions were in any sense compelled by the
EEC Treaty, though they were certainly permissible by reference to it. The Court
constructed a theory of the character of the Treaties and the laws made under
them, no doubt developing something like Dworkinian interpretation guided by

---

[33] [2001] Fam. 255, [2000] 4 All ER at 1066.

a conception of the integrity of the Community. Recall some words quoted in Chapter 6:[34] 'The integration into the laws of the Member State of provisions which derive from the Community, and more generally the terms and the spirit of the Treaty, make it impossible for the states, as a corollary, to accord precedence to a unilateral and subsequent measure over a legal system accepted by them on the basis of reciprocity.' This was, of course, highly contentious at the time, but it has been consolidated over the years and is acknowledged by the Member States for most purposes at least. In turn, it creates further problems of reciprocal coherence.

In particular, the German Constitutional Court found itself unable to accept that the Basic Law's guarantees of democratic and republican government, and of fundamental human rights, could for all purposes yield priority to Community law. For, at the material time Community law as determined by the Treaties had no built-in guarantees of democracy or indeed of human rights. The response of the ECJ was to acknowledge a problem for the global coherence of Community law with Member State law if the Treaty (latterly 'Treaties') were read as mandating purely economic goals without protection for fundamental rights to which all the Member States granted protection, most by way of constitutional entrenchment in some form or another. To deal with this problem, the Court developed the doctrine that the fundamental rights and principles common to the constitutional traditions of the Member States are impliedly guaranteed as part of the constitutional framework of the Community. This was no doubt an audacious step by way of 'interpretation', but the impossibility of sustaining coherence between the interlocking legal orders of Community and Member States shows the strength of the reason for taking the step. In turn, later amendments have written the 'constitutional traditions' into the Treaties, along with reference to internationally recognized human rights. Next the Charter of Rights of the Union was adopted in 2000, but only as a politically binding declaration. The 'Treaty Establishing a Constitution for Europe' signed on 29 October 2004 will finally incorporate the Charter as a binding element of the Union's constitutional law, provided the Treaty is itself ratified by all Member States before the end of 2006.[35]

2. Analogy and Principle: 'Developing the Law'

Some scholars treat argument by analogy as a separate and very special form of legal argumentation. Lawyers reason 'case-by-case', and essentially this is based on some kind of pattern matching between the stories the cases tell, each in its own particular way, but with always some resemblance to each other that is legally (or

---

[34] See Case 6/64, *Costa v ENEL* [1964] ECR 585, [1964] CMLR 425 at p. 593.

[35] A more extended account of these developments in EU law, indicating also the concerns of Italy, is to be found in S. Douglas-Scott, *Constitutional Law of the European Union* (Harlow: Longman/Pearson Education, 2002) 432–62.

in some cases morally) significant. We noted already that at least one of the judges in the *Conjoined Twins* case despaired of finding any 'helpful analogy', *Dudley and Stephens* and its cognates being too remote. But that is not to say that there were no analogies at all.

The Coroner's Inquest into the deaths that occurred at sea after the disastrous capsizing of *The Herald of Free Enterprise* outside Zeebrugge harbour in 1987 recorded one horrible event from the testimony of an army corporal. There was a rope ladder up which passengers could escape. The corporal and a considerable number of other people were in the water near the foot of it, in imminent danger of drowning. But some way up the ladder a young man had become stuck, paralysed either with fear or with cold. After about ten minutes the corporal, taking charge of the situation, ordered that the man should be pushed off the ladder. He was never seen again, but a large number of people, including the corporal, made their way to safety. In *Justification and Excuse in the Criminal Law* (the Hamlyn Lectures for 1989) Sir John Smith argued that a case of this kind was distinguishable from *Dudley and Stephens*.[36] The unfortunate young man was not arbitrarily chosen for death by the others, and, having become immobilized himself he was obstructing others from going where they had both a right and an urgent need to go. Brooke LJ quoted this passage with approval.[37] In the twins' case, this could be considered a rather helpful hypothetical analogy, hypothetical in the sense of not being itself a previously decided case. Mary's use of Jody's heart and lungs, inevitably to be fatal to them both, is similar in that an innocent person, by being where she/he is in relation to others, is impeding their survival while 'designated for death' herself/himself. 'Designated for death' in this context means that the impossibility of a particular person's survival is to do with objective facts of the situation, not contrived by anyone with a view to choosing a sacrificial victim. Another hypothetical analogy, drawn from an actual event in the history of mountaineering concerns the exhausted mountaineer who cuts the rope after an hour's unavailing effort to help the other mountaineer to safety.[37a] Allowing another to drag oneself to death where that other is helpless to save either of us appears to go beyond the most rigorous call of duty in face of the criminal law.

Analogies in this way are relevant to what the judges call 'developing the law',[38] that is extending or restating a legal rule or principle to make it cover, or to show how it covers, novel situations of a kind that Joseph Raz suggests calling 'unregulated cases'. This can also be thought of as using analogy to fill 'gaps' in the law, which is accurate enough in capturing the way judges and counsel dedicate

---

[36] See *Justification and Excuse in the Criminal Law* (London: Stevens, 1989) 77–8.

[37] [2001] Fam. at 229, [2000] 4 All ER at 1041.

[37a] For the true story of this case, see J. Simpson, *Touching the Void* (London: Jonathan Cape, 1988).

[38] Compare the speech of Lord Goff of Chieveley in *Kleinwort Benson v Lincoln City Council* [1999] 2 AC 349 at 378, [1998] 4 All ER 513 at 534: 'In the course of deciding the case before him [a judge] may, on occasion, develop the common law in the perceived interests of justice, though as a general rule he does this "only interstitially" . . .'.

extensive research to satisfying themselves that there really is no prior statute or decision that does regulate the matter in hand.[39] Nevertheless, using the term 'gap' does express the value judgement that on some ground there ought to be a legal provision dealing with the matter in a certain way, namely the way proposed by the 'gap-filling' judgement. The term really expresses a conclusion about what ought to be done rather than a reason why it ought to be done. Juridical consequentialism normally supplies the latter. Alternatively, it can be taken as signifying that a situation fits with an acknowledged principle (or with a freshly statable principle) that covers the very rules which themselves do not cover this case, or that accounts for the analogous case which this one is found relevantly to resemble.

There are many possible illustrations of the process of developing lines of legal doctrine by analogical extension of an originally narrow base. One of the most famous is the line of cases on negligence in many jurisdictions starting from the celebrated Scots case of *Donoghue v Stevenson*[40] in 1932. This made a ruling on the liability of manufacturers of articles of food and drink for harm to consumers arising from defects not discoverable by ordinary inspection. This was expressed to be on the basis of a broader principle concerning people's general duty to take reasonable care to avoid harming persons to whom harm is foreseeable as a result of what one is doing—Lord Atkin's famous 'neighbour principle'. Subsequently, the duty was held to apply to manufacturers of underwear, repairers of elevators, and many other contexts as well.[41] In such a setting it is very clear that the relevance of the analogy depends on the broader principle of which each of the cases can be shown to be an instantiation. In this way, analogical reasoning to fill 'gaps' or to 'develop the law' clearly belongs comfortably within the framework of coherence as a grand-scale legal value, and is simply a particularly vivid illustration of coherentist reasoning.

Some authorities deny this, and suggest that an account of this kind puts the cart before the horse. Bernard Jackson argues that fundamental to human intelligence is an awareness of patterns and of matches between patterns.[42] As we tell the story of one case, we can see how it matches that of another. Our capability to find or to see similar patterns in different stories explains our ability to formulate broad abstract statements of principle that cover the cases. Principled reasoning presupposes analogical thinking, not vice versa. There is a point here

[39] For substantial and wide-ranging study of 'gaps' and 'gap-filling' in many legal systems, see MacCormick and Summers, *Interpreting Statutes* pp. 37–40, 75–82, 131–2, 142–4, 160–1, 174–9, 218–25, 268–77, 313–21, 362–74, 411–22.   [40] 1932 SC (HL) 31, [1932] AC 562.
[41] Compare Zenon Bankowski 'Analogical Reasoning and Legal Institutions', in P. Nerhot (ed.), *Legal Knowledge and Analogy* (Dordrecht: Kluwer, 1991) pp. 198–215, at 199–200. See also P. T. Burns and S. J. Lyons (eds), *Donoghue v Stevenson and the Modern Law of Negligence* (Vancouver BC: Continuing Legal Education of British Columbia, 1991) and particularly therein N. MacCormick '*Donoghue v Stevenson* and Legal Reasoning' 191–213.
[42] B. S. Jackson, *Law, Fact, and Narrative Coherence* (Roby, Merseyside: Deborah Charles, 1988) ch. 2.

that needs to be taken seriously. Undoubtedly, when one reads and tries to make sense of a complex statutory text, or a legislative proposal, it can be difficult to see what it means, unless you try to figure out how it might work in practice. You come to understand it by figuring hypothetical situations it would cover, that is, by figuring stories that match the text. It is, for example, as Jackson points out, a merit of the [English] Law Commission's draft Criminal Code, published in 1985 as *Codification of the Criminal Law*[43] that it has an appendix giving hypothetical cases. By seeing how these would be covered by Code provisions as the Law Commission understood them and wished to commend them, one can form a clearer understanding of them as proposals. It would help no less to understand them as enactments if they were ever to be enacted by Parliament (as now seems unlikely). This is an insight indicating rather clearly the necessary interaction between what are sometimes called 'processes of discovery' and 'processes of justification'.

The process of discovery concerns the steps in thought that lead from first confronting a problem—here, of course, a problem in law, but it could be any other kind of problem, whether theoretical or practical—to figuring out an answer to the problem. After the thinking out an answer has been done the next task is to justify it: to check that it is and show why it is the right answer. As is fairly obvious, judges' opinions in the legal reports of problem cases concern mainly justification, and the question how and why this judicial reasoning is persuasive addresses particularly the issue of its persuasiveness in the process of justification. Nevertheless, it is a mistake to suggest as I have done in previous writing that processes of discovery are totally obscure to us, being purely a matter of psychological contingency, not of reasonable procedures. Bernard Jackson and Bruce Anderson[44] (also Dan Hunter[45]) show that this is quite mistaken. There are rational heuristic steps one can take in trying to work out an answer to a problem, and these are then reflected in the reasons one can give in justifying the conclusion finally reached or decision finally handed down. So there is no need to claim that one discovers or sees analogies because one already knows a principle. The perception of similarity between the problem before a court and problems handled in an earlier decided case can itself lead to or towards the enunciation of a satisfactory decision, ideally involving the formulation of a satisfactory principle. Even in the absence of the formulation of a principle specifically relevant to the legal domain in which a problem is located, there is an overarching principle of justice that prescribes treating like cases alike and different cases differently. This mandates following an analogy once one is satisfied that there is a relevant likeness, even where it is difficult to spell out exactly what is the 'relevance' of the likeness. Of course, to spell out what is relevant in the likeness between case A and C is, in

[43] Law Comm. 143(1985).

[44] See B. Anderson, *'Discovery' in Legal Decision-Making* (Dordrecht: Kluwer, 1996).

[45] See D. Hunter, 'Reason is too Large: Analogy and Precedent in Law' *Emory Law Journal* 50 (2001) 1197–264.

effect, to formulate a legal principle, and this can be characterized as a form of inductive reasoning. For once it is articulated in this way, the procedure works from individual instances to explanatory or justificatory generalizations of these, then returns to the now coherently connected decision about the current problem. In really novel areas of legal development, the principles emerge through the decisions of cases rather than being the pre-established ground for some kind of a deductive inference. It is certainly the case that, having noticed an apparent analogy, one has to test its relevance by seeing whether there is any statable principle that accounts for it. Until this can be successfully done, the genuine relevance of the analogy will remain in doubt. As Bruce Anderson says, the claim to have made a 'discovery' must remain a contestable claim until a satisfactory justification can be stated. On this, Dan Hunter's putative refutation of Anderson seems unconvincing—the claim to have discovered the right answer to a given problem requires to be supported by reasons offered *ex post* to show why the answer is indeed right.

There is perhaps no more far-reaching discovery in natural science over the past half-century than that by Francis Crick and James Watson concerning the structure of DNA, the 'double helix'.[46] But the hypothesis they advanced in their *Nature* article of 1953, for all its elegance, might have turned out unfruitful. Its pre-eminence derives from the huge array of further studies and experiments that have built on it and confirmed the power of the 'double helix' structure in the process of conveying genetic information and operationalizing it in the development of cells through the production of proteins. It was not until some time after the initial discovery that its true character was revealed.[47] The truth seems to be that there is an ongoing interaction between attempts to think through a problem and attempts to show that one has thought through to a convincing answer. In practical thought, such as in legal reasoning, there is not a physical reality that in some way matches or confirms the descriptions and predictions of the 'discoverer'. Nevertheless, the development of acceptable general principles linking the 'discovered' analogy with the general body of the law is in turn somewhat analogous to the confirmation over time of a hypothesis or theory in natural science.

In the legal setting, it is worth remarking that in the adversarial (parts of) legal systems judges find possible answers by listening to counsel or reading their written pleadings or briefs. Counsel, for their part, find possible answers by trying to figure out a basis on which their clients can achieve their own objectives by litigious means. Counsel are constrained by law, both because of a professional duty not to mislead the court and because they are unlikely to succeed for

[46] See J. D. Watson and F. H. C. Crick, 'Molecular Structure of Nucleic Acid: a Structure for Deoxyribonucleic Acid' *Nature* 171 (1953) 737, for the original announcement of the author's theory; and see James D. Watson, *The Double Helix: a personal account of the discovery of the structure of DNA*, Gunther S. Stent (ed.), (London: Weidenfeld and Nicolson, 1981).

[47] See, for example, Matt Ridley, *Nature via Nurture* (London: Harper Perennial, 2004) 235–40.

their clients save by putting together a legally convincing case. So far as concerns analogies, counsel are principally analogy hunters, judges primarily assessors of the adequacy of analogies offered by counsel—along with rationalizing principles, and interpretative arguments, and consequentialist arguments of the appropriate sort. Here the process of discovery is to be understood in the context of a practice in which all that is done has finally to be backed by statements of reasons, *motifs*, of a kind that are acceptably justificatory by reference to law. Where, for one reason or another, counsel are not appropriately instructed, a potentially significant analogy can go unnoticed. Professor J. K. Mason has pointed out[48] that the *Conjoined Twins* case proceeded without discussion of the relevance of the definition of still birth in section 41 of the Births and Deaths Registration Act 1953. A still birth is defined as a child that issued from the mother after the twenty-fourth week of pregnancy and that did not at any time after being expelled from its mother breathe or show any sign of life. Live birth, Mason suggests, must be the converse. Had this point been argued, the court might well have concluded that Mary was never a living person by the law's definition, even though the medical people in the case considered her to be alive.

On the face of it, there is little if any resemblance between shipwrecked ferry passengers crowding round the foot of a blocked rope ladder and two conjoined twins one of whom is wholly dependent on the other for her supply of oxygenated blood. The mountaineer who has held his fallen companion on a rope for over an hour without being able to pull him to safety and who cuts the rope just before his strength fails may also seem only very remotely to resemble either of these. But once you see that all involve situations where a person apparently designated for early and inevitable death has become a potential cause of death to somebody who need not die in the same calamity, things change. Dan Hunter explains such transformation in terms of the propositional and relational similarities one can map between the 'source' examples and the present problem case that is the 'target'.[49] 'Propositionally', an individual is in each case in deadly danger. In each case she/he is in a dangerous situation that has not been deliberately designed by anyone else to this end. Relationally, their death can be the cause of death of another person, who is not otherwise designated for death. Relationally, the possible means to the safety of one is cessation of support being given to the other. Taken in the context of homicide law, it is lawful to withdraw support at the point at which continuing it becomes fatal to the survival of the supporter. Thus stated, the analogy is self-sustaining. But once it is placed in a justificatory perspective,

---

[48] J. K. Mason, 'Conjoined Twins: A Diagnostic Conundrum' *Edinburgh Law Review* 2 (2001) 1–9 at 7; but compare the opinion of Ward LJ at [2001] Fam. 181–2.

[49] In 'Reason is too Large', Hunter reproves my claim (in *Legal Reasoning and Legal Theory*, 190–2,) that it is hard to see ways of discriminating on a cognitive basis between closer and remoter analogies. He shows that, taking the target case and the source case, one can state in a series of simple propositions similar features of the two, and in relational propositions, parallels between relationships in the one and the other. The denser such propositional and relational similarities are, the closer the analogy is. I find this very illuminating.

there is need for formulation of some principle that captures what the relevant similarity is. Once formulated, it probably does no more than confirm the point one has already 'seen'—on the other hand, if every attempt to explicate the similarity failed, one would surely have to doubt, yet again, whether there was an original 'seeing', or only an illusion of 'sight'. A principle that can be shown to be itself anchored in established law it is then relevant to legally justifying the decision in the instant case, albeit the decision is one that in this restricted sense 'extends the law'. In considering how arguments can be made to justify a decision, it does seem correct to say that analogies that work as justifications do so because of the way they instantiate the implementation of some general legal principle that covers both (or all) cases.

Dan Hunter's idea about relative closeness of analogies has another potential for application. In certain contexts the issue of competing analogies can arise. For example, in the *Terrorist Suspects* case, in relation to due protection of persons against detention without trial, a central issue concerned the relevance of the fact that the detainee appellants were not citizens of the UK. They contended that their Convention right to liberty from arbitrary detention (under Article 5(1)(f) of the European Convention and thus under the Human Rights Act 1998) was being infringed in a discriminatory fashion. For the same regime of detention without trial did not apply to UK citizens with similar sinister associations, who thus represented a similar danger in terms of the classifications of the Anti-terrorism Act of 2001. The Attorney-General resisted this argument, on the ground that the closer analogy was with foreign nationals suspected of terrorist links, who could be deported to their country of origin without violating their human rights. (The detainees, by contrast, were persons who faced such threats in their home state that deportation was illegal under another heading of human rights law.) Lord Bingham concluded on this issue as follows:[50]

The question ... is whether the circumstances of X and Y are so similar as to call (in the mind of a rational and fair-minded person) for a positive justification for the less favourable treatment of Y in comparison with X. The Court of Appeal thought not because (per Lord Woolf, para 56) 'the nationals have a right of abode in this jurisdiction but the aliens only have a right not to be removed'. This is, however, to accept the correctness of the Secretary of State's choice of immigration control as a means to address the Al-Qaeda security problem, when the correctness of that choice is the issue to be resolved. In my opinion, the question demands an affirmative answer. Suspected international terrorists who are UK nationals are in a situation analogous with the appellants because, in the present context, they share the most relevant characteristics of the appellants.

The point is that, in addition to being persons designated as terrorist suspects, they are resident in the United Kingdom (with no acceptable option of departure or expulsion). In both respects they resemble UK citizens suspected of terrorism

---

[50] [2004] UKHL para 53.

more than they resemble foreign terrorists who have been deported or who have voluntarily left the United Kingdom.

3. Analogy and Classification: Getting it Right

Analogy does, however, work somewhat differently in cases dealing with problems of classification. Here, what is in issue is some legal norm that deploys a predicate 'P' as a condition of some normative consequence in a relatively complex setting of rules or sets of rules of statute law or case law or both together. Once it is known what can be proved to have happened, or even while simply contemplating what is averred to have happened, the question arises 'Does this count as a case of P?' Previous decisions about what counts as P have an obvious relevance in a precedent-based system, and anyway would have some heuristic value. But every event and person and relationship in the real world is unique. Whatever is an instance of P is in sufficient ways like whatever else is an instance of P, but in other respects they are not identical and may in some ways differ widely. How does one satisfy oneself about, and account to others for, the conclusion that this case is sufficiently like all the other cases of P to count itself as genuinely P?

We took note earlier of the problem who can count as an employee, and in particular whether a controlling shareholder in a company can count as an employee, having resultant rights to redundancy payments against the government in the event of the company becoming insolvent and going into liquidation. The rule is that this is a question of fact to be settled by the industrial tribunal on the basis of the circumstances of each case. Lord Coulsfield said in one case:[51] '[I]t could [not] in common sense be doubted that the fact that a person is a shareholder is a relevant factor. The significance of that factor will depend on the circumstances, and the weight to be given it may vary with the size of the shareholding . . . The decision as to whether a person is or is not an employee must, however, be taken on all the relevant factors at the material time.' In a rather similar case, *Buchan v Secretary of State,* the Employment Appeal Tribunal sitting in England had adopted a different approach, and had ruled that a controlling shareholder could never be deemed an employee.

In the *Bottrill* case[52] the Court of Appeal agreed with the Inner House of the Court of Session and held that there could be no hard and fast rule. There must in each case be a consideration and assessment of the relative bearing of a number of factors on the question whether a genuine employer–employee relationship existed. For this purpose, then, every case has its own particular facts and circumstances relevant to that legally defined relationship and one decision can function as a model or guiding analogy for any other. But except if exactly the same factors

---

[51] *Fleming v Secretary of State* 1998 SC 8 at 12–3, [1997] IRLR 682, at 684 (Court of Session).
[52] *Secretary of State for Trade and Industry v Bottrill* [2000] 1 All ER 915.

recurred with exactly the same weight attaching to them in context, none could be a binding precedent for any other. These are analogies in the context of open-textured language, which must be applied having regard to the merits of the case on each occasion when the problem arises. Of course, as in the coherentist arguments considered in the preceding section, the analogies are relevant precisely because the same concept ('employee' here) is being applied in the context of the same piece of legislation (or, it might be, analogous pieces of legislation). There is a close parallel with the use of analogies in the assessment of what is reasonable, discussed in the previous chapter. In all such cases, the reasons supporting a conclusion one way or the other are 'like the legs of a chair, not like the links of a chain', as the philosopher John Wisdom once famously remarked.[53] The remark has often been taken out of context. When Wisdom's essay is examined more closely, it is apparent that he confined his reading of legal materials to ones that concerned what are in this book styled 'problems of classification'. A penetrating insight relevant to the treatment of these problems should not be assumed to apply more widely.

To conclude on this point, it may be enough to gesture rather weakly towards the many intricate problems there have been in European Community Law concerning the treaty provision, central to successfully establishing a single market, 'Quantitative restrictions on imports and all measures having equivalent effect shall be prohibited between Member States.' Not merely do the courts of all the states, and finally the ECJ, have to decide whether some state activity counts as a 'quantitative restriction' on imports. They further have to decide whether not explicitly quantitative measures can have 'equivalent effect' so that the search for analogies is expressly mandated here by the Treaty, and, moreover, they have to decide what kinds of activity by states relevantly count as 'measures'. The resultant large body of case law abounds with examples of 'legs of a chair' argumentation, and with discrimination between persuasive and unpersuasive analogies. This belongs in the project of trying to establish over time a uniform and principled application of the basic idea of fair dealing among states and among persons in a common market.[54]

---

[53] J. Wisdom, 'Gods' *Proceedings of the Aristotelian Society* 56 (1944), esp. at pp. 157–8; the essay is reprinted in Wisdom's *Philosophy and Psychoanalysis* (Oxford: Basil Blackwell, 1953) pp. 249–54.

[54] On this topic, see P. Craig and G. de Búrca, *EU Law: Text, Cases, and Materials* (Oxford: Oxford University Press, 3rd edn, 2002) ch. 14.

Legal Narratives

Introduction

This chapter deals with some of the matters that arise under the 'problem of proof'. The issue mainly considered is how it is possible to establish true or at least acceptable accounts of past events. Quite apart from detailed specialities of the law of evidence, this is a fundamentally important question in relation to application of the law in individual cases. Very largely this involves claims or accusations based on deeds that have been done and events that have happened. Any justifiable decision about such claims and accusations has to include a satisfactory way of confirming or disconfirming the allegations of fact that back the claim or constitute the accusation. The argument here will be that a certain conception of coherence is essential to the process of proving what was done or what happened, namely 'narrative coherence'. This is comparable in some ways with, but not the same as, the kind of 'normative coherence' that is relevant to justifying decisions on points of law rather than of fact. It depends, among other things, on taking a view about the temporal character of all human activity. It also therefore leads (in the concluding part of this present chapter) to considering how far normative coherence has also an essentially temporal character akin to that of narratives.

1. Time and Activity

This text, as you, reader, are reading it now, was written by me, its author, some time ago. The 'now' of my writing as I write this will become a 'then' for you as you are reading it: 'It was then, in November 2004 that MacCormick rewrote this chapter on legal narratives, using material originating in an address he presented to a colloquium on 29 May 1994 in Sandbjerg, Denmark'. As now (in November) I write it, I look back to words I spoke then. When I spoke at the colloquium, I spoke in a different 'now', saying:

What am I doing now? I am uttering this sentence; presenting this talk; taking part in this colloquium. 'Now' is indexical, but ambiguous, for it points to each of these three: the now of this very instant; the now of this continuing personal project—my presenting a talk over about forty minutes; the 'now' of our common project, to have a colloquium together here in Sandbjerg, starting from Friday 27 May, continuing till Monday 30 May. In the flux of time, 'now' marks an ever moving line between the past that is (as Åke Frändberg argues[1]) fixed and unalterable and the future that is open and still-to-be-determined. But the line can be broader or narrower. It can be a Euclidean line, with no breadth, as in the 'now' of the very instant; or it can be a line drawn with a broader brush, as in the 'now' of an extended talk, the 'now' of a three-day colloquium. These are all different versions of a 'specious present', that which is the present time for us or for me and for our or for my purposes.

We may well ask why it can be that this specious present is variable in range, a broader or narrower line between past and future. To this the answer lies in the very idea of action as an expression of practical reason. Our capacity to do anything, as distinct from simply existing as part of some ongoing and undifferentiated process, depends on our seeing how particular acts belong in larger activities or projects. To say a word meaningfully is to say it in an uttered sentence. But the uttered sentence needs also a context, say the context of the whole of a talk, or of a conversation or reverie. To set the alarm at night is to envisage a rising-early tomorrow; the early rising is to be sure of catching the plane, and that is for the sake of getting to the colloquium, and that is part of a whole way of life as a scholar and professional academic. To do anything as a conscious agent is possible only where the consciousness of the agent can direct itself to a present or present-and-ongoing activity. Particular acts belong to this ongoing activity not, or not only, as present means to future ends but also as present parts of an already present larger project or activity.

Consciousness of the instant 'now' has logically to be based in a consciousness of a broader specious present. The 'now' of each instant is necessarily embedded in the 'now' of some larger project. As Kant showed, our mind must even momentarily be able to comprehend any particular moment as one of a series of moments in time, and must be able to hold the whole series in contemplation while attending to each member as it occurs.[2] When the clock is 'now striking twelve o'clock' there is no single instantaneous moment at which that occurs, yet we have all heard a clock striking twelve. In the case of our own activity, the series unfolds as we envisage it and make it unfold. One of the sad things about the mental deterioration that one observes in people developing dementia is their ceasing to be able to keep a whole sentence in view as they utter each of its words, hence their utterances lack form and meaning as they trail unintelligibly on.

Mogens Blegvad suggests[3] that the ideas of 'past, present and future' are inherently perspectival, for they depend on the temporal situation of a thinking

---

[1] See Åke Frändberg 'Retroactivity, Simulactivity, Infraactivity' in J. Bjarup and M. Blegvad (eds), *Time, Law, and Society* (*Archiv für Rechts- und Sozialphilosophie, Beiheft 64*) 55–72.

[2] See W. D. Lamont, *Law and the Moral Order* (Aberdeen: Aberdeen University Press, 1981) ch. 5, on causality and teleology.

[3] See M. Blegvad 'Time, Society, and Law' in Bjarup and Blegvad, *Time, Law, and Society*, pp. 11–22.

subject. The specious present is the 'now' of perspectival time (past, present, and future time). This perspectival time, henceforward renamed 'real time', contrasts with the 'analytical' time of 'before-simultaneously-after'. The novelist, the historian, the lawyer presenting a case, all seek to construct or reconstruct some series of events by laying them out in a temporal sequence in analytical time, presenting them in their temporal order—some before and some after others, some simultaneously. The student of law applying Frändberg's ideas of the retroactivity, simulactivity, and infra-activity of legal provisions studies them and analyses their effects in analytical time.[4] Any causal explanation also has to have regard to events ordered in analytical time, since the cause must occur before or simultaneously with the effect, not after. So analytical time is also of capital importance in explanations couched in terms of the natural sciences.

The economist Gordon C. Winston (as quoted by Mogens Blegvad) says that 'if we can think in analytical time, we can live and act and decide only in perspective time'.[5] I suggest that there is a converse of this. We are able to act in 'perspective time', that is, real time, only to the extent that we can also envisage our activity in analytical time. The momentary 'now' of the specious present in real time belongs in the broader specious present of an activity or project. But this depends on our being able to comprehend activities and projects as coherent series or congeries of actions or acts linked together under some purpose or value or normative framework. Such a comprehension of activities and projects involves an ability to envisage them in the 'before-simultaneously-after' schema of analytical time. A capacity for thought in analytical time is a condition for acting in real time.

2. Time and Narratives

Narratives are located in analytical time. Narratives, as Paul Veyne observes,[6] have to have a plot. In Aristotle's classical simplicity, they have a beginning, a middle, and an end. You choose a certain beginning point because you already have in view the end of the story, and at least in outline the way the characters will work through the middle of the story to that outcome. This idea of a plot does not differentiate mere fiction—novels and the like—from true histories. History, or at any rate historiography, must make intelligible the events it recounts. It must therefore have principles of selection, of emphasis in accordance with the relative

---

[4] Frändberg, supra, n. 1. Retroactive provisions occur after the events they regulate, simulactive ones at the same time as them, and infra-active ones before them. This notation would be of some value in discussing problems of time and law such as those raised by *Kleinwort Benson v Lincoln City Council* [1999] 2AC 349, [1998] 4 All ER 513, extensively discussed in Chapter 13.

[5] Blegvad, op. cit. at p. 15, citing Gordon C. Winston 'Three problems with the treatment of time in Economics: Perspectives, Repetitiveness and Time', in G. C. Winston and R. F. Teichgraber III (eds), *The Boundaries of Economics* (Cambridge: Cambridge University Press, 1988) ch. 3

[6] Paul Veyne, *Comment on écrit l'histoire* (Paris: Editions du Seuil, 1971). I am indebted for this reference, and for reflection on the idea of a 'plot' in this context, to Patrick Nerhot.

importance of different events, and of ordering. Not every effectively told story or history will use an exactly serial ordering in analytical time. Flashbacks, parallel narratives ('Meanwhile, back at the ranch-house...'), and other techniques can aid vividness, suspense, and even intelligibility. Yet always a key element in intelligibility is temporal ordering. Always, we want to know why things happened as they did, and at least a part of the answer to the 'Why?' question is a causal explanation. Causes cannot succeed effects, so we need to know, within the given framework of explanation, which events were earlier, which later, which simultaneous.

Another aspect of explanation is not causal but motivational, indeed, practically oriented. We give reasons for events in terms of the principles and values acted upon, or the purposes or plans being pursued, by persons both as individuals and as members of groups and organizations, or leaders of them. People acting in real time have reasons for acting, be they principles, values, plans, or purposes. These reasons of theirs become, in narrative, reasons why they did things, thus reasons why things happened, even when that which happened is not exactly the same as was planned. Once we bring in motivational explanation, it adds a certain complexity to causal sequencing, because the future as an agent has envisaged it will have formed an essential part of that agent's deliberation about the action now to be explained. Looked at in simple causal terms, it is the agent A's present mental state (present although in its content future-oriented) that prompts A to act, and the act in turn produces whatever effects it does. (If A is lucky or skilful or whatever, the act will bring about the planned outcome.) But in terms of A's own practical reasoning, A comes to a decision only by forming an intention about the future and the values A thinks achievable or realizable in it. In this sense, the future can have present effects. This has important implications for our approach to explaining the human world.

The programme of any conference or colloquium affords a suitably homely illustration. In the beginning is a decision—by a group or organization to hold a meeting for discussion of some theme; the guiding value here is the pursuit of knowledge, preferably in a stimulating and enjoyable way. Next comes a decision who are to be the organizers, which of them with which roles. A subject is announced and a general invitation for papers on the theme; some particular speakers are invited on the basis of established expertise and reputation in the field. A meeting place is chosen and dates fixed, about two years ahead. Gradually, a programme 'takes shape', as the organizers receive commitments from speakers and plan the best, or some suitable, ordering of sessions, with meal times, rest periods, excursions, and the like worked in. The programme fixes what are to be the beginning the middle and the end of the colloquium. Once published, it gives a basis for planning to those to whom it is distributed. Scholars not engaged to give papers can decide whether it will be of sufficient interest to them to make attendance worthwhile, and can now register to take part, or can choose to let the opportunity pass.

During the run-up to a colloquium, the organizers have to keep in view the temporal structure of the colloquium in analytical terms, set against other related activities and commitments of their own. Once the colloquium starts, the very fact that there is a properly planned beginning, middle, and end of the colloquium gives a common schema for activity to the participants. The whole complex framed by the programme becomes a shared 'now', a shared specious present, even amongst other perspectives of individuals that define broader or narrower now-lines for each of them. After the event, one can (as I do now in the process of my writing) take out and read over the programme as an aide-mémoire to let me reconstruct in memory the colloquium as it happened. The organizers' plan for their colloquium as it is to happen becomes the historian's plot around which to structure a telling of the tale of the colloquium as it did happen. Plots and plans clearly have much in common.

In this case at least, a significant feature of the example chosen is its very public, institutional quality. The planners-in-advance and the describers-after-the-event have in mind the academic colloquium or conference as a recognized form of socio-intellectual activity. David Lodge, eminent professor of literature and prolific novelist, has remarked that:

The modern conference resembles the pilgrimage of medieval Christendom in that it allows the participants to indulge themselves in all the pleasures and diversions of travel while appearing to be austerely bent on self improvement. To be sure, there are penitential exercises to be performed—the presentation of a paper, perhaps, and certainly listening to the papers of others. But with this excuse you journey to new and interesting places, meet new and interesting people, and form new and interesting relationships with them; exchange gossip and confidences (for your well-worn stories are fresh to them, and vice versa); eat, drink and make merry in their company every evening; and yet, at the end of it all, return home with an enhanced reputation for seriousness of mind.

Small World, the novel, or 'romance', from whose prologue this comment is extracted,[7] tells the tale of a young literary scholar, Persse McGarrigle, who falls in love at an April conference in the University of Rummidge with a beautiful young woman, Angelica Pabst, a fellow-scholar. She, unknown to McGarrigle, has an identical twin sister. He pursues her (and occasionally her misidentified sister) through a year's round of conferences and colloquia peopled by other characters involved in other sexual and academic complications of their lives. All bump into each other in a series of sometimes bizarre coincidences, and with in the end a startling denouement, the hero having won wisdom but not his true love. Like all Lodge's novels, it is highly amusing, carries considerable learning very lightly expressed, and is a totally original contribution to our literature. But its originality is not absolute as to form; it very deliberately and overtly depends for its effect at many points on recognition of the literary genre (a novel, indeed 'a romance') within which it works. And it draws upon an understanding of social institutions,

---

[7] David Lodge, *Small World* (London: Martin Secker & Warburg, 1984).

particularly the conference or colloquium, and other institutions of present-day scholarly and touristic life, without some understanding of which it would fail to be an intelligible story.

In the latter point, I claim resemblance to my own example of the colloquium programme as illustrative of the omnipresence of time and narrativity in structuring both our activities as we carry them on and the accounts we give, whether as fact or as fiction, about matters of history, or of the feigned history which we call 'novels'. Human beings are time-bound creatures, and all our efforts to understand ourselves and the world about us have to take account of this. Narratives of various kinds, and reflection upon the character of narratives, are therefore essential parts of any inquiry concerning human nature. One thing to bear in mind is that there is indeed a difference between history and fiction. The prefatory note to David Lodge's *Small World* neatly illustrates this point:

Like *Changing Places*, to which it is a kind of sequel, *Small World* resembles what is sometimes called the real world, without corresponding exactly to it, and is peopled with figments of the imagination. Rummidge is not Birmingham, though it owes something to popular prejudices about that city...The MLA Convention of 1979 did not take place in New York, though I have drawn on the programme for the 1978 one, which did.

To grasp in some way the character of this difference between the sometimes so-called 'real world' and 'figments of the imagination' is a challenge we cannot duck in the philosophy of law.

3. Narratives and Law: Cases

Narratives have an important part to play in legal practice and in law. Steven Burton has well remarked in the context of his *Introduction to Law and Legal Reasoning*,[8] that we read legal cases as stories of a particular kind. This is true when we focus on them as precedents on which to base legal arguments. It is also true when we focus on them in their primary function as determinations of contested legal questions, whether the litigation of claims by citizen against state or against fellow citizen, or the trial of state accusations of crime made against individuals. Compare real decisions at law, especially where the main evidence is circumstantial. In the *Lockerbie* case, discussed in the preceding chapter, the Lord Justice General (Cullen) summed up the character of the case thus: 'The Crown case against the appellant was based on circumstantial evidence. This made it necessary for the trial court to consider all the circumstances founded on by the Crown. In reaching its decision to convict the appellant, the trial court found that the evidence fitted together to form a real and convincing pattern.' By way of finding an illustration

---

[8] Steven J. Burton, *An Introduction to Law and Legal Reasoning* (Boston: Little, Brown & Co. 1985) p. 11: 'As used in this book, a case is a short story of an incident in which the state acted or may act to settle a particular dispute.' From this base he develops an account of reasoning by analogy.

from which to analyse in reasonably simple terms how such a 'real and convincing pattern' can be established, consider *R v Smith*.[9] The short summary of the evidence in the case given in the headnote of the report is sufficient for our purpose:

> The appellant was indicted for the murder of M. who had been discovered dead in her bath after having gone through a ceremony of marriage with him. At the trial evidence was given that subsequently to the death of M. two other women had died in their baths in similar circumstances after having gone through marriage ceremonies with the appellant. Evidence was also given of a consultation between the appellant and a solicitor concerning, *inter alia*, the effect in law of a voluntary settlement made by M., and whether the trustees could buy an annuity without M's permission.

Here, there can be no disclaimer as in Lodge's story. The story of the case *R v Smith* has to be presented and accepted as a story about a murder trial that happened in 'the real world', not a merely credible and coherent account of the world as it possibly was. All the more must the internal narrative be supposed to record events that really happened, such that the conclusion reached by the jury was about a murder of which they convicted George Smith, and the hearing by the Court of Criminal Appeal really took place and did uphold his conviction. His subsequent execution also took place. Moreover, the 'facts' briefly summarized in the quoted headnote depend on accounts given in testimony by witnesses about events they claimed to have really witnessed. The whole story encapsulates smaller stories given under oath, conclusions from these stories drawn by a jury under direction by a judge, and a verdict pronounced on that basis.

The process of 'proof' of the alleged murder is based on the narratives of witnesses and the account of events constructed round these by a prosecutor, and is achieved if the jury decides that the evidence supports the verdict 'beyond reasonable doubt', or achieves a similar standard of convincingness. For the future, the precedent is authoritative in favour of the admissibility of 'similar fact' evidence in cases where the accumulation of similar facts permits the inference that a criminal *modus operandi* is what accounts for the similarity.

The case for us, after the event, is a narrative encapsulating another narrative or set of narratives. For the accused and the police and the lawyers involved at the time, it has not this character. The detectives involved have to gather and piece together the evidence, with deliberation and discussion on the apparent credibility of witnesses, the credibility of the 'bereaved' husband's account of the matter, the availability of expert evidence concerning the possibility of drowning a woman in a bath, and such like. Prosecuting lawyers have to work out how to present the case and how to sustain at law the admissibility of evidence of this kind. Defence lawyers prepare to challenge the admissibility of evidence about one crime in the context of prosecution for a different crime, and generally to consider in consultation with the accused what if any evidence can be found to undermine the credibility of the prosecution case.

---

[9] [1914–15] All ER Reprint 262.

They are deciding what the story is to be. There must be some plan concerning the indictment—for what crime, how specified? What allegations are to be made, what witnesses to give what evidence in proof of them? This planning involves decisions about the narrative to be constructed, indicating the acts committed by the accused. Clearly, prosecuting lawyers in the case must have a view of the story that is to be told, or unfolded, through the presentation of the evidence of witnesses and by other admissible elements of proof. Here, there are strong principles at work to guide the selection of facts to be recounted, witnesses to call, evidence to lead; namely the legal norms governing legal relevance and legal admissibility of evidence. Courts of law can never enter into the raw history of the facts and events they decide upon. They have access to them only after the events, perhaps long after them, only through narrative accounts of things that are said to have happened. Cases as they proceed through time develop narratives about past time constructed so as to be relevant to law then in force, and also in such a way as to invoke the powers of convicting and imposing punishments currently vested in the court.

4. Proof and Narrative Coherence

Civil litigation is in these respects similar to criminal trials. A Scottish judge once remarked that in litigation the parties produce accounts of the past which are 'partial in every sense'.[10] Each party has a case of his or her own to make, and selects facts that uphold the case each seeks to make. One could not in any event tell the whole story of the past, however hard one might try. Every account has to be selective. In law, criteria of relevance and of admissibility play an important part in selection, but always in the light also of the substantive legal provisions that are being invoked and the case the litigant is founding upon them. Suppose I sue for damages for injuries suffered by me in a public washhouse through breach of the duty of care owed to me by the public authority in charge of the washhouse. Then the case I make must focus on some account of the defects in the running of the washhouse machines imputable to some fault of the authority. The necessary partiality of such case-making can lead to a kind of helpless cynicism about legal processes. It can lead to assertions that the law has nothing really to do with truth, only with a competitive system of technical proof. It can lead to acceptance of

---

[10] Lord Thomson J-C in *Thompson v Glasgow Corporation*, 1962 SC (HL) 36 at 52. The case concerned a horrible accident in a public washhouse run by the defender corporation. The pursuer was drying a load of laundry in a 'hydro-extractor'. Her arm got caught in the machine before it stopped spinning and was amputated as a result. The case pled on her behalf alleged that the accident had occurred because of a mechanical failure affecting the guard on the spindle of the machine. During the proof, it became clear that no such failure could have occurred. By this time, the Court held it was too late to amend the pleadings and conduct the case on the basis of a different account of the cause of the accident. This illustrates the necessity to match averments in pleadings with one eye to the law, and with one on the factual narratives that will stand up under the critical scrutiny of a legal process.

such discouraging put-downs as that 'Juries are twelve people chosen at random to decide who has hired the better lawyer.'

It is easy, but perhaps too easy, to take the cynical view. It is indeed obvious that we can scarcely ever be given absolutely certain proof about any single past event; all the more difficult is it to establish with confidence the truth about some complex series or concatenation of events and human transactions. To some extent, of course, we can act with a view to diminishing uncertainty, by careful record-keeping, so that later we can check the record and see what happened. In *Smith*, for example, death certificates were available recording the cause of death of the deceased wives. Memories are not wholly unreliable. Spouses remember each other with absolute confidence during days apart. I remember with a fair degree of confidence the main events of the colloquium in Sandbjerg at which I gave the talk presenting an early version of what has become the present chapter. (As noted earlier, it helps me that I can still refer back to the programme, though it was made for purposes other than to constitute a record of the proceedings.)

Two truisms are therefore worth stating at this point: not all memories are false; and not all records are inaccurate or misleading. To this, may be added a third, of some importance: not all statements are dishonest or insincere. In short, three forms of scepticism are impossibly self-defeating if taken in an absolute sense: memory-scepticism, record-scepticism, and honesty-scepticism. It is no doubt wise to approach every particular memory-claim, particular record, and particular averment with a critical, even a moderately sceptical, view that is alert to the possibility of mistake or falsehood in the given case, and seeks to test each item rigorously. Adversarial legal processes provide a highly effective (some people think a too aggressively effective) instrument for systematic critical testing of evidence. Opinions about matters past are sometimes pure conjectures. But sometimes they are seriously held opinions, however cautious and tentative, about the way things really were, or really did happen. These depend upon the truisms I have mentioned. They depend upon some memory, or some memory-claim made by someone, or on some item of record; and thus on the truisms about memory, record-keeping, and honesty.

But this is not all. For we also rely on two vital principles of explanation and understanding mentioned previously. We rely on the principle of universal causation, according to which all that happens is prima facie capable of being explained in terms of some cause occurring not later than the event to be explained, itself in turn explicable in terms of some anterior state of the world. And we rely on the principle of rational motivation, according to which human decisions based on reasons of the kind discussed earlier have a distinctive part to play in such explanations. In turn, human decisions constitute a partial exception to the principle of universal causation. If an event is explicable in terms of a rational decision to bring it about, there is no need to explain that decision in terms of causes rather than in terms of reasons. (It is, however, probable that one can give a plausible social-historical, and at least partly causal, account of how reasons of the kind the agent relied on came to be recognized as reasons having a certain degree of force.)

A further consideration of the *Smith* case will illustrate this. Smith's defence lawyers had objected at the trial to admission of evidence about the fact that his two 'wives' subsequent to M had died by the same 'misadventure' as M. The defence had also sought to exclude the solicitor's evidence about Smith's enquiries concerning the money he stood to inherit, and the possibility of its being converted to an annuity by his wife's trustees. As noted earlier, the Court of Criminal Appeal held that the evidence had been properly admissible, and therefore upheld the conviction.

But why was this evidence so damaging? Why so vital to the defence to have it excluded? In a common-sense way, the answer is obvious. A man is to be pitied if he loses one wife by drowning in a bath, to be somewhat suspect if he loses two in this way, and to come under the gravest suspicion of murder if he loses three. A man whose wife dies is to be pitied. A man whose wife suffers a sudden death shortly after he has checked to ensure that her death will benefit him financially comes under suspicion as a possible murderer. Accidental drowning in a bath is possible, but occurs very rarely in the case of ordinarily healthy people. An unlikely misadventure of this kind can happen by way of sheer accident, if a person is bathing on her own and falls asleep or faints while in the bath. (Smith testified that he had gone out of the house after filling a bath for his wife.) If materially the same unlikely misadventure occurs three times in similar circumstances to successive wives of one man, it is not plausible that any one of the deaths in this series occurred by sheer accident. An alternative account, supported by expert forensic evidence, shows that a person immersed in a bath of the kind involved in the case is unable to resist if her feet are pulled up at the foot end of the bath, immersing the head with the upper body wedged into the top end and the arms immobilized. Drowning can occur quickly and with no outward signs of violence to the deceased. Three such events so interrelated are likely to have a common cause. The cause in question is the deliberate act of the husband. A motive for this act was established, if the solicitor's testimony was correct: Smith had been informed that capital owned by his wife might be converted into an annuity, with the result that he would not inherit it in the event of her death. If he wished to be sure of inheriting, he had reason to desire her early death. His act of checking on this issue with a solicitor suggested that he was concerned about it, and knew he stood to gain if she did die.

Consider the following four propositions:

(1) 'The first Mrs Smith died in her bath, and Smith was nearby at the time.'

(2) 'The second Mrs Smith died in her bath, and Mr Smith was nearby at the time.'

(3) 'The third Mrs Smith died in her bath and Mr Smith was nearby at the time.'

(4) 'Before the first Mrs Smith died, Mr Smith checked up on the probability of his inheriting her money.'

These propositions (1) to (4) are not themselves contradictory of either

    (5) 'All the Mrs Smiths died by sheer accident' or

    (6) 'Mr Smith wilfully killed all the Mrs Smiths in their baths.'

Yet, in the absence of some further propositions that diminish the plausibility of (6), it coheres with (1) to (4) in a way that (5) does not. This justifies concluding that we have less ground to doubt (6) than to doubt (5). Whether this puts (6) 'beyond reasonable doubt' so as to justify deeming it true for the purposes of the criminal law, or whether that calls for further evidence, such as was provided at Smith's trial, are questions that can be put to one side just now. As things stand, we are able to hold that the story [(1) to (4) plus (6)] is coherent in a way that [(1) to (4) plus (5)] is not.[11] Why is this so, and how can that justify concluding that (6) is the probable truth of the matter?

The principles of universal causation and of rational motivation as outlined above supply the basic answer to this, coupled with more detailed scientific theories and common-sense generalizations about probability. Accidents that occur without human intervention have to be explained in a non-intentional and non-motivational causal or probabilistic way. The probability of the conjoint occurrence of the necessary causal conditions for any person's drowning in a bath is low. Even lower is the probability of these conditions occurring three times in the case of three persons successively enjoying the same relationship with a given fourth party. But the probability that a human agent can intentionally bring about the realization of these necessary conditions is so high as to approach certainty. And the probability that someone who has a strong motive would do this intentionally is much greater than the probability of the 'sheer coincidence' hypothesis. Given those explanatory principles, we can weakly derive (6) from the combination of (1) to (4) and the relevant explanatory principles. This is not a deductive derivation of (6) from the other set. Rather it is the case that [(6) plus (1) to (4)] belongs within a single rational scheme of explanation of events; whereas [(5) plus (1) to (4)] does not. It cannot stand up unless further evidence becomes available, or further explanatory hypotheses can be produced, that add further propositions to set [(5) + (1) to (4)] in a way that enhances its coherence (or add to the other set in a way that weakens its coherence).

Narrative coherence so illustrated is our only basis for upholding conclusions, opinions, or indeed verdicts about matters of past fact. A certain idea of rationality

---

    [11] In the case of so-called 'cot deaths' (Sudden Infant Death Syndrome), it has been treated as a ground of *Smith*-like suspicion if a succession of infant children of particular parents suffer sudden death while asleep. But there is now a seriously advanced theory that a genetic account exists to show why some families are at high risk of respiratory failure in childhood. Here is a case where the analogue of [(5) + (1) to (4)] acquires substantially enhanced probability, especially since parents are not normally motivated to kill their children except in exceptional cases of depression or the like. There appear to have been some horrifying examples of wrongful convictions prior to the development of improved understanding of these matters. See especially *R v Cannings* [2004] EWCA Crim 1.

plays an important part in this. Neither intellectual nor practical experience is a mere chaotic succession of Humean impressions and ideas. As both Hume and Kant recognized (though putting the point differently—perhaps less differently than is commonly supposed), we could not conduct ourselves as agents in the world if our consciousness consisted of a mere succession of ideas and impressions. Implicit in all our practical and speculative activity is a reliance on basic explanatory principles as mentioned above. These, together with an ever-growing body of scientific theories which in a way count as specialist elaborations of the basic principles, make our world an intelligible world for us. One of the conditions of intelligibility is the supposition that what we perceive is real. Another is the supposition that whatever is real is rationally related under some explanatory principle to whatever else is real. Therefore, whatever propositions about unperceived events fit into our explanatory schema in rational relationships with true propositions about perceived events are, under the second supposition, true propositions about the reality of the unperceived events. The difficulty, however, is that the suppositions have to be tentative, for three reasons: one is the always-revisable quality of our explanatory schemes; another is the incompleteness of the information derivable from perception—there could be other relevant things that we failed to perceive, that we 'did not notice' (Nobody, till Holmes came on the scene, had noticed that the dog had not barked[12]); the third is the known delusory character of some of our perceptions, in particular the possible inaccuracy of memory-claims even when we feel we recall some event exactly.

This indicates why 'truth is stranger than fiction' at least sometimes. Fiction, historiography, and legal proofs all have narrative coherence in common. But in fiction the 'perceptions' are imaginary ones. We can imagine as many as we want so 'the facts' of the story can always be as complete as the storyteller wants them to be. The storyteller can also decide in advance which perceptions or memory-claims by his characters are going to turn out to have been mistaken. In real life we decide only tentatively and *ex post* which must have been mistakes, precisely because they do not fit our present tentatively held explanatory scheme. Finally, in science fiction at least, the novelist is allowed to present an imaginary world for which a perfect set of explanatory principles is available. Thus can the world of fiction be a more coherently understood universe than the 'real world' ever is for us who inhabit it and try to make it intelligible to ourselves. The price of this is that the world of fiction is at some remove from the real world.

---

[12] Conan Doyle's Sherlock Holmes stories, give ample illustration of the force of 'narrative coherence'. The case of the dog that did not bark in the night is in point. A valuable racing horse has been taken from the stable by night. The trainer has been found dead on the Downs nearby. A suspicious-looking stranger has been picked up by the police and held on a murder charge. But Sherlock Holmes elicits from reliable witnesses the information that they did not hear the stables' dog barking by night. 'The dog did not bark' and 'a stranger took the horse' are not mutually contradictory. Yet if, as a generalization, dogs bark at strangers, then, under this common-sense principle, the dog's not barking becomes incompatible with a stranger's taking the horse, unless there is some further explanation, or some relevant exception to the general common-sense generalization.

In a similar way, superseded explanatory principles come to be reckoned as 'fictions' or 'superstitions' by those whose world-view is shaped by new explanatory principles. Think of our view of the Homeric Gods or the Ptolemaic spheres. We do not suppose there is no possible world or universe explicable in those terms (otherwise we would not understand how godly arbitrariness or Ptolemaic astronomy could count as an explanation at all). But we do suppose that no world or universe so explicable is our real one. It is our awareness that our successors will do for our explanations what we have done for our predecessors', and for the same good reasons as we have done so, that should encourage us to a proper tentativeness about our own explanations. But this critical tentativeness is not to be equated with full-blown scepticism.

Be that as it may. To sum up on narrative coherence: this provides a test as to the truth or probable truth of propositions about unperceived things and events. The test is of the explicability of the tested proposition within the same scheme of explanation as explains propositions considered true on the basis of perception. The relative probability of one or other of two mutually inconsistent propositions relating to the same unperceived event (e.g. the drowning of a Mrs Smith) depends on the number of other events which have to be supposed to have occurred to allow of coherence. Also relevant is the character and credibility of further auxiliary explanatory hypotheses that are assumed or explicitly taken into account in the process of establishing coherence. The most coherent story among mutually inconsistent stories is that which involves the lowest improbability by such a test. Few such stories allow of certainty about the truth of the proposition to be proved. Such a test justifies beliefs, and thus justifies decisions about matters of past fact because (a) it is a necessary condition of the intelligibility of the phenomenal world; and because (b) rationality requires us to make the phenomenal world intelligible. This may involve and would not be inconsistent with a transcendental presupposition that there is a noumenal world which is so ordered as to be perfectly intelligible, and that the phenomenal world perfectly replicates the intelligible structure of that noumenal world. So the propositions which satisfy truth conditions set within our schemes of explanation could be true about the reality of things. But we could never be sure that they are.

So much for narrative coherence. An account of a past event or complex of related events is credible only if it is coherent. This requires that there be no inexplicable logical inconsistencies between any of its factual elements,[13] and that there be some causal and motivational account of the whole complex of events

---

[13] The idea of an inexplicable inconsistency depends on the thought that a degree of inconsistency between witnesses or even in a single person's accounts of a past event is to be expected, because memory and perception, especially in relation to traumatic events, are imperfectly reliable. Some mistakes or elements of vagueness may thus make a story more plausible, because they less arouse a suspicion that they have been 'cooked up' after the event. But after discounting explicable inconsistencies, what remains must be non-contradictory and satisfactorily coherent in what remains after the discounted elements are dropped out.

stated in the factual statements that, as a whole, constitutes in itself a satisfactory account of them. In the case of two or more minimally coherent accounts, those which rest upon the more plausible causal or motivational hypotheses and/or the more ostensibly credible memories, records, or witness-statements are to be preferred to those making less plausible assumptions.

Narrative coherence so understood is a necessary but not a sufficient condition of real-world credibility. For, as noted, fictional narratives share narrative coherence with historical or forensic or other non-fictional ones. Non-fictional ones have to be somehow 'anchored' in reality.[14] The essential anchoring point of non-fictional narratives to the real world lies in the truisms about perception, memory, record-keeping, and honesty. These truisms come into operation when there is testimony by witnesses concerning what they heard or saw, what they remember, and what records they kept, or when some record of a legally probative kind is produced. Whereas some statements factual in content are conceived and/or presented as conjectural or purely imaginary, others are presented as reporting present or remembered perceptions, or readings of records of events that were made contemporaneously with the event they record or authenticate. So far as concerns observation of actions and imputation of motives or reasons, or ascription of meanings to records or to things said, we require not just perception but also interpretation. And interpretation in turn involves application of coherentist reasoning, hence an absence of certainty from the outset. Nevertheless, a claim to having perceived or remembered or to have referred to a record, together with any necessary element of interpretation, when honestly made, is a claim to be giving an account of the real world. Such an account, if the person who makes it is in fact honest and also accurate, is rationally acceptable as a probable account of things that have happened.

Thus mere cynicism or absolute scepticism about the possibility of reasonable procedures for finding out or reaching well-founded conclusions about past events ought to be rejected. It is not the case that we cannot get at the truth about the past; only that we can rarely if ever be absolutely certain what the truth of a given matter is. The legal system has to deal with this either by regulating in some way procedures for making and proving or challenging assertions about the past, or by abandoning the attempt as futile. To abandon the attempt as futile, however, involves abandoning a main purpose of contemporary legal systems, namely the purpose not merely of guiding action prospectively but also of taking action,

---

[14] See W. A. Wagener, P. J. van Koppen and H. F. M. Crombag, *Anchored Narratives: the Psychology of Criminal Evidence* (cited hereafter as *Anchored Narratives*) (London: Harvester Wheatsheaf, 1993), as discussed in W. Twining 'Anchored Narratives: A Comment' in his *The Great Juristic Bazaar* (Aldershot: Ashgate/Dartmouth, 2002) 425–33. Part B of Twining's book, entitled 'Lawyers' Stories' is of the greatest value in relation to all the matters covered in the present chapter. *Anchored Narratives* warns against too ready reliance on a good story as solidifying belief in 'facts' established by it. This is an important warning, but it does not seem that there is any way out of constructing narratives based on the best evidence one can find if anything at all is to be established for any purpose about past events.

coercively if necessary, in respect of breaches of law that can be shown to have been committed. Inevitably, such breaches are past events before sanctioning action can be taken. The common response of legal systems, of course, has been not to abandon the attempt to establish the truth about the past, but to regulate it, ordinarily by way of adopting, at least formally, a stance of moderate scepticism. Whatever is asserted about the past is to be disbelieved unless either admitted by those against whom it is alleged, or supported by coherent evidence up to a stipulated standard of proof. This may be the 'intimate conviction' of the trier of facts; or proof 'on the balance of probabilities', or proof 'beyond reasonable doubt'.

Certainly, all such processes of proof have this weakness: they do not operate in a self-applying, objective way, but always require some subjective exercise of judgement. Whether or not an adequately coherent narrative has been put together, whether interpretations offered of acts and records and motives are reasonable ones, whether witnesses are sound of memory, records authentic, statements honestly made—to decide on such points always requires the passing of judgement by somebody. The suggestion that this has been done mistakenly can only be tested by subjecting the same evidence and proofs to other judges, and if their view should be challenged, the same would apply again, and so on.[15]

Further, when we look at the whole process from the point of view of the person or persons appointed to be trier or triers of issues of fact, we can see that their process of judgement may have a doubly narrative aspect. A dossier has to be studied and witnesses heard; or a case has to be put through judicial examination, cross-examination, and re-examination of witnesses. After this, the trier of fact has two connected stories or narratives to reflect upon. The first is the story put before the court as material to the claim or complaint, and any challenges to it offered by the other side. The second is the story of the trial as it unfolded, the arguments put, the witnesses called, the rival emphases and interpretations, the different accounts of discrepant elements in different stories: Who says which other witness is lying? Which conflicting pieces of testimony should be disbelieved? Can any safely be believed? Only by reflecting over this self-narration can one find a basis to uphold or reject a story put to the court as decisive for the result—civil claim upheld or rejected, accused person convicted or acquitted. This is, as was remarked in Chapter 4, an instance of a 'truth certifying procedure'.[16]

The time-bound character of all human experience suggests indeed that a sense for the coherence of narratives is fundamental to our whole process of obtaining access to the past and of making judgements about it in which we can repose sufficient confidence to justify taking any action upon them. This is why real-time activities must always be structured through reflection about analytical time.

---

[15] For an exhaustive exploration of how to handle this problem, and for a discussion of the problems about circumstantial evidence, see *Megrahi v HM Advocate* 2002 JC 199.

[16] Chapter 4 section 6, above, discussing Z. Bankowski, 'The Value of Truth: Fact-Skepticism Revisited.' *Legal Studies* 1 (1981) 257–66.

5. Narrative and Normative Coherence Distinguished

In the preceding chapter (Chapter 10), I discussed another kind of coherence, 'normative coherence', different from narrative coherence as explained here. Normative coherence is at least as important for legal reasoning as is narrative coherence. Narrative coherence relates necessarily to the flux of events in time. Narratives replicate in analytical time events supposed or imagined to have occurred in real time. A coherent narrative fits events and acts together in sets ordered through time, that is to say, in convincing diachronic linkages. Normative coherence, by contrast, is at-one-time, rather than through-time, coherence; normative coherence has an essentially synchronic character, contrasting with the essentially diachronic character of narrative coherence.

To explain: modern legal rationality focuses on legality in terms of system, or systemic quality. Under the Rule of Law, conforming to a norm of law means conforming to a norm identified as a member of the relevant legal system. Legal systems are institutional normative systems. Systems of state law are territorial and coercively backed also. Other systems, such as church law, regulate members of religious communities in an in-principle non-territorial way, and rely rather on sanctions of exclusion than of coercion, except in contexts in which religious law interacts with state law. Systems like that of European Community law are territorial, but not directly coercive, though they are in effect enforced through organs of Member States.

The 'system' element of legal order in this modern conception of it is at least partly ideal rather than actual. As Joxerramon Bengoetxea[17] has put it, the reality of 'system' is its reality as a 'regulative ideal'. Because, and to the extent that, those who implement norms do so on the ground of their particular origins or sources, and treat all the norms of common or coordinate origin as being systemically interrelated, 'system' is at least partly realized in the implementation of law. The scholarly activity of those who engage in doctrinal legal study and writing ('legal dogmatics') plays a large part in the rational construction or reconstruction of legal materials conformably to an idea or ideal of system, and this helps to reinforce the practical implementation of law as guided by the idea of systematicity. This in turn helps to justify the doctrinal construction of law as system, for it is the case that the system idea does actually animate the activity of law-implementation, even if the idea (or ideal) is never perfectly made actual. Doctrinally constructed legal systems (or subsystems like criminal law, property law, or contract law, or family law) are thus in part descriptively accurate, even though they neither are nor should be perfect or complete descriptions of the totality of legal activity.

[17] Joxerramon Bengoetxea, 'Legal System as a Regulative Ideal' *ARSP Beiheft* 53 (1994) (eds H-J Koch and U. Neumann) 66–80.

Highly significant for this ideal of system is coherence in its specifically normative sense. A system of law is to be understood as an interrelated set of norms all having a common ground of formal validity, some final normative source presupposed in the very act of interpreting norm-set as norm-system. This idea derives from Kelsen's *Grundnorm* concept, of which Hart's 'Rule of Recognition' is a variant that draws attention more explicitly to the possibility that complex sets of ranked criteria of validity may be necessary for the purpose of defining normative sources for formally valid norms.[18] Ranked criteria of validity are a presupposition neces- sary for securing consistency of norms in a system. A simplified example might be of a system whose criteria of validity are (i) enactment by the legislature and (ii) precedents of the highest appeal court. These are themselves ranked hierarchically, so that any act of the legislature repeals any contrary precedent- based rule. One must add at least these two further priority criteria: *lex posterior derogat priori* and *lex specialis derogat generalibus*. According to these, later enact- ments derogate from earlier ones, and special provisions make exceptions to general ones. Thus we have a basis to ensure that at any moment the rules of the system can be considered mutually consistent. This is because any legal actor who finds her- or himself confronted by a pair of mutually contradictory rules can apply priority criteria to determine which has to be considered abrogated and to what extent. (This presupposes that the two norms in question, and perhaps the priority criteria also, have been subjected to interpretation. This is a complication to be considered shortly.)

Coherence differs importantly from consistency defined in that way. Coherence stipulates that norms should not merely not contradict each other, but should also hang together purposively. L. L. Fuller made much of the idea that law is a 'purposive enterprise', an enterprise of submitting ourselves purposively to a 'governance of rules'. That way of putting it is perhaps excessively voluntaristic. But it is true that rules belonging to a system can be envisaged as determinations of particular values or principles, and that the way different norms relate to common principles or bodies of practical principle enables us to see them as coherently, not just consistently, interrelated. This was argued in detail in the preceding chapter.

For a fresh example, let us take the rule that requires a person who is in breach of a contract to pay damages to the other party on account of the breach. This might be thought of as simply an arbitrarily posed rule, set for no particular reason. Alternatively, it might be thought to be a form of punishment for wrong- doing; or it might be thought to be a form of compensation to the innocent party for loss arising from the other's breach. A connected issue concerns the possibility of mitigation by the innocent party. Suppose a person against whom a contract

---

[18] For recently expressed doubt about the soundness of the 'ranked criteria' approach, see N. W. Barber, 'Sovereignty Re-examined: the Courts, Parliament, and Statutes' *Oxford Journal of Legal Studies* 20 (2000) 131–54 at 134–42. But compare MacCormick, *Questioning Sovereignty* pp. 86–91.

has been broken has an opportunity to take steps at relatively low cost that will reduce the loss she or he suffers from the breach. There are two possible rules each of which is consistent with the rule that requires damages to be paid. One says: 'the innocent party shall take all reasonable steps to mitigate loss'. The other says: 'the innocent party is free to take or not take steps to mitigate loss according to her/his own choice'.

The mitigation rule is coherent with the damages rule if the damages rule is deemed a concretization or determination of the compensation principle. The no-mitigation norm is coherent with the damages norm if the latter is deemed a concretization or determination of the punishment principle. The same points carry over into the law of reparation for civil injuries (torts or delicts). Are damages here to accord with the compensation principle? May there be punitive damages in some circumstances? If so, how are the special cases of punitive damages differentiated from the general run of cases where the rule is for damages as compensation only?

My task here is not to give yet another extended account of this or any other particular branch of the law. It is enough to indicate how the idea of legal systematicity involves the idea that law is not arbitrary or pointless, but an expression of reasonably tenable values or principles concerning human social interaction. This then yields a notion of normative coherence distinct from the idea of consistency in the logical sense. Consistency is absence of logical contradiction between two or more rules. Coherence is axiological compatibility among two or more rules, all being justifiable by reference to some common principle or value. Each of consistency and coherence is supposed to obtain among norms that are, in Frändberg's useful term, 'simulactive', valid at the same time. Hence normative coherence is a character of systems viewed synchronically (as what Joseph Raz calls 'momentary systems').[19]

Why does coherence in this sense matter? The answer is in terms of justice as requiring a kind of common rationality in treatment of members of a complete community under law (citizens of a state, communicants of a widely distributed religious community, citizens of member states of a transnational community). The role of the European Court of Justice within the European Community gives a vivid contemporary illustration. It is not enough that the same norms of Community law be merely formally operative in different Member States; they must be operative in the same sense, and be seen to be so. Hence the need for the Court to have a jurisdiction to receive and answer questions posed by the judges of Member States concerning the proper interpretation of points of Community law where these interact with national law. The same norms (treaty provisions, regulations, directives, or whatever) being applicable everywhere, they ought to be applied according to a common and determinate understanding of the principles that underlie them. The ECJ as the common court of the whole Community,

---

[19] Joseph Raz, *The Concept of a Legal System* (Oxford: Clarendon Press, 2nd edn, 1980).

staffed by judges from all the legal traditions of the Community, is entrusted with this responsibility, and has on the whole discharged it impressively well up to the present. If it were not so, there would be no common justice in the Europe of the Community.

Whether or not the Community, or any state within it, has achieved substantive justice either in the distributive or in the corrective sense, there is a prior demand of formal justice. This is the demand that everybody be treated the same according to the same rules under the same interpretation, and in a way that makes some overall sense, rather than being capricious and arbitrary. This requires common rules to be underpinned by common principles. Where millions of people are to be brought into a large and complex normative order, governed by elaborately interlocking representative organs and parallel bureaucracies, the imperative to construct that normative order as a coherent system has great force. This is both a matter of the practicalities of even partially effective governance and a matter of perceived, not to say actual, fairness among different people, and *a fortiori* different peoples. This is necessary for securing acceptable terms of association among many diverse persons and interests.

Of course, it oversimplifies the value of coherence to treat it as though coherent rules are simply those that express the requirements of one common principle. That is true, but must not lead us to overlook the fact that in conditions of complex legal order, many principles are in play, and securing a balance or equilibrium among principles is also required as a condition of coherence in the full sense. Mikail Karlsson has advanced a critique of certain approaches to the idea of 'repressed memory' as this can function in litigation concerning child sexual abuse and initiated by an alleged victim in adulthood.[20] The particular problem he had in view arose in a case in which the normal limitation period for time-barring an action was waived to permit the case to be tried, Waiving the time-bar allowed evidence to be given concerning incidents in respect of which the plaintiff and expert witnesses on her behalf testified to her recovery of memory of grave assaults. Karlsson criticizes the decision on the ground that statutes of limitation, setting time limits on the raising of actions for (*inter alia*) civil damages, afford a safeguard against acting on old and unreliable information. On that account, it seems to him both imprudent and unjust to make an exception to the normal limitation period so as to enable an individual to sue in adulthood for wrongs allegedly suffered in childhood, but forgotten because of repression till the memory was reactivated through therapy. There may, however, be other rationales for limitation of actions. For example, the principle of damages as compensation may be considered to have or imply a corollary that a person who has a right of action must exercise it in a reasonably timely way, or lose it. This in turn may reflect the idea that, in justice, a potential defender of a claim of damages should

---

[20] M. Karlsson 'Time out of Mind: Memory, Sexual Abuse and the Statute of Limitations' in Blegvad and Bjarup, *Time, Law, and Society* pp. 41–54.

be able after a reasonable time to discount the possibility of fresh actions arising from former transactions or activities. In business, the ability to close files after a time is important for efficiency. But if these are the defining principles, or are among them, the case of wilful wrongdoing to a child may fall outside their scope, and the importance of rectifying the wrong may be given priority over the purely cognitive disadvantages of relying on stale evidence and contested memories. Moreover, if memory is recovered only after a period of time, it is not the case that the person in question has neglected to take action, for she did not know till a later date that the ground of action existed.

Such a case reminds us of the complexity of legal argument from principles of law, and thus of the ideal of coherence as one element in systematicity as a guiding ideal for the construction and reconstruction of modern legal order. Finally, this leads us to the point of acknowledging a complexity passed over earlier in the discussion of normative consistency in law. All legal norms or rules are subject to interpretation in the process of applying them. In particular, wherever there is a prima facie conflict between norms valid according to some criterion, there must be interpretation of each to see whether, once each is properly interpreted, there remains an actual contradiction. The priority criteria that allow abrogation of one of the pair of contradictory norms come into play only when the process of interpretation reveals that one on its proper interpretation does conflict with the other on its. Thus, although consistency and coherence are distinguishable as different elements in systematicity, they interact in practice.

6. Normative Coherence as Narrative Coherence?

The diachronic character of narratives defines the kind of coherence they must have, and this differentiates narrative coherence from normative coherence as a property ascribed to, or an ideal property of, normative systems viewed synchronically. This seems satisfactory, but it may be open to an objection. The objection says that this picture ignores the crucially diachronic character of legal interpretation, and ignores the way in which legal doctrines and norms themselves develop through time.

Kevät Nousiainen's Finnish-oriented version[21] of a widely held critique of the criminal law concerning self-defence and provocation gives a good illustration. In many jurisdictions, this is governed by similar principles: self defence is lawful wherever a person uses in self-defence force reasonably proportional to the violence offered against him/her, in circumstances where self-defence is necessary. Self-defence is deemed necessary only when, under immediate attack, there is

---

[21] Kevät Nousiainen, 'Time of Law—Time of Experience', in Blegvad/Bjarup, *Time, Law, and Society* pp. 23–40.

no reasonable alternative to resisting through counter-force. Provocation is a mitigating or excusing defence, where one person acts toward another in such a way as would arouse a reasonable person to anger or resentment, and where the result is a loss of self-control expressed in an immediate and violent response to the act of provocation.

Doctrines of self-defence and provocation broadly similar in terms exist in many legal systems. One can account for the underlying principles in terms of a principle of fairness, according to which a person is not required to surrender life where it can be saved by immediate and forceful resistance, nor excessively punished for an immediate and violent response to outrageous conduct by another. Balanced against this principle of fairness is another principle of public order, according to which persons are required not to take the law into their own hands beyond necessity, and may not resort to force out of vengeance or resentment after cool reflection upon some attack or insult. These principles seem reasonable in themselves, and the balance struck between them in the defences of self-defence and provocation has been received as satisfying well the demands of coherence in the criminal law.

Yet feminists have put forward a critique based on the differential exposure of men and women to violence, especially domestic violence. A woman subjected by husband or male partner to frequent acts of potentially deadly violence, or to regular violent and provocative behaviour, may have no real, or no perceived, opportunity either to escape or to resist within the scope of the traditional legal defences. Yet her perceived situation may seem to leave no course open but that of violent self-protection, in circumstances where the public protection of the law's agencies is substantially unavailable. As Nousiainen points out, this may even be characterized in terms of differences of temporal perspective (in real time) between women and men in respect of their experience of violence and their sense of its immediacy as a threat. Hence it may be argued that the balance between fairness and public order has hitherto been struck in a manner which is itself unfair, since based on a gender-biased view of violence. If this argument were accepted, one would expect to see developments in legal interpretation and in case law (so far as case law as such is recognized in any given system) restating and adjusting doctrines of self-defence and provocation in a more gender-sensitive way. In some, but by no means all, jurisdictions, this process is already under way.

As this suggests, and as is in any event true, legal rules, principles, and doctrines are themselves time-bound, have themselves a history of critical development over time. The act of legal interpretation, especially an interpretative act by a superior court, is an act in a process of historical development of legal doctrines or legal principles. Ronald Dworkin has illuminatingly proposed the analogy of the 'chain novel'.[22] Each court that faces the task of interpreting the law, for example on

---

[22] R. Dworkin, *Law's Empire* (Cambridge, Mass.: Harvard University Press, 1986) pp. 228–32.

self-defence, has to consider the previous decisions, the previous 'chapters' in the story of this doctrine's development. Then it has to render its own decision as the best or most persuasive fresh chapter of the unfolding story, and has to do so in full awareness that others will later write further chapters carrying the story on from this one. In a similar vein Bernard Jackson and Jan van Dunné have contended that normative coherence is not something distinct from narrative coherence, but rather a subspecies of it.[23]

Discussion through the last few chapters of the *Conjoined Twins* case has certainly indicated that judges, certainly judges in systems like those of the United Kingdom, think it is right and necessary to take a long view of the development of legal doctrine in handling difficult problems of interpretation. In that case, discussion of the idea of necessity in relation to homicide started with Bracton in the thirteenth century, continued through Sir John Fortescue in the fifteenth, and lingered over theorists of the seventeenth and nineteenth centuries as well as case law from the mid nineteenth century onwards. It is certainly true that legal interpretation, and the development of legal principles and doctrines, do indeed have the diachronic quality suggested by Dworkin, Jackson, and van Dunné. This also answers to another of the demands of the Rule of Law set out by Fuller—the idea that law should exhibit a reasonable constancy over time, not always subject to sudden and radical changes. However, this does not deprive of sense the distinction between synchronic normative coherence and diachronic narrative coherence. As Dworkin says, it is important for human institutions and their laws to exhibit a kind of integrity. Even though the law cannot stand still, it is a matter of fairness that the decisions issued at one point in time be capable of rational reconciliation with those issued at an earlier time. A man held in jail after a failed defence of self-defence in a murder case will want to know why a woman accused of murder is later treated differently. There could, however, be a coherent explication through interpretation of the underlying idea of fairness to the defence, showing why different considerations apply in the case of women and men in such matters. If this is so, it will at least make the difference of outcome acceptable to a reasonable bystander, an interested citizen with no personal involvement in either case. It ought therefore to make the position more acceptable to the aggrieved male prisoner too.

The value of integrity interpreted in this way does call for a certain coherence over time in the development of legal norms and their interpretation. This is not a substitute for, rather it is a requirement additional to, the coherence that we demand as a matter of formal justice among all the norms in force in a system at a given time. Ideally, at least, the diachronic normative coherence that integrity demands is coherence across a system which at each moment in its development

---

[23] B. S. Jackson, *Law, Fact and Narrative Coherence* (Roby, Merseyside: Deborah Charles Publications, 1988); J. M. Van Dunné, 'Normative and Narrative Coherence in Legal Decision-Making' *ARSP-Beiheft* 69 (1998) 194–205.

ought (so far as humanly possible) to exhibit synchronic coherence as a momentary system. The system as a system comprises general rules and norms at various levels of generality. That these are applicable to individual cases by a process that involves (though is never exhausted by) logical subsumption is a point which Chapter 3 tried to establish.

12

Arguing Defeasibly

Introduction

The main subject of this book is the examination of kinds of argumentation and reasoning that are persuasive rather than demonstrative. From the beginning, it has been assumed that legal syllogisms are helpful as a way of posing legal issues, and at least some systems of legal pleading give the lawyer's preliminary statement of a claim against the client's opponent a somewhat syllogistic shape. In some legal systems also, the form of judicial opinions, or, rather the 'motivation' of the judgment of the tribunal or court, is quasi-syllogistic. As everyone knows, however, the appearance of purely deductive or demonstrative argumentation, so far as it exists, is nearly always misleading. The deductive element is rarely sufficient to conclude any contentious matter in law, and other arguments have to be deployed of all the kinds studied in the previous chapters, and perhaps more as well.[1] Here we deal with arguments or reasons that are relatively stronger or weaker than others, or that have (in one way of putting it) to be 'weighed' or 'balanced' against each other. Differences of opinion are frequently to be found, most obviously where a judge or judges in an appeal court have and, when appropriate, use the right to state a dissenting opinion alongside of the majority view.

It is itself a contentious issue whether these differences of opinion show that there is truly no right answer to legal questions of the kind raised in such cases. That issue will be dealt with in the next chapter. Meanwhile, the reference to the 'persuasive' rather than 'demonstrative' character of legal arguments concerning proof, relevancy, interpretation, or classification should not be interpreted as begging that question. Whether greater or lesser persuasiveness is an objectively decidable matter remains an open question, but the difference between legal arguments and demonstrative logical or mathematical proofs is sufficiently obvious. Hence the study of such arguments belongs to the domain of 'rhetoric' in at least one of the senses of that term.

Many lawyers put much time and effort into trying to ensure that no such arguments need be encountered in affairs in which they are engaged for their own

---

[1] Nevertheless, as Arend Soeteman points out, the deductive and non-deductive elements are present together, and the persuasiveness of the whole argument depends on both. A. Soeteman, *Logic in Law* (Dordrecht: Kluwer Academic Publishers, 1989) 18–20.

behalf or that of others. They write wills for clients or draft commercial leases or private house sales or trust deeds or insurance policies that will stand up in even unusual circumstances, hence avoiding the costly and imperfectly predictable risks of litigation. When things go wrong, or when accidents occur or wilful wrongdoing seems to have taken place, great efforts may be put into finding compromise solutions that produce a reasonably satisfactory outcome for an aggrieved party while avoiding litigation. If litigation becomes inevitable, there is need for skills of analysis of what are often very complex issues both in fact and in law, and for skills of drafting to draw up what is as nearly as possible a compelling and unanswerable legal claim against the other party. In that case, the hope will again be that the other party will choose to cut its losses and settle in full or offer a reasonable compromise solution.

The legal ideal of certainty in law once again shimmers before our eyes. Business people and ordinary people going about the ordinary affairs of their life have obvious and strong reason to prefer situations in which the law, or at least the law as it currently impinges on their activities and interests, is clear and suscept-ible of statement with certainty. Even if it impinges in an unwelcome way, at least they know where they stand. Not knowing is extremely uncomfortable. One of the most strongly advertised merits of the Rule of Law is that, where it flourishes, legal certainty flourishes also, as part of it. Much current thought on 'better regulation' and 'better law-making' has in its view the desirability of clear drafting of legislative instruments. This should aim for clear and achievable legislative objectives, with wording transparently geared to those objectives and as little as possible reliance on such vague or open-textured terminology as is involved in the use of standards rather than descriptive predicates in the framing of rules.[2] To the extent that they can enhance certainty (it is, of course, never completely achievable) such efforts at exactitude in drafting are laudable, though not if carried to the extent that they generate such a proliferation of details in legislation as to undermine its clarity and ready intelligibility. Where there is no or little statute law, case law predominates, and where there is statute law, it inevitably acquires a surrounding aurora of interpretative precedents of a kind laboriously itemized already. Here also, the hope for certainty appears, taking the form of a desire for clearly articulated rulings in law on points of doubt that have emerged.

Despite all this, litigation still occurs, and malefactors or alleged malefactors commit crimes (alleged crimes) and prosecutors prosecute them. When this happens, what was called in the last chapter the legal system's 'stance of moderate scepticism' comes into play. It cannot be taken for granted that a claim is well-founded just because it has been stated and placed in proper form before a court of law. It cannot be taken for granted that a person indicted on criminal charges has actually committed the crimes charged, just because such a charge has been

---

[2] See, for example, the European Parliament decision P5_TA(2003)0426 on the conclusion of the inter-institutional agreement on *Better Law-Making between the European Parliament, the Council and the Commission* (2003/2131(ACI)).

solemnly laid by the state's prosecuting authority. The presumption of innocence matters greatly, and is one fundamental aspect of the respect for persons that human rights instruments encapsulate. Likewise, civil claims must be proved before courts can order their enforcement, except that defenders may admit liability and settle matters voluntarily (or settle them without formal admission of liability), or may fail to appear in response to the claim and suffer a default judgment against them. Criminal charges must be proved, to a high standard of proof, except if the accused pleads guilty to the charge or charges laid.

1. Pragmatics and Defeasibility

It is necessary in this light to face up to the pragmatic aspect of legal processes. Cases come to courts because private parties or public officials bring them there. In so doing, in state courts, they commence the mobilization of the coercive power of the state in a world in which states claim the monopoly of legitimate coercive power within their respective territories. This is a serious matter, and (as was said in the opening chapter) the Rule of Law itself demands that those against whom the state acts or is activated have the right to deny what is alleged against them and put the other side to proving it. Further, they must also have the right, if they so choose, to present counter-evidence to any evidence that is given against them and to challenge, by any of the routes we have studied, the rectitude and relevance of the legal grounds asserted as grounding the claim or accusation against them.[3] All adversarial legal processes and also (though in a different way) inquisitorial processes have a dialogical character, assertion versus denial, assertion versus counter-assertion, and so on up to a pre-determined limit on the number of iterations to be permitted. In charge of such processes, there has to be an impartial judge who presides over the dialectical process and who in the end makes whatever findings of fact are required (unless there is a jury as fact-finder) and forms and states an opinion as to the legally justified conclusion on the point or points in issue. Finally, the judge issues the decision that accords with that conclusion.

This pragmatic setting has a bearing on the important topic of defeasibility. The idea of the 'defeasibility' of legal concepts has received a great deal of attention at least since the time of H. L. A. Hart's early essay on 'The Ascription of Responsibility and Rights'.[4] That essay was subsequently disowned by its

---

[3] For this reason, it is a matter of urgent concern that there should be some approximation to 'equality of arms' between parties. Large corporations against small businesses or individuals of even moderate means can involve unequal battles, and in this case the normal inhibitions about not having too quick recourse to law may be greatly weakened. Where counsel are permitted to charge 'contingent fees' (fees proportional to damages won, payable only in the event of victory) the balance can slide the other way. Anyway, some arrangements for competent legal assistance for all persons are vital and cannot be presumed to exist.

[4] Hart, 'The Ascription of Responsibility and Rights' *Proceedings of the Aristotelian Society* 49 (1948–49) 171–94.

author,[5] but later rehabilitated by G. P. Baker,[6] and the topic has recently attracted the attention, among others, of Fernando Atria,[7] Richard Tur,[8] and myself. Indeed, a substantially similar idea, not there labelled 'defeasibility', was introduced in 1973 in my 'Law as Institutional Fact'.[9] The idea there concerned 'ordinarily necessary and presumptively sufficient' conditions for the validity or legal soundness of legal arrangements such as those discussed a moment ago, where lawyers try to organize affairs in a way that will immunize them against the risk of future dispute or de-validation. This attempted immunization relies on the use of legal rules defining relevant arrangements[10] or instances of 'legal institutions' like contract, trust, mortgage, will, and so forth. The problem is that such rules may turn out not to have been as watertight as envisaged, since they may be subjected to a fresh interpretation in the light of some significant legal principle in some relatively unusual circumstances. One stock example is of a very strictly drawn statute concerning wills that a court then interpreted as not applying in favour of the named beneficiary when he shot the testator, his grandfather, to prevent him from altering the will.[11] The reason for this was that, even in the face of quite categorical terms in the statute, the court considered it right to limit the application of the rule it laid down so as to defer to the broad legal principle that no one should be able to found a legal claim on their own iniquity, or to profit from their own wrongdoing. This gives an example of defeasibility. An arrangement that was designed to achieve certain legal effects ceased to operate so as to achieve them because of the occurrence of anomalous circumstances.

The point about defeasibility is that every appearance of validity may attach to some arrangement set up under legal rules or some legal state of affairs ostensibly arising from some set of rules and events. Yet it can still happen that this arrangement or 'institutional fact' is subject to some kind of invalidating intervention. That which was initially, or on the face of it, valid turns out to be open to attack, and under attack to lose its initial validity, or be revealed as never having been valid, despite all appearances. That is, the arrangement (or whatever) in question is defeasible, and invalidating events bring about its defeasance.

The easiest case of this to imagine is that of what we might call 'express defeasibility'. As an example, one might think of a rule about a right R, where the rule

[5] H. L. A. Hart, *Punishment and Responsibility* (Oxford: Clarendon Press, 1968), preface.

[6] G. P. Baker, 'Defeasibility and Meaning', in P. M. S. Hacker and J. Raz (eds), *Law, Morality and Society* (Oxford: Clarendon Press, 1977) 26–57.

[7] F. Atria, *On Law and Legal Reasoning* (Oxford: Hart Publishing, 2001) 37–44, 122–40, 172–84.

[8] R.H.S. Tur, 'Defeasibilism', *Oxford Journal of Legal Studies* 21 (2001) 355–68.

[9] N. MacCormick, 'Law as Institutional Fact', *Edinburgh University Inaugural Lecture* No 52, (Edinburgh: Edinburgh University Press, 1973) also *Law Quarterly Review* 90 (1974) 102–29, reprinted as ch. 2 of N. MacCormick and O. Weinberger, *The Institutional Theory of Law: New Approaches to Legal Positivism* (Dordrecht: D. Reidel, 1986).

[10] On 'arrangements', see N. MacCormick, 'Institutions, Arrangements, and Practical Information' *Ratio Juris* 1 (1988) 73–82.

[11] See *Riggs v Palmer* 115 NY 506; 22 NE 188 (1889), and cf. in the UK, *Cleaver v Mutual Reserve Fund Life Association* [1892] 1 QB 147; *Re Crippen* [1911] P 108; *Smith* 1979 SLT (Sh Ct) 33.

expressly states the positive conditions for the vesting of R in an appropriate person, but also expressly makes this subject to some exception or proviso. So the formulation of the conditions in relation to R is in such terms as 'if conditions c_1, c_2, c_3 are satisfied then R vests in A as against B, but not if B shows that exceptional condition e_1 exists'.

The point of this formulation has to do with the pragmatics of right-claims and right-enjoyment. Under it, all A need do to establish a good claim to the subject matter of R is satisfy, or show to be satisfied, c_1, c_2 and c_3. Under the rule as formulated, it is not up to A to show that the situation is not exceptional. It is up to the other interested party, B, to show that the case is exceptional in that e_1. By so doing, B defeats A's otherwise good claim. Any assertion by A of a claim to the right (or its subject matter) on the footing of c_1, c_2 and c_3 is defeasible, and will be defeated if B can indeed show or prove that e_1. Where there is no dispute, A's confidence in her claim, or in secure enjoyment of the right or its subject matter, depends on B's being unable to show or to prove that e_1. For total security, it must actually not be the case that e_1 exists.

For example, A's claim to the proceeds of an insurance policy is usually made out by A's showing the insurers that the contingency has occurred against which insurance was taken out. It is not up to A to show the absence of every possible vitiating circumstance that might defeat his entitlement to the insurance payment. But a failure to give a timely intimation that the contingency has arisen may defeat the claim.[12] There are other cases where defeasance of a right depends on B's taking timely action. If A fraudulently purchases goods from B, for example, by giving a dud cheque under a false name, A acquires a voidable title to the goods, and can pass the title to a third party unless B in the meantime takes appropriate steps to rescind the transaction. So long as A retains the goods unsold, A's title is a defeasible one, and effectual rescission by B defeats it. An innocent third party who purchased from B after rescission would in turn have only a defeasible title, pending recovery of the goods by B. There may be many other examples of express defeasibility in this sense. Still, it does not seem that what is here called 'express defeasibility', important though it is, exhausts the idea, or perhaps even captures its most interesting cases. Indeed, if it is the case that the express formulations of institutive rules of legal institutions are always properly regarded as stating only 'ordinarily necessary and presumptively sufficient' conditions for the arrangements they regulate, implicit defeasibility afflicts all instances of legal institutions. Even in cases of express defeasibility, there may be possibilities of implicit defeasibility over and above the explicit conditions of defeasance.

In the context of this book, it is easy to see why this is so. The principles and the implicit values of such a system interact with the more specific provisions to be found in the texts of statutes or in the more narrowly defined *rationes* of binding precedents. Well-known examples of this are found in the cases from many

---

[12] Compare *Bass Brewers Ltd v Independent Insurance Ltd* 2002 SC 167; 2002 SLT 512.

jurisdictions dealing with the problem of the murderous legatee. One such case has already been noted, where the anticipated right of succession under the will is defeated by the principle that the law should not enable persons to profit from their own crimes. Nowadays, in the great majority of jurisdictions, the case law in respect of wills is now so well settled that this exception can be taken as constituting a settled rule in the given context.

It remains the case, however, that the underlying principle extends more broadly than to wills and murderers. It can still generate new restrictive interpretations of other statutes. A comparatively recent illustration is provided by *R v National Insurance Commissioner ex p. Connor*.[13] A woman applied for a widow's pension on the ground that her husband was dead, and she was therefore a widow. In fact, she satisfied all the explicit statutory conditions of entitlement to a widow's allowance, for her husband had died and his record of contributions to the National Insurance scheme satisfied the statutory conditions. The alert clerk to whom application was initially made, however, recognized the widow in this case as one who had been widowed by her own hand, through accidentally stabbing her husband with a carving knife during a quarrel. In consequence, she had been convicted of the manslaughter of her late husband. The clerk refused to make payment and in due course this refusal was upheld by the National Insurance Commissioner, and then by the Divisional Court on an application for review. The principle that the law will not uphold rights arising directly out of criminal misconduct was held to apply to the pension statute as well as to other sorts of entitlement arising on death. The court considered that the principle does not automatically disqualify, but requires judicial scrutiny of all the circumstances of a particular unlawful killing. It also considered that the unlawful killing in this case did have the effect of defeating the statutory right that had ostensibly vested in the widow. There was no issue concerning a dishonest or fraudulent claim in this case. It was accepted that Mrs Connor claimed her pension honestly and in good faith. What defeated the claim was an established legal principle that in these circumstances generated a novel exception to the express statutory conditions for vesting of a right, through the exercise of a discretionary judgment concerning the materiality of the principle to the type of situation in hand.[14]

Conceptually, what is going on here? Is the right to a widow's allowance itself defeasible? Or is it nearer to the truth to say that, despite initial appearances, this widow never had any right at all? Is the situation one in which she claimed that to which she had no right, even though she and her advisers honestly thought she was entitled to it? Was the claim defeated because the right never existed (despite appearances) or was there here a right that proved defeasible and was defeated?

---

[13] [1981] All ER 770. I am grateful to John Bell for having drawn this case to my attention in the present context.

[14] See now the Forfeiture Act 1982, the first two sections of which add to the partly discretionary 'forfeiture rule' a judicial discretion to mitigate the effects of forfeiture in appropriate cases; so now forfeiture itself is explicitly defeasible.

Taking account of the pragmatics of the legal process, it seems most appropriate to focus on the claim as being that which is defeated. There is not a right that first exists and then is defeated. There is a claim that was put forward, which was ostensibly justified by the explicit provisions of the statutory text. As such, it might well have succeeded had a different clerk been on duty that day. No fraud was involved in this. Nevertheless, the claim was put forward on what turned out to be (at least, was subsequently ruled to have been) an inadequate or incomplete understanding of the legal conditions for acquisition and enjoyment of the right. In the given instance, the misunderstanding involved treating the express statutory conditions as themselves not only necessary (which indeed they are) but also sufficient for acquisition of the right conferred by statute.

The 'right' is, after all, a theoretical object, an institutional fact. Such facts exist only where there is perfect and undefeated satisfaction of all conditions (the implicit as well as the explicit) actually required in a given case. It is the *ascription* of a right, or the *asserting of a claim to one* (or to what one purports to be entitled by the right, e.g. payment of a widow's allowance), that can be defeated, in which case there is no right at all, not a defeated right. So it is not after all the concept that is defeasible, but some formulated statement of conditions for instantiating the concept in given cases, or some assertion, ascription, or claim based on a certain understanding of those conditions.

It is easy to see why academic or practitioner-directed expositions of legal rules about contracts or wills or pensions may yield defeasible formulations of relevant legal rules. For almost any right or other legal institution there may well be certain exceptional or abnormal conditions whose presence will vitiate the vesting of a right, but their very abnormality makes it unfruitful to state the necessity for the absence of those conditions in every formulation of the right. Even the draftsman responsible for statutory formulations of the conditions for vesting of rights of given types is subject to constraint on the exceptions and provisos that can practicably be made explicit in the legislative formulation of such matters. Conversely, it is equally easy to see how a citizen or even a legal adviser can perceive a claim as sufficiently justified when all express statutory or doctrinally stated conditions are shown to be met in a given case. Yet there is the risk that what is expressly stated in law can be trumped by recourse to some unstated condition that is deemed to be implicitly overriding, given the principles and/or values at stake.[15]

The present view of defeasibility connects with a related view about one omnipresent problem concerning the formulation or articulation of the law. The problem is in one aspect that of limits to accuracy or exhaustiveness in statements of the law, and in another aspect that of the reliability with which one can draw inferences from the express statements in which law is formulated. Law has to be

---

[15] Compare J. Wróblewski 'On the Unstated in Law: Implicit Presuppositions and Conventions', in P. Amselek and N. MacCormick (eds), *Controversies about Law's Ontology* (Edinburgh: Edinburgh University Press, 1991).

stated in general terms, yet conditions formulated generally are always capable of omitting reference to some element which can turn out to be the key operative fact in a given case. The difficulty concerns the multiplicity of possible conditions which may arise from the interaction of different parts of the law with each other and the interaction of explicitly enacted rules, or doctrinally formulated restatements of rules, with principles and values in the manner indicated. It would be extremely difficult, perhaps impossible, to attempt a formulation of every conceivable precondition of validity in every statement of every rule. Even if possible, it would have disastrous effects for the clarity and intelligibility of the law. On that account, general formulations of rights are apt to leave many background conditions unstated, especially those which arise only in rather exceptional cases. The presence of unstated elements appears to be a general feature of law. Certainly, different legal traditions at different times take different characteristic lines on the degree to which statutory draftsmanship should tend towards completeness in each statutory formulation, rather than giving broader allowance to a reading of statutes in the light of their whole systemic context.

In any system, those who formulate rules for widows' pensions are unlikely to focus their (or the citizens' or the legislators') attention particularly on the comparatively rare instances of widowhood that occur by the widow's own act of wrongfully killing her husband. Statutes tend to contain more concise prescriptions of the positive conditions for a certain entitlement, without always listing every possible negative condition that might defeat the vesting of the entitlement. But these prescriptions are then subject to defeasance when the exceptional cases do turn up. Exceptions come to be formulated when particular events in issue bring into operation some legal principle or value of sufficient importance to override the presumptive sufficiency of the conditions stated expressly as conditions for the vesting of the right. The special situation activates some background factor that exceptionally vitiates the vesting of a right whose vesting would otherwise be unproblematic. The general statement of the right is adequate if it stipulates what is necessary and sufficient for establishing the right in the common run of cases, subject to any express exceptions or provisos for regularly occurring and readily foreseeable (or doctrinally well-documented or case law established) defeating factors. But the operation of background principles can be seen as raising the possibility of rather open-ended exceptions in cases of an exceptional or unusual sort.

One feature identified in the earlier discussion of express defeasibility remains highly significant in relation to implicit defeasibility. For again the pragmatic aspect looms large. It would be absurd if it were the case that a party relying on the explicitly stated (even if only presumptive) conditions of the rules stated in statute or precedent or both bore the burden of first imagining and then disproving every possible defeating condition that might make these inoperative. The burden has to be on some other interested party, or some public official, to raise a relevant and effective challenge. Defeasibility again finds its explanation in the pragmatics of legal processes. Where a claim is made with some prima facie justification in law and grounding in facts that are proven or assumed to obtain, it is up to whoever challenges the claim to show what is wrong with it in the context. It must be shown that there are sufficiently adverse features for it to be defeated when these are considered and given significance proportional to the principles and values that bear on them.

An example that may reinforce the point can be drawn from one particular doctrine concerning burden of proof. One such doctrine concerns the difference between qualifications upon an entitlement and exceptions to it. If *A* has a right upon certain conditions but subject to a certain negative qualifying condition, then in any action in which *A* claims that right, *A* bears the burden of proving that all its conditions are met. Naturally, this includes proving the absence of any of the negative qualifying circumstances. If, however, *A* has a right under certain conditions, but the vesting of the right is expressed to be subject to a certain exception, then, in a parallel situation of making a claim to the right, *A* does not bear the burden of proving that the exception applies. The evidentiary burden shifts to the other interested party or parties to show that the exception does obtain.

So a shipowner who shows that a chartered ship has been sunk can claim a right to be exempted from liability under the charter party. For the contract is terminated by impossibility of performance ('frustration of contract') through the loss of the ship. But legal doctrine concerning frustration of contracts establishes that the events which make the contract impossible to perform must not themselves have come about through the act of the party relying on it. Frustration must not be self-induced. If non-self-inducement is properly taken to be a qualification intrinsic to the concept of frustration, this will leave the onus on the shipowner to show that the ship's loss (e.g. by torpedoing in wartime) was not due to faulty navigation. But if non-self-inducement counts as an exception to the normal rule of frustration through loss of the ship, it will be the charterer who bears the burden of proving that there was some fault on the shipowner's (or the master's or crew's) part. It will not be for the shipowner to disprove such fault.[16]

There is on this point an argument by the late Julius Stone which, if sound, would undercut the present thesis in relation to this very example. Stone finds here one of his 'legal categories of illusory reference'.[17] I treat the rather technical distinction between qualification and exception as neatly exemplifying the presence or absence of express defeasibility. Stone, however, challenges the roots of this difference or alleged difference between a qualification included in a rule and an exception extraneously limiting its application. He argues that there is no logical difference between 'for all *x*, if *x* is *F* and *x* is not *G*, then *x* is *H*' and 'for all *x*, if *x* is *F* then *x* is *H*, but not if *x* is *G*.' So legal qualifications and exceptions are

[16] See the *Joseph Constantine* case, [1942] AC 154.
[17] See J. Stone, *Precedent and Law* (cited hereafter as *Precedent and Law*) (Sydney, NSW: Butterworths, 1985), 61–77, esp. at 68–73, and compare the earlier Stone, *Legal System and Lawyers' Reasonings* (London: Stevens, 1964).

logically indistinguishable. Accordingly, says Stone, there can be no logical justification for the differential burden of proof which the law proclaims to be dependent on exactly this differentiation. The practice of differential allocation of burdens of proof cannot be one that is logically compelled by the supposed difference in different kinds of legal condition. For they do not differ logically. There must be some other explanation for it altogether. A difference justified (if at all) on some other ground is being dressed up as depending on the (after all bogus) logic of 'qualification' versus 'exception'.

There is an important point here (though not as convincing in relation to his concrete examples as Stone claimed[18]). A truth-functional logic that allows only of conjunction ('and'), disjunction ('or'), negation ('not') and material implication ('if...then...') does indeed lack the capacity to handle the distinction we are dealing with. This is (*inter alia*) because it has to treat 'but' as simply a form of 'and'. For such a logic, qualification and exception are indistinguishable, as Stone says. But this does not mean that the distinction is for all purposes an illusory one. As we have seen, there is a real and important difference located in the pragmatics of legislation, doctrinal rule formulation, and claim-making in particular cases. This is in a way acknowledged by Stone, in so far as he accounts for the use of the 'categories of illusory reference' in terms of the pragmatic development of the common law by the judiciary. Judges, he says, can by the use of these categories achieve the reality of legal change and development while preserving the illusion of timeless continuity in the common law. This does not defeat the present argument, but if anything reinforces it.

It must be admitted that in such an area as this, the vagueness or malleability of law-formulations, whether in statute, or case law, in doctrine, or in contractual documents, create scope for judicial discretion in the way indicated by Stone. But it must also be said that the broader view of legal pragmatics here proposed gives a more complete account of the phenomenon, and shows why in its proper setting the difference between qualification and exception is not illusory. That it would be so in the context of a purely truth-functional propositional calculus merely shows that this would be an insufficiently rich logical notation in which to handle concepts like conjunction, qualification, and exception in law. To say there is no logical difference is to invite the challenge: from the point of view of what logic? Only if the qualification–exception doctrine is interpreted in particular logical terms is it an identity masquerading as a distinction. But in the present argument, the difference is real. This difference, like other cases of defeasibility, ought primarily to be understood in terms of pragmatics. So if a rule is formulated in the terms that a right vests on conditions c_1, c_2, c_3, but this is subject to exceptions in case e_1, e_2, ..., we are to take that express formulation as one conventionally used to signal one allocation of the burden of proof, while the other formulation,

---

[18] Compare MacCormick, *Legal Reasoning* 145–6, and the reply by Stone in *Precedent and Law* pp. 4–6, and p. 79, n. 32.

in terms of positive and (qualificative) negative conditions of vesting signals the opposite allocation. Where a formulation is vague on this point, the issue is how best to interpret it in the light of an underlying rationale for the distinction. For the issue is (as much as anything else) which type of formulation to choose.

Due allowance ought to be made for the difference between what it is reasonable to formulate as the ordinarily necessary and presumptively sufficient conditions of some legal entitlement, and rather exceptional or unusual conditions which another interested party may be able to adduce as objections to finally granting the entitlement. Conditions of the latter sort are then more properly treated as defeating conditions than as ordinary negatively qualifying conditions of vesting in the first place. The particular example can best be handled in terms of the general account developed here of defeasibility as a concept belonging to the pragmatics of legal processes. What logical calculus or notation would be needed to model this, for example for the purposes of developing legal expert systems or other intelligent knowledge-based systems, is a question beyond the competence of the present book and of its author. Others such as Giovanni Sartor have, however, made notable advances on this front.[19]

2. Pragmatics and Realism

What has been said so far, although claiming a base in pragmatics, might be criticized as far from pragmatic enough. Considered in the perspective of what Robert Summers has dubbed 'pragmatic instrumentalism',[20] or more particularly in the perspective of legal realists of the stripe of Oliver Wendell Holmes, Jr,[21] the present account may be thought much too accommodating to shadowy 'institutional facts' behind the plain facts of how the law is actually administered. In 'The Path of Law', Holmes delivered a broadside against any ontological assumptions about legal rights and duties. Such terms were of value solely in the context of predictions about what the courts would order people to do or desist from doing under sanction of some punishment or enforceable civil remedy. There was in his view a risk of metaphysical or moral confusion if people imagined the law conjuring into existence shadowy objects such as rights or duties independently of what one could count on the courts and judges actually doing.

---

[19] See G. Sartor, 'Defeasibility in Legal Reasoning' in Z. Bankowski, I. White and U. Hahn (eds) *Informatics and the Foundations of Legal Reasoning* (Dordrecht: Kluwer Academic Press, 1985) 119–67, responding, among other things, to ongoing discussion of 'defeasible logic' in the artificial intelligence community.

[20] See R. S. Summers, *Instrumentalism and American Legal Theory*, (Ithaca, NY: Cornell University Press, 1982).

[21] O. W. Holmes, Jr, 'The Path of the Law', in *Collected Legal Papers* (London: Constable and Co., 1920) pp. 167–202, containing at 168–76 a counterblast to any ideas of rights as objects subsisting apart from predictions of what courts will do in certain circumstances.

Some will say that just such a metaphysical confusion befogs the present account on the ground of its postulation of rights as existing in law independently of claims made about them, and as that which lies behind the (justified) judicial upholding of claims by appropriate remedial decrees and orders. Coupled with this could well come an objection to the idea about the conditions of implicit defeasance as these were sketched above. For the idea was developed that there might objectively be principles and values of a system which, rightly weighted and weighed, intervene so as genuinely to defeat a legislative or case law or doctrinal statement of conditions for a right, or an individual's claim to a right in a given case. Surely, it will be insisted, the moment of defeat is not the occurrence or presence of supposedly objective defeating factors. The moment of defeat is that at which a court holds that despite appearances some claim made by somebody is an unsound one. And, just as Stone argued, this is a matter more of judicial policy-making and principle-expounding than of some objective pre-existing legal state of existence or non-existence of a right. Rights only do exist when voluntarily respected or judicially upheld given an absence of voluntary respect. There is no point in any other way of speaking about rights. Entities should not be needlessly multiplied.

Pursued rigorously, this line of objections would lead not to a rejection of the idea that defeasibility is all about pragmatics. It would say that it is exactly about pragmatics, but above all the pragmatics of law enforcement. You can think yourself as secure as you like in some legal arrangement or legal advantage, but your ultimate security lies in judicial enforcement and nothing else. What the courts will in fact uphold for you is the sum total of your patrimony or aggregate of rights; you may think or hope you have more, but such thoughts or hopes are defeasible. The source and meaning of defeasibility can be traced simply to the insecure predictability of the judicial decision in difficult cases. Defeasance occurs when a court upsets expectations, as courts are always capable of doing. Defeasibility is simply the possibility of such defeasance. Express defeasibility is simply defeasibility that is strongly predictable in the light of statute or case law.

In at least some circumstances of defeasibility, such as those noted above in *Connor's* case, the principle whose application generates the exception has been interpreted in a way that requires a discretionary decision each time the issue arises. In each relevant case of unlawful killing, a judgement has to be made about the degree of heinousness and culpability, so as to determine whether the case requires defeasance of the prima facie right or not. These facts may be considered to give further strength to the Holmesian line of argument we have been considering. However that may be, the weighing of principles and values against express rules with a view to determining whether they support an exception is clearly a matter of judgement on any view. Discretion of some sort[22] is involved here. The

---

[22] For discussion of different senses of—or analyses of—discretion, see R. Dworkin, *Taking Rights Seriously* (London: Duckworth, rev. edn., 1978) 31–9; but cf. MacCormick, *Legal Reasoning* 264–5, and MacCormick, *H. L. A. Hart* (London: Edward Arnold, 1981) ch. 7.

only open question is whether this imports a purely subjective judicial choice, or a judgement involving in-principle objective factors. The best answer seems to be that there are objective factors here, but they are necessarily mediated through judicial subjectivity. The process is one of determination,[23] not of deduction.

In any event, the difficulties of a predictive rather than a normative interpretation of legal categories have been sufficiently often explored to require no restatement here. The normative interpretation is to be preferred, even when there is built into it allowance for the necessity of judicial intervention in some types of case. A right is what legally ought to be (and thus probably will be) upheld by the courts, or what will *justifiably* be upheld by the courts. Defeasibility concerns legally justifiable exceptions to ordinarily necessary and presumptively sufficient conditions; exceptions which ought to be made when the question is put to a court. This normative interpretation as developed here depends on the theory of legal institutions that is part of the institutional theory of law, as sketched in the prologue to this book and more extensively developed elsewhere.

3. Defeasibility, Powers, and Institutions

Here, it is sufficient to say that legal powers in private law, such as the power to enter into contracts, or powers in public law, such as powers of public authorities to make local by-laws or to grant or refuse planning permission for new building developments, are subject to many conditions laid down by law. In the case of bilateral powers (as when contract-making requires reciprocal acts of both parties) the conditions affect both parties. The explicit requirements and explicit defeating conditions concerning the exercise of such a power are stated in great detail. Provided these are all satisfied in a given case, each exercise of the power brings about an instance of the legal institution in question, one with its own determined express terms concerning the contractual duties to be performed on each side, or the precise permission for the type and scale of building permitted, or whatever. Given that the power has been validly exercised, the duties or permissions, with any attached conditions, become operative, and set particular norms for the conduct of the parties, by reference to which mutual claims may be made or challenges answered. But this is subject to a continuing risk of defeasibility. This is a low risk, sometimes practically no risk at all, but everything depends on an array of positive and negative conditions being satisfied and no exceptional circumstances. Whether a duty or permission can be asserted or not is therefore a complex matter, not a simple one. So what one ought to do or may do depends

---

[23] This Thomistic idea of *determinatio* or 'determination', I derive from John Finnis, 'Natural Law and Legal Reasoning' in *Natural Law Theory: Contemporary Essays*, R. George (ed.), (Oxford: Clarendon Press, 1992), and from his 'The Critical Legal Studies Movement', *American Journal of Jurisprudence* 30 (1985) 21–42 at 40–2; repr. in J. Eekelaar and J. Bell (eds) *Oxford Essays in Jurisprudence: Third Series* (Oxford: Clarendon Press, 1987) 144–65 at 163–5.

not on any single fact, but on a complex set of facts governed by the institutional rules in contract law (or a special branch of it, like consumer credit or insurance) or in planning law, or whatever.

This draws to attention an aspect of the debate between particularists and universalists postponed from Chapter 5. Jonathan Dancy makes an argument for particularism based on the thought that somebody's having made a promise is not always a reason to do the promised act—sometimes it is, sometimes it is not. Here is an example based on one of his.[24] Consider this train of thought: '(1) You made a promise, (2) you did not make it under duress, (3) you are able to keep it (4) there is no greater reason not to keep it (5) so you ought to keep it.' Quite rightly, Dancy points out that if (2) were negated, and you did make the promise under duress, (5) would not hold good. Likewise, if (3) were negated (roughly on the analogy of frustration of contract) (5) would not hold good. So there is no universal rule that promises ought to be kept. Some should, some should not, and some need not, be kept. A particular promise is a reason to do the particular promised act only if certain enabling conditions are present and if some disabling ones are absent. Reasons for acting hunt in packs, as it were, and only on scrutinizing what exactly are the reasons you have for and against acting in a given case can you decide what (you ought) to do. Sometimes the fact of having made a promise tells strongly for acting as promised, sometimes not. It all depends. And the same goes for any other particular reason that might favour your acting in a certain way in one case. In a different case, with a different constellation of reasons, the reason may not have the same polarity as before (that is, it might become an 'against' reason, rather than a 'for' reason). That there will be a lot of people about is sometimes a reason to go to a certain place (when I feel lonely, perhaps); sometimes it is a reason not to go there (since I feel inclined to the pleasures of solitude).

Promises and contracts are not identical. But they are cognate instances of obligations voluntarily undertaken, whether in a moral setting or in a legal one.[25] So far as concerns the law, however, there is no ground for supposing that contracts can be understood simply as speech-acts each of which in its own way generates reasons for action in appropriate circumstances, or against it in others. They certainly do generate reasons for acting, but there is a reason why they do. Contracts are structured and regulated by elaborate rules, and whole textbooks are given over to explaining these. In acting to fulfil a contract one acts in conformity with relevant rules of contract law, with the blanks (as it were) filled in from the terms of the particular contract. If the contract is vitiated from the start (say, by fraud or mistake) or ceases to bind (say, because of frustration), the resultant liberation from obligation is also a matter of applying rules, and perhaps also relevant principles.

[24] J. Dancy, *Ethics Without Principles* (Oxford: Clarendon Press, 2004) 38.
[25] See N. MacCormick, *Legal Right and Social Democracy* (Oxford: Clarendon Press, 1982), ch. 10 'Voluntary Obligations'.

One could not credibly reconstruct contract law and contract-practice in terms of particularistic reasons paralleling Dancy's analysis of promissory obligation. The rules of contract law set the legal conditions for the validity of contracts, and for exceptions, exemptions, and the like. They are many and quite complex. They include positive conditions to be fulfilled (capacity of both parties, agreement actually reached, proper formalities observed, consideration[26] moving from each party, intention on both sides to create legal relations, etc) and defeating conditions which must be absent (no fraud, no duress, no fundamental mistake, no illegal or immoral purpose, etc). Termination of contracts may occur before the time due for performance (e.g. by supervening impossibility or illegality of performance). Hence, while it is of course an important principle of law that seriously made contracts must be kept, it is not an absolute or universal rule. The rules come in sets ('institutive, consequential, and terminative'). They are quite detailed, and are universal in character. They include rules about defeating circumstances (express defeasibility) and they cannot be, or anyway are not, insulated against the risk of defeasance by the force of countervailing principles and values in unusual circumstances. Contract law and the omnipresent practice of making and keeping contracts works, but not because of an absence of rules, and not through simple case-by-case operation of each constellation of particular contract-related reasons. We would not know what a contract or a contract-related reason was if we did not have the body of law—rules and principles and values—that give meaning to the concept and to the obligations undertaken by contracting parties. Claims based on contracts are defeasible claims, but are quite rarely actually challenged, far less defeated.

There is room to debate how far and in what way promises in ordinary life are likewise encapsulated in elaborate institutional rules[27] (certainly not institutionalized ones). But the weak analogy of legal contracts with social promises suggests that moral particularism concerning promises and much else may be rebutted on grounds similar to those that apply here.

Enthusiasm to refute as respects law and to cast doubt as respects morality on Dancy's particularism should not lead to exaggeration the other way. It has to be repeated that the rules that structure institutions like contract or trusts or corporations or the like[28] should be considered as stating 'ordinarily necessary and presumptively sufficient conditions' for the normative consequences they attach to the operative facts they stipulate. To ignore this is to ignore the way principles of law interact with rules of statute law and of case law, and, above all, with doctrinal or judicial formulations based on the source materials provided by statutes and 'written laws' of all sorts as well as by judicial precedents.

---

[26] A requirement only in English common law and systems deriving therefrom—not applicable in Scotland, for example.

[27] For one attempt at an answer to this question, see MacCormick, *Legal Right and Social Democracy* pp. 201–7.

[28] That is, 'institutive, consequential and terminative rules', to use the terminology proposed in MacCormick 'Law as Institutional Fact', cited n. 9 above.

4. Defeasibility of Rules?

Both Fernando Atria and Richard Tur[29] argue that defeasibility is on that very ground a feature of legal rules. Atria assigns law to the class of 'regulative institutions' on the ground that law has the function of regulating social coexistence in the service of certain aims and values that are independent of the activity of regulation. Hence the rules formulated by legal agencies are always defeasible for the sake of better pursuing these aims and values through an appropriately nuanced interpretation of them, and with a regulated discretion in applying them. In this they contrast with 'autonomous institutions' such as games, whose point is that they use rules to constitute a kind of activity whose point is intrinsic to it. Hence rules of games are typically, or perhaps universally, non-defeasible. Defeasibility of rules is built into the kind of activity that regulative institutions define through these rules. On different, Kelsenian, grounds, Richard Tur likewise argues for the intrinsic defeasibility of legal rules. The same fundamental point is to be found in his work as in Atria's—too much is at stake when laws are being applied in real life to make acceptable any flatly formalistic approach to law-application. Regard must always be had to consequentialist considerations, and to overarching moral concerns.

As is obvious, both these authors take lines that are much in sympathy with the theses advanced in this book. In some ways they are engaged in the enterprise of pressing further along parallel, or perhaps converging, lines in a way that challenges me to live up fully to implications present in the lines of my own argument developed elsewhere and redeveloped here. Nevertheless, there is a case for retreating at this stage from ontology into pragmatics again. Is it rules that are defeasible, or certain formulations of them, or claims made on the basis of such formulations, including legal-doctrinal statements based on the text of legal 'sources' such as the statute-book or the law reports?

For the present, it seems sufficient to rest content with the pragmatic account of defeasibility, and leave ontological considerations to another place.[30] As with rights, so with rules, it is not the statute nor the precedent that is defeasible in the light of exceptional circumstances relevant to legal principles, when we deal with implicit defeasibility. It is the claim based on a particular formulation or interpretation of the rule that is defeated in the light of the principle. Thereafter, more cautious formulations of the rule, or doctrinal expositions that draw attention to exceptions established by case law, will be called for. The reasons for this approach have already been stated at sufficient length.

Finally, therefore, it is opportune to consider how the idea of defeasibility applies to legal reasoning itself. This affects the question of the universality

[29] Cited above at nn. 7 and 8 respectively.
[30] The next work in my quartet on 'Law, State, and Practical Reason', will be *Institutions of Law*, dedicated specifically to ontological questions concerning the existence of law.

or universalizability of legal claims, defences, and decisions. It connects with H. L. A. Hart's suggestion that 'A rule that ends with the word "unless..." is still a rule.'[31] Whatever can be claimed can be rebutted, though the rebuttal may not deserve to succeed and may in fact fail. Whatever suggested ruling one puts forward in a debate on relevancy or interpretation (or, sometimes, classification) to cover and justify one's own particular claim, somebody else may see a potential exception, possibly relevant to my very claim, and may argue that the exception applies and defeats the claim. Judges deciding cases may or not be (or consider themselves) restricted to dealing with points actually argued by the parties, but they surely have to deal at least with those points. They do have to give some ruling, at the very least implicitly, to cover their conclusion in the case and make clear the reason for the decision. They should give arguments that in their view justify the ruling they give while explaining the inapplicability or relative weakness or unpersuasiveness of the arguments on the other side. But still a question posed in its essence by Steven Burton recurs: 'how can one tell that there will not be new cases to which the ruling in question, though by its terms applicable, is not appropriately to be applied? Unforeseen exceptions can always turn up.' It seems that we have an example again of what Hart called 'rules hav[ing] exceptions incapable of exhaustive statement'. So it appears to be also with rulings. Decision makers, and advocates for one decision or another, have to frame rulings that are testable as universals, and they have to test them as ingeniously as they can with counter-examples and apparent problem-cases actual or hypothetical. But they do universalize defeasibly. Circumstances turn up for which the most carefully crafted ruling and the most elegant justification are simply inept and call for a rephrasing of the original or a new and perhaps radical exception to it. Defeasible universals are, however, still universals.

---

[31] Hart, *Concept of Law* p. 139. The whole passage is worth quoting in relation to the present argument: 'We promise to visit a friend the next day. When the day comes, it turns out that keeping the promise would involve neglecting someone dangerously ill. The fact that this is accepted as an adequate reason for not keeping the promise surely does not mean that there is no rule requiring promises to be kept, only a certain regularity in keeping them. It does not follow from the fact that such rules have exceptions incapable of exhaustive statement, that in every situation we are left to our discretion and are never bound to keep a promise. A rule that ends with the word "unless..." is still a rule...'.

13

Judging Mistakenly?

Introduction

The argument up to this point has established that the apparent antithesis between the arguable character of law and the ideal of legal certainty implicit in the Rule of Law may be a resoluble tension. It all depends on the extent to which there are genuine constraints upon legal argument, so that the process of making determinate that which is indeterminate and developing that which appears to need development can be accepted as non-arbitrary, being based on good grounds of a distinctively legal kind. The issue therefore focuses on the persuasive character of legal arguments, beyond the point at which these can be cast in a simple legal-syllogistic form, when the issue is about establishing premisses rather than about drawing conclusions from them. Let us recapitulate upon the matters established so far.

The syllogistic form is indeed important, for it shows that the application of law is rooted in the idea of applying universalistic rules in particular cases that do instantiate the facts the rule stipulates as being legally operative. This can, however, be problematic, and it is frequently problematized in law. Challenges can be raised about the relevancy of the major premiss or about its proper interpretation, or about the proper classification of the particular facts that allegedly instantiate the rule's operative-fact predicates, or about the appropriate application of a value predicate (a 'standard') included in the rule. And there can be problems of proof that intertwine with the other problems. Add to this the fact that the interpretation of the normative consequences stipulated in a rule can be as problematic as the interpretation of the operative facts when it comes to applying a rule.

Dealing with these problems calls for the exercise of practical reason, and accounting for what is done requires a statement of reasons. The stated reasons are justifying reasons in respect of law-applying decisions sought by citizens or their counsel and made by judges. Such reasons have certain characteristics that have been explored at length. They are universalistic, or at least universalizable. The universals they deploy have to be tested in respect of their consequences, most particularly in respect of their juridical consequences. This involves evaluation by reference to values of a kind appropriate to law in general and/or to particular branches of law. Arguments from precedent illustrate these points, and interpretative argument exhibits a similar concern for teleology in the light of reasonable objectives imputed to particular statutes or other legal instruments, while at the same time having due regard to the linguistic and systemic context of the text of the instrument. 'Reasonableness' illustrates one of the pervasive values deployed by lawmakers and judges, and shows how multi-factored are arguments concerning such values in the legal context. The requirement of coherence, both in its normative and in its narrative senses, imposes a significant constraint on what is acceptable by way of arguments toward legal conclusions, and indicates the essential role both of principled argument and of arguments from analogy in law. Both in the application of legal rules and in the proposing of (universalistic) rulings to resolve problems of law application, the defeasibility of legal premises and conclusions is an always present feature of law, and of its necessary openness to unanticipated developments.

If practical reasoning and argumentation in law do have these characteristics, what are we to say about their persuasiveness? Are we in the end dealing only with the capability of arguments to move a particular audience into a particular frame of mind, resulting in their holding a new belief?[1] Or is there, truly, a quality of rational persuasiveness such that some arguments are really better than others, and can be received as justly convincing because of this quality they have, while those that have it in greater measure than others must be acknowledged as better arguments? Then the audience would come to its conclusion because it grasps the arguments one way and assents to the conclusion by virtue of their quality as arguments, in preference to arguments the other way after these have been equally well grasped and appraised. Its members could therefore account for why they were persuaded, by giving their own reasoned opinion about the quality of the arguments.

1. On Matters of Opinion

One point of undeniable certainty is that very often the issue which is the best or the better argument on a given point is much disputed. In great landmark decisions of highest courts and equally in more run-of-the-mill cases before intermediate appellate tribunals or courts or tribunals of first instance,[2] dissenting judgments are frequent in those legal systems that allow for such dissents. Where single collegiate judgments of a court are the rule, the judgment finally pronounced often shows the signs of having been a compromise. Though judicial propriety calls for non-disclosure of any disagreements during the private

---

[1] George Christie, *The Notion of an Ideal Audience in Legal Argument* (Dordrecht: Kluwer Academic Publishers, 2000), at 193–9, argues sympathetically in favour of Perelman's notion of an ideal universal audience, but warns that in real life the orientation of particular arguments is and has to be relative to variations of legal culture.

[2] Of course, where first instance tribunals comprise a single judge, no issue of dissent arises!

deliberations of a judicial college, it is an open secret that such disagreements do take place and have to be handled as far as possible by compromise solutions or, finally, by a vote, such as openly takes place in tribunals of the other kind. These judicial disagreements concern points on which opposing counsel have deployed the best arguments they can, typically rather convincing ones, for one or another interpretation of the prevailing rules of law in the light of underlying principles and relevant values. If there are right answers, we may say, they are not always obvious right answers.[3] (One reason why, in France, for example, collegiate courts do not permit dissenting opinions is precisely because the function of the courts is deemed to be that of '*bouches des lois*' and to state the law with a single voice rather than undermine confidence in the clarity and certainty of the laws.[4])

This rules out of serious consideration any kind of naively cognitivist view about the quality of better or worse in arguments. It would be deeply implausible to claim that in this process there is something one simply 'sees' in a straightforward way. Whatever faculty we have for coming to conclusions on such finely balanced matters, it is not well assimilated to any of our basic senses, of sight, smell, taste, sound, or touch, nor is it like 'internal' feelings such as pain or pleasure that are immediately present to us. It is more like our faculty for thinking out the answer to complicated theoretical or factual matters, as in judging the probable truth of a complex narrative (see Chapter 11). It is a matter of opinion or of judgement, not a matter of what you see just because it is there in front of your eyes, or mind's eye. It is a matter of reflective and strongly contextual judgement, not of immediate perception or even hunch (though one may often start from a hunch—and then confirm or disconfirm it on maturer reflection). Material to this is a remark of Lord Hoffmann in *Kleinwort Benson Ltd v Lincoln City Council*, concerning what counts as a mistake of law. Does a person who acts on one view of the law count as having acted on the basis of a mistake if a subsequent judgment by a superior court lays down a ruling in law that contradicts the view that person held at the time she or he acted?[5]

I have to confess that on this point I have changed my mind. At the end of the argument I was of opinion, perhaps not in a very focused way, that a person who pays in accordance with what was then a settled view of the law has not made a mistake. In fact it seemed to me that one could go further and say that if he had acted in accordance with a tenable view of the law, he had not made a mistake. In the first case he was right, and in the second neither

---

[3] John Alder, 'Dissents in Courts of Last Resort: Tragic Choices?' *Oxford Journal of Legal Studies* 20 (2000) 221–46 argues that dissents indicate collisions of incommensurable values that cannot both be satisfied, e.g. in clashes of principle and expediency ('policy'), hence the tie-breaking vote is always in a sense arbitrary. Scott Veitch, *Moral Conflict and Legal Reasoning* (Oxford: Hart Publishing, 1999) 169–71 can be read in a similar sense. The present argument opposes this view.

[4] Compare M. Troper, 'Statutory Interpretation in France' in MacCormick and Summers (eds) *Interpreting Statutes* 171–212 at 199; M. Taruffo, 'Institutional Factors affecting Precedent', in MacCormick and Summers (eds), *Interpreting Precedents* 437–60 at 451.

[5] *Kleinwort Benson Ltd v Lincoln City Council* [1999] 2 AC 349 at 398; [1998] 4 All ER 513 at 552.

right nor wrong, but in both cases his state of mind could be better described as a failure to predict the outcome of some future event (scilicet, a decision of this House) than a mistake about the existing state of the law.

On reflection, however, I have come to the conclusion that this theory was wrong, both in its stronger ('tenable view') and in its weaker ('settled view') form. The reason, I think, is that it looks at the question of what counts as a mistake in too abstract a way, divorced from its setting in the law of unjust enrichment.

This suggests that what is in issue is a reflective formation of opinion, taking account of a number of relevant factors to which one ascribes weight in the light of the particular context.

In the Scottish case that was a precursor to *Kleinwort*, namely *Morgan Guaranty v Lothian Regional Council*,[6] considerable efforts were made to trace back to its roots the ground of the duty in Scots law to repay money paid by one party to another in error. The basic principle is that one person should not profit by another's loss ('*nemo debet locupletari aliena jactura*' in the original civilian sources), and this is received in Scots law as a principle of equity. It appears, however, that there is no reason in equity to distinguish between errors of law and errors of fact when the issue is of one person gaining from another's error, and the matter is considered as between these two parties only. Certainly, in the case of errors of law, the effect of a decision declaring that a certain view was erroneous may have implications for transactions among other parties, with a consequential weakening of certainty in completed commercial and other transactions. But this, the Court of Session argued, was not itself an equitable consideration, it was one of expediency. Moreover, it was susceptible of being, and had to some extent been, guarded against by legislation on prescription and limitation of actions. House of Lords precedents that had influenced the Scots courts in adopting a rule against restitution of money paid under a mistake of law were shown to have been arrived at in ignorance of the then prevailing Scottish authorities, the true character of which was revealed by historical research. Further, in other mixed civil-and-common law jurisdictions, and in many Commonwealth jurisdictions, the old doctrine that precluded restitution in cases of a mistake of law, based on the English decisions of the nineteenth century, had been abandoned.

All in all, there was in the court's view, no sufficient justification to retain the rule against restitution in cases of mistake of law, though it was necessary to remain alive to equitable considerations militating against repayment as these might appear in various classes of case—it would in such cases be a matter for the defender to lodge an appropriate plea. The Court also held that there was no need to leave it to Parliament to abrogate the old rule, since what was in issue was reassertion of a long-standing principle of Scots law that had been effectively overruled from the standpoint of English doctrines imposed at a time when the House of Lords had no effective Scottish legal input in its decision-making. In

---

[6] 1995 SC 151.

Morgan Guaranty, the Court of Session, sitting as a Full Court of five judges, reached its decision unanimously. It seems right to say that, as summarized here, the arguments do bear considerable cumulative persuasiveness, provided the objection to law reform by judicial decision is considered to have been satisfactorily met—no court does or should lightly overturn a precedent that has stood for many years. Taking it as a whole, the argument reviews and assesses many factors, and these do support each other 'like the legs of a chair, not the links of a chain'.

The difficulty concerning judicial law reform was considered even more acute in the *Kleinwort* case in England, where indeed the majority was a bare three to two in favour of abolishing the 'mistake of law' rule. Moreover, as noted, Lord Hoffmann acknowledged that his initial inclination had been towards the opposed view. So it was in every sense a finely balanced issue. The rule barring restitution of payments made under a mistake of law stood to be reversed by judicial decision, despite the fact that the Law Commission had recommended a statutory rather than a judicial redetermination of the law, in order that the new dispensation might at the same time deal with consequential problems about the potential weakening of certainty in relation to concluded transactions. Lord Goff and the majority that decided in favour of revoking the 'mistake of law' rule acknowledged, indeed, that this was a case of 'developing the law'. It did indeed involve changing a long-established rule, with an inevitably retrospective effect, in view of the prevailing declaratory theory of precedents (discussed further below). Even so, they considered that this was a legitimate use of the judicial power, not an invasion of the domain of the legislature, although the latter can legislate prospectively while at the same time regulating the impact of new law (or even retrospective new law) on transactions already effected. The minority found this deeply alarming, as the following quotations from Lord Lloyd of Berwick make vivid:[7]

Nobody now suggests that the common law is static. It is capable of adapting itself to new circumstances. Is it then capable of being changed? Or is it only capable of being developed? The common sense answer is that the common law is capable of being changed, not only by legislation, but also by judicial decision. This is nowhere clearer than when a long-standing decision of the Court of Appeal is overruled. Indeed in a system such as ours, where the Court of Appeal is bound by its own previous decisions, the main justification for the existence of a second tier appeal is that it enables the House [of Lords] to re-direct the law when it has taken a wrong turning.

If it is right that the House of Lords can change the law by overruling a previous decision of the Court of Appeal, it must follow that a person relying on the old law was under no mistake at the time, and cannot claim to have been under a mistake ex post facto because the law is subsequently changed. This is obviously true where the law is changed by legislation. In my opinion it is equally true when the law is changed by judicial decision.

What are the consequences [of reversing the mistake of law rule, without excluding reliance on a 'settled view of the law' as non-mistaken]? One consequence is that in all

---

[7] See [1999] 2 AC 349 at 393, 394, 397–8; [1998] 4 All ER 513 at 547, 548, 552.

those cases where the House of Lords has overruled a previous decision of the Court of Appeal it would be open to those who have entered into transactions in reliance on the previous decision to seek to re-open their transactions. This is a consequence which, in the commercial field at any rate, I view with alarm. My noble and learned friend Lord Hoffmann accepts that there is a problem, but considers that the solution can be left to Parliament…But in the meantime there will be an inevitable period of intense uncertainty.

Lord Browne-Wilkinson spoke with equal alarm about the risks of uncertainty in law consequential on the line taken by the majority—and with considerable doubt about the apparent justice of the matter, since people who pay on the prevailing view of the law make no mistake, even if subsequently that view of the law ceases to prevail by virtue of a decision by the ultimate appellate tribunal.

In such a situation, what are we to say? If Lord Hoffmann had decided on reflection that his own original inclination had been right, the decision would have gone the other way. The difference between the House of Lords and the Court of Session did not really turn on a fundamental difference of principle between Scots and English law at the present day, but on the element of 'expediency' concerning the risk of reopening long-settled claims that may turn out to have been settled on a subsequently altered ruling in law. As Lord Hope (who sat in both cases) put the point:[8]

[I]n some cases a mistake of law may have affected a very large number of transactions, and…the potential for uncertainty is very great…I think that the risk of widespread injustice remains to be demonstrated. If the risk is too great that is a matter for the legislature. The problem does not arise under the statutory scheme which applies in Scotland. The prescriptive period of five years under section 6 of the Prescription and Limitation (Scotland) Act 1973 applies to any obligation based on redress of unjustified enrichment: Schedule I, para.1(*b*). It may be extended only where the creditor was induced to refrain from making a claim by fraud or error induced by the debtor's words or conduct or was under a legal disability. Mistake on its own is not a ground for relief.

It is worth noticing that Lord Hope speaks here of 'widespread injustice'. While it is true that the risk of uncertainty is from the point of view of any two parties simply a matter of policy or expediency that does not affect the balance of equity between the parties, in a wider perspective it is also a demand of justice that the institutions of the state protect citizens from needless uncertainty concerning their rights. However that may be, the position under statute law in Scotland concerning prescription and limitation is decidedly different from that in England, where time only runs against a person when she/he has discovered that she/he was mistaken, or reasonably should have so discovered. Clearly this considerably affects the balance of convenience, however much weight attaches to this. In the upshot, two of the Law Lords voted not to discontinue the 'mistake of law' rule since it was impossible at the same time to introduce an exception according

---

[8] [1999] 2 AC at 573; [1998] 4 All ER at 569.

to which one who acts on the settled view of the law at a given time cannot afterwards complain of having made a mistake of law in the event of new case law that unsettles the previously settled view. The other three voted to abrogate the rule, with no such exception attached.

What account should be given of such differences of judicial opinion? The first point to make, assuredly, is that it is of opinion—carefully considered opinion— that these are differences. Law is not the only discipline or practical art in which the most highly qualified experts can come to different opinions about cases. Difficult medical diagnoses, and prognoses predicated on different possible courses of treatment can also occasion diversity of opinion among the most highly qualified and highly skilled specialists, and the same goes for consulting engineers, architects, accountants, and, one must suppose, practically all professional or, indeed non-professional, domains of expert judgement. Certainly, the way the patient or building project turns out in the light of the advice that was followed is one test of its wisdom, though it must remain purely conjectural how things would have turned out had different but equally expert advice been followed. To some extent, innovative judicial decisions can be appraised in the light of how they work out as precedents in later cases, and sometimes leading decisions are fairly swiftly limited or abandoned.[9]

Matters of opinion, it may seem, stand opposed to matters of fact; but that is not quite so. Medical opinions may be largely about matters of fact, but about complex matters of fact concerning what inferences to draw from symptoms and diagnostic tests, and what predictions to make about probable future developments of a certain condition in a patient. The problems are about the interpretation of symptoms and other diagnostic aids, and relating these to current (often imperfect) understandings of complex causal processes. The value of an opinion where such interpretative issues matter depends on who holds it, and how they came to it. A person's expertise and established skill give credibility to that person's opinion against another's, on the matters in which their skill is established and in relation to which they have had time to give careful first-hand attention to a specific problem. Judges do not prescribe for heart diseases nor cardiologists decide law suits. Wisdom is the fruit of trained intelligence and long experience, coupled with some initial aptitude to a certain domain of activity.

Those who have practical wisdom in the inquiry of right, '*juris prudentes*', jurisprudents, are those whose opinion is of value concerning the law, and in litigation before the highest tribunals, the very senior judges sitting there have the benefit of hearing (or reading) long and carefully—and persuasively—stated arguments which put either point of view (all points of view in multi-party

---

[9] For example, the ruling in *Pepper v Hart* [1993] AC 593 according to which Hansard may be consulted for assistance in relation to statutory interpretation, has been drastically restricted, and if not quite reversed: see J. Steyn (Lord Steyn), '*Pepper v Hart*: a Re-Examination', *Oxford Journal of Legal Studies* 21 (2001) 59–72; Aileen Kavanagh '*Pepper v Hart* and Matters of Constitutional Principle' *Law Quarterly Review* 121 (2005) 98–122.

situations) in the strongest terms counsel can devise, with reference also to academic experts.[10] As appeal tribunals, they also have the advantage of being able to consider and ponder the judgment(s) of the trial court and any intermediate appeal court. Even then, in highly problematic cases, differences of judgement and opinion can persist. Partly, this is imputable to the relevance of consequentialist argument, where there may be differences of apprehension concerning what may happen if the precedent is followed. In *Kleinwort*, for example, there was a clear disagreement concerning the degree and extent of uncertainty implied by the decision in its universalized application, and the commercial or other damage this would involve. It can also concern the likelihood of legislative action, either as an alternative to judicial decision on the one hand, or as a necessary curative of uncertainty arising. This may also (again as in *Kleinwort*) go alongside of substantial agreement on other main points, for example, the unfairness and inexpediency of distinguishing different cases of money paid under an erroneous view that one has an obligation to pay it, depending on whether the error concerns the legal or the factual basis of the obligation in question.

Such differences of opinion are endemic (though, over time, people may come to a different view from the one they originally held). To them one's general political and ethical outlook makes a real contribution (as is highly visible in constitutional courts such as the US Supreme Court or the German *Bundesverfassungsgericht*; also the European Court of Justice, which however decides collegially without disclosure of individual judges' opinions, given the potential sensitivity of national differences for the character of the EU, at least at this stage in its development). This is inevitable. For, however sincerely judges and others attempt to insulate the courts from the partisan controversies that are built into representative democracy and that dominate legislative debate, the values and principles implicit in law and explicitly deployed in the most problematic cases are also political values and principles, in many cases representing the never-permanent outcome of past political struggles.

It is important to stress that disagreement, although endemic, is focused, episodic, and local, not all-pervasive and universal across the whole range of the law. If the latter were the case, the state and civil society would be on the verge of collapse, or over the verge, and the law would be a battlefield not a by-and-large established and functioning system of institutional norms. Disagreements concerning deep and important matters of opinion exist. But they are disagreements among persons who share a view of the points that are in issue in the argument, whilst assigning different weight to different components, singly or in some combination or combinations. In this sense, they are reasonable disagreements among reasonable persons, persisting after careful and thoughtful debate and deliberation.

---

[10] Note how, in the *Conjoined Twins* case, Ward LJ contrasts the constraints of time the trial judge had worked under with the opportunity the Court of Appeal enjoyed to consider a much wider and deeper range of arguments [2001] Fam. at 180, [2000] 4 All ER at 988; note also the weight now accorded in such cases to academic opinions.

Practically speaking, there is only one generic way to handle such disagreements, which is by some form of hierarchy of authoritative judgment, and some system of majority voting in multi-judge tribunals, whether this involve voting in public or only in private. A reasonable decision-making procedure is the only appropriate solution to interpersonal disagreement, where all or most of those affected by it accept that the disagreement is indeed reasonable, not simply the polite face of the powerful addressed to those with less power. Such a procedure is then in its inherent character law-determining, at any rate on a case-by-case basis. The rights or wrongs of parties, and the remedies or penalties prescribed after such argument are, or become by the very act of deciding, the operative rights or lawful liabilities of those parties in the terms laid down according to the majority (or, when possible, unanimous) opinion of the tribunal in question. Under a system of binding or persuasive precedent, such decisions also spill over from each particular case and are received as law-stating, or authoritatively law-interpreting and-determining, so far as concerns everyone else in the jurisdiction.

2. Precedents and the Declaratory Theory

All modern western systems acknowledge precedent in one or other way,[11] and law reports record the most significant among them, in great profusion. It may be and may remain an open question in an intellectual sense which set of arguments in *Kleinwort* or any other case was truly the strongest. But for purposes of practical governance, the argument is over, for the time being. Critique in law journals and political or popular press may build up a head of steam for a reconsideration of a questionable decision, and indeed the issue may be transferred into the legislature, which can (in some situations at least) enact legislation that redetermines the issue for the future. The long history of struggle between courts and Parliament concerning the legalization of Trades Unions in the United Kingdom in the nineteenth and early twentieth centuries (resumed again in the nineteen sixties) is a salutary example, and a reminder of the standing risk of class bias in legal institutions.[12]

The way in which the issue of mistakes in law arose in *Kleinwort* adds a certain piquancy to the issue whether judges can make mistakes. If there is a single right answer to a legal question of this kind, the very fact that the judges disagreed indicates that one or other of them must have been in error, even if it is difficult to tell which is, or if commentators in turn disagree on the question which is. Perhaps the truth is that either answer was one that could be asserted with good supporting reasons as well as serious opposing reasons, so that each would have a

---

[11] See MacCormick and Summers (eds), *Interpreting Precedents.*
[12] Compare J. A. G. Griffith, *The Politics of the Judiciary* (London: Fontana, 5th edn, 1997) 63–102.

reasonable claim to being true, on condition that, in that case, the other is false. As noted already, this looks like a difference of reasonably formed opinion among reasonable people who are themselves wise and well informed, and deeply learned in the matters at stake. Accordingly, the method of resolution by voting is required here, and that which has the majority is the operative decision, that which, under a doctrine of binding precedent establishes (defeasibly, at least) what is to be the rule on this matter in the system henceforward. Whatever the prior truth of the matter, the act of deciding institutes a new truth in law, namely, that mistake of law does not preclude restitution in cases of payment by mistake.

What may have been false thus becomes true for future purposes of the law. The same goes, after all for all cases of acquittals or convictions that were erroneous. Smith did it, but was declared 'not guilty'; Robinson did not do it but was declared 'guilty'. Possibilities of appeal apart, such verdicts settle the matter internally to the legal system, whatever controversy may rage externally to it.[13] There is, however, a particular problem about a decision like that in *Kleinwort*, and more generally in other cases. This has to do with the so-called 'declaratory theory' of precedent. According to this, the task of judges is not making the law but declaring what it is, and applying it as it is. The underlying problem both in *Morgan Guaranty* and *Kleinwort* arose out of transactions between banks and local authorities of a kind known as 'interest rate swaps', aimed at enabling local authorities to get compensating advantages to cover losses arising out of interest rate fluctuations. These the parties (naturally) presumed to be legal under the financial powers conferred on local authorities under relevant Acts of Parliament. However, the question of legality was raised by the Local Government Auditor, and finally settled on appeal in 1991 to the House of Lords, which determined that the transactions involved were beyond the statutory powers of the local authorities, and hence illegal.[14] The transactions in question took place between 1983 and 1989; at issue was whether the Local Government Act 1972 conferred power to enter into transactions of the kind exemplified by these interest rate swaps. The Lords answered that it did not.

The case was one of first impression; hence it was the first time the relevant sections of the 1972 Act had been judicially construed in respect of this aspect of local authorities' powers. Necessarily, such a decision says what the Act means and has meant all along, ever since laid down in 1972. To take it in a different sense, and to contend that this changes the law (or changes understanding of the law),

---

[13] Consider, for example, the 'Appin Murder' of 1747 in Scotland, controversy about which is central to R. L. Stevenson's two classic nineteenth century novels *Kidnapped* and *Catriona*, and about which controversial historical commentaries still appear from time to time (e.g. S. Carney, *The Appin Murder* (Edinburgh: Birlinn, 1994). The better view appears to be that James Stewart of the Glen (*Seumas a' Ghlinne*) did not commit the murder of Colin Campbell of Glenure for which he was convicted, hanged, and his corpse exhibited for many years on a gibbet near the mouth of Loch Leven. Other continuing controversies concern whether or not Lee Harvey Oswald murdered President Kennedy single-handed in Texas in 1963, and whether the conviction in the *Lockerbie* case was justified on the evidence.　　　[14] *Hazell v Hammersmith and Fulham LBC* [1992] 2 AC 1.

and hence can have only prospective effect, would be paradoxical. For it would amount to saying that, as the Lords interpret the Act, it does not confer and never has conferred the relevant power, but nothing can be done about the erroneous exercise of power as it has been carried on till now, and only if it continues will it be effectively illegal. On the other hand, it does necessarily follow that in declaring what the law has meant all along, the House of Lords (or a different court) affects the meaning of the law for all who have acted under it. The decision necessarily implies (because of universalizability) that any other local authority's interest rate swap was invalid for the same reason. (This is exactly what led Kleinwort Benson to sue Lincoln City and other local authorities for return of the excess sums they had paid under the swap contracts.) Transactions undertaken by parties on a certain understanding of the law turn out after the event (after the making and implementation of the contract) to have been invalid—and then the issue of 'mistake of law' by the parties arises with a vengeance.

Retrospectivity of this kind is, in the view of Lord Goff, who gave the principal speech in *Kleinwort*, 'inevitable', a point with which it seems necessary to concur.[15] Here is the gist of the argument:[16]

In the course of deciding the case before him [a judge] may, on occasion, develop the common law in the perceived interests of justice, though as a general rule he does this 'only interstitially', to use the expression of O.W. Holmes J.... This means not only that he must act within the confines of the doctrine of precedent, but that the change so made must be seen as a development... of existing principle and so can take its place as a congruent part of the common law as a whole. [Usually such developments are modest in extent, but sometimes they can mark major steps in reconfiguring the law in the light of changed times and circumstances.]

[T]he law which the judge then states to be applicable to the case before him is the law which, as so developed, is perceived by him as applying not only to the case before him, but to all other comparable cases, as a congruent part of the body of the law. Moreover when he states the applicable principles of law, the judge is declaring these as constituting the law relevant to his decision [so]... what he states to be the law will, generally speaking, be applicable not only to the case before him but, as part of the common law, to other comparable cases which come before the courts, whenever the events which are the subject of those cases in fact occurred. It is in this context that we have to reinterpret the declaratory theory of judicial decision. We can see that, in fact, it does not presume the existence of an ideal system of the common law, which the judges from time to time reveal in their decisions. The historical theory of judicial decision, though it may in the past have served its purpose, was indeed a fiction. But it does mean that, when the judges state what the law is, their decisions do, in the sense I have described, have a retrospective effect. That is, I believe, inevitable.

---

[15] But Lord Rodger of Earlsferry draws attention to ways in which the 'intertemporal' interaction of different legal authorities (e.g. European Human Rights Court in relation to courts in the UK) can have a bearing on the possibility of prospective overruling. See 'A Time for Everything Under Law' *Law Quarterly Review* 121 (2005) 57–79 at 75–7.

[16] [1999] 2 AC 349 at 378; [1998] 4 All ER 513 at 534–5.

The sharp contrast between this and the view of Lord Lloyd already quoted is of some importance. Lord Lloyd treats it as being a matter of obvious common sense that the judges change the law, hence they should change it only with great prudence. On such a view, to state that people who acted earlier on a different, but widely held, understanding of the law acted under a mistake about the law is wrong. They were right then, but the law has changed now. Lord Goff's view is that judges indeed 'develop' the law, and this does involve change; but of a special kind: 'the change so made must be seen as a development . . . of existing principle and so can take its place as a congruent part of the common law as a whole'. Lord Goff's 'congruent' expresses the same idea as 'coherence' in Chapter 10, in which also the idea of 'development' of law was discussed. This means that some changes in operative rules, as likewise adoption of particular interpretations of enacted law, have to be in a certain sense already derivable from the existing materials of the law, deploying established principles and values in new contexts. This amounts to change within genuine continuity, and is distinguishable from the kind of more radical change that is legitimate only through the legislative process and after all the associated forms of deliberation through green papers, public consultation, commissions of inquiry, and all such like matters leading up to debate and decision in the legislature.

If this alleged difference is illusory, then the declaratory theory breaks down into incoherence, and there would be nothing for it but to embark on a new approach to decision-making and the interpretation of precedent. Probably by legislation, it would be appropriate to introduce a practice of 'prospective overruling',[17] through rules stating some criteria to limit the retrospective impact of any decision, and to ensure its appropriate prospectivity of effect as a precedent. On the other hand, even if the difference is not illusory, it does not follow that every exercise of the judicial power is or will be a sound or prudent one. Judges who professedly and indeed actually adhere to the applicability of the constraint of 'coherence' (or 'congruence' in Lord Goff's usage) may on occasion overstep its boundary. For the theory is necessarily one according to which judges, even those of highest authority, are capable of making mistakes. The anguished protests of Lord Browne-Wilkinson and Lord Lloyd of Berwick in *Kleinwort* alert us to the possibility that the majority in that very case may well have erred on the merits and on the acceptability of using this opportunity to overturn a long-established rule rather than leaving this task to the legislature, which could have dealt with the whole problem prospectively.

The declaratory theory presupposes that there is some way of achieving a right answer to questions of the kind we are considering. This is not because there is in existence some item of law that can be 'read off', so to speak, but because

---

[17] See R. H. S. Tur 'Time and Law' *Oxford Journal of Legal Studies* 22 (2002) 463–88, esp. at 474 and compare his 'Varieties of Overruling and Judicial Law Making: Prospective Overruling in a Comparative Perspective' *Juridical Review* (1978).

appropriate arguments applied to the established body of law can persuasively establish one conclusion on the given problem as more acceptable than any other.[18] The only possible alternative to this view is a decisionist one. On the latter view, what a court decides is right because that court has decided it, and it has not (or not yet) been reversed on appeal. Judges may decide in an unwise or impolitic way, but they can't actually make mistakes about the law in problem cases, since there is no anterior truth of the matter about which they could be mistaken.

3. Decisionism: An Example

The approach I will take to considering the persuasiveness of decisionism in this context is through examining a legal decision triggered off by the Suez crisis of 1956, from which emerged one of the path-breaking decisions in the reshaping of United Kingdom administrative law that took place in the third quarter of the twentieth century. From judgments passed in it, it I will cite two quite extensive passages. The case is *Anisminic v Foreign Compensation Commission.*[19]

One of the results of the ill-considered British intervention in the conflict over, and attempted repossession of, the Suez Canal in 1956, was a large-scale seizure by the government of the United Arab Republic (UAR) of assets belonging to British nationals (including corporations) in that country. In due course, after considerable diplomatic activity, an agreement was struck between the UK and UAR governments for payment by the UAR of a large sum of money in compensation for all British property seized and retained by it in the Sinai Peninsula and elsewhere. The Foreign Compensation Commission is a statutory body set up to decide about claims for compensation for losses suffered by British nationals overseas in circumstances in which the United Kingdom government has received compensation from a foreign government for distributing among injured British nationals. It was given the task of appropriately distributing the compensation fund for property seized in Egypt to persons and corporations who were able to make a justified claim, showing that they had suffered a loss of relevant assets. The regulations (technically, 'Orders in Council') concerning the process of making and deciding these claims included a provision that claims could be made by the original owners of seized assets and any relevant 'successors in title'. But both owners and successors in title had to be British nationals at the dates stipulated in the regulations.

The Anisminic Company was one claimant, but the Commission rejected its claim, on the following ground: although Anisminic had lost property in Sinai, it

---

[18] Compare John Bell 'The Acceptability of Legal Arguments' in N. MacCormick and P. B. H. Birks, *The Legal Mind: Essays for Tony Honoré* (Oxford: Clarendon Press, 1986) pp. 45–66; also Klaus Günther, *The Sense of Appropriateness: Application Discourses in Morality and Law* (trans. J. Farrell), (Albany: State University of New York Press, 1993) p. 224. The whole of the present work deals with what Günther calls 'application discourses', since what is in issue is not primarily the justification of general rules of law, but their application case-by-case.   [19] [1969] 2 AC 197.

had already succeeded, through applying commercial pressures, in negotiating some compensatory payments directly from the government of the UAR, which, after seizing the company's assets, had passed them to an Egyptian body called 'T.E.D.O.'. The Foreign Compensation Commission took the view that the result of these independent negotiations was to make T.E.D.O. the 'successor in title' to Anisminic in respect of its mining operations in Sinai. Since T.E.D.O. was not a British national, this disqualified Anisminic from obtaining compensation under the regulation concerning 'successors in title'. But according to Anisminic's view of the matter, this decision was based on a wholly wrong interpretation of the concept 'successor in title'. They said that T.E.D.O. had clearly no right to be considered any kind of successor to Anisminic's claim for compensation, which was based on the very fact of UAR seizure of the mining operations and transfer of them to T.E.D.O..

Anisminic therefore initiated an action in the High Court in London to obtain a declaration that the decision against the company was invalid on the ground of the fundamental legal misinterpretation involved. In doing so, they faced a formidable obstacle. Section 4 of the Foreign Compensation Act, the Act which established the Commission provides as follows: 'The determination by the Commission of any application made to them under this Act shall not be called in question in any court of law.' A provision of this type, protecting administrative decisions from judicial review, is by no means uncommon in legislation of the United Kingdom Parliament that establishes special commissions, authorities, or agencies for carrying out special functions in the public domain, giving them some form of decision-making power. The question has been how far such a provision does actually exclude supervision by the courts of the legality of actions of such special public bodies. By contrast with other European countries, the United Kingdom never developed superior administrative courts or tribunals with general public law powers, on the model of the French Conseil d'Etat or of the German Administrative Courts. Indeed, according to one highly authoritative view,[20] the special feature of the British version of the 'Rule of Law' has been that the same courts as decide matters of private law between citizens also decide public law issues between citizen and state.

Governments have, however, been hostile to excessive interference by the courts in the business of the state, and have prevailed upon Parliament to include in many Acts dealing with public powers privative clauses such as section 4 of the Foreign Compensation Act, severely limiting, if not totally excluding, the power of the courts to make decisions that override those of the specially con-stituted public agencies. Then the question is whether respect for the Rule of Law requires the courts to give a broad construction to the exemption of such agencies from their interference, or to construe such 'privative clauses' narrowly, to enable

---

[20] See A. V. Dicey, *An Introduction to the Study of the Law of the Constitution* E. C. S. Wade (ed.), (London: Macmillan & Co, 10th edn, 1964) chs 4 and 12.

the citizen to challenge through the common law errors or abuses by public bodies exercising statutory powers. The increasing tendency of the second half of the twentieth century was to build up a body of administrative law within which the power of the courts to exercise judicial review over the decision-making of public agencies expanded, and doctrines governing the proper exercise of public powers were thus developed.

The *Anisminic* case was one landmark in this development. For the company to succeed in its case, it had to argue not only that the Commission had made a legal error in rejecting its claim for compensation, but had to argue also that the error was of such a kind as to render ineffective the protection that the privative clause conferred on a 'determination' by the Commission of questions raised with it under the Act. According to the prevailing administrative jurisprudence, this required that the error must have been of a kind that deprived the Commission's decision of any valid legal effect, making it from a legal point of view a nullity, not a 'determination' at all. The judge of first instance in the High Court held that Anisminic had made out such an argument; the Court of Appeal held that it had not, and overruled the judgment at first instance. On final appeal, the House of Lords overruled the Court of Appeal, and reaffirmed the judgment at first instance.

Perhaps even that brief, all-too-summary, description of the way the case went forward indicates why it may have a bearing on the title question of this chapter. In such a case, nobody could come to a decision without having some theory about the possibility of judging mistakenly, even in a highest appellate tribunal. Any judge faced with Anisminic's claim for a declaration against the Commission had to ask and answer the question whether the Commission had made any kind of mistake and, if so, what kind, and what the effects of its mistake were. All the judges at each level in the hierarchy of appeals did ask and answer this question, and gave an extended justification for the answer given. The issue about decisionism versus judicial mistakes is posed sharply by two conflicting justifications for two opposite decisions on the main issue, respectively by Lord Diplock (Lord Justice Diplock as he then was) and Lord Reid, two of the most influential judges of the twentieth century, each given by a judge of exceptionally high repute.

First, then, as for what Lord Diplock had to say:[21]

Lawyers, when they talk of 'error', whether of 'fact' or of 'law' ... are dealing not with absolutes but with the opinions of human beings. A statement that there exist particular facts which give rise to specified legal consequences is 'right' if it is made by a person to whose opinion as to the existence or non-existence of those facts, and as to their legal consequences, effect will be given by the executive branch of government. Such a statement from being 'right' may become 'wrong', however, if subsequently a contrary statement is made by some other person to whose opinion as to the legal consequences of those facts effect will be given by the executive branch of government in substitution for

---

[21] See [1968] 2 QB 862 at 887–8; [1967] 2 All ER at p. 993.

that of the person who made the first statement. It is then the later statement that is 'right'; but it may be that effect will be given to the substituted opinion of such other person as to the legal consequences of facts only, and not as to the existence or non-existence of the particular facts which give rise to those legal consequences. In that event the original statement that particular facts exist remains 'right' and must be so treated by the person to whose substituted opinion as to the legal consequences of facts effect will be given.

Against this way of considering the matter, a real contrast can be found in the following dicta of Lord Reid:[22]

It has sometimes been said that it is only where a tribunal acts without jurisdiction that its decision is a nullity. But in such cases the word 'jurisdiction' has been used in a very wide sense, and I have come to the conclusion that it is better not to use the term except in the narrow and original sense of the tribunal being entitled to enter on the enquiry in question. But there are many cases where, although the tribunal had jurisdiction to enter on the enquiry, it has done or failed to do something in the course of the enquiry which is of such a nature that its decision is a nullity. It may have given its decision in bad faith. It may have made a decision which it had no power to make. It may have failed in the course of the enquiry to comply with the requirements of natural justice. It may in perfect good faith have misconstrued the provisions giving it power to act so that it failed to deal with the question remitted to it and decided some question which was not remitted to it. It may have refused to take into account something which it was required to take into account. Or it may have based its decision on some matter which, under the provisions setting it up, it had no right to take into account. I do not intend this list to be exhaustive. But if it decides a question remitted to it for decision without committing any of these errors it is as much entitled to decide that question wrongly as it is to decide it rightly. I understand that some confusion has been caused by my having said in *Armah v. Government of Ghana* that, if a tribunal has jurisdiction to go right, it has jurisdiction to go wrong. So it has if one uses 'jurisdiction' in the narrow original sense. If it is entitled to enter on the enquiry and does not do any of those things which I have mentioned in the course of the proceedings, then its decision is equally valid whether it is right or wrong, subject only to the power of the court in certain circumstances to correct an error of law.

The points these extended quotations make are worthy of analysis. Lord Diplock starts from the undeniable thesis that answers to questions of law are matters of opinion. He derives from that thesis the conclusion that the answers cannot be subject to any absolute standard of rightness or wrongness. Thus, for legal purposes, according to Lord Diplock, what is 'right'—and he puts 'right' in quotation marks—is definable only in terms of the authoritativeness of a person's opinion, authoritativeness being in turn a function of the preparedness of executive organs to act in response to decisive statements of opinion. Since these questions before the court are matters of opinion, argues Lord Diplock, there is no, or no available, independent ground or test for rightness of opinion other than this: whose is the opinion and how will other persons react to statements of that person's opinion? Let us call this decisionist conception of rightness the 'Diplock view'.

[22] See [1969] 2 AC 147 at 171; [1969] 1 All ER at p. 213.

By contrast, Lord Reid's opinion keeps distinct the concept of the validity of a decision and that of the rightness or wrongness of the decision given. Lord Reid envisages that there are various modes or forms of error or mistake in decision-making (he gives quite a list of these modes), and that some of those go to the issue of the validity of a decision, while others do not. What is the test for validity? The test, certainly, is primarily in terms of the authority conferred on a decision maker. The decision made by the person authorized to make it in accordance with the grant of authority, within the jurisdiction granted, is a valid decision. This is different from the rightness or wrongness of a decision. What is the test for that? The test is to be posed in terms of a variety of grounds, and Lord Reid gives a long but not exclusive list of these. Of them all, however, we must note that they are stated in terms independent of the decision maker's authority and of the decision maker's opinion. We may observe, therefore, that this is an authority-independent conception of rightness, which henceforward will be dubbed 'the Reid view'.

It should now be obvious what bearing this contrast of theses has on the title of the present chapter: is it possible for judges to judge mistakenly? Here, we have two judges advancing mutually contradictory views, admittedly at the level of theory, but still mutually contradictory views, upon the selfsame question. It follows, by the logic of excluded middle, that both cannot be right, hence that at least one is mistaken. In the history of the world, then, at least one judge has made a mistake, though so far we deal only with mistakes of a certain sort, mistakes in legal theory. (From the presence of such a mistake, it does not follow that judges are also capable of mistakes on practical questions of law.) Moreover, the Diplock view has an ostensibly paradoxical character. Like Epimenides the Cretan, who held that all Cretans were liars, Lord Diplock seems to be right only if he is wrong, and yet wrong if he is right. For in this particular context, Lord Reid's is relatively the more authoritative opinion, being given in a House of Lords decision which reversed the decision of the Court of Appeal in which Diplock participated. So, if it is true that the rightness of an opinion depends upon the authority of its maker, Lord Diplock is wrong. On the other hand, if Lord Reid's thesis as to mistakes is both correct and generalizable, then his (Lord Reid's) opinion is not self-authenticating. Reid's view acquires no necessary rightness by being issued by a judge in the ultimate instance of appeal. For the theory is one that yields an authority-independent conception of rightness. One could logically accept Lord Reid's approach to the theory of rightness and of mistakes without having to suppose that the rest of his decision was right. Indeed, one can on that very ground argue that his (and the House of Lords majority's) decision in the particular case was wrong though based on the right theory; while perhaps Lord Diplock's decision was right though based on the wrong theory.

That theory, anyway, is one which supports the view that judges (or at least some judges) logically cannot make mistakes. To be sure, it has to be put a little more guardedly: every judicial decision, in virtue of the deciding judge's authority, is right until (if ever) it is declared wrong by some higher judicial authority. Further, so long as the executive will enforce its rulings, the highest judicial authority cannot be wrong except in so far as its earlier decisions can be overturned in its later ones. In case of such rejection, the latest decision of the highest court is always and necessarily right and remains so as long as it is not (or until it is) subsequently declared wrong by the same court on a yet later occasion. Rightness depends on what is the prevailing view of the highest authority, nor, on the Diplock thesis, can there be any other test for what is right in law.

By contrast, on the Reid view, it is possible always for any judge to make a mistake. The concepts of the authority held by a decision maker, and of the authoritative character of his or her opinions, and thus also of the validity of a decision given in the exercise of that authority, are kept distinct from the issue of the decision's rightness or wrongness. In other words, the possibility of judicial error or mistake is not precluded by the fact of a judge's being in authority, even in final authority, upon the answering of a given legal question. Thus the question which (if any) judges solved a given problem correctly must be kept distinct from the question which judges handed down the most authoritative and finally valid decision. The European Court of Justice, when it decided that the Rome Treaty and associated Treaties must be interpreted as establishing a new legal order, separate both from international law and from the domestic law of Member States, or when it decided that this law formed necessarily a part of Member State law, and yet enjoyed supremacy over it in virtue of the transfer by Member States to Community of part of their sovereign rights, decided with final authority in the framework of the law of the European Community. The German Constitutional Court, on the other hand, decided that, though the ratification of the Maastricht Treaty was valid as a matter of German constitutional law, and not incompatible with the fundamental guarantee of democracy in the Basic Law, yet any further transfer of powers might violate that guarantee, and that it would be violated by any interpretation of Community Law as granting competence-competence to Community organs, including the European Court of Justice. In so doing it for its part acted with final authority under the German Constitution.[23] Yet, if the thesis of judicial fallibility is correct, either or both of these approaches might be challenged as wrong even though for the moment authoritative. Some would indeed say that the conflicting quality of the approaches shows that one at least is wrong, though legal pluralists would plausibly contend that each could be right within the particular frame of reference provided by the legal system in question, that of Germany or that of the European Union.

[23] These matters are more fully discussed in N. MacCormick, *Questioning Sovereignty* (Oxford: Clarendon Press, 1999) ch. 7; also 'The Maastricht-Urteil: Sovereignty now' *European Law Journal* 1 (1995) 259–66.

4. Against Decisionism

The question about mistaken judgments has a serious point. The arguments respectively by Lord Reid and by Lord Diplock, have each at first sight considerable persuasive force. This shows how much the question before us is a live one, and not just a live one for theorists, but also for judges and practitioners themselves. The rivalry of these two doctrines matters at several levels and in several ways. First of all, let us consider it on the level of the history of legal theory or jurisprudence; we can see how the two judicial opinions parallel and find alliance in different approaches to legal theory. To think of Lord Diplock's view for a moment, that great swelling of opinion and exciting outburst of theorizing in the United States in the early part of the twentieth century, which we know as the 'American Realist' movement, was saying the same thing as Lord Diplock. Law is not a matter of a brooding omnipresence in the sky, as Oliver Wendell Holmes Jr. put it,[24] it is a matter of the decisions and opinions of yesterday and today, and all the more of tomorrow. Knowing the law is knowing how to predict what the authoritative decision makers will decide, not knowing some abstract set of propositions that might be written in a legal textbook.

Again, this view receives support from a very different thinker, Hans Kelsen, who, especially as his career proceeded, grew more and more sceptical of the possibilities of applying logic in the sphere of the normative world of the rules and principles that stipulate what people ought to do. Especially by the end of his life, Kelsen's 'pure theory of law' embraced the view that decisions by authorized persons are necessarily right since no demonstrative argument can be made to show that they are contrary to the law, there being no possibility of logical and demonstrative argument using the raw materials of the law, which are decisions, not assertions, acts of will not acts of thought.[25] In yet a different way, the Critical Legal Studies movement in the contemporary United States makes much of the fact that, as they say, there is never final closure in law. Somebody could always decide something different, there is no final rightness and those who teach or suppose otherwise commit the sin of reification, talking about law as though it was something 'out there', discussable, objective, whereas all it is in the last resort is the decision of the moment by those in power for the moment.[26]

---

[24] Per O.W. Holmes J., in *Southern Pacific Co v Jensen* 244 US 205,222 (1901).

[25] H. Kelsen, *Reine Rechtslehre*, 1st edn 1934, reprinted 1985, S. L.Paulson (ed.), (Aalen: Scientia Verlag, 1985) section 38, pp. 97–9; and see later editions, and *Allgemeine Theorie der Normen* (Vienna: Manzsche Verlags- und Universitätsbuchhandlung, 1979), chs 57–9; Kelsen grew more and more convinced of the gap between logic, applicable to acts of thought, and legal decisions as acts of will, hence either valid or not, and even valid in the last instance if carried out by a highest-level decision maker whose 'incorrect' decisions cannot be corrected within the system. See also Chapter 4 above.

[26] See particularly M. Kelman, *A Guide to Critical Legal Studies* (Cambridge, Mass.: Harvard University Press, 1987).

Lord Reid's view, if we were lining up champions for it, would certainly find not a few. One might start in the early modern version of natural law theorizing that was so influential in the development of institutional legal writing throughout Europe. For example, Lord Stair in his *Institutions of the Law of Scotland* advances a natural-law theory of the structure of legal orders as principles defining the right, qualified by principles of public and private utility. Judicial decision-making requires always a balancing between the demands of the right and those of the useful. In this, individual decision makers may easily go wrong. Accordingly, it may take time for a line of decisions to emerge that deserve full respect as settled law. Statute law is less likely to be accurate, since the lawmaker has to get everything right all at once.[27]

To move in one jump from the seventeenth century to the twentieth, Ronald Dworkin as long ago as in the nineteen seventies challenged the 'no right answer' thesis that many (myself then included) then took to be implicit in the soundest theory of law, some form of legal positivism based on the work of H. L. A. Hart. Dworkin contended that actually for nearly every legal decision there is just one right answer, even although quite often human beings, including human judges, fail to find it. Thus the rightness of propositions of law is not a function of the authority of the asserter of the proposition at all.[28] This attacked the thesis that sometimes the law runs out and judges just have to decide in a more or less legislative way what it is to be, and then apply it. Even so, in some respects Hart's view was actually closer to that of Reid than that of Diplock.[29]

These observations have further implications. They carry us into the question what the business of academic lawyers really is. It is already, and ought to be even more, a discussed question among legal academics what exactly it is that members of this profession are here to do. What is it that they are here to teach, research, and instruct about and argue about? Is it something such that it can be an objective ground of the rightness of opinions regardless of whose opinions they are, or is it on the other hand a matter dependent only upon the opinions of currently authoritative persons? Obviously, the proper approach to the teaching and discussion and writing of the law will be affected by which view one takes on the basic question.

---

[27] James, Viscount Stair, *Institutions of the Laws of Scotland*, D. M. Walker (ed.), (Edinburgh: Edinburgh University Press, 1981) (reprinting second edition of 1695), Book I, ch. 1, paras 10, 18–22.

[28] See R. M. Dworkin, *Taking Rights Seriously*, (London, Duckworth, revised edn, 1978), end-note, 'No Right Answer?' *Law's Empire* (Cambridge, Mass.: and London, Harvard University Press, 1986) pp. 225–76.

[29] H. L. A. Hart, *The Concept of Law* (Oxford: Clarendon Press, 1961); ch. 7, arguing with American Realists, Hart draws attention to the difference between the idea of finality of judgment and that of incorrigibility; however, in his posthumously published addendum (see *The Concept of Law*, (Oxford: Clarendon Press, 2nd edn, 1994), with postscript, P. Bullock and J. Raz (eds)), he vigorously attacks Dworkin's version of the 'Right Answer' thesis at pp. 272–6. My own view started out on the sceptical side; see *Legal Reasoning*. pp. 246–58; but for a later statement see 'The Interest of the State and the Rule of Law' ch. 3 of *Questioning Sovereignty*, published in an earlier form in *Essays in Memory of Professor F. H. Lawson* (London: Butterworths,1986) 169–87.

On one view, there is nothing to teach and nothing to know but what the judges decided last and will probably decide next. That, and nothing else, will be the law. On the other view, there will be something, some mysterious essence perhaps, which jurists will be trying to capture in their debates and lectures and seminars and tutorials, which will be the ground of the rightness of the decisions that are authoritative among us but which will not be constituted wholly and solely by these decisions themselves. Perhaps there is also space for an intervening view, a more constructivist one, which allows that law is a partly theoretical object, constituted by an interaction of human practices and theorizing about them, yet which gives this construct sufficient depth and objectivity (without mysterious essence) to give an independent basis for arguments about rightness and wrongness, and judgements between them of the kind postulated by the thesis of judicial fallibility.

Again, outside academia, answering the question will have implications for the way judges should go about the job; and, indeed, therefore also on the way legal counsel should go about their job. If Lord Diplock's view were correct, surely what will be most important of all will be that decisions be clear, rather than that they be in some other sense right. For there is no other sense. The crucial task of a court will be to state clearly what it now decides, what it now holds, what it now opines, and leave it to others to get on with their business in the light of that. On the other hand, if the Reid view is correct, then it would be very important for the judges, as far as time and pressures of business permit, to hear and to offer fine-grained argument and discussion and debate about what is right on a given question and try to ground their decisions in that. Rightness may matter even more than clarity in this view. Alan Paterson has drawn attention to certain significant fluctuations in the style of decision-making and reporting of opinions in the House of Lords at periods material to our discussion.[30] During the period in which, as his earlier study had shown, Lord Reid was the dominant personality in the House of Lords organizationally, the normal practice, ever more so towards the later tenure of Lord Reid, was for each decision in the House on any matter of moment to be spoken to by all the sitting Lords. Thus even at the highest level of decision-making there was debate among the judges what the right answer was, a teasing-out of the right answer from a multiplicity of opinions. By contrast, when subsequently Lord Diplock became the leading figure in the House of Lords, the style shifted quite sharply towards one judge being delegated the task of writing a single opinion which would clearly state the law. Lord Reid, in his address to the Society of Public Teachers of Law in Edinburgh in 1971, gave this account of the approach he favoured:[31]

We are often told that there should only be one judgment instead of, it may be, five speeches in the House of Lords. At first sight that seems good sense: the law will then be

[30] See A. A. Paterson 'Appellate Decision-making in the Common Law World', in R. Dhavan *et al* (eds) *Judges and the Judicial Power* (London: Sweet & Maxwell, 1985) pp. 158–64.
[31] Lord Reid, 'The Judge as Law-Maker' *Journal of the Society of Public Teachers of Law* 12 (NS) (1972) 22–9, at p. 29.

clear and judges and others who have to apply it will know where they are. The trouble is that it won't work and experience has shown that. As you know, until recently there could only be one judgment in the Privy Council and now if there is a dissent there can only be one judgment on each side. If you compare the quality of Privy Council judgments with speeches in the House of Lords for a long time back I think you will agree that from the point of view of developing the law Privy Council judgments have been much inferior. They are perfectly adequate to decide the particular case but not often of wider importance. Yet the same Law Lords have sat and they have taken just as much trouble. The reason is that a single judgment must get the agreement of at least all in the majority so it tends to be no more than the highest common factor in their views. So often in the House of Lords it is the second or third speech which now carries the greatest weight but we would not have had it at all if there had been only one judgment. Or take another example. For a time it was customary in the House of Lords to have only one speech in criminal appeals. But after the disaster of *Smith v. D.P.P.* we changed that: I don't believe that decision would have been so bad if there had been more than one speech. Differences would have been expressed which would have taken the edge off it.

The truth is that it is often not possible to reach a final solution of a difficult problem all at once. It is better to put up with some uncertainty—confusion if you like—for a time than to reach a final solution prematurely. The problem often looks rather different the second time you deal with it. Second thoughts are not always best but they generally are.

Lord Reid's words show clearly the implications of a rejection of the decisionist conception of rightness in judgments. Certain styles of judging, which would fit that conception, do not fit Lord Reid's own.

It is not, however, only at the level of legal theory, or of law teaching, or of judging, that the difference between the two approaches matters, there are also profound political, sociological, and constitutional considerations and questions that focus upon this topic. If we take the Diplock view, the view that rightness lies in the decision by the person with authority to decide, it would seem to follow that judges become in a very pure sense political actors, people who decide the law on the basis of their opinion and whatever they take to be relevant to it, there being no law other than what they decide in the cases that come before the courts. In terms of sociology or of political theory this implies the existence of a judiciary placed firmly in the front line of the political law-making process. Rightness in legal matters is what judges say it is, and that's all there is to it. They are law-makers in being law-sayers. And, of course, this view of them is not uncommonly proposed, for example by the Critical Legal Studies movement as mentioned earlier. At that rate, it becomes a crucial and urgent question in a democratic polity, how we should select and appoint judges, how representative they should be of the country that appoints them to be the deciders of the law. That issue is raised now and again, often under some assumption of the infallibility of judges.

On the other view, the judges will still be political actors of a kind, but only in the sense that their decisions upon the law are matters that unavoidably concern the well-being and utility of the polity, and the upholding of equity within it, as Stair said. Both their errors and their sound judgments will have effects on the public weal. But they will not be law-constituters, they will not be in the strong sense lawmakers, they will remain in some important sense law-finders. The rightness of matters will be what they are there to discover, not what they are there to create. This again will bear upon the issue of judicial selection, among other matters. A sound policy for recruitment will then run rather more along the lines of the best appointments being those of the people wisest and most experienced, as Stair put it, 'in the inquiry of right', a phrase which reminds us how at one time the English-language equivalent of the German '*das Recht*' was still 'right', not yet always and exclusively 'law'. Rightness, or a capacity to discern it, would be deemed more important than the supposedly representative character of a judge. Mark you, it would still be important that judgment should engender a public sense of rightness. And so even on this view it ought to be widely acknowledged that the procurement of a conviction of rightness would still depend upon some confidence in the community that its judges were properly its representatives in the inquiry of right.

5. Judicial Fallibility and the Rule of Law

Further and finally, at the highest and grandest level of political and constitutional theory, the whole issue of the 'Rule of Law', or of the character of a law-state, a *Rechtsstaat*, is put in issue by the question of judicial fallibility. If the Rule of Law means a government of laws and not men, then it is impossible if the judicial infallibility thesis is true. For the governance of law turns out to be just the governance of the people that do the legal deciding. On the alternative view, the idea of the Rule of Law will acquire a different sense. The idea will be that the persons who do the deciding are charged with upholding and implementing the law rather than making it by their opinions. Thus our belief in law and order, if it is a belief in the rule of law, will be greatly coloured by which opinion we take on the question whether judges can make mistakes.

How, finally should we therefore answer this question? By what method? One very important, and not to be neglected way, would be to ask the judges themselves, in order to find out what they say upon the question of their capability of erring, when we put it to them. Alan Paterson made a path-breaking and important contribution in this line of inquiry in the UK through his empirical sociological study of the House of Lords, interviewing in depth both the judges themselves and a broad sample of the advocates who had argued cases before them in the period of the study.[32] Still, if we were to take the fruits of judicial questioning (and he does not so take them) as more than just evidence upon the point, good

---

[32] See A. A. Paterson, *The Law Lords* (London: Macmillan, 1982); compare Ward LJ in the *Conjoined Twins* case, noting the growing frequency of life and death decisions in medical law, which 'are always anxious decisions to make, but which are invariably eventually made with the conviction that there is only one right answer and that the court has given it'. [2001] Fam. at 155.

evidence, we would be begging the question. To do so would be to assume the Diplock view by supposing that the judicial view upon the question 'Can judges make mistakes?' is a self-authenticating one. The judicial self-perception is an important piece of evidence, but not a conclusive one.

It remains, therefore, important to look beyond what they say they do[33] to what they do. What they do is to decide cases at law and give reasons for their decisions. Judicial opinions are markedly not blank opinions, but reasoned and justified opinions; the whole of this book hitherto has been devoted to reflection on the kinds of reasons and justifications the Law Reports contain. One way to try to get at the answer whether and why mistakes are possible is to think about the intrinsic nature of this activity of reasoning and justifying in the decision-making game. What are its presuppositions? Clearly, there is no point in offering an argument unless it tries to show something, to show at least why some opinion or opinions are legally better or sounder than others. To reason and argue at all in that way implies not quite the existence of, but a rooted belief in the existence of, objective interpersonal criteria of legal soundness.

In the sense already discussed, the application of such criteria is a matter of opinion, concerning how the grounds of rightness are to be stated and how, as stated, they apply in given particular cases. Opinions carry weight by virtue of the expert quality and the practical wisdom of those who put them forward. But they are not self-authenticating in the Diplockian way simply by virtue of being authoritative opinions issued by persons with legally vested decision-making authority. This is what was argued above in relation to *Morgan Guaranty* and *Kleinwort*. No one has a judgement other than his or her own to apply to these questions and the result reached can only be a matter of that person's judgement, including, possibly, the judgement that the advice of a wiser and more experienced person should be sought. That judgement, however, is one about the possible grounds of rightness.

The kind of reasoning which goes forward in legal decision-making, legal argumentation, and indeed in legal thought in all its forms and levels is, as this book in common with other contemporary authors maintains, a form of practical reasoning. All practical reasoning works on the presupposition that there may be some matters upon which opinion can be right or wrong. It proceeds under a pretension to correctness, an implicit claim to being correct, not just to being boldly or confidently asserted.[34] That does not, however, conclude the matter even if the theory here outlined is a sound one. Just as it is notorious that practical

---

[33] Anyway, what they say may not be perfectly self-consistent. In his earlier quoted essay 'The Judge as Law-Maker', Lord Reid famously remarked that it was a 'fairy tale' that judges do not make the law. Here, I am taking other remarks of his to support a thesis that developing the law is a different thing from making it in the legislative sense, and one which is subject to rationally persuasive argument using materials from established law. John Finnis, 'The Fairy Tale's Moral' *Law Quarterly Review* 115 (1999) 170–3 is powerfully to like effect.

[34] See on the 'claim to correctness', Alexy, 104–8, 214–20.

reasoning proceeds in roughly the way I have been suggesting, it is also obvious that our practical reasonings and disputations are not infrequently inconclusive. When we think about how to argue over matters of practice, morality as much as law, we do notice that, while on some points we can hold quite conclusively that 'that view is wrong', on many other points there remain open questions where, so far as we can judge in practical terms, both views, or more than one view, is reasonable. Robert Alexy, on whose theses I draw here, argues that in our practical discourse and practical reasoning we can and do exclude many approaches to a question as being impossible because unreasonable. But among the surviving reasonable or 'discursively possible', answers there can be a plurality of apparently open possibilities. There can be inconclusiveness not because reasonableness and rightness cannot be objective, but because it can be actually inconclusive among rival opinions.[35]

Some people have put forward the argument that a prime reason why we have to resort to so-called 'positive law' at all, the reason why we set up or sustain courts, and judicatures, and parliaments and legislatures, is precisely that in human practical life, although exclusions of what is unreasonable may settle much, they don't settle enough. We have therefore to construct institutions, or to sustain historically evolved institutions, for settling matters at a level of detail and with a degree of clarity substantially greater than that which general practical reasoning apart from such institutional devices could achieve.

On that view, the point about law and about legal reasoning is to make more determinate things which our general ideas of reasonableness could not but leave too indeterminate. And so, experimentally over time, as Stair put it,[36] we develop rules and principles, grounds of decision and argument, and practices of reasoning and of trying to secure reasonable decisions, decisions reasoned and reasonable within an institutional legal framework, upon these matters. Our law as it develops becomes, as Kelsen put it, more concretized, more exact, more capable of dealing with more and more fine-grained questions; also, of course, by the same token, more complex at each level of its development. With this we may compare Niklas Luhmann's theory of legal systems as autopoietic systems, continually solving problems of complexity, though always at the price of generating new complexities.[37]

Anyway, we can establish to a very large extent objective grounds of rightness among us, things about which we can be mistaken or about which we can give right answers. Surely this is more or less the truth of the matter. What earlier chapters explored about the constraints of coherence and consistency in argument about law do set rather formidable tests which lawyers and judges and all the rest

---

[35] Alexy, *Argumentation* 207, 287–9.   [36] Stair *Institutions* I.1.16.

[37] N. Luhmann, *Law as a Social System* (trans. K. A. Ziegert), (Oxford: Oxford University Press, 2004) 267–9, and cf. 317 'Accordingly, the reduction of complexity serves to increase complexity'. Compare also E. A. Christodoulidis 'The Inertia of Institutional Imagination: a Reply to Roberto Unger' *Modern Law Review* 59 (1996) 377–97 at 383–5.

of us have to respect. Many are the times at which it can be clear that what is right is fully determined by respect for the facts and the rules and these other canons of good argument and sound legal interpretation. Where I think the Diplock view comes back somewhat into its own is, however, on the point that always beyond these settled domains of certainty, or even of obscure rightness, there do remain some questions on which the best determinacy-generating law remains incompletely determinate. Here, as Alexy has remarked, we go back from specifically legal reasoning to general practical reasoning. Judged by reference to that, sometimes one of the legally possible answers is on reflection capable of being characterized as unreasonable, or less reasonable than the alternative, and then the right thing will be to decide for the more reasonable view. But still again, there could be cases where neither the law nor our common sense of the reasonable will finally determine this, and there we can have no recourse other than to let there be some authoritative person who decides and, provided they behave reasonably, to whose decisions authority is ascribed. In such a case, there may be nothing for it but to accept the authority of an authoritative opinion. But this is not to say that such an opinion is for all purposes self-authenticating and rationally incorrigible.

It is itself a discussable question, for any given topic of rational discourse, whether the topic is one which does admit of two or more 'discursively possible', that is essentially reasonable, outcomes. Hence the claim that a certain matter was one on which there was nothing to be done but make an authoritative decision is one which it is always reasonable to problematize in a further discourse. The fact that legal finality imposes a closure for the law's practical purposes on such decision-making cannot insulate it from further inquiry at the bar of critical reason. Hierarchies of courts, with majority voting rules in the highest court, are, as already argued, necessary to achieve finality in practical affairs. They do not show that legal questions have only arbitrary answers, nor even that there is nothing to choose between any two.

Perhaps no better way to conclude on this point can be found than to quote from the translation of Robert Alexy's work. The following remark seems absolutely right on the present topic: 'Questions', he says, 'about the nature of argumentation in general, and legal argumentation in particular, are not only of interest to legal theorists and philosophers of law. They are pressing issues for practising lawyers and a matter of concern for every citizen active in the public arena. Not only the standing of law as a scientific discipline, but also the legitimacy of judicial decisions, depends on the possibility of rational legal argument.'[38] Rational legal argument, according to the view advanced here, is not demonstrative argument. Except in very straightforward and essentially undisputed situations, it does not amount to logical demonstration of the correctness of the result reached in the light of uncontested legal and factual premises. It is rationally persuasive, rather than rationally demonstrative. Its study is one

---

[38] R. Alexy, *Argumentation* p. vii.

department of rhetoric. A studying such as the present one of legal arguments does show how they can be rationally persuasive, as summarized in the introductory section of the present chapter.

The second chapter of the book commenced with a conflict between the two commonplace propositions that the Rule of Law has value in promoting certainty and predictability about potentially coercive interferences in people's lives, and that the law on any point is perennially arguable. Better acquaintance with the rhetoric of legal argumentation shows that the arguments there can be about legal problems range only over the scope of reasonable disagreement as outlined here. Within that scope, it is everyone's right to develop the best argument they can on any problem they raise within the possibilities explored in the chapters of the present book. That right is also grounded in respect for the Rule of Law. Obfuscating tactics beyond these constraints can be and are from time to time utilized by lawyers. That is not within the legitimate rhetoric of their profession, but is a betrayal of it.

The opening words of this book, taken from Lord Nicholls' speech in the *Terrorist Suspects* case were a reminder of the urgency that issues about the Rule of Law have in times of justified public alarm. When the way of life of civilized societies comes under threat, it is urgent for their citizens to reflect on the question what most matters in that threatened way of life. Erosion of the Rule of Law would not be a good way of warding off threats to civilization, but a way of yielding to them. Taking practical reasoning and legal argumentation seriously does not weaken one's respect for the Rule of Law; it enhances it.

Index of Names

Index of Subjects